The Novels of the German Romantics

Friedrich von Hardenberg (Novalis). Oil painting by Franz Gareis, 1799. Original in Städtisches Museum, Weissenfels.

The Novels of the German Romantics

By ERIC A. BLACKALL

Cornell University Press

ITHACA AND LONDON

PUBLICATION OF THIS BOOK WAS ASSISTED BY A GRANT FROM
THE PUBLICATIONS PROGRAM OF THE NATIONAL ENDOWMENT FOR
THE HUMANITIES, AN INDEPENDENT FEDERAL AGENCY.

First published 1983 by Cornell University Press.
Published in the United Kingdom by Cornell University Press Ltd.,
Ely House, 37 Dover Street, London W1X 4HQ.

International Standard Book Number (cloth) 0-8014-1523-3
International Standard Book Number (paper) 0-8014-9885-6
Library of Congress Catalog Card Number 82-22104

Printed in the United States of America

*Librarians: Library of Congress cataloging information appears
on the last page of the book.*

*The paper in this book is acid-free and meets the guidelines
for permanence and durability of the Committee on Production
Guidelines for Book Longevity of the Council on Library Resources.*

For Roger on his
sixteenth birthday

Contents

Plates

[9]

Preface

THIS book is addressed primarily to a general cultivated audience and does not assume a knowledge of German. It is the first extensive treatment in English of the subject and its purpose is to give an account of these romantic novels, as well as to explain what I conceive to be their importance. But since these works, with a few exceptions, are also not all that well known to those who do read German, it is my hope that what I have written may also appeal to those who already have some acquaintance with the material, especially since the only book in German specifically on this subject was published as far back as 1916. With this latter purpose in mind I have given references to the original sources of the quotations which, when German, I have translated in my text, and also a selected list of books and articles on these authors and their novels, both for those who read German and for those who do not.

None of what follows has been published before, except that part of Chapter 11 is a reworking of certain sections of my article "Moonlight and Moonshine: A Disquisition on Eichendorff's Novels," which appeared in *Seminar*, VI, no. 2 (1970). I am grateful to that periodical for being allowed to rework those sections.

I am also indebted to the Prussian Bildarchiv in West Berlin for permission to reproduce the pictures of Friedrich Schlegel, Dorothea Schlegel, Jean Paul, Hölderlin, Arnim, Hoffmann, and Eichendorff, to the Bildarchiv of the National Library in Vienna for the picture of Tieck, and to the Freies Deutsches Hochstift in Frankfurt for that of Brentano. The portrait of Novalis is reproduced from the edition of his works published by Kohlhammer of Stuttgart, with their permission.

Various students of mine helped me assemble preliminary material for this book and I am deeply grateful to them for their diligent searchings. Cornell University Press has made this book a reality; to its staff, and also to my two outside readers, I would like to express my thanks for their encouragement and valuable advice.

ERIC A. BLACKALL

Ithaca, New York

The Novels of the
German Romantics

CHAPTER ONE

Introduction

SOMETHING very important happened to the novel during the romantic period. And we of the last quarter of the twentieth century are better able to appreciate it than were the generations of 1850, 1890, or even 1920. For we have experienced a complete transformation of the novel away from traditional linear modes of narration and self-contained realms of representation toward a more complex amalgam of fantasy, myth, and poetry, with more emphasis on seeking than on telling, more concern with ambiguity than finality, more awareness of the insufficiency of all statement, and greater self-reflexiveness. Because we have experienced notable attempts by novelists to express time as something more than chronology, because we have been given novels in which the author himself is the organizing principle to a degree far greater than ever before, because we have come to appreciate that fragmented form may have greater cohesion of truth than rationally organized structure, because we have been made to see that images seek meanings just as meanings seek images, we can now more easily understand the complete revolution in the conception of the novel as a form that took place between about 1795 and 1830, most notably in Germany, and the resulting narrative patterns that emerged. We are no longer wedded to chronologically developing, "linear" narration, nor to the type of mimesis exploited so brilliantly by the great novelists of the post-romantic nineteenth and early twentieth centuries. For the great novelists of our own time have asserted and demonstrated that reality was inadequately captured by literary "realism," that it contains much that is intangible, even at times nonrepresentational and non-representable, except by intimations, images, shapes, or patterns of sounds—a tissue of affinities, contiguities, and memories which clock-time and defined location cannot account for and which yet are essentially part, perhaps the very texture, of reality. All this was fully realized by the German Romantics, in their own way. And in their novels they sought to give expression to it, each in his own peculiar way.[1]

Essentially what happened was that the novel was declared a poetic form, whereas in the eighteenth century it had been considered a prose form. In Germany the assertion was more categorical than elsewhere, embodied in such statements as Novalis's "A novel must be poetry through and through" [*Ein Roman muss durch und durch Poesie sein*], or Friedrich Schlegel's "The novel is a romantic book" [*Der Roman ist ein romantisches Buch*]. But also in England and France we find testimonies during the romantic period to the poetic potentialities of the genre, for instance by Scott in his assessment of Mrs. Radcliffe, and by Victor Hugo in his review of *Quentin Durward*, where he terms Scott's novel "picturesque but prosaic" and calls for a novel that shall be "picturesque but poetic, real but also ideal."[2] We have various statements—from Laclos, from Fanny Burney, from Mme. de Staël, among others—that the novel was considered a lesser form of literature in the eighteenth century, albeit the most widely read.[3] But by the last quarter of the century it had achieved a greater measure of respect, and was already the subject of critical discussion, for instance as to whether it had "rules" of its own and whether it was the legitimate successor of the epic or a legitimate, or illegitimate, rival to drama. In large part this shift in evaluation was due to certain qualities in some of the novels that the second half of the century had produced—the dramatic nature of *Clarissa*, the epic dimension in Fielding, the lyrical intensity of *Werther*, and the almost Cornelian tragic confrontation of passion and duty in *La Nouvelle Héloïse*. What became clear was the fact that the novel could engage both intelligence and feelings in a measure far transcending the demands of a leisure entertainment. It could embody statements every bit as important as those of drama, epic, or lyric. It was becoming more than the escapist diversion of storytelling, it analyzed the springs of action, it interpreted. In the wake of Richardson the novelists of sensibility concentrated more on characters than on events, on inner life rather than on external action. But there were also others, such as Fielding, Lesage, and Smollett, who maintained the primary interest of events in the structure of their fictions, without, however, disregarding the reaction of characters to these events. It was Schiller who declared that the structure of a novel must needs be organized by the understanding [*Verstand*], presumably because the novel must have a plot based on cause and effect. This made it for him a prose form, and he was troubled by what he called the "impure" form of Goethe's *Wilhelm Meisters Lehrjahre* in which he found an uneasy combination of "prose sobriety and poetic boldness." It was difficult, he thought, to depict what he called "poetic states" in the novel.[4]

The Romantics did not see why this should be so. Their view did, however, imply a different concept of the genre, one in which the novel was not to be organized by the understanding alone. In Germany this argument proceeded out of reactions to *Wilhelm Meister* which contrasted it with the "prose" depictiveness of eighteenth-century novels in general, and coincided with a revival of interest in Cervantes, in medieval romances, and in certain novelists—Sterne and the Diderot of *Jacques le fataliste*—who had penetrated deeper below the surface of everyday reality and allowed the novel to reflect on itself and emphasize its own fictiveness, breaking through a normal rational structure of time, place, and causality in the interests of greater truth. In England an important factor in the change of emphasis was the revival of interest in the romance with Walpole's *Castle of Otranto* and the subsequent development of the romance alongside the novel, culminating in Scott's delineation and justification of both genres in his *Essay on Romance*. The basic distinction, as formulated by Scott, was that the romance depended on "marvelous and uncommon incidents" for its appeal, and could tolerate a looser structure than the novel.[5] Indeed the structure was often developed in order to emphasize the marvelous and the unusual rather than the normal workings of causality. This meant that a whole realm of experience not easily accountable for by the workings of normal causality came into the novel. And Goethe was right in declaring that chance belongs legitimately to the subject matter of the novel. He made no distinction between novel and romance, and both German and French use the same word for both. Only in English is the distinction clearly enunciated. The important fact is that with the revival of the romance, the range of the novel expanded to include the supernatural.

If by "supernatural" we mean what is not accountable for or contained within the finite world of space and time, and yet is part of sensed, although perhaps not observed or known, experience, then the relationship of this "supernatural" to the "natural" or finite experience of reality is one of the cardinal concerns of romantic thinking. We find it everywhere, either in religious form or in secularized transformations. We find it in Blake, in Wordsworth, in Hölderlin, in Chateaubriand, in Hoffmann. It is the basis of various romantic mythologies, and of recurrent romantic images such as "the golden age" or "chaos," images of a primal unity of all things, of finite and infinite, anterior to the dichotomous fragmentation of modern life but also still transcendently present as a reality to which all the seeming vagaries and contradictions of finite experience are mysteriously attuned and into which they will all ultimately be resolved. Poetry, according to the Romantics, achieves this resolution. Therefore without this integration of the real with the "supernatural," as I have been using the word in this paragraph, there can be no poetry. This was basically the reason for Schiller's hesitations regarding the novel as a form. In his view, and as the great eighteenth-century novelists had demonstrated, it had to deal with the real stuff of life, and yet, for him, poetry emerged only when the real was elevated to what he called *das Ideal*—by which he meant both "ideal" and the "realm of ideas," not the romantic "supernatural." He was prepared to accept *Werther*, as presenting the tension between "real" and "ideal," but in *Wilhelm Meister* he felt that the two were disturbingly present side by side without being brought thematically into a meaningful relationship.[6] He was referring predominantly to what we might term the "romantic" elements in the book—Mignon, the Harper, the Society of the Tower, the "marvelous and uncommon incidents" that Scott claimed for the romance in general. Schiller recognized that these proceeded from a truly poetic mind—how could he have thought otherwise, being so richly attuned to Goethe's whole creative processes?—but he was somewhat uneasy, as many others have been since, at their presence in a novel. For *Wilhelm Meister* to be a really successful novel, it needed more "sobriety."

Novalis, on the other hand, thought it had too much.[7] He found Goethe's novel "thoroughly prosaic" and once called it a "Candide against poetry"; for in his view—and here again many others since have agreed—poetry was completely ousted from the book by the prose of everyday domestic existence. His own novel *Heinrich von Ofterdingen* is to a certain extent an anti-*Wilhelm Meister*, or perhaps one might better say a *Wilhelm Meister* as it should have been. For it is undeniable that, despite his harsh strictures on Goethe's novel, Novalis would never have written *Heinrich von Ofterdingen* without *Wilhelm Meister*. Goethe's novel revealed to Novalis by what he considered its imperfections as an achievement the potential for poetry that lay within the confines of a novel properly conceived and executed. The poetic elements that Schiller viewed with mistrust were for Novalis the positive aspect of the work. Friedrich Schlegel in his remarkable essay of 1798, "Über Goethes Meister," observed that this was far more than a novel concerned with personages and events. It had much wider implications, embodying what he called a "sense of the universe" [*Sinn für das Universum*], though more as premonition than as demonstration.[8] It was this evocation of the universal through the particular that made the novel interesting. Schlegel pointed to a similar quality in the narrative structure: each book of the novel summarized the preceding books and contained the germ of the following ones. This was what his brother was to call "organic form," the adumbration and extrapolation of a germinal idea. Hence, said Friedrich Schlegel, the coincidences, mysterious apparitions and such like are all premonitions of what is to come, and therefore poetically justified. He also praised the irony of the book, the self-contemplation in it (what we would nowadays call its self-reflexiveness), the constant returning into itself which, far from limiting the work, in fact broadened it out. For him the structure of *Wilhelm Meisters Lehrjahre* was therefore refléxive, organic, and, by its sense of the universal, symbolic—all of which made it poetic. By his emphasis on the novel's self-reflexiveness, Schlegel was affirming the importance of the author's personality being within the novel itself and both contributing to and conditioning its structure. He once jotted down in his notebook a remark to the effect that a novel should combine absolute individuality and absolute universality.[9] By universality he did not mean objectivity, for he scoffed at novels that claimed to present an objective picture of life, manners, or what not. But by individuality he did mean subjectivity, and, as we see, demanded it. The correlative "universality" refers to the nonempirical world of universals or absolutes, the ideas (in the Platonic sense) behind the accidentals of finite existence, the infinite embodied in the finite. By passing through the alembic of the poet's individuality, the ideal becomes real. And the individuality is always consciously present both to itself and to the consciousness of the reader, absolute because independent and unlimited, able to dissolve and reconstitute its own construction at will and at any time, connecting and disconnecting by virtue of its deeper and wider vision. It is the young Friedrich Schlegel who worked out in greatest detail and in characteristic paradoxical aphoristic richness the fundamental romantic conception of the novel as a poetic form, and it is therefore to him that we must turn for the basis of our investigation.

CHAPTER TWO

The Novel as Romantic Book:
Friedrich Schlegel

FRIEDRICH SCHLEGEL (1772–1829), the younger of two brothers famous in the annals of criticism, began his literary career with the publication of several essays on Greek poetry, the most important of which, entitled *Über das Studium der griechischen Poesie* [On the Study of Greek Poetry], appeared in 1797. This essay contrasts Greek poetry as idealizing and objective with modern poetry, which is individual and characterizing [*charakteristisch*]. On the whole the essay avers that modern poetry is inferior to Greek poetry, but it also testifies to Schlegel's concern with and interest in modern poetry. What was lacking, however, at this early point in his career was a true system of poetics adequate to account for modern poetry. This he worked out in the various notebooks he kept, in the Fragments that he published between 1797 and 1800, and in the *Gespräch über die Poesie* [Dialogue on Poetry] of 1800.[1]

In order to understand Friedrich Schlegel's pronouncements on the novel as a poetic form, we must first examine his conception of poetry. The central statement is to be found in the 116th of the Fragments that he published in the programmatic critical journal *Das Athenäum*, edited by himself and his brother August Wilhelm, in 1798. Beginning with the definition of romantic poetry as "progressive universal poetry" [*eine progressive Universalpoesie*], Schlegel develops first what he means here by "universal": poetry is to reunite the separate genres and reestablish contact with philosophy and rhetoric, embrace all that is poetic whether artistically articulated or not, combine poetry and prose, enthusiasm and critical stance, and maintain a free equipoise between what is represented and the representing agent, each mirroring the other to a higher and higher power, in mutual and continual reflection. He then explains that by "progressive" he means that poetry is not established as a given, but is and will always be in process of developing itself, can never be completely realized, and cannot be characterized by theory or critically analyzed—only "divinatory criticism" can describe what it is and what it is out after.[2]

In speaking of articulated and unarticulated poetry I am paraphrasing what I believe Schlegel to mean in this passage by the terms *Kunstpoesie* and *Naturpoesie*.[3] Romantic poetry, he says, is to combine both, and he goes on to make a distinction between artistic "systems" and "the sigh, the kiss which a child breathes out in artless song." Schlegel writes "das dichtende Kind," meaning that the child is thereby making poetry. There is, Schlegel said elsewhere, a poetry in all of us. Each of us has his own individual poetry, and it is up to each of us to develop it. More than that, poetry is in all nature. Without this "formless and unconscious poetry in the stirring of plants, the gleaming of light, the smiles of a child, the shimmering blossoms of youth, the glowing love of women, there would be no poetry of words."[4] This *Naturpoesie* is the divine spark within us, and it would seem that Schlegel means by it a striving outward in joyous response to the world around us, and the intimation of the eternal. To be a poet, one must have this sense, which is a kind of religious urge, an individual view or experience of the infinite. "The life and force of poetry consists in going out of oneself, detaching a piece of religion, and then returning with it and making it a part of oneself. It is just the same with philosophy."[5]

This conception of poetry is to be what animates the *Roman*, which word we would normally translate as "novel." Hans Eichner, the distinguished editor of Friedrich Schlegel, asserts, however, that Schlegel uses the word to mean a work of romantic poetry and not to designate a particular genre.[6] He points out that the word had a somewhat wider connotation in the late eighteenth century, and quotes from a section of Herder's *Humanitätsbriefe*,[7] which says that the representative genre of postclassical poetry was "der Roman," that it originated in the confusion and mixture of genres in the late Middle Ages, and that it was used by Shakespeare to present a great breadth of subject matter and to convey a great expanse of time and place, so that in each of his dramas there was a perfect "philosophical novel." The use of this same form to contain a vast range and variety of material was testified to, said Herder, by the development of the English novel during the eighteenth century. We know that Schlegel read this work on its appearance in 1796, for he reviewed it, albeit perfunctorily and without referring to this passage. Eichner points out that three ideas basic to Schlegel's concept of the *Roman* are present here: its predominant place in modern literature, the central position of Shakespeare in its development, and the designation of variety of content—and of form—as its overriding characteristic.[8]

It is true that Schlegel in various places affirmed that Shakespeare was the link between the modern *Roman* and the Middle Ages, that he termed Dante's *Divine Comedy* a "Roman," and that he made a notation for himself to the effect that Shakespeare's tragedies were a mixture of classical tragedy and *Roman*.[9] His brother August Wilhelm asserted in his famous Berlin lectures of 1803–1804 that all modern drama should be judged on the principle of the *Roman*. But would it not seem that Herder and both the Schlegels were all using the word *Roman* in the manner that we English speakers would use the term "romance"? This makes better sense, both as regards the Middle Ages and with respect to Shakespeare, or Dante—or *Don Quixote*, heralded by Friedrich Schlegel quite early as a seminal work and as the "only completely romantic *Roman*."[10] It is clear that Schlegel recognized that a romance could be in prose or in verse, or preferably in both. The term could therefore be applied to Ariosto as well as to *Jacques le fataliste* or the plays of Shakespeare which, as he asserted, were either rooted in romances or were romances. And it is used consistently to mean "romance" throughout the Boccaccio essay of 1801, for Schlegel recognized that many early romances were in fact collections of novellas that together made up a romance.[11] His specification of what constituted the form of romance, as distinct from its content, was to be refined progressively, resulting in a broadening out of the concept *Roman* to include novels that would not normally be termed romances (such as Diderot's *La Religieuse*) and in various attempts at a typology of the *Roman*.

When Schlegel made his famous statement "Der Roman ist ein romantisches Buch,"[12] he was therefore thinking primarily, it would seem, of the romance rather than the novel—a distinction, as we have noted above, that German is unable to make—but he was also implying that to satisfy the demands of romantic poetry all novels should be romances. He was at the same time distinguishing the novel from other poetic forms by his use of the word "Buch," implying both something to be read (hence not a drama) and something extensive (hence not a poem or a novella). As he himself said, the statement is not so tautological as it might at first sight appear. We should add that it is proscriptive as well as descriptive. The statement occurs in the "Brief über den Roman" [Letter on the Novel], published in the *Athenäum* in 1800 as the third main section of the *Gespräch über die Poesie*. During the preceding three years Schlegel had been consistently preoccupied with a specification of the concept, as his notebooks amply show. Let us therefore first follow the progress of his thinking through these private notebooks before turning to his published statements on the subject, the most important of which are the essay on *Wilhelm Meister* (1798), the "Brief über den Roman," and his Vienna lectures of 1812. In what follows I shall use the word "novel" when Schlegel uses the word *Roman*.

In his earliest surviving notebook, which belongs to the years 1797 and 1798, Schlegel traced the origins of the novel to mixed forms of the later Middle Ages.[13] He also observed that "most novels are just compendia of individuality."[14] The notion of the novel as compendium was to be taken up again in one of his earliest published fragments, which states that "many of the best novels are compendia, encyclopedias of the whole intellectual life of an individual of genius; works of that nature, even though in quite a different form, like [Lessing's drama] *Nathan the Wise*, acquire thereby something of the quality of a novel. And every man who is cultured and self-cultivating has within himself a novel, though he need not express it in writing."[15] It is therefore unnecessary for anyone to write more than one novel, he says[16]—assuming, we would add, that the novel is of this postulated ideal type. We note the stress here on inner life and the individual, rather than on the depiction of outer reality. The novel, he says, again in this earliest notebook, tends naturally toward digressions—especially to what the ancients called *parekbasis*, where the author speaks directly to the reader—or at least the "philosophical" novel does, and he discredits "empirical" novels that depend too exclusively on external plot.[17] In a first attempt at categorization Schlegel distinguishes four types of novels. There are "poetic" novels, either "fantastic" or "sentimental," and "prose" novels, either "philosophical" or "psychological."[18] All of these he calls "imperfect" novels. A perfect novel would presumably be a combination of all

Fiedrich Schlegel. Drawing by Philipp Veit, 1810. Original in Goethe Museum, Frankfurt.

four. It should, he said elsewhere, like all poetry, combine the "fantastic," the "sentimental" and the "mimic."[19]

Some explanation of these terms would seem to be desirable before we proceed further, for Schlegel uses them in a very particular sense. By "mimic" he means what we would be more likely to call "mimetic," that is to say "realistic," the representation of the real stuff of the finite world of human experience—persons, events, places, times. By "fantastic" he means the opposite of this; unreal material, fantasy, purely imaginative worlds. By "sentimental" he most definitely does not mean sentimentality in the normal sense, and expressly says so in the "Brief über den Roman": he is using this term to mean material in which feeling predominates, real and not affected or excessive feeling, and "spiritual" rather than sensual feeling.[20] Schiller had used the term *sentimentalisch* to denote poetry of reflection in which the person of the poet is very much present as a constitutive factor. Schlegel uses *sentimental* in the same general sense but specifies it to mean involvement in the sense of a meeting between mind and world that arises from an urge outward, the source of which, as he says in the "Brief über den Roman," is ultimately some form of love.

The "sentimental" novel is characterized as epic in material, elegiac in spirit, and idyllic in form,[21] here taking up Schiller's contrast of elegiac and idyllic in his essay "On Naive and Sentimental Poetry" as two modes of "sentimental" or reflective poetry. By a "philosophical" novel Schlegel means one primarily concerned with a thesis or philosophy, with ideas or philosophies; by a "psychological" novel he means one centrally concerned with character, though also with the interaction of character and events. A "psychological" novel is declared to be essentially analytical, its greatest power residing in its "unshakable coldness."[22] The "fantastic" novel is for the senses and the imagination, the "psychological" novel for the intellect, and the "philosophical" novel for the reason.[23] There should be "no love" in the psychological novel[24]—by which Schlegel probably means none from the author, cold objectivity. Everything is clearly accounted for and worked out in the psychological novel, whereas in the philosophical novel everything should be "boldly touched on, brilliantly flung out [*genialisch hingeworfen*], like lightning and storm—almost caricature—everything extreme and eccentric," in other words not elaborately developed, not integrated into a causal structure, but moving from one flash of an idea to the next.[25] The psychological novel has clear protagonists around which the other characters arrange themselves in graduated importance, but in the philosophical novel there should be no main character and no completely passive ones, for all the characters together make up the novel.[26] There should be interplay of wit in the philosophical novel, says Schlegel. A philosophical novel, he suggested, should always have a dunderhead [*Dummkopf*] and a clown [*Narr*] in it,[27] a dunderhead presumably being one who is unwittingly foolish and a clown one who consciously propagates folly. He seems to be thinking of a sort of philosophical dialogue such as is to be found in several novels of the eighteenth century, and the dialogues of Plato were obviously also very much in his mind, for in one of the earliest published fragments he expressly stated: "Novels are the socratic dialogues of our time. *Savoir vivre* has fled the halls of academic philosophy and taken refuge in this liberal form."[28] The Fragment I have just quoted was published in 1797. In the previous year Schlegel reviewed a famous philosophical novel of the eighteenth century which had just come out in a revised edition, Jacobi's *Woldemar*, a pretentious [and bad] novel that claimed to be dealing with serious ethical topics but did so clumsily and superficially. Schlegel rightly remarked that the book had no philosophical unity despite its claims to philosophic intentions, for its "philosophy" was merely a distillate of Jacobi's own personality, and the characters, situations, and emotions were woefully poorly used to demonstrate any ideas whatsoever.[29]

Schlegel was not satisfied with his nomenclature for the two types of prose novel, and later in the notebooks we find him using "critical" for "psychological" novel, and then using "mimic" and "political" and finally "ethical" as categories of prose novels. It is not always easy to understand the implications of this changing terminology, but by "political novel" he would seem to mean one dealing with the life of a nation, or larger community, whereas the "mimic" novel would be concerned with an individual person's experiences (for instance Don Quixote's) and the "absolute mimic novel" would be biographical.[30] In Dante, he says, the *Inferno* is predominantly mimic, the *Purgatorio* sentimental, and the *Paradiso* fantastic.[31]

The purpose of the ethical novel is to poeticize life [*das Leben zu poetisiren*]. It would therefore seem to be synonymous with his concept of what a romantic novel should be.[32] In one fragment, expressed in mathematical symbols, he draws a distinction between the poetic novel as "ethos taken to the power of infinity" [*unendlich potenziert*], the philosophical novel as "ethos taken to its infinite root" [*unendlich radiziert*], and the ethical novel as "both."[33] Relevant is also this entry in the notebooks: "In the ethical novel the greatest cohesion, flow, no gaps or jumps; conversations, dreams, letters, recollection. Fine loquaciousness. —*Confessions* [presumably Rousseau's] belong to the romantic novel." And this: "In every ethical novel an absolute chaos of character [*ein absolutes Chaos von Charakter*] necessary: but preferably only inward and in all [*besser aber nur innerlich und in allen*]."[34] Faced with such a cryptic utterance as this last, we must never forget that it is a jotting in a notebook and does not represent a considered formulation. Nevertheless it seems to be trying to say something important. Interpretation hinges on the two key words *Chaos* and *Charakter*. The former is used by Schlegel (and others of the German Romantics) to denote not muddle but unity, "chaos" in the sense of the chaos of Genesis, prior to the creation of the world and its dichotomies, and to the emergence of consciousness. The "chaos" that the Romantics *sought* was a harking back to a unity lost in the modern world. Another entry in these notebooks describes the form of the desired novel as "a formed, artificial chaos" [*ein gebildetes künstliches Chaos*],[35] artificial in the sense of something constructed by art, formed in art. But what does Schlegel mean by "absolute chaos *of character*"? Is he referring to the general character of the work? Does he mean "character of chaos"? Or is he referring to the characters, the personages in the novel, as the concluding dative plural *in allen* might suggest? If we look through the notebooks, we find that Schlegel uses *Charakter* in both these senses.[36] Leaving aside the possibility that Eichner is his deciphering may have misread *in allem* as *in allen*, which in view of his general meticulousness seems to me unlikely, we are left with the impression that in this particular statement Schlegel has moved from the sense of "general character" to that of "the characters," who of course are part of the general character. The concept of "chaos," as Schlegel understands it, is therefore not incompatible with "cohesion," for it implies a unitary although manifold whole. Digressions and "fine loquaciousness" are part of the cohesion, and Schlegel praises Sterne's loquaciousness as "good because it springs from the endless variety of self-contemplation" [*aus der unendlichen Mannichfaltigkeit der Selbstanschauung*].[37]

Perhaps the best way to get at these distinctions is to look at some of Schlegel's examples, though here again he is not always consistent. But Ariosto's is a "fantastic" romance, Tasso's is "sentimental," *Jacques le fataliste* is a "philosophical" novel, *La Religieuse* a "psychological" one. *The Tempest* and *A Midsummer Night's Dream* are "fantastic," *Romeo and Juliet* and *Hamlet* are "both sentimental and philosophical," but the "philosophical" predominates in *Hamlet* and the "sentimental" in *Romeo and Juliet*.[38] Eventually Schlegel's categorizations in the notebooks seem to reduce themselves to the triadic "fantastic sentimental mimic" as a typology of the novel in which, as Eichner has pointed out, the mimic represents the ideal of fullness of life, the fantastic means the free play of fancy, and the sentimental embodies love.[39] One might add that the mimic and the fantastic represent outer finitude and inner infinitude respectively, and the sentimental a mediating power reaching out and drawing back in, the force of what is called in the 116th *Athenäum* Fragment "poetic reflection."

There are in these notebooks various comments on *Wilhelm Meister* which imply that Schlegel thought it was tending toward what a romantic novel should be without completely getting there. He wished for a greater range of style and topics. It provided a "philosophy of the universe," but it was not "mystical" enough, though it was poetic, at least in its form.[40] But the true form of a novel should be "elliptical," he says, if it is to be an "absolute" book and have "mystical" character, "mythological character," "personality."[41] By "elliptical" Schlegel means having two centers. Mysticism was for him a philosophy that, in contrast to empiricism, recognized the existence of the supernatural and infinite, and posited as its basis an Absolute involving a tension out of which a philosophic system was dialectically evolved. The "elliptical" form that Schlegel desired for the novel implies such an opposition within a cohesive whole. Hence the image of the two centers, which probably also implied that a novel should move simultaneously on two planes, one of which should be transcendental. His remark to the effect that *Wilhelm Meister* was not mystical enough would in that case seem to mean that the transcendental dimension was not sufficiently developed to satisfy him completely. These remarks are elaborated further in the *Wilhelm Meister* essay of 1798. For instance the "poetic" nature of the form is there shown to lie in its progressiveness, in which each book of the novel takes up what has been achieved in the previous book and also contains the germ of the following book, so that the whole has progressive "organic" form. The phrase "philosophy of the universe" has been significantly modified to "sense of the universe," for this is obviously not a "philosophical" novel in Schlegel's use of that term. And the novel's cohesion—"no gaps or jumps; conversations, dreams, letters, recollection"—is described as a "magic hovering between forwards and backwards," with the image of the theater predominating (even the Beautiful Soul lives "theatrically," he rightly says), an apprenticeship in learning how to live according to one's nature.[42]

The *Fragmente* published in the *Athenäum*, also in 1798, contain expansions and reformulations of some of the germinal ideas in the notebooks. Schlegel here discredits those novels where everything revolves around a hero who is the author's spoilt darling. The constitution of a novel should definitely be republican, he says.[43] This seems intended to apply to all novels, whereas in the notebooks the point had been made only with regard to "philosophical" novels. He now repeatedly talks of the union of philosophy and poetry in a novel, which may well mean that he was by now moving away from the acceptance of a purely "philosophical" novel. If a novel is to teach anything, he says, the lesson must emerge from the whole, not from individual parts.[44] We can also observe in the *Athenäum* Fragments a further development of his notion of *parekbasis*, a development that leads him to the important concept of the arabesque as a mode of romantic form. He admires what he calls the "arabesques" fashioned from old tales in Tieck's *Franz Sternbalds Wanderungen* and considers them an important part of the richness of that truly romantic novel. He also admires its "sense of irony," representing the reflexiveness that he had advocated in the 116th Fragment, to which we referred at the beginning of this chapter.[45] On Jean Paul Richter, perhaps the most famous novelist of the day apart from Goethe, he is ambivalent. He admires his grotesque humor, for this constitutes his poetry. But he also considers the arabesques (or digressions) of *Siebenkäs* "leaden" and the prose of the novel either heavy or sentimental (in the bad sense).[46] He seems to have as yet no understanding of the poetic force of Jean Paul's cohesive discordance and purposeful disjunctiveness (which I will describe further in a later chapter). He is, however, feeling his way in these Fragments toward a validation of the grotesque as a poetic mode, or at least as a poetic element, and in this he is working outward from his reading of Jean Paul as he previously worked outward from his reading of Cervantes and *Wilhelm Meister*.

The full florescence of all these germinal ideas is attained in the *Gespräch über die Poesie*, published in the *Athenäum* in 1800, and especially in that section of it entitled "Brief über den Roman." This is the third of the four main sections of the work, the sections being linked with each other by dialogues between fictive interlocutors. The introduction justifies the dialogue form. Every human being has his own poetry, and each such "poetry" is different from all the others, whereas reason is one and the same in all of us. Reason therefore unites men in their likeness to each other, poetry unites them in their differences. Each of us has a longing to develop his own poetry, and does so by experiencing the poetry of others. This "poetry" means individuality, an innermost power of self-development, connected more with the imagination than with the reason, a "self-made unreason" [*selbstgemachte Unvernunft*],[47] self-expanding from the desire produced by what it has already attained, the primal urge for expansion in man, the desire to embrace more and more of the inexhaustible world of poetry, individuality striving to realize itself by extending beyond itself by its own powers. Poetry is therefore the transcendence of individual bounds by the assertion of individual power, the progressive assimilation of the created "poem" of the universe by our own poetic power. By means of the dialogue form of this work Schlegel aims at presenting the different "poetries" of individuals who can connect because of a common "center" [*Mittelpunkt*],[48] namely poetry itself. For poetry, thus conceived, is born of the spirit of love (in its desire to embrace other poetries) and leads naturally to communion with others. In fact life should be the continuous expansion of one's poetry toward ever greater comprehensiveness, total comprehensiveness being attainable only in death.

The first main section of the dialogue is a contribution read by one of the characters on "Epochs of Poetry," a historical survey from the Greeks to the present, with interesting comments on the mixture of genres in Ariosto and assertion of the prime importance of Cervantes and Shakespeare. This leads to a conversation in which demands for a theoretical delimitation of genres are raised on the one hand and countered on the other by assertions that this is useless, that it does not produce poetry, and that poetry is indivisible. The second "paper" read is addressed to the reasons for the decline of poetry since the times of Shakespeare and Cervantes, attested by the previous speaker, and declares that the reason for this is that modern poetry lacks a center such as mythology provided for the ancients, and hence the modern poet has to create such a center from inside his own work, an individual center and not one shared by the communality. Another solution to the problem would be the creation of a new mythology, which the speaker considers thoroughly possible. From his remarks it is clear that he, and Schlegel, consider mythology to be the organizing of the disparate "chaos" of experience into a meaningful and therefore "harmonious" whole. ("Only that confusion from which a world can spring, is [a true] chaos,"

Schlegel said elsewhere.[49]) Greek mythology achieved this, and it is apparent that the Romantics have the same aspirations for poetry. This speaker reiterates the point, already made several times by Schlegel, that poetry should fuse with philosophy, especially with idealist philosophy, which was also a search for a center, and with recent natural philosophy or "physics," which was also working toward a "mythological" conception of nature. The difference between the old and the new mythology would be that the latter would proceed from the intellect whereas the former had evolved from the imagination playing on sensory experience. But though its roots would be in idealism, the new mythology should produce a new "realism"—by which he means a new understanding of the real world, of reality as opposed to ideas—and "this new realism, because it is of idealist origin and must float [*schweben*] above idealist ground, so to speak, will manifest itself as poetry which is based on the harmony of ideas and reality."[50] All mythology is the hieroglyphic expression of surrounding nature as transfigured by human imagination and love. It is a securing in terms accessible to our minds and senses of that which otherwise evades the comprehension of our consciousness. It is "all connection and transformation." The "wit" [*Witz*] of romantic poetry—the power that connects and transforms imaginatively—is therefore a sort of indirect mythology. We find it in Cervantes and Shakespeare, and . . .

> Yes indeed, that artfully ordered confusion, the attractive symmetry of contradictions, the wondrous constant alternation of enthusiasm and irony operating even in the smallest elements of the whole, seem to me to be a sort of indirect mythology. The organization is the same and the arabesque is certainly the oldest, original form of human fancy. Neither such wit nor any mythology can exist without some such original, [which is] primal and unreproducible, essentially indissoluble, in all of whose transformations its original nature and strength shimmer through, and the glint of reversals and dislocations, of the simple and the stupid, is visible in its unreflective depths. For all poetry begins by disrupting the process and laws of rationally thinking reason and transporting us back into the beauteous confusion of fancy, the original chaos of human nature for which I would know of no better symbol so far evolved than the motley throng of the ancient gods.[51]

The speaker then calls for a revivification of this old mythology transfused by the spirit of Spinoza and by the new insights provided by physics. He also advocates the investigation of other mythologies.

Spinoza and physics? The speaker goes on to refer to the "dynamic paradoxes" of physics, meaning presumably its revelation of the polar oppositions and contrary motions in nature. And Spinoza? Presumably because his whole philosophy was based on a concept of substance which was primal, unitary, and eternal, rejecting Descartes's distinction between extended substance, thinking substance, and God, and asserting that all substance was God. Earlier Schlegel had said that it was difficult to understand how one could be a poet and not revere Spinoza because his philosophy embodied the alpha and omega of all fancy [*Fantasie*], the basic ground and general state on which all individual imagination rests and from which it breaks forth separately. His philosophy provided the general foundation for every individual kind of "mysticism," which, as we have seen, is for Schlegel closely allied to poetry. Mysticism, in contrast to empiricism, posited an Absolute, and Spinoza's "God" was of course such an Absolute.[52]

The third main section, the "Brief über den Roman," begins with a defense of the novels of Jean Paul Richter. Charges brought against these were on the one hand that they were muddled and had no perceptible plot, and on the other hand that they were too subjective. The speaker, Antonio, asserts that such combinations of the grotesque and the confessional were the only truly romantic products of an unromantic age, and then proceeds to a spirited defense of Sterne as "arabesque" in form, and of *Jacques le fataliste* as an arabesque without Sterne's "sentimental admixtures" [*sentimentale Beimischungen*].[53] He vindicates the arabesque as a literary form where the fantastic (or fanciful) can find expression in an age that is not naturally inclined toward the fantastic. If one can appreciate Swift, Sterne, and Diderot, then one is well on the way toward an appreciation of the divine wit and fancy of Ariosto, Cervantes, and Shakespeare. He places Jean Paul above Sterne because his fancy is "sicklier" [*kränklicher*] and therefore weirder and more fantastic. He is much wittier than Sterne, and because of this even his "sentimental aspect" is "lifted above the sphere of English sensibility" [*durch diesen Vorzug erhebt sich selbst seine Sentimentalität in der Erscheinung über die Sphäre der engländischen Empfindsamkeit*].[54]

There then follows the famous definition of romanticism as "that which portrays a sentimental subject in fantastic form" [*was uns einen sentimentalen Stoff in einer fantastischen Form darstellt*], and Schlegel's explanation, already quoted above, that by "sentimental" he does not mean tearfulness or flabby, comforting moralizing, but that which is imbued with feeling [*Gefühl*] appealing to our minds, not our senses [*nicht ein sinnliches, sondern das geistige*].[55] The contrast is therefore between real feeling appealing to the mind, and simulated feeling delighting the senses. There is also the contrast between "sentimental," meaning real feeling, and "fantastic," meaning the product of the imagination, the fictive. In a romantic work the two are to merge, for this "sentimental" urge is a form of love, a hieroglyphic of eternal love, a striving from the real toward a realm attainable only in the imagination. "Only imagination [*Fantasie*] can grasp the mystery of this [eternal] love and present it as a mystery, and this mysterious quality is the source of the fantastic in the form of all poetic representation."[56] Since the Infinite reveals itself only indirectly in the reality of the finite world, it is necessarily only to be comprehended by that faculty of the fancy which Schlegel calls "wit" [*Witz*].

Schlegel uses the term *Witz* to designate the faculty of perceiving similarities and of making connections. This was a usage current in the eighteenth century, and is ultimately based on Locke's distinction between wit as the perception of likenesses and judgment as the observation of differences. The Enlightenment was not, however, entirely satisfied with this distinction. It was pointed out by several thinkers, for example by the influential German philosopher Christian Wolff, that judgment was a necessary part of wit, for wit proceeded from a combination of perspicacity and imagination, and was really the discovery of *hidden* likenesses. Schlegel seems to be using the term in this extended sense of establishing connections that normally escape the logical operations of the reason, connections between seemingly disparate and quite unconnected things, connections perceived or fabricated by this faculty of the human mind or spirit. It is a "combinatory" force, divinatory, even prophetic at times, the product of inspiration, emitting flashes of insight, related to genius, and therefore opposed to systematic reasoning.[57] Since the connections established by *Witz* may sometimes be highly personal, even eccentric, the term often has the added connotation of producing something "witty," or being witty, ingeniously or amusingly formulated. In referring to Jean Paul as being wittier than Sterne, Schlegel is using the term in both these senses. One result of this is that in romantic poetry there is not, and cannot be, any greater validity given to visible truth than to fiction or semblance, no poetic distinction between the historically attested and the imaginary. Hence its combination of the confessional or real with the arabesque or imaginary.

The novel is not a specific genre: it is a "romantic book," and should ideally embrace all genres. If a particular novel does not do so, the reason lies in its individual character. What was best in the best novels so far, was the more or less veiled confessional element, "the fruit of his [the novelist's] experience, the quintessence of his individuality." The "arabesque" element usually only makes itself felt in the endings when "bankrupts regain funds and credit, poor suckers get to eat, pleasant rogues turn honest and fallen women turn virtuous again"[58]—in other words in the contrived fictions with which novels are often brought to a close. It is clear from the tone that Schlegel is not satisfied with these forced finalities: the *Confessions* of Rousseau and Gibbon's *Autobiography*, he says, are better novels than *La Nouvelle Héloïse*.[59]

The final section of the *Gespräch* is an essay comparing the style of Goethe's earlier and later works, praising the progressivity of his production to date and pointing to the centrality of *Faust*, at this time still a fragment, though a published fragment. *Götz von Berlichingen* with its manifold richness and its "formless" form seems to Schlegel less dated than *Werther*, and he notes with approbation the harmonious portrayal of disharmony in *Torquato Tasso* and its mysterious ending, the dissonances presented in *Egmont*, and the progressive nature of *Wilhelm Meister* from an artist-novel to a much broader conception, combining a modern sensibility with antique spirit. All these works are described as if they were novels, and all of them are interpreted romantically.

References to Cervantes are constant throughout the *Gespräch über die Poesie*, and it is clear that *Don Quixote* has become a touchstone for Schlegel in evaluating novels. It was, as he had said, the nearest approximation to his ideal of the romantic novel. It had the self-reflexiveness that he so much desired, for in Part Two the novel "returns into itself, working down to its very depths with unfathomable understanding," creating from within itself a central point of reference during the process of its own evolution.[60] In his Paris lectures of 1803–1804 to the brothers Boisserée he called Cervantes the "most profound, most inventive, most artistic of all novelists," and linked him with Boccaccio as the progenitors of the modern novel, now categorized as "a romantic book . . . in which all forms and genres are mingled and intertwined," a form that makes possible the most manifold complexity, the "primal, most individual and most perfect form of romantic poetry," as exemplified by *all three* of Cervantes's larger works (that is to say, *Don Quixote*, *Galatea*, and *Persiles*).[61]

In the twelfth of the Vienna lectures of 1812 he contrasts the poetic portrayal of life in *Don Quixote* with the prosaic representation of life in later novels. But in no age, he says, is life unfavorable to or unsuitable for poetic presentation. A poet can give new illumination to what seems banal or unpoetic by what Schlegel calls "the higher transformation of things in a magic mirror" in which past, present, and future appear and time becomes the eternal fullness of time.[62] In eighteenth-century France, he remarks in the fourteenth of these lectures, the novel became a favorite vehicle for the expression of ideas and emotions that did not easily fit into "the old forms" of literature. Thus Voltaire, Rousseau, and Diderot each made of the novel something personal to him, and different, Voltaire making it the perfect vehicle for his wit, Rousseau for his own particular rhetoric, and Diderot to indulge his caprice [*Muthwillen*]. The English novelists of the time were more concerned with the prose rendering of events culled from everyday life, and Richardson, for all his gifts, proved that on such lines the novel could not become a poetic form. And Jean Paul, he says in the sixteenth of these lectures, portrayed in his own peculiar way the rich variety of a chaotic and dissonant age, but with wit and feeling and a style that corresponded in its own dissonance and motley colorfulness exactly to the very world that it described.[63] In neither of these two sets of lectures was Schlegel largely concerned with the novel, but what he said there indicates that his concept of what a novel should be had not radically changed from what he had sketched in those early notebooks and developed in the published fragments and the *Gespräch über die Poesie*. The great difference between the notebooks and the *Gespräch* is that in the latter he has abandoned all attempts at a typology of the novel. Another significant development is the greater stress on form, culminating in the concept of the arabesque as the expression of *Witz*, and the reiteration in even stronger terms that a novel should cultivate a mixture of modes and styles to present poetically a fusion of the real and the fanciful, in which the categories of rational observation are displaced and superseded by wider vistas and deeper premonitions, and the stuff of life imaginatively transfigured to capture that eternal, primal unity which our fragmented experience of the finite world reflects, a unity that embraced and contained variety.

In a section of the notebooks headed "Von der Schönheit in der Dichtkunst" [On Beauty in Poetry] Schlegel asserts that beauty has three constituent components: oneness, multiplicity, and wholeness (or: unity, variety, and totality).[64] These, as Eichner has pointed out,

are Kantian categories (of quantity), but applied here to the work of
art to mean coherence, breadth, and the fusion of finite and infinite.[65]
The wholeness of poetry is the expression of a dialectical interplay
between unity and variety, the two key concepts of all Schlegel's
philosophizing. The search for absolute unity is the predominant
characteristic of philosophy, particularly of idealist philosophy which,
for instance in Kant, becomes the analysis by the mind of itself. And
yet Kant had revealed the limitations of the reason and denied the
possibility of our knowing any unitary Absolute. Fichte had posited
such an Absolute in his concept of the Ego, but the world, nature in
all its variety, was, as non-Ego, opposed to the free activity of the
Ego. Schlegel rejects this, because the plenitude of nature is for
him a necessary concomitant to that unity striven for by the mind—
and the prime task of poetry is to embody this interplay in its totality. Hence his affection for Spinoza, whose concept of substance
posited an identity, not an opposition, of absolute unity and absolute variety. And recent discoveries in the physical sciences (oxygen, electricity, galvanism) with their assertion of a unitary life-
force in the multiplicity of natural phenomena seemed to him to
be tending in the same direction. Basically he was concerned with
evolving a philosophical system that should combine the absolute
unity of substance with the absolute variety of its manifestations,
persistence with change, Being with Becoming. Ernst Behler asserts
that by interpreting change as motivated by striving and longing,
and by asserting that the absolute unity is this same force, which he
called "love" and saw therefore as a manifestation of the divine,
Schlegel was working his way toward some kind of solution, though
he never was able to express this in an articulated philosophical
system.[66] Nor did he need to, we may add; for the true expression of
all these ideas was for him poetry, which was to combine absolute
unity with absolute variety. Behler suggests that irony and wit can be
seen as the manifestation of the tension between these two basic
concepts of unity and variety. Both irony and wit are functions of
the free play of the mind. Freedom was the key concept for Fichte,
as also for Schlegel. Irony is for Schlegel "constant self-parody" of
the mind, and consciousness of the "infinitely full chaos" of the
world (and all experience).[67] In an article of 1803 he expressly states
that the novel is the genre preeminently suited to dissolving the
opposition of poetry to reality by poeticizing the real, and it therefore should always show a tendency toward mythology. As an example he cites Novalis's *Heinrich von Ofterdingen*.[68] By the exercise of

caprice, *Willkür*, the poet displays his absolute freedom in digressions, in arabesques, in "artistically arranged confusion."[69] Wit, *Witz*, Schlegel defined, in an essay on Lessing of 1804, as "the innermost mingling and interpenetration of reason and fancy," as the freedom of the mind operating with plenitude of thoughts.[70]

In 1794 Friedrich Schlegel had contemplated writing a novel of his own, of which a plan is preserved,[71] but he did not get down to writing it until the winter of 1798. The plan indicates that the novel was to be concerned with two characters who together constitute a whole—a man cultured and basically pure, but ingenuous and enthusiastic, who is to develop through love, friendship, and worldly experience into a coordinated human being, and a woman of enthusiasm and high culture who preserved femininity (in contrast to a secondary female character of rich culture who does not), the whole to be elevated but easy and joyful in tone. *Lucinde*, published in 1799, represents the development of this plan, but the focus is more on love and friendship than on worldly experience. Indeed it seems to say that the only educative experience is love. We have already noticed the central position that Schlegel accorded to love in his literary theory. Love means for him not merely the great transfiguring force in human experience, but also the experience in which above all others the inner and outer world become one. Thereby it becomes in romantic thinking (for we shall find similar statements about love in others of the German Romantics) the Absolute in which all that is individual is contained and sustained, the one primal force and the one life force, the infinite in the finite, that which gives man the sense of unity with the universe. As regards form, this means that the individual personages of a poetic work become metamorphoses of this one central force, and that persons and world become one.

For Friedrich Schlegel love in our finite individual experience combines both the sensual and the spiritual, and any attempt to divide the two or devalue the one in favor of the other is deprecated. This is the theme of *Lucinde*, and it grew to a certain extent out of his own personal experience. For in July 1797 he met Dorothea Veit, his future wife, and was swept off his feet by her combination of intelligence and sensuality. Four years earlier he had encountered Caroline Böhmer, later to become his brother's wife and still later the wife of the philosopher Schelling, who had a similar combination of qualities, as history was indeed to show. In an essay "On Diotima" (published in 1795), he was already attacking conventional ideals of masculinity and femininity in society (masterful aggressiveness and selfless devotion) and asserting that in the full life neither such extreme can have any place but both must merge and enrich each other.[72] And that is love.

The form of *Lucinde* is as unconventional as its content. Being concerned with reflections rather than events, with inner rather than external experience, it has no "story" as such and therefore eschews any attempt at chronological narration, except in the seventh section, which is entitled [Apprenticeship to Manliness], "Lehrjahre der Männlichkeit" a *Bildungsroman* in miniature that traces the development of the "hero" Julius up to the point where the novel begins. This is flanked on either side by six shorter sections, reflections in various literary forms on the theme of love, arabesques surrounding the central "confessional" narrative. Quite early on in the book the hero Julius, who is also the fictive author of the novel, claims to have discarded a progressively unfolding narration as unsuited to the subject and chosen instead to give us discrete fragments he has written at various times without order—"a strange mixture of different memories and longings."[73]

The first section is a letter from Julius to Lucinde and announces the theme: their love is a mingling of spirituality and sensuality; wit and delight characterize their embraces, which are "romantic confusion" and can be described only in "a charming confusion" [*einer reizenden Verwirrung*]. The work has already become self-reflexive, in that Julius is here describing the novel in which he figures. Straight progression would falsify the subject, and indeed nothing of the kind is given us. We progress therefore nonprogressively to a "Dithyrambic Fantasia on the Most Beautiful Situation," which restates the theme of the first section around the witty idea that the reversal of roles in the love act is an allegory of the perfection of masculine and feminine into full, whole humanity. The metaphor is somewhat shocking, or was in 1799, so the third section, the "Portrait of Little Wilhelmina," leads up to an attack on false modesty; Wilhelmina kicks her legs immodestly in the air, is unabashedly sensual and yet at the same time very intelligent, is impelled by fancy rather than intellect [*Verstand*], and in that is like a poet. This, says Julius–Schlegel, is a portrait of the ideal he has before him as he writes (more self-reflexiveness). Wilhelmina is the novel itself. We are then given, as the fourth section, an "Allegorie von der Frechheit"[Allegory of Insolence], which is a jocular allegory of how *Lucinde* came to be written, or might have been (but surely wasn't). The poet stands within a "chaos" of beautiful flowers, is jumped at by what seems to be a monster but turns out to be a frog, and is then told by Wit, *der Witz*, the creative force *per se*, that this "monster" is public opinion. Since the poet turns it on its back and then deems it to be nothing but a frog, he implies that he does not care a fig about public opinion. Wit then shows him four young men at a crossroads, representing the four novels that he could be about to write, all faced with the choice between modesty [*Delikatesse*] or insolence [*Frechheit*]. One of the novels (obviously the about-to-be-written or being-written *Lucinde*) chooses the latter, and *Witz*, his creative mind, approves of the choice. (Don't worry, dear reader. You are not getting any more confused than Schlegel intends you to be!) The poet now feels a new power within him, sees the world as a "carnival of lust and love" but then dissolves it in a flash and hears the words: "Destroy and Create, One and All," and the admonition that it is time for him to proclaim the sanctity of nature and health. There follows a rhetoric of love, interspersed with comments on the reactions the novel is likely to provoke among its readers.

Having attacked modesty and prudery and defended insolence, the novel now demolishes useful occupation and defends laziness in an "Idyll of Indolence." Love has no purpose but itself. The general busyness of most human beings is really based on an antipathy to the world, which can be understood only in leisurely reflection. A parable at the end of this section contrasts Prometheus, as representing the ethic of work and enlightenment, with Hercules, the goal of whose labors was to enjoy fifty girls in one night, an activity of "noble indolence." He got to Olympus, but Prometheus didn't. The sixth section, "Treue und Scherz"—"Devotion and Diversion" might be the appropriate translation—is a dialogue between the lovers during love-making, simultaneously serious and joking, for, we are told, "society is chaos that can achieve form [*Bildung*] and harmony only through wit, for if one does not joke and play with the elements of passion they coagulate into thick lumps and darken everything."[74]

The first six arabesques have been cast in a variety of forms such as Schlegel required of a novel: letter, fantasia, portrait, allegory, rhetorical excursus, idyll, and dialogue. The "Apprenticeship to Manliness" which follows is a third-person narration tracing the successive stages of Julius's sensual-spiritual development up to the point of his meeting with Lucinde. The progression is from emotion-without-a-target through a succession of sexual experiences involving an innocent girl, a society lady, a prostitute, a soul-friend, a sister-figure, an educated girl who recoils from the act, and finally Lucinde, a free-living artist, in whom he finds love, himself, and the impulse to art—so that he can now look back on his narration, self-reflexively, as a work of art. He realizes that his narration has involved transformation of experience by his present state of mind; and this realization leads to the first of the second set of arabesques, the eighth section, "Metamorphoses," concerned with metamorphoses of the loving mind. It begins with a parable of the union of external and internal worlds in love, and emphasizes the fact that full love is not elevation from the mortal to the immortal but a complete union of the two. In its description of the three successive stages of objectlessness, narcissism, and mutuality, this section is a metaphorical recapitulation of the apprenticeship narrated in nonmetaphorical terms in the preceding section, an interpretation in poetry of its prose.

The ninth section consists of two "letters" from Julius to Lucinde. The first begins by his expression of joy at her impending motherhood, which he views as a sign from the gods that their love is part of the great chain of all living things. The letter has an arabesque form and consists of a series of disconnected fragments dealing with aspects of the love-relationship, reaching its climax in a passage that relates their love to the general life-force of the universe, returning thereby to the tone of the beginning of the letter, which therefore has something of a circular form. The second letter expresses his anguish at Lucinde's illness, his relief at her recovery, and yet his satisfaction at being able to see pain as an image of the eternal dissonance of the universe and therefore interpret it meaningfully. Lucinde, he says, had become the mediator between his "fragmented self and indivisible, eternal humanity," as he contemplated the possibility of her death and subsequently her return to life.[75] This second letter is a continuous statement, not broken into fragments, not circular but progressive, progressing toward the assertion that what he has experienced is the thought of dissolution in freedom and the fact of reestablishment in hope. We note that in these two letters the "action," if one may call it such, has proceeded beyond the point at which the novel started. In contrast to the seriousness of these reflections, section 10 is a parodic reflection in the vocabulary of Fichte on sexual powers in humans and other forms of life. It ends with the observation that Nature seeks an eternal circle of experiments, each of which is completely new, but is in its individual separateness likewise an image of the ultimate inseparable Individuality, what Fichte calls the "absolute Ego" and what Novalis (see below, p. 110) calls the "personality of the Universal.")

The eleventh section consists of two letters from Julius to a friend named Antonio. The first of these explains that their friendship had declined because Antonio is too ready with negative criticism to encourage frankness, the essential basis for any friendship. What is friendship? The second letter distinguishes between "external" [*äusserlich*] friendship, which takes in more and more persons, and "inner" [*ganz innerlich*] friendship, which depends on the sympathy and symmetry of minds, demands repose and humble reverence for the "divinity" of the other.[76] This leads over to the twelfth section, which is entitled "Sehnsucht und Ruhe" [Longing and Repose], a lyrical dialogue between Julius and Lucinde on the curious fact that in repose one experiences deep longing. Repose is here interpreted as *undisturbed* longing, its image is Night, Lucinde is priestess of the Night, and the mood of the dialogue moves close to Novalis's *Hymns to Night* and the second act of Wagner's *Tristan and Isolde*, both of which authors were familiar with Schlegel's novel. To die in the ecstasy of love is a serious note to strike in a novel that Schlegel himself had described, albeit proleptically, as "light-hearted"[77] [*leichtfertig*], and indeed this second set of arabesques, even including the Fichte parody, has become increasingly serious. So Schlegel rounds it all off with some "Tändeleien der Fantasie" [Dallyings of Fancy], asserting that there is something to be said in favor of letting the fancy float on a stream of images and feelings without further purpose—delighting in play and resulting in a motley dance of life, without ulterior motives. We end therefore with a paean to the imagination and a degrading of the *Verstand*—the intellect always concerned with purpose and intent—just as we had begun with praise of imaginative confusion and a rejection of logical consequentiality.

Lucinde cannot be treated as an illustration of the ideas expressed in the *Gespräch über die Poesie*, because the latter was not worked out until after Schlegel stopped writing the novel. The title page of *Lucinde* indicates that what was published was only the first part of a novel. Its appearance was greeted with general consternation, although some persons, notably the philosopher Schleiermacher, spoke up in its defense.[78] Its ethical message was misconstrued, even by writers as acute as Hegel and Kierkegaard. Kierkegaard did realize that Schlegel was reacting against prevalent eighteenth-century notions that love was either sensual or spiritual, but he did not appreciate that Schlegel was arguing (indirectly, for there is not much argument in the book) for a fusion of the two as the nature of true love. That Schlegel did not get his message across to most readers was largely owing to the fact that the sensual occupies much more space in the book than the spiritual. In short his moral failure was due to some degree of aesthetic failure. Nevertheless the novel is a fascinating experiment, in its use of arabesques, its combination of genres, its irony, and its self-reflexiveness.

CHAPTER THREE

Traditions and Innovations

IMMEDIATELY after completing the first part of *Lucinde*, Schlegel informed his publisher that he would soon be sending him the manuscript of Part Two. But work on this was delayed by the completion of other projects, including the *Gespräch über die Poesie* and in fact the second part was never written. As a result of the ideas worked out in the *Gespräch* Schlegel became increasingly aware that the first part of *Lucinde* did not entirely correspond to his conception of what a novel should be, particularly in its lack of lyrical elements. He therefore composed numerous poems designed for the second part (eventually seventy-one in all!), but never arrived at a systematic plan for it. It has been suggested (by Eichner) that he may have had in mind as a model Cervantes's *Galatea* or (by Josef Körner) Boccaccio's *Ameto*, both of which combine prose and poetry in a striking way.[1] He also seems to have considered giving the characters of the second part an allegorical dimension. Several prose fragments for this second part have been reprinted from Schlegel's notebooks, one of which deals with the subject of irony. But it is impossible to deduce any structural pattern from all this. The second part of *Lucinde* does not exist.[2]

Meanwhile Dorothea Schlegel (1763–1839) had tried her hand at writing a novel. The result was *Florentin*, published in 1801.[3] At the time she was writing it, that is, between the fall of 1799 and the summer of 1800, Dorothea was not yet married to Schlegel, but she was living with him in Jena, and she asserted that she wrote her novel in order to bolster their extremely slender financial resources.[4]

[44]

This statement is not very convincing, for neither she nor Schlegel could have expected to earn much by this means, and there were presumably other and better ways for her to earn money.

Florentin is not a romantic novel, though it has as its main personage a romantic type. It does not deal with essentially romantic preoccupations nor with specifically romantic states of sensibility. It does combine in its structure different modes of presentation, but the effect is more artificial than integrated, and the result in no way approaches the mixture of genres that Schlegel had in mind. Dorothea obviously knew *Lucinde* and was influenced by it in a positive direction (despite objections from various quarters that she herself was Lucinde and the book was too personal), and some people have suggested that the protagonist of her novel was in fact Friedrich himself. This is hard to believe, for the details of Florentin's elaborately recounted life story bear no resemblance whatsoever to those of Friedrich's life. All one can say is that Florentin has a restlessness, passionate idealism, and uncertainty as to where he was headed similar to those of the young Friedrich Schlegel, but that is as far as the resemblance goes.

Dorothea's novel is therefore, in the context of what we are here considering, a transitional work, whose structure employs familiar narrative methods but is primarily concerned with the delineation of a basically romantic temperament. It does tentatively suggest here and there certain romantic narrative devices, but none of these becomes an organizing principle as in the novels of Novalis, Brentano, Hoffmann, or Eichendorff—not even to the extent that they do in *Lucinde*. There are occasional moments of self-reflexiveness as when at one point the description of a character is called (by the author) "perhaps too detailed,"[5] or when Juliane says she would never have believed that Florentin could talk (he is telling his life-story) so coherently.[6] Comic scenes alternate with serious encounters, though rather too consciously, and there is a shot of irony when Florentin falls asleep at a carefully arranged assignation.[7] A ghost story is injected into the narrative, seemingly without much reason, and commented on. The flow of the prose is constantly interrupted by songs, but very few of these have the quality of quintessentially expressing a situation or of conveying something transcending the bounds of prose; far too many of them are just interludes. These romantic features give all too often the effect of being grafted on to a basically conventional structure. But they are there, and even though they are not very artfully used, their presence shows the way things

Dorothea Schlegel. Oil painting by Anton Graff, c. 1790. Original
in Nationalgalerie Stiftung Preussischer Kulturbesitz, Berlin.

were moving. *Florentin* is not a compelling novel, but it is an interesting one. Interesting most of all, perhaps, because although it apparently never arrives at a conclusion, Dorothea asserted that for her it did.

It was published by Friedrich Schlegel, with no indication of its authorship on the title page but with the subtitle "Volume One." In a "Dedication to the Editor" (Schlegel) which was not published with the novel, Dorothea talked very interestingly about the composition of *Florentin*. It arose from various "little stories" that she wrote down or told orally without any sense of an organizing principle other than that of her own fancy, her "quicksilver fancy" [*quecksilberne Phantasie*].[8] As for the ending, she herself was satisfied with it. What was a "satisfactory ending" anyway? Getting married, or dying? Who could Florentin possibly marry? And death? . . . this she implies would have been no solution. She does not want finality from a book: "I am never satisfied if an author leaves me nothing to add, in thoughts or in dreams. I can delight myself for a long time by occupying myself with a story that could end this way—or that way. My book is therefore finished, because Florentin's influence did not extend any further."[9] At the end of the book he disappears, leaving the persons he has so much affected. Dorothea muses, adding in thoughts and in dreams: maybe he changed in that he no longer treated serious matters lightly, maybe he did abandon civilization for his "beloved natives" (in America, presumably), becoming a leader of a nation. We don't know what has happened to him since. Perhaps he is still alive, and telling his grandchildren "about the maleficent wonders and glittering misery of the Europeans."[10] This is not, I think, to be taken as the sketch for a continuation, but, like Novalis's remarks on what he had not written of *Heinrich von Ofterdingen* and Hoffmann's on what the continuation of *Kater Murr* should be, an indication of how it *could* continue. She did think about this, perhaps even in the months immediately preceding publication of the first part, but soon gave up, and in July 1805 Friedrich Schlegel reported that *Florentin* "gave her no real pleasure any more," a fact that Dorothea herself confirmed in the spring of 1808, after which there is no further mention of the novel, either by her or by Friedrich.[11] A novella exists in various incomplete manuscript versions that seems to have been intended for the second part of the novel, because it shows connections with some of the characters of the first part. Hans Eichner has examined these in an article presenting a reconstructed "text" from the manuscript fragments.[12] In general it can be said that the novella was to have accounted for some of the mysteries left un-explained in Part One. But Dorothea clearly did not want to do this. She never really seriously envisaged a second part. As far as she was concerned, there was no need for one. She obviously decided that the novel was better left as it was. The character of Florentin was not one suited to finality, for he was always seeking without knowing what he was seeking. It was therefore right that he should just dis-appear. Never mind the rest; the point had been made. And the only really "satisfying ending" was, in Dorothea's thinking, an open ending. This is the most strikingly *romantic* aspect of her novel.

Florentin is prefaced by two sonnets, addressed to "the editor," that is to say, Friedrich Schlegel, the second of which declares that love is the "inner center" of the novel. This is true in the sense that the book deals with the presence or absence of love, its joys and sorrows, and with the longing for love. Florentin is torn between a Rous-seauesque desire to flee society and the need to seek society in order to find the woman who will flee it with him. He envisions but has never encountered the love that he seeks. Circumstances bring him to the estate of a Count Schwarzenberg which embodies eighteenth-century enlightened ideas of husbandry and community,[13] a world of harmony and order, presided over by the count and his cultured wife in a spirit of love that extends to their relationship to each other. Florentin, who was really on his way to fight with the colonists in America, finds himself unexpectedly drawn to this world of order, repose, and fruitful (though unsensational) activity, and agrees to stay till the wedding of the count's daughter Juliane to a young man of parts named Eduard. As the action progresses—and it progresses very slowly, being constantly interrupted by songs, Florentin's life story, and other digressions—Florentin realizes he is in love with Juliane and because of the respect and affection he bears for Eduard and for all that the Schwarzenberg world represents, he declines Eduard's offer to live there as friend of the soon-to-be-married cou-ple, and departs to the house of Juliane's aunt Clementina, who has tried to delay the marriage because she feels that it will not be based on love. Clementina speaks of the "sufferings of love," whereas Eleonore, the Countess Schwarzenberg, is made to represent the joys of love. Clementina projects sorrow, and Eleonore projects joy, but each into some form of external creation. Eleonore combines old and new in the tasteful furnishing of the old castle, and the count has abolished feudal villeinage and encourages the peasants to do their own job while he provides them with the wherewithal. It is a community of healthiness. Clementina on the other hand devotes herself to those who need to be helped back to health, especially children neglected by their parents, and to music. Florentin's attempt to disrupt, in Clementina's circle, an impending marriage in which there is no love leads to a violent confrontation, during which the newly married pair Juliane and Eduard arrive to receive Clementina's blessing. "May you never know the sorrows of love," she says to them. They inquire after Florentin, but he has vanished.

Various mysteries are (purposely) left unsolved. Florentin seeks to find out who his parents were: and where has he gone at the end of this "Part One"? Clementina is obviously nursing some secret sorrow, which may well be connected with the "sorrows of love." She herself is in poor health and her devotion to sickly or neglected children suggests that this might be compensation for a lost or neglected child of her own. When she first sees Florentin—during the performance of a requiem of her own composition—she faints. One suspects therefore that she is in someway related to him, that maybe she is his mother. But who is the father? This motif of a child brought up by persons he thinks to be his parents but is then told are not, and his subsequent search for his real parents, especially the mother, is a commonplace in narrative literature from the Middle Ages on. It begets one form of the structure of a quest, that which becomes a quest for identity. In *Florentin* this traditional motif is used to express the search for purpose or destiny; Florentin decides to seek in a new life to forget what had tormented him so far, "he had to find the solution to his destiny and his birth"—in other words discovery of the past in order to discover the future.[14] Various other traditional motifs are present in the book, for instance the two estates representing orderly existence such as he has not been able to create for himself. One thinks of various novels of the period of the Enlightenment, of Clarens in *La Nouvelle Héloïse*, and the concluding books of *Wilhelm Meister*. Anticlericalism figures largely in Florentin's retrospective account of his early life, together with the motif of his sister's being forced to become a nun and his attempt to abduct her from the convent, and the hateful tutor he is subjected to—all of which is highly derivative. Venice appears in this narration as the city of sensuality and intrigue, Rome as the city of political intrigue and German painters, two English lords as squanderers of riches to dissipate their deep-set ennui, millers representative nature and the contentment of circumscribed activity close to the soil. All this is sickeningly familiar, as is the general plot of a hero on a journey, staying longer than he intended at certain places, forgetting the purpose of his journey and becoming involved in emotional entanglements. The long life story is crisp, straight narration that contrasts with the involutions of what surrounds it, just like the "Lehrjahre der Männlichkeit" section in *Lucinde*. In structure the novel is an amalgam of derivative narrative modes. It is the character of Florentin himself and the way that his own uncertainty is paralleled by the open ending that give the book its interest. Tieck's *Franz Sternbalds Wanderungen* (1798) had a similarly open ending, and for the same reasons. Which reasons Dorothea Schlegel perfectly understood, and she stuck to her decision to leave things unexplained and unresolved and let the reader add more on his own "in thoughts or in dreams."[15]

In order to appreciate the transitional quality of *Florentin* and the other novels that I shall describe in this chapter, it would seem desirable for us to pause for a moment and consider what types of novel and what types of novel structure had established themselves by the end of the eighteenth century. To understand a revolution one needs to know the situation from which it arose, and to comprehend the innovative nature of the romantic view of the novel one needs to place it in its context. To speak of "traditions" in so recently emerged a form as the novel may seem exaggerated: but one can observe various trends in novel-writing of the eighteenth century and the evolution of certain delineable types. The seventeenth century had produced novels of two main types: courtly romances that derived ultimately from the chivalric romances of the Middle Ages (via *Amadis of Gaul* and with admixture of the pastoral tradition) and antiromances of parodistic or realistic tenor (or both simultaneously). The former were massive in scope, artificial in setting (both as regards time and place), idealistic in sentiments (concerned mostly with valor and constancy), and complex in the external plot, which involved violent events (shipwrecks and abductions prominent among them), disguises, mistaken identities, and coincidences, with hosts of personages and with multiple action. The latter were shorter, dealt with real people and fewer people, mostly in a contemporary setting, emphasized flesh-and-blood rather than fantasies, and eschewed or ridiculed all artificial language and idealistic sentiments. But the two types had certain structural elements in common, and these are still to be found as active ingredients in novels of the eighteenth century. For instance the use of episodic narratives to diversify the plot, the presence of digressions of various types, the employment of dialogue and discussion, the preference for unusual events over everyday occurrences, and the role of chance.

The two greatest novels of the seventeenth century, *Don Quixote* and Grimmelshausen's *Simplicissimus*, might be said to combine a "heroic" structure with an antiheroic ethos. By "heroic" structure I mean a narrative of adventures; by antiheroic ethos I mean that these are not presented idealistically. War becomes a hideous reality in *Simplicissimus*, chivalry a laudable but anachronistic ideal in *Don Quixote*. Both these novels aim primarily at captivating the reader with a string of interesting, sometimes even harrowing adventures, and are therefore still in the tradition of the romance. But they also hope to make the reader think for himself about the lasting validity of what has been described. Don Quixote dies and Simplicius retires from the world, both of them disillusioned: the latter disillusioned by humanity in general, the former disillusioned at his own illusions. The world of these novels is therefore a real, not an artificial world, even though the narrative structure continues the artifices of the medieval romance. The supernatural appears in both, but not as fantasy, for the descent to the Cave of Montesinos and the descent beneath the surface of the Mummelsee are descents and at the same time elevations into a realm beyond space and time, a world unsullied by the transience and follies of earthly life, and therefore represent a kind of absolute vantage point, a true supernatural and infranatural of deeper meaning than mythological incursions as such. Both these novels are novels of development, both deal with journeys through life, both are panoramic in effect, both are concerned with character as much as with external events, both contain extensive digressions and numerous episodes. Both are masterful examples of the adaptation of a tradition to a changing world. And each contains structural features that were to become paradigmatic for later novelists—in *Simplicissimus* the use of a highly personalized narrator, in *Don Quixote* a certain degree of self-reflexiveness and the use of two contrasting but complementary protagonists.

The eighteenth century was certainly also a changing world, and the novel changed accordingly. Erich Kahler has spoken of the "inward turn of narrative" and Ian Watt of the movement toward more private concerns.[16] Depiction of the inner life was, of course, found before Richardson, but this aspect of the developing eighteenth-century novel was reinforced at this time by other forms of confessional writing. We know that *Pamela* emerged from a collection of letters, and we know that some German novels of the time owed much to pietistic self-examinations, with real autobiographies giving way to fictional ones. Two main types are distinguishable here: letter-novels and memoir-novels, the basic difference being that in a letter-novel the narration is on-going whereas in the memoir-novel it is retrospective. In both cases a first-person narrative is usual: indeed in France the use of a third-person omniscient narrator is, scholars tell us, not common until late in the century, though it is found earlier in England and Germany. A middle position is provided by a narrator who communicates to us a manuscript by someone else, letters or memoir, to give fictive credence to its being a record of true events. Letters had figured in earlier novels as vehicles of communication or, when misplaced, misused, or misdirected, as causes of misunderstandings between the characters (as in *La Princesse de Clèves*)—in other words, as incidental elements in the plot. But in the eighteenth-century epistolary novel, letters became the narrative medium. By "on-going" narration I mean the communication of events and reactions to events as these occur, or soon after. The justification for this narrative method was the attainment of immediacy, which therefore brought this mode into close proximity to drama. Many scenes in *Clarissa* are like altercations in a drama, as are the debates in *La Nouvelle Héloïse* and the developing machinations in *Les Liaisons dangereuses*. On the other hand the single letter-writer of *Werther* gives us what is in effect a protracted dramatic monologue. Another argument for the epistolary mode was that it gave the illusion of authenticity to what was actually a fiction.

The illusion of authenticity was also a constituent factor in the memoir-novel. Here the narration is retrospective, the author looking back on his youth (or, with the advent of the third-person narrator, on someone else's). The illusion created here is different from that in the letter-novel, the author viewing what he describes from his present position. The opening sentences of these novels often emphasize this fact: "J'entrai dans le monde à dix-sept ans, et avec tous les avantages qui peuvent y faire remarquer"; "Je suis obligé de faire remonter mon lecteur au temps où je rencontrai pour la première fois le Chevalier des Grieux"; "My father had a small estate in Nottinghamshire; I was the third of five sons"; "My life has for several years been a theatre of calamity."[17] "Pourquoi voulez-vous m'arracher à ma solitude et troubler ma tranquillité?" exclaims Duclos as he begins to narrate the *Confessions du Comte de D****. In *Roxana*, *Robinson Crusoe*, *Le Paysan parvenu*, *La Religieuse*, and *Tristram*

Shandy (and many others) the narrator goes back to his birth. The
memoir pattern is a device for retrospective narration. There are
also mixed types in which on-going narration gives way to retrospective narration, or vice versa, often with alternation between first-
person and third-person narration. Thus in *Werther* the first-person
narrator of the letters becomes a third-person in the retrospective
narration of the "editor" at the end of the novel. There are also
on-going narratives, many of them, in which a third-person becomes
a first-person narrator when he tells his life-story retrospectively;
and there are retrospective third-person narratives in which such
retrospective episodic narrations, either first-person or third-person
occur. In the "found manuscript" type, a third-person becomes a
first-person in the communicated document, with movement from
on-going to retrospective narration, as in Marivaux's *Mariane*.

What I have been describing is all part of a technique of illusion,
in which the reader is constantly kept clearly in mind, as receiver of
a communication. Indeed one of the most significant developments
during the eighteenth century is that the reader becomes a much
more active participant in the narrative experience. He is addressed
directly by the author, either in forewords, introductions, or other
framework material (thereby replacing in effect the patron that the
seventeenth century usually addressed, for a novel is now its reader's
possession, not the patron's), or directly in the course of the unfolding narrative. One thinks of Fielding's opening chapters to the
various books of *Tom Jones*, of the footnotes provided for the reader's enlightenment by Rousseau and others, and, more subtly, the interplay maintained between author and reader that pervades *Tristram
Shandy*, the novels of Wieland, and Diderot's dialogues—a continual
converse, overt or covert, not an episodic, occasional establishment
of contact. Wieland never writes "straight narration" (if indeed there
is such a thing) but always attunes his exquisitely malleable style to
the sensibility and expectations of a clearly envisioned (albeit imaginary) audience—as if they were listening instead of reading. With
Sterne the role of the reader is different: no longer putative, he is an
active participant in the dialogue. And so he is with Diderot, whose
narrative dialogues are the most ingenious meetings of epic and
drama.

We shall return to Diderot and Sterne in a moment. For the present let us briefly consider the relations of the novel to both drama
and epic in the eighteenth century. Approximation of the novel to
drama had begun in the seventeenth century, and it developed more

closely in the eighteenth. Experiments were made in writing novels exclusively in dialogue. Dialogues as in a play with speakers' names given became quite frequent in novels, and there were dialogues on philosophical topics which, because attitudes became substantivized in personages, took on narrative character, in which the dialogues of Don Quixote and Sancho were by no means forgotten. The novel became generally viewed either as successor to the epic or as rival to the drama, according to whether the main emphasis was on the external action or the inner life of characters. Both types of novel continued to flourish and permitted two types of general plot-line: the logic of drama excluding chance and demanding strict causality, the "epic" type less rigid and inclusive of contingency, even luxuriating in it. But the two types are rarely found pure: there is coincidence in as "dramatic" a novel as *Clarissa*, though not so much as in *Tom Jones*, and there is a logic of causality in both, so the distinction between "epic" Fielding and "dramatic" Richardson is hardly clearcut. And one could equate the causality of inner experience with what Schlegel called the "confessional" element, and the external contingencies of the "epic" type with his concept of the "arabesque."

So the eighteenth-century novel is not all inward narrative. Peter Brooks, speaking mainly of French novels of the period, has used the term "novel of worldliness" to characterize what he sees as a part of the "literature directed to man's self-conscious social existence."[18] This literature is therefore concerned not just with the private but also with the public sphere, and Brooks asserts that the image of society in the major French novelists of the period derives its "realism" from the great moralists of the seventeenth century, particularly from La Rochefoucauld and La Bruyère. Here again we note the fact that the novel is deriving much of its character from other types of writing. And indeed it is interesting to reflect on how many of the great novelists of the period came to the novel from other forms of literary expression: Defoe from factual reporting, Fielding and Lesage from drama, Jean Paul Richter from satire, Voltaire from a combination of philosophy and satire. The result of this is a broadening of the scope of the genre to include not only novels of external incidents and novels of private worlds, but novels concerned with philosophies of life, with political education (usually of a future ruler), with the debased state of society, with pure fantasy, or with urgent social problems. Episodes and digressions (both narrative and argumentative or expository) are found everywhere, and in Sterne this digressive element becomes in itself the substance of the novel so that it is really no longer digressive because there is hardly anything to digress from. It is important for our considerations here that it was Sterne and Diderot who, of all eighteenth-century novelists, particularly appealed to Schlegel. He liked them because they did not operate within a restrictive plot, because the author himself was continuously present (not just intervening occasionally) as a manipulator, and because this high degree of individuality was complemented by the universality of multiple perspective.

Both *Tristram Shandy* and *Jacques le fataliste* break with the concept of chronological narration, but both employ a combination of ongoing and retrospective narration. Digressions and episodes retard any steady progress of the plot, to such an extent that plot becomes subservient to the deviations. In both these novels the "plot" consists not in a developing action, but in a series of side-trackings. It is therefore virtually impossible for the most part to distinguish between what is central and what is peripheral because contiguity is the central concern. Early on in *Tristram Shandy* Sterne asserts that his work is digressive and progressive at the same time: "I have constructed the main work and the adventitious parts of it with such intersections, and have so complicated and involved the digressive and progressive movements, one wheel within another, that the whole machine, in general, has been kept a-going." The progression is indeed through the digressions—"Digressions, incontestably, are the sunshine;—they are the life, the soul of reading! . . . All the dexterity is in the good cookery and management of them"[19]—but if the progression is not chronological, what sort of progression is it? It is not the progression of an unfolding idea, and no climax or resolution is achieved (or sought). It is one continuous conversation, broken only by the author's account of his travels in Book Seven, a conversation that goes round in circles governed only by the concept of the "hobby-horse," the various hobby-horses, which direct its gyrations and constitute the stopping points of its motion. We constantly return to Uncle Toby's hobby-horse or Walter Shandy's, but each return is a variation on the last, so that repetitiveness is avoided but continuity preserved in a series of arabesques. The structure of the novel is therefore highly contrived, and the personality controlling it projects itself into the novel as a character in it, so that the narrator and the act of narrating become parts of what is narrated. There are also various fictive readers in the novel who are allowed to reflect on it as part of its progression. These are of course different from actual readers of the novel such as ourselves, who are presented with a whole set of interlocking viewpoints, contrasting but complementary, including those of the author and the fictive readers he uses as sounding boards, both of which extraneous perspectives emphasize the fictionality and extrapolate the process of narration. Peter Michelsen asserts that *Tristram Shandy* is not so much the product of one particular "subjectivity," but "a play of subjective worlds," born of a relativism with no absolute set against it, and in this lies the essence of Sterne's humor and his tolerance. Thus Uncle Toby's "heart" and Walter Shandy's "head" are, according to Michelsen, complementary opposites, as are the wit and the sentiment of the book.[20] Perhaps one might more truly say that this is not a "play of subjectivities" but one integrated subjectivity which embraces opposite standpoints, broad and generous, open rather than confined— what Goethe called a *"free* view of life."[21] Its effect is to invigorate the mind. "If 'tis wrote against any thing," said Sterne, " 'tis wrote, an' please your worships, against the spleen."[22]

We know that Diderot was a great admirer of Sterne,[23] and the outer framework of *Jacques le fataliste* is an elaborate extension of a few pages from *Tristram Shandy*, those pages in Book Eight where Corporal Trim tells the story of his falling in love with someone who was massaging his wound. *Tristram Shandy* is a protracted conversation between various characters both in and outside the plot; *Jacques le fataliste* is a dialogue, for the most part between Jacques and his master, though other characters enter in—including the author and a fictive reader—and there are reflective digressions and short narrative links between the various dialogues. A similar relativism pervades both novels, but the movement of Diderot's novel is more oscillatory than circular. The oppositions in *Tristram Shandy* can, as I have suggested, be seen as valid and mutually enriching standpoints, the expression of a truly broad, and free, human spirit. But Diderot is not so easy to sum up. It is hard to say where we come out at the end of *Jacques le fataliste*, much harder than at the end of *Tristram Shandy*. Henri Bénac has asserted that one of the difficulties with Diderot is that none of his works can be accounted for by one idea, that one cannot give a résumé such as one can give of, say *"Candide*, a discourse of Rousseau's, or even *La Nouvelle Héloïse*."[24] Of course one could hardly give such a résumé of *Tristram Shandy*, though one can give an overall summation of what the book is about. But what is *Jacques le fataliste* about? When it starts out, it looks like an argument (albeit a jocular one) about free will and predestination. But as it proceeds, the opposition becomes blurred—not muddled, but developed in all its complexities. Like Sterne, Diderot delights in the presentation of opposing standpoints, but with him the standpoints are mutually contradictory, not complementary as with Sterne. For despite Walter Shandy's outbursts of anger at Uncle Toby, and the latter's disregard of his brother's cerebrations, they respect each other and we respect both. But Diderot presses one line of thought to its extremity, and then another, so that what we are essentially left with is a view of life as a series of paradoxes with no ultimate *coincidentia oppositorum*. Hence although the philosophy of *Jacques* is basically deterministic—in accordance with Diderot's idea that all life is action and reaction within a universal *sensibilité*, and that good and evil are the results of tendencies within that sensibility for which we are not responsible and which we cannot control—nevertheless we do experience pleasure and pain, there are human feelings in all of us, and we do have a sense of responsibility. All these contradictions are expressed brilliantly and convincingly in *Jacques le fataliste*.

The basic *donnée*—the account of Jacques falling in love while being tended for a wound (which stops just before the climax that Trim's story did reach)—is stretched out on to the account of a journey undertaken by Jacques and his master, with plenty of the elements traditional in such journey-narratives—chance encounters, stays at inns, adventures, misunderstandings, misfortunes, conversations, interpolated narratives, odd characters, peasants, monks, bandits, long-lost friends—all of which keeps it going and gives variety. It also permits Diderot to express all sides of his nature, to reflect satirically on novels while writing one himself, to combine humor with serious portrayal of *mœurs*, to penetrate far more deeply into female psychology (in the tale of Mme. de la Pommeraye) than Sterne ever did, and, in the anecdotes concerning the various women who seduced Jacques, to indulge in his own particular kind of lewdness, which was every bit as individual as Sterne's, though quite different. As in *Tristram Shandy* there are sentimental episodes (Uncle Toby and the fly, Le Fever, poor Maria; Denise and her garters, the hostess's dog, Jacques's captain and his poor friend), and there is wit, but Diderot's is a more sophisticated and essentially French wit. There is nothing in *Jacques* to compare with Sterne's comments on "the right end of a woman," the disquisition on "noses," the discomfiture of the Abbess of Andoüillets, or the question "are children brought into the world with a squirt?" There is more grotesqueness in *Tristram*, and Sterne's humor is certainly, as Alice Green Fredman has said, "more abandoned," with more indulgence in farcical comedy as compared with what she terms Diderot's intellectual satire.[25] The associative progress of conversation is an important structural element in both books, but more consciously so in Diderot. Both authors ironically protest against the absurdities, incongruities, and improbabilities of novels. Fredman concludes: "Diderot and Sterne could agree that everything is the proper stuff of fiction and that rather than work within restrictive rules, the artist should experiment freely to do justice to his content."[26]

The narrative structure of *Jacques* is extremely intricate, with the account of Jacques's *amours* running side by side with the account of those of his master, each interrupting the other. There is plenty of self-reflexiveness. The author is constantly telling us that a particular situation could develop, or rather be developed, this way or that way, or intervening to pacify the (fictive) reader's impatience and curiosity. At one point he invites the "reader" to chat a while during the time that Jacques and his master are separated so that he "cannot" for the moment continue the story; at another he suggests that what he has just narrated is the conclusion Goldoni *should* have given to a particular comedy.

Both Sterne and Diderot refer to Cervantes. It was Cervantes's humor that particularly appealed to Sterne, what he once called in a letter "the happiness of the Cervantic humor" that arose from "describing silly and trifling events, with the Circumstantial Pomp of Great ones."[27] In the novel itself Sterne refers to the "honest refinements of the peerless knight of La Mancha, whom, by the bye, with all his follies, I love more, and would actually have gone farther to have paid a visit to, than the greatest hero of antiquity."[28] And elsewhere: "Was I left, like Sancho Panca, to choose my kingdom, . . . it should be a kingdom of hearty laughing subjects." For his book was "wrote . . . against the spleen."[29] Diderot refers to the essential inseparability of the Don and Sancho—"Jacques and his master are only of any good when they are together and worth no more apart than Don Quixote and Sancho. . . ."[30] It would seem therefore that both authors understood the complementary nature of Cervantes's two characters and respected it. The whole structure of *Jacques le fataliste* is modeled on Cervantes, even though the characters are quite different. And the relationship between master and servant, even at one point the question as to who is "master," is integral to Diderot's novel.

What was the particular appeal of these two novels for the German Romantics? Precisely, I would think, in those very aspects which most troubled some readers of their time and have troubled some others since, namely the apparent formlessness and the uneasy combination of wit and sentiment, or even, certainly in Sterne, of wit and sentimentality. Not that the Romantics favored sentimentality, but they did believe that a purely rationally or intellectually grounded presentation of experience must needs be incomplete, and asserted the claims of feelings unaccountable to reason and going beyond it as part of truth. This goes further than anything in Sterne or Diderot, neither of whom ever deals with the transcendent in his novel, except ironically, even jokingly. But the concept of wit and sentiment as conflicting, though perhaps complementary, attitudes, was something that fed into the romantic sense of the dichotomous nature of human experience, an experience in which irreconcilables were acceptable and no attempt was made (or desired) to integrate them into a harmony by humanizing wit and refining sentiment, as some writers of the Enlightenment, notably Wieland, had attempted. Both *Tristram* and *Jacques* suggest that all statement is only partially and relatively true—hence their cultivation of multiple perspectives. The Romantics were of the same opinion, although in contrast to the relativism of Sterne and Diderot (in these two novels), they did recognize an Absolute, transcendental but perceptible, sensed though not rationally known. The "formlessness" of these novels, with its disdain for chronological progression, its ironical and self-reflexive incursions, its combination of seriousness and mirth, and the expressive use of various styles of discourse would obviously appeal to a Friedrich Schlegel, as did their juxtaposition of sentiment and wit. He may well have sensed in them the dichotomy of head and heart that he had striven to overcome in *Lucinde*.

Nevertheless, there is much in the romantic view of the novel that is not represented by *Tristram* or *Jacques*. In them, there is no mingling of genres, and neither novel can be called a work of poetry. No German romantic novel is really like either of these novels. Sterne and Diderot were admired for what they had achieved in revealing new possibilities for the novel, but neither was taken as a model by any of the German Romantics. Goethe's *Wilhelm Meisters Lehrjahre* may owe something to his reading of *Jacques le fataliste* in its irony, its polyperspectivism, and its discussion of fate and chance, and the novels of Jean Paul certainly owe a great deal to Sterne's wit and sentiment. But both Goethe and Jean Paul did elevate the novel into a poetic form whereas Sterne and Diderot did not.[31]

There is another French novel of the eighteenth century which Schlegel repeatedly refers to as "Faublas," and always with approba-

tion, praising its wit and ingenuity. The forty-first of the so-called
Lyzeum Fragments declares that few books could compare with
Faublas in social wit and social gaiety: "It is the champagne of its
genre."[32] Schlegel is here referring to *Les Amours du Chevalier de Faublas* by Louvet de Couvray, which appeared in three parts between
1787 and 1790.[33] The boudoir encounters, the succession of mistresses, piquant situations, *quiproquos*, and relished deceits, combined
with real comedy-farce situations with lovers hidden in closets, secret
staircases, exquisite misunderstandings and unabashed licentious-
ness—all this is typical of its period, though Louvet handles it brilliantly, writes well, and fails only when he goes on too long (the third
part is infinitely inferior to the first, because it is verbose, repetitious
and, at the end, theatrically sensational). We do not know for sure
whether Schlegel read all three parts (which fill 820 pages in the
Pléiade edition). But whether or not he did, what appealed to him
about Louvet's novel is basically all in the first part. What might this
appeal have consisted in? Fundamentally in the basic *donnée*, of a
man dressing up as a woman and living out the part until he finds
himself in a certain situation of by no means uncertain character and
uses his feminine guise for masculine purposes. He is a full-blooded
young man, who initially assumes the role of a woman to cloak his
native shyness (he is only sixteen at the time) and yet achieve entry
into adult society, to *le monde*. This first experiment has unexpected
results in that he arouses the interest of a marquise (to whom he
hints that he is not what he seems) and simultaneously of her husband (who is not vouchsafed any such hint). From this initial situation a complicated plot evolves, fundamental to which is the fact that
in order to obviate suspicions he continues to dress as a woman most
of the time. Amused by all this, the sophisticated marquise, who is
herself only in her twenties, dresses as a man when she visits him.
Thus accoutred she rides with him in the Bois, and at one point
fights a (short) duel with a cast-off admirer (pre-Faublas) who tries
to expose her socially. In the last of the three volumes there is an
absurd situation in which Faublas's second mistress, a countess (aged
sixteen) finds herself between him dressed as a woman and the
marquise dressed as a man! "L'amour est un enfant qui s'amuse de
ses métamorphoses,"[34] the marquise had said in Part One, and the
word *métamorphoses* may well have struck a spark in the man who was
to write *Lucinde*. But Louvet's novel is not just *jeux d'enfants*: it has
deeply serious moments, as when the marquise expatiates on the lot
of women under the *ancien régime*, early sacrificed to the purely

social-economic institution of marriage, victims at an early age of
men they do not know or love, and dishonored in the eyes of society
when they do find a man they love, despite the fact that those who
revile them have all gone through the same experience themselves.[35]
The possibility of divorce is only touched upon, not treated compre-
hensively as it is in Mme. de Staël's *Delphine*. Behind the novel as a
whole is the sense of the double standard applied to the conduct of
men and women, and to the stereotypes of what are womanly qualities and what are male characteristics. But this is not presented in a
spirit of outrage. It is treated jocularly. For instance: the marquise
masquerading as "Vicomte de Florville" has taken Faublas in the
guise of "Mademoiselle du Portail" to a pretty little house in St.
Cloud, where the following conversation takes place:

> Je voulus donner un baiser au vicomte: "Mademoiselle, me dit-il,
> c'est à moi qu'appartient l'attaque." Il me prit par la main, me fit
> quitter la table, et voulut m'embrasser. Je le repoussai vivement:
> "Monsieur, laissez-moi, vous êtes un impertinent." Le vicomte, plus
> obstiné qu'entreprenant, semblait vouloir ne dérober qu'un baiser,
> et riait beaucoup de la résistance qu'on lui opposait. Apparemment
> plus accoutumé à résister qu'à poursuivre, il déployait dans l'at-
> taque beaucoup d'adresse et peu de vigueur. Mademoiselle du Por-
> tail, au contraire, renversant tous les usages reçus, mettait dans la
> défense peu de grâce et beaucoup de force. Le vicomte, bientôt
> épuisé, se laissa tomber sur un canapé: "C'est un dragon que cette
> fille-là, s'écria-t-il, il faudrait un Hercule pour la subjuguer! Que la
> nature est sage! elle a fait les autres femmes douces et faibles. Je
> vois bien que tout est pour le mieux dans le meilleur des mondes
> possible! Allons, que tout rentre dans l'ordre. Maligne demoiselle,
> apaisez-vous. Je ne suis plus que la marquise de B***; le vicomte de
> Florville vous cède tous ses droits."[36]

And so the stereotypes persist. But Louvet is mocking them, as
Schlegel does in the section of *Lucinde* dealing with "the Most Beautiful Situation," and Louvet's bantering tone—there are many conversations in his novel like the one just quoted, and some that are
much wittier—was probably what Schlegel was striving after in the
dialogue of the lovers in the "Treue und Scherz" section (see above,
page 40). He hardly succeeded because of the admixture of a rather
high-flown seriousness and because of his attempt to combine the
spiritual with the sensual, which Louvet never pretended to. Schlegel
may also have been attracted by the theme of androgyny, which
lurks beneath the surface of Louvet's novel and was to be developed

here and there in the novels of the German Romantics. Goethe's Mignon is androgynous, and we also find "masculine" women in the demonic females of some of the popular novels of the time, about which more later. There is also irony in Louvet's novel, though not of the self-reflexive type, except in the various prefaces—especially in the one entitled "A mon Sosie," where Louvet the author addresses Louvet the political orator. Louvet played a significant part in the Revolution. He made a famous speech against Robespierre in 1792, and spent two years in hiding after the fall of the Gironde, returning to Paris only after Robespierre's execution.

Louvet asserted that his novel had serious moral import, but its appeal undoubtedly lay more in its wit than in its wisdom. It belongs to the entertainment literature of the eighteenth century, though it does have literary qualities because of its elegance, liveliness, and portraiture. The century spawned a great mass of popular novels, most of which had no literary and certainly no poetic pretensions. These books belong to that substratum of literature that the Germans call *Trivialliteratur*, and everybody read them. They catered on the one hand to the lust for exciting adventures, for thrills and shudders and titillations, and on the other to the sentimental strain that there is in all of us—combined in many cases with a moralistic or pseudomoralistic streak (even in *Faublas* the avid mistresses and profligate seducers all die violent deaths and Faublas himself endures a spell of madness). These popular novels varied in tenor according to the differing climates of taste in England, France, and Germany. But many of their motifs were taken up by novelists with more serious artistic purpose. This was certainly true in Germany, where German *Trivialromane* had a considerable influence on the novels of the Romantics.

Marion Beaujean has examined the various kinds of German popular novels found in the eighteenth century, and noted the enormous increase in their number and the emergence of certain influential types toward the end of the century.[37] A moral-didactic type embodying Enlightenment values and interests had led to novels of social criticism, both humorous and serious, to novels of education, sometimes embodying pedagogical theories, and to family novels. Most of these dealt with contemporary German conditions, but around 1785 we begin to get novels about the past, specifically about the German past, in which the German Middle Ages are made to incorporate ideals of virtue, valor, and solidity in contrast to modern times. The figure of the noble knight becomes the incorporation of ideals of morality that belong not to the religiously oriented world of the true Middle Ages but to the secularized ethos of the Enlightenment. Some of these novelists were troubled by the incompatibility of the facts that they found in historical sources and the ideals they wished to impose upon them. One solution was to incorporate the ideals in invented characters and keep the historical personages and facts in the background.[38] Scott and Arnim were to work in a similar direction, but they were not the first to think of it. One interesting thing about these "historical" novels was that in them the interest in adventures *per se* again appears, whereas the earlier German moral-didactic novels had been heavy on message but thin in plot. So the old joy in a good yarn combined with the desire for moral edification (the latter perhaps stronger in Germany than elsewhere) was agreeably provided for. Between 1787 and 1798 a certain Leonhard Wächter, writing under the pseudonym of Veit Weber, produced a series of novels entitled *Sagen der Vorzeit* [Tales of Yore] which, according to Beaujean, present a wish-fulfillment in their accounts of the "Middle Ages" in which knights embody both Enlightenment virtues and *Sturm und Drang* toughness, resolutely avenging wrong and maintaining right.[39] All this was not without its effect on the Romantics' equally nostalgic, equally imaginary but much more imaginative "Middle Ages."

But the Middle Ages had its own supernatural, its world of marvels and wonders which represented its own recognition of values beyond the rationally explicable. This "marvelous" was consonant with the medieval world-view, but created difficulties for these novelists of the eighteenth century. In their re-creations of the past they could not ignore it, nor did they wish to, as writers with a good eye on their public, for everywhere in the later eighteenth century there were signs of a hankering after mysteries. We see this in the power that purveyors of mystery like Cagliostro, Mesmer, and St. Germain exerted over the public imagination, and we see it particularly in the growth of secret societies in the later decades of the century. What had begun as philanthropic and Enlightenment organizations, such as the lodges of Freemasonry, took on an increasingly occultist character and participated in what Marianne Thalmann, in her important study of the influence of these trends on the popular novel, has called a movement toward mystification (rather than toward enlightenment), as testified by symbols, ceremonies, secret archives, and general paraphernalia. Beaujean points out that, with the harking back of Freemasonry to the medieval Order of Templars, an imaginative contact was made between the late eighteenth century and the Middle Ages.[40] We therefore find in these "historical" novels not just individual "knights" but whole societies avowedly engaged in the propagation of justice and freedom. One of Veit Weber's novels was entitled *Die Brüder des Bundes für Freiheit und Recht* [The Confraternity for Freedom and Right], and it contains an opposing organization bent on sinister *Realpolitik* and obscurantist reactionariness. The novels that Thalmann examined abound in mysterious occurrences, persons, and objects, many of the incidentals being fictional counterparts of elements of the rituals and practices of the secret societies. But—and this is very important—the mysteries were nearly always resolved rationally at the end, and what had thrilled the readers as manifestations of the uncanny turned out to be the work of some secret *Bund*, even at times of a political organization. So the public could be chilled by horrors and yet restored to a belief in an orderly, explicable universe. Nevertheless, as Thalmann pointed out, there was an attempt in these novels to present the demonic even though its power is ultimately dispelled. This demonic is often very contrived—dark landscapes, ominous presentiments, blue flames, mysterious strangers, fateful days of the year, revenants, secret vaults, mysterious caskets, elixirs, secret writing, magic mirrors, rings and books. But the sense of evil "fate" is always external. What happens with the Romantics is that they take over much of this paraphernalia, but give it a deeper metaphysical basis, presenting a true "marvelous," not an illusory one. Among the motifs of this provenance that we find in romantic novels are: unknown parentage, visions and dreams, warning figures, initiation rituals, journeys in the service of something, disguises for a purpose, mysterious towers, vaults, and caverns, archives, secret societies with a Superior representing their spiritual aims and an Emissary or "Genius" who is sent out to accomplish some practical aim and often guides (or misleads, if the *Bund* be evil) a developing hero, so that life becomes a process of education. Anyone who has read *Wilhelm Meister* will recognize how much of all this was used by Goethe for his own artistic purposes, including the freeplay of his irony. We have already encountered some of these motifs in *Florentin*, and shall find them again in Jean Paul, Tieck, Hoffmann, and Arnim. Certain type-characters also recur: evil monks and serene hermits, all-too-impressionable youths, androgynous females, demonic women, madmen. In general what happened was that external elements became internalized, related meaningfully to the inner life of the characters, often (but not always) symbolically; and an experienced magic and mystery replaced a fictitious, illusory one.

CHAPTER FOUR

Toward a Poetic Novel:
Jean Paul and Hölderlin

IT seems fairly obvious that these popular novels of the German eighteenth century catered to a desire to rise above the dull prose of ordinary everyday life—both in their authors and in their readers. They sprang from an antiprose urge and yet remained prose. For the superimposition of the mysterious onto the clear face of events, especially when such mysteries were finally "explained" and therefore ceased to be mysteries, was merely a narrative device to sustain interest and excitement, although it was a reflection of the quest for mystery represented by the occult dabblings of the later eighteenth century. One could argue that by playing on the human urge to believe in the uncanny, these novels were somehow reaching out to the incommensurable. Those who have studied these novels extensively tell us, however, that no deeper interpretation of the world is involved. Nowhere is there to be found the richer insight of the poet that attempts to account for what defies the categorizations of the understanding. One cannot say that the novel has here become a poetic form.

When Friedrich Schlegel and Novalis spoke of the novel as poetry, they meant that it should provide an extended statement of the poet's heightened vision. And this vision implied a greater sense of the unity manifest in the multiplicity of experience, of the infinite vistas opened up by the finite, of the ultimate rootedness of the determinate in the indeterminate, of the indifferentiation behind all individuation—those revelations of man's inner sense which transcend and relativize the perceptions of his outer senses. No novelist of the eighteenth century would, I think, have made a statement like Novalis's "a novel must be poetry through and through." Goethe might have accepted such a statement as one possibility, an extreme possibility, but he was critical of the omnium-gatherum of romantic aspirations (as we see from his comments on Jean Paul and on Arnim) and of talk about art without a true sense of what art is (as we see from his comments on Tieck's *Franz Sternbalds Wanderungen*).[1] There is certainly poetry in his own novels, which are full of the mystery of life, its irony, and its incommensurableness. The world of his novels is a poetic universe, whose reality embraces the worldly and the extraworldly, accepts the validity of chance in the finite world but relates it to a higher realm, sensed but not rationally interpretable, where chance becomes a relative concept, perhaps a non-concept. Mignon is as important to him as Philine, Ottilie as Charlotte, and Makarie as Hersilie. The characters who live according to the insights and dictates of their inner sense maintain their position alongside those who are more empirically grounded. In short: the poetry exists alongside the prose—Schiller was right, though this is not a fault—but the prose is the foundation of it all and these novels are not "poetry through and through." Perhaps just because of this tension within their structure, the poetry of these novels emanates with correspondingly greater power. Goethe might not have subscribed to the absoluteness, the proscriptive quality of Novalis's statement. But he did show that the novel could embrace poetry, and therefore occupies an intermediate position between the eighteenth-century assertion that the novel was prose and nothing but, and the romantic position that the novel was all poetry. The two novelists I shall consider in this chapter seem to me to represent a similar position. Neither completely embodies the romantic ideal of the novel, but both are working toward a poetic conception of the genre. Both are intimately concerned with the contrast and connection of the finite with the infinite.

Jean Paul Richter who, following his own preference, is usually referred to as "Jean Paul," is of all German authors perhaps the most difficult to interpret to a foreign audience—nor, one should add, is he all that easy for German readers.[2] This is largely due to his style, or rather to his combination of two seemingly incompatible styles. A highly indirect style characterized by oblique (and often obscure) references, extravagant (but often amusing) metaphors, and constant ebullition of wit (including brilliant wordplay) alternates with a direct style less concerned with effect than with the close observation and depiction of persons and things—both of which styles embody a virtuosity of language, inventive and reproductive, the speech of a man of unbounded curiosity who made lists and indexes of strange words and facts for potential use in his fictions. The pyrotechnics seem, at first reading, to consort ill with the meat-and-potatoes, as does the rapturous ecstasy with the intimate genre-painting, the sentimentalism with the ironic wit, the idealistic "higher" beings impelled by dreams and longings with the small-town parsons, schoolmasters, and housewives going about their daily business. High flights of fancy are combined with sharp delineations of small-town pettiness, lyrical expansiveness with satirical reductiveness, moon-flooded landscapes opening into eternity with walled-in interiors of ordinary simple homes. But Jean Paul grows on one, "le bon Jean-Paul, toujours si angélique quoique si moqueur" as Baudelaire called him.[3] And what may seem at first acquaintance an incongruous and puzzling mixture becomes with more attentive reading a meaningful depiction of the warring concurrence of opposites, a dualistic and discordant world, whose very essence lies in its disharmony. To this Jean Paul gave expression of incomparable forcefulness and breadth. It is a romantic theme, this tension between aspiration and reality, between restlessness and security, between indeterminate longings and determinate satisfaction, including self-satisfaction. But the form of Jean Paul's novels is not completely romantic. He does not combine the genres, he does not reject chronological narration, he does not always prefer "geometrical" to "arithmetical" progression as Novalis advocated (a point we shall return to in a later chapter). But he does combine the "confessional" with the arabesque, using Sternean digressions extensively. He constantly operates with multiple reflection between narrator and what is narrated, or between different strands of the narrative—even between one novel and another, for characters from one novel appear in a different novel as commenting voices. And he himself is always present, either as the master puppeteer, the sovereign god controlling his creations, or even directly as one of the narrators, sometimes with the help of his wife or his sister, or as an actual character in the action. Nowhere in the whole range of German fiction is irony used so manifestly or so manifoldly. The plots are skeletal structures de-

Jean Paul Richter. Oil painting by Friedrich Meier, 1810. Various versions extant.

rived from combinations of motifs from the *Trivialromane*: unknown parentage, education in a foreign or unusual environment, mysterious strangers and emissaries, secret operations of seemingly mysterious forces, including "spirits," mistaken or exchanged identities, family strife, presentiments, dreams, visions, warning figures, "magic" mirrors, and the like. Much of the mystery is cleared up in the end, but the sense of being surrounded by things beyond one's comprehension and forces beyond one's control is never entirely dispelled. And this emerges all the more powerfully because of the contrast with the world of those characters who do not look beyond the confines of a limited existence which they have accepted or are resigned to, contentedly or not. This "other" world of Jean Paul derives from the depiction of all the problems of petty domesticity, for parents, for children, and for small-town officials, such as he knew from numerous novels and comedies and from living in such an environment himself.

Jean Paul acknowledged several times the importance that Swift and Sterne had for him.[4] His earliest works were satirical sketches but with time this "vinegar-factory" style (as he often called it) gave way to a more benign humor, though the spirit of Sterne never completely ousted the sharper bite of Swift. The most Swiftian character in Jean Paul, the librarian Schoppe in *Titan*, does indeed go mad, aping in his last days several details of his English model. But there is still plenty of satire in the later novels, of both the small-town bourgeoisie and the absurdities at the courts of petty princes. The high-flown, sometimes overblown, sentiment remains an important element in all his novels except the last. It was not a pose, not a sop to a certain class of readers, but represented his attempt to come to terms with those moments in our experience when something far greater than we can comprehend wells up in us. He sets these moments in symbolic landscapes, usually at night, and does not hesitate to include all the accoutrements of ecstasy or eternity—moonlight, nightingales, aeolian harps, echoes, mirages. The "other" world has its own imagery: pots and pans, darned clothes, petulant wives, spendthrift husbands, and pedantic schoolmasters. There is no monotony, for the range of his humor extends to fops, *arrivistes* and bigots—doctors, lawyers, unscrupulous magistrates—calculating politicians, incompetent rulers, and lustful princesses. In this world, as in the "higher" world of those who live poised between the here and the beyond, there are successes and failures; there are those who continue to respond to some higher vision, some of whom find it in life, others in death, and some never. There are three recurrent images in the "higher" range of Jean Paul's novels. Sudden accession of blindness and recovery from blindness are symbols of turning inward and then awakening to higher revelation. Seeming death (including simulated death) and then the return to life are images of similar tenor. And then there are various events used as images of alienation, particularly of alienation from the self, loss or abandonment of identity—purposeful disguises or exchanges, impersonations, masks, uncommon degrees of likeness with another person, identical twins, and so on—also hallucinations, distorting mirrors, doubles, split personalities, delirium, madness.

Jean Paul was a voluminous writer who was widely read in his lifetime. He had some following in England, appealing particularly to Carlyle and De Quincey both as a humorist and a moral idealist. He lived from 1763 to 1825, first in Hof, a small town in Franconia, then later in Weimar, where he became acquainted with Goethe and Schiller but was intellectually closest to Herder, then in Berlin, where he had contact with Friedrich Schlegel, Tieck, and Fichte, and finally in Bayreuth, where he settled in 1804 as a married man with several children. His favored medium of literary communication became the novel, his major novels being *Die unsichtbare Loge* [The Invisible Lodge] (1793), *Hesperus* (1795; expanded edition 1798), *Siebenkäs* (1796–1797); *Titan* (1800–1803), and *Flegeljahre* [Fledgling Years] (1804–1805). He also wrote several shorter narrative works, part idyllic and part satiric, and a treatise entitled *Vorschule der Ästhetik* [Preschool of Aesthetics] (1804; second, expanded edition 1813). In later life he wrote several political works, a treatise on education—education had always been a central preoccupation in his novels—and another novel *Der Komet* [The Comet] (1820–1822), which embodies a different, and no longer romantic, conception of the form.[5]

Die unsichtbare Loge is an amalgam of various novel-types of the eighteenth century—humorous, satirical, and sentimental novel, plus novel of education and novel of adventures.[6] But the highly individual quality of Jean Paul's style and concerns is already evident in this his first major foray into novel-writing. He protests that this is a real life story, a *Lebensbeschreibung*, and ironically marks it off from works that are mere novels, just as Diderot had in *Jacques le fataliste*. Within the novel (for *we* may surely call it such) one of the characters manipulates one of the other characters so that he may write a novel about him—much to the disapproval of Jean Paul who is in the novel not only as its named narrator (though when he is sick, his sister

continues the story) but as the tutor of the hero Gustav. The romantic ideal of multiple reflection is therefore well represented here.
Combination of genres there is not, but the characteristic combination of what we have above called his two main styles activates the
basic tension of the novel. This tension is prefigured in the Preface
(dated 1792) of the first edition, where, in the fashion of Sterne's
Sentimental Journey, Jean Paul addresses various people in his thoughts
as he travels. He says that to perceive certain truths and certain
beauties we must develop the heart as well as the head. "Between
heaven and earth there hangs a great mirror of crystal into which a
hidden new world throws its great images; but only an untarnished
child's eye perceives them, a besmirched animal-eye does not even
see the mirror."[7] Having reached the summit of a mountain and then
descended, he comments on the heights and valleys of human experience: "I come down again, and yearn upward and downward at
the same time. For errant man—the Egyptian deity put together
from animal heads and human torsos—stretches out his hands in
opposing directions, toward a first life and a second: spirits and
bodies assail his mind. . . . And this conflict, which no human resolves, you will find, dear reader, in these pages."[8] Toward the end of
Part One of the novel there is a digression on *hohe Menschen*, those
higher beings characterized by "the ability to rise above the earth, a
sense of the pettiness of all earthly activity and the incongruity of
heart and place, their countenance lifted above the confusing thicket
and loathesome sticky slime [*Köder*] of the ground, the wish for
death, the glance above the clouds."[9] There are, he says, four such
characters in this novel: Gustav, Ottomar, the Genius, and Dr. Fenk.
Gustav is the idealistic hero whose life is traced by Jean Paul in a
strictly chronological narration (with no romantic jumps) from birth
to imprisonment. Ottomar, the illegitimate son of the prince, longs
for "cataracts of passion" and scorns all moderation and stoicism.[10] Dr.
Fenk is a humorist who writes a satirical journal, scornful of follies
and all extravagances of spirit, whether these be in Gustav or in
Ottomar, but possessed of a generous heart, much concerned about
the problems of all the young people he comes into contact with, a
sort of stable center to a world flying out in all directions, who
transmutes everything into irony. The Genius is an emissary from
some other place, imported by Gustav's pietistic mother as his first
tutor, a gentle, unsullied youth the memory of whom remains with
Gustav and incorporates into itself certain other people that Gustav
meets through life. What we have here, then, are four distinct varia-

tions on what constitutes a superior human being but, except for the Genius, these are all divided characters tormented by some greater vision they can never completely fulfill.

Contrasting with these four are the lesser mortals of the small-town capital of the mini-state Scheerau: Professor-of-Morality Hoppedizel, Inspector Peuschel, the priest who prepares Gustav for his First Communion, Legation Secretary von Oefel—ladies' man, would-be novelist, and place-hunter—the world of full-titled officialdom with heads empty of everything but ambition, a world of pretense, persiflage and license presided over by an indolent, philandering prince. Against this are pitted the young lovers Gustav and Beata, against this the scorn and restlessness of Ottomar. Gustav has, at his mother's request, been educated underground for the first eight years of his life by the Genius, who prepares him for his ascent to the light by talking of "resurrection from the grave," and when this takes place it is presented as the acquisition of a sight of the "second world," of moving out of earth toward Heaven. In the middle of the novel the same image is taken up in a sequence of striking scenes. First there is the account of the death and burial of the gentle Amandus who, like Gustav, had loved Beata. Then Gustav and Fenk encounter another funeral, for it seems that Ottomar is dead too. Beata, consumed with grief at the death of Amandus, comes upon Gustav asleep by Amandus's grave. When he wakes he tells her of the dream he just had, in which Beata and Amandus, both dead, had urged him to join them in eternity, so that he thought he too was dead. But he was awakened to life by hearing the organ playing in the adjoining church, awakened to life and to the realization of the love that binds him and Beata. But who is playing the organ at midnight? It turns out to be Ottomar, who has woken up out of seeming death, though this transcendent experience has made him more negative than ever toward the things of this earth. The motif of death-into-life is therefore used here as a double-faced image, an expansion of the simple upward motion of Gustav's earlier "resurrection."

The plot, as always with Jean Paul, is of extreme complexity—basically of the adventure-novel type but cast in the mold of an education or development. As a result we have a tissue of sensational and often mysterious events but at the same time a sense of some overriding design. In this particular novel the design is never revealed, though the title hints at it. The "Lodge" is a lodge in the sense of Freemasonry, a secret society. No such lodge has figured in the action of the novel, which is unfinished. But the letter from Fenk to Jean Paul, with which the novel as we have it ends, implies that Gustav had become involved in the operations of a secret society to overthrow the prince, a society in which Ottomar was the leading spirit. The novel was therefore to be given some external cohesion by a familiar motif from the *Trivialromane* of the time. But this is really only external and superficial, as are Jean Paul's "plots" in general. They are merely devices to give some semblance of connection to the divisiveness he so ardently portrays, devices also to sustain the reader's attention on the most primitive level. We do not read Jean Paul for such plots, and they do not embody the real essence, the lasting interest of his work. They are merely machinery—one might even say gadgetry—to enable him to organize the confrontations of experience as he saw them. They also enable him to sheer off into digressions, many of which are little essays, usually humorous or satirical in tone, on general topics aroused by the nature of the incidents, the quality of behavior, or the drift of conversations. We move easily in and out of these digressions, we reflect and catch our breath, but these are not romantic arabesques in the sense of variations on the theme of the book. They are rather interstices. They depend on the essentially combinatory nature of wit, in the romantic sense of that term. There is an interesting passage in this novel in which Jean Paul instructs his pupil Gustav on how to perceive similarities from quite different branches of knowledge "and thereby invent":

> For instance anything big or weighty moves slowly: hence oriental princes—the Dalai Lama—the sun—crabs don't move at all; wise Greeks, according to Winkelmann, moved slowly—so does the hour-wheel—the Ocean—clouds in fine weather. Or: in winter humans, the earth, the pendulum goes quicker—Or: concealed was the name of Jehovah—of oriental princes—of Rome and its tutelary god—the sybilline books—the first old Christian Bible—the catholic [Bible]—the Veda etc. It is amazing what nimbleness [*Gelenkigkeit*] this gives to children's minds.[11]

Also to Jean Paul's mind. There could be no better description of how it worked.

There are, however, two real arabesques in this novel—or rather not in it but attached to it. One is the "Life of the Contented Little Schoolmaster Maria Wutz in Auenthal," which Jean Paul attached to *Die unsichtbare Loge* as an appendix or tailpiece. He called it "a kind

[73]

of idyll," There is a superficial connection with the novel, for Jean Paul had told us that while writing it he was staying in the house of Wutz's son. There is also a substantial connection in that Wutz, though belonging to the lower world of Jean Paul's novels, participates in their higher world through his imagination, combining his outer and inner experience in a way, says Jean Paul, not given to us ordinary mortals.[12] But the contentment is based on living out disappointments and frustrations by transforming them in wistful recollection, and by making his own versions of books which he knows only from the titles in publishers' catalogues, a process in which, for instance, the *Sorrows of Werther* become *Werther's Joys*. It is therefore a tenuously grounded idyll—only "a kind of idyll." Moving, but sad. The second arabesque follows, in the form of "Seven Last Words to the Readers of the Biography and the Idyll" in which Jean Paul dwells on the loneliness of the *hohe Menschen* in the chaos of this fragile world and works up to a final ecstatic vision of the "second" or higher world, the eternal world of the spirit gleaming above the pettiness and divisive misery of the world below.

It was his second novel, *Hesperus*, that made Jean Paul famous. Walter Höllerer has described it as being basically a rewriting of the same idea as that embodied in *Die unsichtbare Loge* but with sharper delineation of the court-world and of revolutionary tendencies opposed to it, and with improved stylistic means.[13] Jean Paul was thinking it out while he was writing *Die unsichtbare Loge*, which may be one reason why the latter was never finished. In both novels we find the same three spheres of external plot: a *Residenz* or court which is depicted critically, scenes in a middle-class community, part idyllic and part humorous, and the same great dream-landscapes and symbolic enclaves of joy where the higher visions emerge and the deepest revelations are vouchsafed. There are even references in *Hesperus* to the earlier novel. Character types recur, for *Hesperus* contains further developments of what Gustav, Amandus, Beata, and the Genius had represented in the earlier novel. Jean Paul, his sister Philippine, and Fenk appear in both novels, and at one point in *Hesperus* the hero Viktor reads *Die unsichtbare Loge*.[14]

The external action, every bit as complicated as that of the earlier novel, abounds in similar motifs from popular novels (confusions, exchange of children, intrigues, mysterious hints, revolutionary factions, secret societies) and there is the same basic concern with education. There is the same characteristically Jean Paulian use of digressions, the same dazzling virtuosity of language, an equally complex narrative situation with narrators within narrations, shifts and mutual reflexiveness, the same ironical "discrediting" of fiction ("if this were a novel, such-and-such would probably follow, but not here" and the like), and intrusive authorial presence. But the technique is much more deliberate and much more advanced. There is greater self-reflexiveness. At the end of the first chapter the narrator introduces himself as the author of *Die unsichtbare Loge*, now living on an island mentioned in that novel, to whom a dog brings each section of the present story. These communications are signed "Knef," who is later revealed (as if we didn't guess) to be none other than Fenk. Jean Paul has agreed to report this story, so long as he is allowed to let his imagination work on the "truth." At one point he expresses concern at the many improbabilities in the story and asks Knef, via the dog, to explain what is really going on, which Knef declines to do for the moment, saying that everything will be explained later—a reply that Jean Paul terms "wretched."[15] At another point he jokes with the reader about the difficulty of sorting out Viktor's various women friends and deciding who is the most important—a process always dependent on what the dog will bring next. Sometimes the "dog-post" is late, so when the seventh chapter doesn't arrive on time, the author talks with the reader and decides to insert a "leap-day" (*Schalttag*—"leap" as in "leap-year") after every four "dog-post-days," a scheme that he sticks to pretty well, but not absolutely. These *Schalttage* are the major digressions, some of them embodying material that Jean Paul had written earlier and separately; but there are also minor digressions, *Extrablätter*, within the various "dog-post-days." Basically this is parody of the epistolary novel and of the novel with philosophical digressions. And the novel of political intrigue is parodied in the ridiculously complicated external action. Jean Paul as author made a good point in pretending that Jean Paul as narrator was impatient with Knef! We are in a world of mirrors.

The external action has been interpreted straight as typical of a certain type of *Trivialroman*. In a novel entitled *Dya-Na-Sore* (claiming to be a translation from the Sanskrit but actually the work of a certain Wilhelm Friedrich von Meyern, published between 1787 and 1789), which we know Jean Paul to have read,[16] we have a father bringing up four sons to save the Fatherland, which is in the hands of enemies. When they are grown these four young men are sent out into the world where, without their knowledge, they are directed by a secret society. The tenor of the secret society is antimonarchical;

but the monarchic party, headed by the minister of the king, wins over the youngest and weakest of the young men, though in the end both king and minister are killed and the country set on a democratic-republican course. The earliest drafts for *Hesperus* present a somewhat similar scheme, which is obviously a reflection of occultist and republican tendencies of the period.[17] But in the final scheme of *Hesperus* the pattern is developed to the point of absurdity—and, I would think, consciously so. For the four young men are illegitimate sons resulting from the journeyings of Prince January, ruler of a petty German state, left in various places and unaware of their paternity. The prince has asked his chief adviser, Lord Horion, to bring these four sons back to Germany, but he "discovers" that three of them had been kidnaped in the same night and the fourth had disappeared. There is also a fifth "adopted" son, the so-called "Infante," the child of Horion's niece who had previously had relations with the prince. Horion himself had married a relative of the prince, but she had died in giving birth to a son Viktor, the hero of the novel. Viktor had been educated first in England, together with the Infante and Flamin, the son of the court chaplain, by a tutor named Dahore, then at the home of the chaplain, who lives in the country, together with Flamin—the Infante having gone blind from smallpox and been left behind in England. This is the "truth" reported by Knef. But Jean Paul allows his imagination to run riot over this skeletal scheme adopted from novels like *Dya-Na-Sore*, thereby situating the reader in something that seems appealing and familiar but then playing with it parodically throughout the novel. Of these five sons, three appear in the novel as republican-minded "Englishmen," the fourth is Flamin (for Viktor, not Flamin, is the chaplain's son), and the fifth turns out to be none other than Jean Paul himself. *Hesperus* is therefore ridiculing self-reflexively a traditional novel-type, the novel of unexpected revelations in high places which combines personal adventures with political purposes, but Jean Paul uses this type of plot, and was to do so again in *Titan*, to introduce a variety of characters, a variety of content, and the sense of shifting uncertainty in human experience. For although the external action is only an envelope, and we do not read Jean Paul for his plots, it becomes in his hands a metaphor for the mystery of selfhood, for hardly anyone in this novel is actually what he thinks he is. This quest for the self was to become a leading motif in the romantic novel.

When the novel begins, the chaplain and his family are preparing for the arrival of Viktor, who has trained to be a surgeon, and of Lord Horion, his putative father, who needs to have a cataract operation. Viktor successfully performs the operation, though Horion is not aware who has operated on him till he regains joyous sight. This opening sequence is followed first by the explanation of the dog-post technique, then by the account of the prince and his children. Now, says Jean Paul, "we can go straight on with the story," and he does. Lord Horion is to go to London to fetch the Infante and a new bride for the prince, while Viktor is to become the prince's physician and keep tabs on him till Horion returns. Although he hates the atmosphere of the court, Viktor agrees to do this in order to help humanize the prince. Viktor is an interesting character. He is warmhearted but at the same time addicted to wit, with "more inclination to raptures [*Schwärmereien*] than disposition [*Ansatz*] toward them, for his negative-electric philosophy was always striving to maintain a balance with his positive-electric enthusiasm—and from the ferment of both these spirits came nothing but humor."[18] He is therefore philosophic, sentimental, and "humorous"[19] (in the sense of being inclined toward adopting a humorist's stance), a truly complex character. It may be true, as has been asserted, that in Viktor we have Jean Paul's most elaborate and successful attempt to portray the combination of opposing forces within himself. Be that as it may, the whole novel embodies these oppositions as basic to the fullness of life. And it was primarily the fullness of *Hesperus* and the richly rounded-out character of Viktor that accounted for the enormous success of the novel on its first appearance. It had everything: sentiment, adventures, mysticism, humor, and republicanism.

Viktor differs from the Gustav of *Die unsichtbare Loge* in that he is a mature character in an established profession at the outset of the novel. Nevertheless, he has to learn to equilibrate the various tendencies in his nature. This comes about mainly through his relationship with two persons: a girl named Klotilde and her beloved teacher, the Indian sage Emanuel (who as Dahore had also been the teacher of Viktor, Flamin, and the Infante). The scenes with Emanuel are the most celebrated passages in the novel. Into these Jean Paul has woven his enthusiasm for the Sanscrit play *Sakuntala*, which he read in Forster's German translation—with its figure of the teacher-priest, his female pupil, and the flower imagery.[20] These scenes are set in an idyllic, symbolic landscape, a landscape of the spirit, here called Maiental and akin to the Lilienbad of *Die unsichtbare Loge* and the Lilar of *Titan*, the place where "higher humans" commune.

Emanuel is a mystic who foretells the moment of his death and prepares himself longingly for this transfiguration into the "second world." He is attended by a blind youth named Julius, whom Viktor and Jean Paul suspect to be the "Infante," and who, we are told at one point, is really the son of the chaplain, though Emanuel before he dies tells us that Julius, not Viktor, was the son of Lord Horion! But to revert to the inner meaning of the book: this curious image of blindness, which had already played its part in *Die unsichtbare Loge* either as blindfolding or damaged eyes and is to recur significantly in *Titan*, is always associated with heightening of the inner life, inner vision replacing external sight. Emanuel is characterized by complete "harmony between his heart and external nature,"[21] both being for him animated by the spirit of God:

> God is Eternity, God is Truth, God is holiness—He has nothing, He is everything—the whole heart grasps him, but no thought can; and He thinks only us when we think Him. All that is eternal and incomprehensible in man is His reflection: but let your wonder think no further. Creation hangs like a veil woven of suns and spirits over the Eternal, and Eternities move past the veil, not removing it from the brilliance it conceals.[22]

In Emanuel's presence Viktor feels his argumentative ratiocination, the "baser" side of his nature, falling away.[23] The ecstasy of this language was perhaps more appealing at the time it was written than it is nowadays. But its purpose is clear: somehow to express transcendent states of experience where the incommensurable touches us and moves us.

The themes of the novel are friendship, love, and republicanism. The latter is more explicitly developed than in *Die unsichtbare Loge* and in two ways: direct connection is made with the ideals of the French Revolution, and the "lodge" in the background of the earlier novel is replaced here by a definite "club." Gustav's friendship with Amandus and with Ottomar coalesces into the intense friendship of Viktor and Flamin, which becomes strained when they both fall in love with Klotilde—a situation that is resolved artificially and ironically by the revelation that Klotilde is Flamin's sister (Jean Paul never flirted with incest). Flamin is a more impetuous character and more inclined toward violence—less divided in himself than Viktor but also less self-assured, more dependent on others and especially on Viktor and Klotilde, too credulous of the malicious lies of self-seekers, and with no sense of the "second world." The contrast between the two is well developed, with Klotilde standing in the middle. She, a much more interesting character than Beata, is also the intermediary between Emanuel and Viktor. It is she who brings them together and bridges the two worlds that they represent, so that Viktor, because of her mediation and the love that she inspires in him, is able to partake of both and to fuse them into a richer attitude to life.

There is one extraordinary image in the novel that we should note before leaving it. When they unwillingly leave for the court, both Viktor and Flamin have wax images made of themselves to remain in the chaplain's house. This implies some kind of separation of the self-as-it-is from the self-as-it-is-to-become. Later Viktor recites a funeral oration over his wax image, which Klotilde has been tearfully observing.[24] It is a leave-taking from a life that has become for him a death-in-life, now that the higher vision has been vouchsafed him. Viktor's quest is the quest for unity within himself. At one point he implores eternal *natura naturans* to give him *one* soul, "just *one* . . . to my poor pining heart, which seems so hard and is so soft, seems so joyful and is so sad, seems so cold and yet is so warm."[25] This is the pervasive melody of the novel, and it is Jean Paul's own basic problem, a problem which *Hesperus* does not solve. It remains a statement of discordance, of an essentially romantic dualism.[26]

The full title of *Siebenkäs* sounds very baroque: *Blumen-, Frucht- und Dornenstücke oder Ehestand, Tod und Hochzeit des Armenadvokaten F. St. Siebenkäs* [Flower, Fruit and Thorn Pieces of Matrimony, Death and Marriage of the Poor Man's Lawyer F. St. Siebenkäs]—baroque in its clashing antitheses and its placing of death between matrimony and marriage, the state of matrimony on earth and marriage of the spirit. But it is non-baroque in that Siebenkäs's marriage of the spirit is not transcendental but here on earth. And the death referred to is a simulated death, not imagined as in Gustav's dream or mistaken as in Ottomar's "death," but a willed "death" like Viktor's destruction of his waxen image. We know that Jean Paul in 1790 had a terrifying vision in which he saw himself dead. We know also that on another occasion he had the experience of being separated from his Self and confronting it. These two traumatic experiences of early life were to pervade his whole work as metaphors of dissociation and dislocation. In *Siebenkäs* the protagonist decides he must go through the pretense of death and burial in order to liberate his spirit from his oppressive environment. In this novel the three worlds of the earlier two novels are reduced to two—the court, with all its intrigues and political factions, plays no part, and we concentrate on the clash between ordinary bourgeois existence, set as before in a small town with all the usual types of people, and the aspirations of the restless spirit. No reconciliation of the two is offered or even envisioned: to partake of the latter Siebenkäs must decide to die to the former. It is the most agonizingly dualistic of all Jean Paul's novels—agonizing because the life that Siebenkäs departs from is that between husband and wife. We watch the marriage gradually disintegrating, which is also an agonizing experience because our sympathies are divided between Siebenkäs and his wife Lenette. She is indeed obsessively domestic and disturbs his "writing" by the clatter she makes in cleaning the house. But he is not engaged in the composition of some great masterpiece, only in satirical *Selections from the Devil's Papers* (which Jean Paul himself had published in his "vinegar-factory" period). There is indeed more vinegar than wine in Siebenkäs. Then there is Lenette's attachment to her possessions, but these are so very few that we can sympathize with her unwillingness to have them pawned to pay her luckless husband's debts. Everything is bathed in Jean Paul's humor at its very richest: one's sympathy with the well-meaningness of it all is shot through with one's sense of its absurdity. It is indeed dark comedy. Her world is restricted and petty, but it was a world of contentment until disturbed; his aspirations are comprehensible but pretentious, and his is a world of discontent. Neither respects the other because neither can share in the other's world. Hers is homespun but at least real; his is the world of a searching, frustrated imagination but somehow false because he does not have the intellect or the soul to be a "higher man," though he thinks he has. And so we watch as the radiant young girl and the loving bridegroom of the beginning of the novel develop through constant hagglings, mistrust, and suspicion into a shrew and a tyrant. It all begins with his amusement at her provincialisms of speech. He is given to irony but what at first was gentle mockery steadily degenerates into quite cruel denigration.

As a cross-rhythm to this, there is the relationship between Siebenkäs and his double Leibgeber. The latter is harsh, cynical, and prone to anger; the former is gentler, satirical but stoic by nature. Leibgeber has the brittle laughter that proceeds from feverish anguish of spirit: "only an oppressed breast could laugh like that, only a too feverish eye around which the fireworks of life float like flying play-sparks [*Spiel-Funken*] fluttering before the black cataract [*schwarzer Star* = amaurosis], could see and draw such feverish pictures,"

[80]

says Jean Paul.[27] Leibgeber therefore comes out as negative, but stimulatingly and dangerously so, to us as we read the novel. Siebenkäs describes himself in a letter to Leibgeber as follows: "I hate sentimentality [*Empfindelei*], but Fate has implanted it in me so fixedly that the satirical Glauber Salts one can usually take to good effect, have to be taken by me in tablespoonfuls and even then without any noticeable improvement."[28] In other words both Siebenkäs and Leibgeber are attempting to bury their real natures by assuming a second nature, a persona which in each case is compensatory—for Leibgeber the superiority of scornful wit, for Siebenkäs the defense mechanism of satire. The conflicting forces in Viktor's personality are objectified here in two opposing but complementary characters, two *friends*. Once again Jean Paul takes conventional plot-elements and uses them metaphorically. The hoary old motif of two persons so alike in physical appearance as to be indistinguishable in the eyes of the world is the basis of the complexities of the plot of *Siebenkäs*, but is given psychological depth by the fact of their inseparability. For Leibgeber can become Siebenkäs, and vice versa—and at will, not by any enchantment or force outside their control. They have exchanged names before the novel begins, they exchange names again after Siebenkäs's "burial," which is instigated and origanized by Leibgeber. And Leibgeber can appear as Siebenkäs's "ghost," and Siebenkäs, as "Leibgeber," take over Leibgeber's post as inspector in Vaduz (which Leibgeber is anxious to avoid) and affect his moods. But then we must remember that this "Leibgeber" was really Leibgeber all along, because of the change of names. To point this up Jean Paul uses a second all-too-familiar motif of novelists, one that was to persist even to the age of Dickens and George Eliot: the disputed inheritance. But here again this becomes a metaphor: at the beginning of the novel Leibgeber comes into an inheritance, but since he has changed his name to Siebenkäs he cannot claim it until he can prove he is really Leibgeber, which he cannot. This means that by an act of will he has lost his real identity.

When he buries himself he is voluntarily renouncing his Siebenkäs identity. One might expect that by becoming "Leibgeber" he would regain identity and security. But he cannot dissociate himself entirely from his Siebenkäs self. He has found what he believes to be the ideal woman for him—intelligent, cultivated, serene, the very opposite of Lenette—and her name, Natalie, is curiously enough the same that Goethe was to give to the ideal woman for Wilhelm Meister, though *Siebenkäs* was finished before *Wilhelm Meister*. But when Siebenkäs–"Leibgeber" arrives in Vaduz we are told that "all of his old world was submerged in a deluge of tears, and nothing floated up but the two limp funeral wreaths of [his] dead days, Natalie's and Lenette's corsages, the medicinal sublimates [*Arznei-blumen* = flores, cf. "flowers" of sulphur] as it were of his sick soul, the border-plants of flower beds laid waste."[29] Before his "death" he had provided death benefits for both of them, but when he finally does get the legacy it is to "Siebenkäs's widow," that is, Lenette, that he directs it to be paid. And in the final scene of the novel he returns to his native town on the anniversary of his death. Why? To see his grave, to "do penance" properly, to catch a glimpse of Lenette and perhaps of her child (for she has married his friend the local schoolmaster), maybe to get some news of Leibgeber, and to "celebrate" his "death."[30] But things turn out differently. When he reaches the cemetery he finds a new grave, that of Lenette, who has died in childbirth. He now regrets the suffering he had caused her. "That's what we all say," the author comments, "when we bury those we have tormented."[31] One can extend the image to include Siebenkäs, for he had tormented himself. And had hoped to bury his torment, but obviously has not, especially when he learns that Lenette's last words expressed the hope that she would be rejoining him in the beyond. When he returns to the cemetery he finds Natalie bent over *his* grave. She takes him for a ghost, but only now does he tell her what has happened, for he has made no attempt to approach Natalie since his "death," having provided for two "widows." The novel ends with Natalie's resolution that they shall stay together, couched in the form of a prayer to God: "O All-loving One—I have lost him—I have found him again—Eternity is on the earth—make him happy with me."[32] When they had last seen each other, they had parted with a "death-kiss," resolving never to see each other again but to live on the memory of that moment.[33] The two scenes must be viewed together. Although at their very first encounter she had mistaken him for Leibgeber, it was his Siebenkäs nature that she loved. And it is significant that no Leibgeber, neither the one nor the other, is present in this closing sequence.

To understand this final scene fully we must relate it also to another earlier passage, a scene in this same cemetery.[34] Only then can we appreciate the close texture of this great novel—and its all-pervasive poetry. Among the items pawned to pay their debts had been a nosegay of silk flowers given to Lenette by Siebenkäs on the day they were engaged—a white rose, two red rosebuds, and a border of forget-me-nots. She was willing to let it go, implying that the red rosebuds of joy not yet full had lost their meaning, and the white rose—what that meant, she had forgotten. So the nosegay went the way of so much else among Lenette's possessions. Then some time later Siebenkäs, feeling sentimentally generous, decides to buy real flowers to replace the nosegay, hide them in some dark place, and then surprise Lenette with them on an evening walk. It is autumn, and although he gets the red and white roses from a greenhouse, he cannot buy forget-me-nots, which have long since been left in the fields. So he goes to the pawnbroker to redeem the flower-piece and take the forget-me-nots from it—only to find that it has already been returned to Lenette by another, an unsavory character who had made unsuccessful advances to her and of whom Siebenkäs is unnecessarily jealous. All he can do is take other silk forget-me-nots that happened to be in the pawnshop. Armed with this curious bouquet—half real, half artificial—he goes to the cemetery and puts it on a fresh grave, the grave of a young mother and her newborn child. Shortly before this, in a tense conversation between Siebenkäs and Lenette there had been a reference to the childlessness of their marriage. And we know, and Lenette does, that he had legally defended a young mother charged with infanticide to save her from torture (though not of course from death). Now, when Siebenkäs, Lenette, and the schoolmaster (another "rival," who does marry Lenette after Siebenkäs's "death") walk past the place where the flowers lie, Lenette mistakes these in the darkness for her own silk flowers, and thinks that her husband, angry at discovering that someone else had returned them, had placed them on this particular grave to scorn her childlessness, or to scorn her in general. Red and white roses—the roses of love and death—that they were *real* roses, she hadn't noticed; and forget-me-nots, but not her own—that she couldn't know.

The conversation in this first churchyard scene had turned on themes of death and corruption, rotting bodies and blooming flowers, sacrifices and memorials, the smallness of the world and the looming presence of the beyond. This is followed in the novel by one of the most extraordinary passages in all Jean Paul. Originally it was to have been placed elsewhere, perhaps not in this novel at all, but, as it now stands, it is linked to the conversation in the churchyard—thematically, for its style and tone are quite different. It takes up again the theme of eternity. And with it the theme of Godhead. Without belief in a God, eternity is a cloud-covered realm and the cosmos but "the cold iron mask of shapeless eternity."[35] Without belief in God the universe of the spirit shatters into numerous quicksilver Egos without direction, without unity and consistency. There follows the account of a dream in which the author awakes among the dead in a dead landscape. The dead ask Christ: "Is there then no God?" And he replies: "No." We, including him, are all fatherless orphans. At this the world destroys itself and dissolves into nothing, and Christ implores those mortals who are still alive to *believe* and worship. Else "He", God the Father, will be lost to them forever. The dreamer awakes to the joy of still being able to worship God, and his prayer is for belief. The dream is a therapeutic nightmare. In a second digression, which follows, Jean Paul gives us a second vision—the vision of the "second world," the eternity of the believer and therefore neither clouded nor shapeless, an eternity, like Natalie's, that is "on the earth," a dream in which both worlds meet in a mythological fantasy of longing, love, and redemption.

The higher world of the visions of Emanuel is therefore, here in *Siebenkäs*, taken out of the novel proper and put into the digressional arabesques. But there are also plenty of satirical digressions as well, in which the usual pyrotechnic display of wit is given full expansion. The "lower world" is, as we have seen, as vividly portrayed as in the earlier novels—even more so, for there are elaborate scenes (such as a Kermesse, and a shooting festival) of great realistic vitality which were to endear this particular novel of Jean Paul's to later realist writers. Ironical self-reflexiveness, contributes to the texture: in the Preface, Jean Paul reads the *Extrablätter* from *Hesperus* to a merchant to put him to sleep, so that he may read the digressions of his new novel to his daughter, but the merchant wakes up and objects to his putting such "novel-nonsense" into his daughter's head. To which Jean Paul objects: does not this man know that he, Jean Paul, is the son of a prince, as *Hesperus* had shown? And later the characters of *Hesperus* reassemble to discuss love, hate, and moral principles. There is also a reference forward, to *Titan*, which he was already thinking out. All the main features of Jean Paul's art are therefore well represented in *Siebenkäs*. What distinguishes it from his two earlier novels is greater realism, and greater integration—integration of opposites, but not reconciliation. Unless this be seen in Natalie's closing words. But those are a prayer. They are words of hope, not a statement of achievement.[36]

Titan (1800–1803) does work toward a reconciliation, though not very convincingly. It is Jean Paul's most elaborate and longest work, and he spent ten years writing it.[37] Again we have, as the shell of the action, a highly intricate plot, with all the usual elements: mistaken parentage, "supernatural" incursions, political intrigues, doubles, mysterious messengers and mysterious prophecies, plus some new twists such as distorting mirrors, deceiving wax effigies, ventriloquism, and a talking jackdaw. Throughout the novel the hero Albano has the sense of being manipulated by "spirits"—and doesn't like it. He longs for enlightenment, to know the truth both about the past and regarding his present state and future destiny; but this revelation is constantly delayed. *Titan* has a much wider range of characters than Jean Paul's earlier novels, and much more interesting ones. And it is the portrayal of these characters—especially of Albano, Roquairol, and Schoppe, the three "heroes," that gives the book its fascination. The three main women characters—Liane, Linda, and Idoine—are also far from uninteresting, though the last mentioned is perhaps more of an idea than a person. The petty but insidious schemings at the *Residenz*, and the richer because more honest and less self-seeking life in the country, again form one of the main contrasts—and this is essentially a novel of contrasts, contrast of characters, ideals, styles as well as settings. There are more of the symbolic landscapes we have become accustomed to from Jean Paul's earlier novels: this time there is a long sequence in Rome and another around the Bay of Naples, including Vesuvius but centered mainly on Ischia. There are the same great outpourings of ecstasy, both waking and in dreams, together with scenes of vivid realism as in *Siebenkäs*, and a somewhat greater range of humorous characters. But what makes the book especially memorable are the tragic characters—Roquairol, Liane and Schoppe. There is plenty of authorial commentary but less self-reflexiveness, for this is a much more assertive and self-reliant novel than the others. It does not relativize what it says, preferring rather to display inconclusiveness in the characters themselves—but Albano, especially in conjunction with Idoine, moves toward a completeness and finality that the others never achieve, remaining divided even in death. For Liane, Roquairol and Schoppe death is not the serene consummation that it was for Emanuel. It is for them merely the final working out of the agony within them. But Albano is made to work through to a unity, though only an envisioned and future unity, and therefore perhaps for that reason and because it is so worked at, it may not convince (and has not convinced) all readers. The novel could well have ended otherwise, with the discord unresolved, and many wish that it had. Indeed there is some evidence that *Titan* may at first have been intended to end thus, but Berend's detailed examination of the huge mass of preliminary drafts suggests that quite early on Jean Paul decided in favor of a conclusion that should be a resolution. Much of what had at first characterized Albano became the basis for the character of Roquairol.

In Jean Paul's original conception, this novel was to be a study of the good and bad sides of genius. In fact, the first title we have recorded was *Der Genius*. For Jean Paul the characteristic of genius was being ruled by the imagination, and he was particularly concerned with the dangers of being excessively or exclusively so directed. This is the root of the inability to live productively and happily, from which several of the characters suffer, and it is one strong element in Albano, though he has an attachment to reality to counterbalance it. Much of the novel is concerned with this division within Albano, a discord that is only resolved when he discovers that he is to be ruler of a state and determines that his idealism will be combined with a sense of practical responsibilities in his high office.

This has often been presented as a victory for Weimar humanism. Of the great men of Weimar, it was Herder in particular who meant most to Jean Paul, and especially during the decade when he was working on *Titan*. However, the idea that Albano should by the end of the novel have developed into an integrated personality seems to have emerged quite early in Jean Paul's thinking, though maybe at that early stage not precisely in terms similar to *Wilhelm Meister*. Jean Paul once stated that the novel should perhaps be called "Anti-Titan". . . "every heaven-stormer finds his Hell, just as every mountain finally makes a level plain out of its valley."[38] This is from a letter he wrote in September 1803, by which time the whole novel was virtually completed. It cannot, however, be asserted that this turn toward humanism eclipsed the "real" Jean Paul, for *Titan* is as full of dualism and anguish as the other novels. Only the end is different. Furthermore, he worked out the other alternative in a section of the "Komischer Anhang" [Comic Appendix] that forms part of this immense novel, the section entitled "Des Luftschiffers Giannozzo Seebuch" [Giannozzo the Aeronaut's Seabook]. This travelogue by a balloonist who levitates above the earth because of his distaste for it is the diary of an idealist who scorns the vanity, hypocrisy, injustice, and folly of the world, exulting in his lonely superiority, only to find one day that he cannot descend, as he has regularly done, and crashing to death in the Swiss mountains. It is "comic" only because of the series of satires that it contains. It is an obverse to the story of

Albano, with which it forms a sort of double-novel, a typically romantic form in that each reflects on the other. There are plenty of
Giannozzo moods in *Titan*, and dreams like Albano's and fears like
Schoppe's in "Giannozzo." The two are an indissoluble whole, and a
characteristically Jean Paul whole.

He had from quite early on in the composition of *Titan* planned
various supplements to the main structure in which he would freely
indulge his fancy. These form the "Comic Appendix," the first part
of which was published together with Volume One of the novel in
1800, and the second part with Volume Two in 1801 (the novel is in
four volumes). In later editions of the complete novel these two
parts of the appendix were printed together at the end. The first
part of the appendix is in the form of contributions to a fictive
journal, by Fenk, Siebenkäs, Viktor, and Jean Paul himself. The
second part consists of a sort of, and very Jean-Paulian, "essay on
criticism" and "Giannozzo." It is Leibgeber for whom Giannozzo
wrote his journal, and who communicates it; and it is Leibgeber who
is declared to be the author of the "Clavis Fichtiana" (1800) which
was originally written for inclusion in the "Comic Appendix" but
then withdrawn—a satire (and a very perceptive one) on Fichte's
philosophy to which, we are told by Jean Paul in footnotes, Leibgeber was addicted. Apart from "Giannozzo" and the "Clavis Fichtiana," the "Comic Appendix" is pretty tedious reading, mainly
because it has no structural coherence other than being a collection
of satires—similar to those Jean Paul had written before he turned
to novels, though less vinegary. They are not easily referable to
sections of the novel, except for "Giannozzo" and the "Clavis," and
although as digressions or arabesques *within* a novel they might have
had functional value, standing alone they have none. But the fact of
their existence in this form is significant. What Jean Paul has done is
to take arabesques *out* of the novel and treat them as supplements.
There are digressions within *Titan* but far fewer than in the earlier
novels, and mainly only in the first two parts; the reflective passages
in the third and fourth volumes occur in letters, diaries, or authorial
commentary. What this all seems to indicate is a turning away from
the basically Sternean construction with digressions of the earlier
novels; but also an unwillingness, or inability, to abandon them entirely, and the incorporation of them primarily into supplements,
not emerging from the action but appended to it, resulting in a new
form that is not entirely successful because it is unduly fragmented.

The external plot of *Titan* is far too complicated to be summarized here. Basically it is the same sort of plot as that of *Die unsichtbare Loge* and *Hesperus*, dependent on mysteries and eventual demystifications, with even more emphasis on the operations of "spirits," which turn out in this case to be purposeful machinations of an "Uncle." It has a similar contrast between a world of the spirit and the world of *Realpolitik* in a petty state, and the same general theme of the education through life of a hero—the main difference being, as we have already noted, in the resolution of dualism foreseen at the end. Like the other novels of Jean Paul, it deals with friendship and with love, and differentiates between them. It builds on contrasts of characters, but attention is divided more equally among these than in his earlier novels, so that we have here what amounts to multiple heroes and multiple heroines, all of whom are made to engage our interest and to a certain extent our sympathy. In the education of Albano three women—Liane, Linda, and Idoine—play major roles, successively but, in a total view of the novel, complementarily. And of the men, Roquairol, Schoppe, and Gaspard (whom Albano erroneously believes to be his father) are the strongest influences on his development. Gaspard is a further development of Lord Horion, Roquairol is a much profounder and more interesting study of the basic type represented by Ottomar, and Schoppe is Leibgeber thought through to his logical, tragic conclusion—and recognized as such by both Siebenkäs, who enters the novel at the end, and Leibgeber, the recipient and transmitter of Giannozzo's journal. All three are titanic in one way or another: Gaspard is consumed by the drive for power and position, Roquairol by passion and cynical contemplation of the havoc it creates for others and himself, Schoppe by cerebration and obsession with the Absolute. When Schoppe dies, Jean Paul takes leave of him in words that suggest he is the tragic hero of the novel:

> The earthly globe and everything terrestrial from which fleeting worlds are formed, was too small and light for you. For you sought something higher than life, something behind life, not *your* Ego, nothing mortal, not *an* Immortal, but *the* Eternal, the Primal, God. —All appearances here below, good and bad, meant nothing to you. Now you rest in true Being, death has withdrawn the sultry cloud of life from your dark heart, and the eternal light that you sought so long now stands revealed; and you, its beam, dwell once again in its radiance.[39]

These three men begin as friends but end as frightening examples of where titanism of feeling or thought can lead, except for Gaspard with whose world, but not its opportunism, Albano becomes reconciled. All three stand in opposition to Albano—Gaspard by his coldness, Roquairol by his violence, Schoppe by his nihilism. None represents the attitude to reality that Albano desires. Gaspard is calculating, Roquairol ruthless, and Schoppe self-destructive. The three women, on the other hand, are all positively contributive to Albano's development whereas the men contribute, as it were, negatively. Roquairol is first viewed by Albano as Karl Moor, Hamlet, Clavigo, Egmont—heroes of tragedies; and the plural is significant because Roquairol is always play-acting. When he first enters the novel he has been to a masquerade dressed as Werther and, rebuffed, has shot himself—but only in the earlobe: finally he shoots himself successfully in the performance of a play of his own composition. Schoppe, too, longs for freedom from his ego, but also for love. In his madness his obsession is a fear of the Absolute Ego, the hypostasization of Spirit or Mind, the nightmare of an idealist philosopher. Albano, on the other hand, though endowed with a rich life of the spirit and therefore affectionately devoted to Schoppe, is eager for action, for participation in the active world, especially for participation in those causes which he considers as embodying higher aspirations of the spirit, such as that of the French revolutionaries. Gaspard is, for Albano, too pragmatic to have his undivided approval. Liane is too little of this world, absorbed as she is with certainty of impending death and communion with a dead woman friend, but she represents a purity of spiritual life that remains with Albano as a constantly recurring vision. Linda is a much stronger character, proudly self-reliant, determined to realize her self, basically opposed to marriage, and to the belief that fulfillment is found only in external action. She tries to argue Albano out of fighting for the French revolutionaries and asserts the satisfaction of being "something for oneself, not for others".[40] She is nonetheless confused, because although she wants freedom for herself, she loves Albano. Only when she is seduced by Roquairol masquerading as Albano does she withdraw completely. Albano in Rome is oppressed by the sense of the dead past in contrast to the living present, which for him is concentrated in contemporary France. Idoine, who presides over a model community and combines high ideals with practical activity, represents a solution to what was lacking in Liane's spirituality and Linda's confusion. She is very much in the spirit of *Wilhelm Meister*[41] and her device could well also have been: "Here or nowhere is America"—or France. She, together with Albano's assumption of the duties of a prince, provides the resolution.

It is by these characters that *Titan* lives, all very vital and not as schematic as my account may have suggested. And there are many others, including a goodly number of excellent comic types, splendid court intriguers, vivid representatives of the common people, a foppish music master, a village pedant, and a saintly old hermit who is the real moral center of the book. It is a rich canvas of oppositions and potentialities constantly relativized by being balanced off against each other, a welter of marvelously graphic scenes, a thicket of experience through which the hero battles toward light and harmony, a hero who has always had a thirst for greatness and may well at the end be on his way to achieving it. May well be . . . maybe . . . may be not. . . ? In the last pages of the novel Albano anticipates a rule of happiness for his subjects, of "highest justice," and reconciliation with old enemies. He looks forward to the greenness of the future. Could it be that this ostensibly closed ending is implicitly just another uncertain one, a romantic open ending, leading "this way or that way" in Dorothea Schlegel's terms? The reader is certainly left with plenty to think about.

Jean Paul began writing *Flegeljahre* while he was working on *Titan* and for a time intended it to be part of *Titan*, a counterpoint in the form of a counter-theme expressing a nontitanic character and his education to life.[42] By April 1799 he had decided to separate the two novels, but he continued to work at both simultaneously.[43] *Flegeljahre* finally appeared in four volumes in 1804 and 1805. The title refers to the fledgling inexperience of youth (not in the present meaning of "hooligan years"). It is the story of twin brothers, the dreamy, credulous, good-hearted idealist Walt and the unsentimental, incredulous, ironic realist Vult. Throughout the novel they complement each other in mutual affection and assistance, but in his last message to Walt, Vult admits that neither has really changed the other: "I leave you as you were, and go as I came."[44] The novel, as we have it, ends with Walt recounting to Vult a dream he has had, a cosmic dream of a higher, *true* world—"das rechte Land"—in which all things come together in a new creation, a dream of longing, hope, and resolution. But Vult's reaction is to tell Walt to go on dreaming, and leave, without Walt's realizing that he has left forever. No real resolution of what Walt and Vult represent is therefore achieved or even suggested. The novel ends with a reinforcement of the dualism. We know that Jean Paul contemplated a continuation; in his sketches for the fourth volume (which ends in the manner I have described) he spoke of an eventual resolution of the conflict as "victory of simplicity over world" [*Sieg der Einfalt über die Welt*],[45] and he planned that Walt should marry the daughter of a Polish general with estates in Germany, acquire an ecclesiastical living and settle down to a comfortable and peaceful life. But Jean Paul never proceeded with such a continuation. Various reasons can be adduced for this. The external plot had too many loose ends and Walt's character had shown no progress toward mastery of life. Indeed throughout Book Four Jean Paul's sympathies seem to be equally centered on Vult, who becomes the more unfortunate of the two. Another factor might have been that the novel had not received the general acclaim that its author may well have expected. With time, however, it has become the best liked of his novels, and that perhaps because it expresses most sharply and in more easily accessible form than the others the basic dualism in Jean Paul, the dualism inherent in all romanticism—indeed in all of us and all our lives. No one understood this better than Robert Schumann, who transformed Walt and Vult into Florestan and Eusebius, and turned into *Papillons* the great masked ball of the penultimate chapter of what he once called "a book akin in kind to the Bible."[46] For all his love of Walt, Jean Paul could not let Vult drift out of the novel, only to reappear (why, and as what?) in Pastor Walt's house. Vult meant far too much to him for that. His penetrating gaze contrasts with Walt's ingenuous, too-ready acceptance of things at face value, but his distrust of enthusiasm is not really nihilistic because it is based on a sense of truth. He pits wit against effusiveness, but respects true love and shows it toward his brother. He is also in no wise a philistine or a representative of prosaicness, for he is an accomplished artist, and the sounds of his flute—sometimes strident, sometimes enticing—resound throughout the novel as a lonely commentary on life. And so Walt recounts his dream and Vult goes off playing his flute, "his second windpipe, his firepiece," as it is elsewhere called.[47] And perhaps that is the only way, and the best way, the novel could end.

Flegeljahre lives predominantly through its humor, which is not that of the "vinegar factory" but the benign humor of reflective maturity. It is full of richly comic incidents, of ludicrous mistakings and absurd *contretemps* viewed with the loving laughter of a tolerant and understanding narrator. Jean Paul himself is commissioned by the town council of the small town of Hasslau to report regularly on the doings of Walt, who is to come into an inheritance so long as he fulfills the extraordinary conditions of the will. The testator is a local Croesus who went under the name of Van der Kabel, but whose real name was Friedrich Richter. The novel begins with the reading of the will from which seven relatives—five of them small-town officials, one a book dealer, and the seventh just "Flitte from Alsace"—hope to profit, but will not unless Walt, a virtual unknown, fails to fulfill the conditions. These latter are aimed at giving him education to life, but in odd ways—such as proofreading for the bookseller, tuning pianos for a day, tending a garden for a month, being a notary for a year, fulfilling the wishes of all the other presumptive "heirs" for a week each, being a schoolmaster, and finally becoming a parson. The seven relatives are obviously concerned to prevent Walt's compliance. So this initial *donnée*, which sets the humorous tone, serves as a means to bring Walt into relationship with petty bourgeois such as Jean Paul reveled in describing, and also to provide the skeleton for a complicated external plot that will introduce variety and constant shift of superficial focus. I say *superficial* focus, for the real essence of the plot soon becomes focused on Walt and his brother, and the latter, of course, hopes to benefit from Walt's inheritance. In fact the complicated machinery of the external plot soon breaks down, with only very few of the conditions fulfilled before the novel ends, and this may be another reason why Jean Paul never attempted a continuation. Perhaps one could say with truth that Jean Paul viewed his "plot" with the same bemused irony that he bestowed on the complicated conditions imposed by the "plot" of *Titan* on Albano. But it does give rise to several superbly funny sequences, such as Walt's notarial activity for General Zablocki, which includes making an "official" copy of his travel memoirs under the title of *mémoires érotiques*, the advantages enjoyed by a piano tuner in getting to know the daughters of the household, and the connections established by proof-reading with the book dealer (who is also a publisher) from which Walt hopes to get his novel placed—or rather *their* novel, for the two brothers are cooperating on a novel in which Walt provides the substance and Vult the digressions. Its title is to be *Hoppelpoppel or The Heart*, from which we might assume that *Hoppelpoppel* refers to irregular cardiac activity. But in fact it is a name for scrambled eggs mixed with meat and potatoes.

So we have here a novel within a novel. The relationship between *Hoppelpoppel* and *Flegeljahre* is complex. By the time *Flegeljahre* ends, the twins have not succeeded in getting *Hoppelpoppel* published. After two silent rejections they send it to the Berlin critic Merkel (who had made some particularly nasty attacks on Goethe and the Romantics and also reviewed *Titan* insensitively), and this elicits the comment that Walt's contributions were tolerable but Vult's were just "echoes of that cuckoo Jean Paul who without his cuckoo-clock of imitation would be boring anyway."[48] When Vult had first suggested that they write a novel together, his idea had been: "I will laugh in it and you will weep or fly high—you the evangelist, I the beast of the field in the background [*das Vieh darhinter*]—each will set off the other—and everybody will be satisfied. . . ."[49] As a title he had suggested "Flegeljahre," but Walt had rejected that as "too blatant, and too wild." So Vult then suggested a double title, such as a certain popular author prefers (Jean Paul himself, naturally), to indicate the double authorship. Walt begins by writing about the hero's longing for a friend, and Vult adds an ironic digression on love of woman interrupting male friendship, adding salt to sugar, as he says, "for the sweet parts will gain most from the sharp parts, for behind a sharp fingernail lies the softest, sentimentalest flesh."[50] Walt lives his life and relives it more intensely in his novel; a summer day begets a lyrical description of that season for eventual use in the novel, and a dinner party sees him observing characters that he could also use. Meanwhile Vult counters his ecstatic experiences with satirical digressions—on talking in concerts, on the limitations and pretenses of aristocrats, on a "disconcerting concert" that took place after a concert in which the members of the orchestra fell to blows over the relative superiority of Italian or German music, a *zertierendes Konzert*, a concert without the con-. Jean Paul, the most ingenious etymologizer in German literature, removes the *kon* from the verb *konzertieren* (to make music) and is left with *zertieren*: but *Tier* means animal, *vertieren* would mean "to make into animals," and *zer-* is a disjunctive prefix meaning "breaking up." One can therefore appreciate Jean Paul's appreciation of Vult. Walt sends Vult chapters, and Vult sends Walt digressions. By two-thirds through the novel, *Hoppelpoppel* has become the only real link between the brothers. Jean Paul breaks off one of the digressions by saying that it belongs in *Hoppelpoppel* and not here, and in one of his reports to the executor of the will he includes passages from a diary kept by Vult, which say that Walt could be the hero of a novel called "Tölpeljahre eines Dichters" because he is as innocent as a cow [*Vieh*], can only love poetically, and reveres in quite ordinary people "badly daubed saints' pictures of his inner images of life and soul."[51] *Tölpeljahre* is merely a derogatory synonym for *Flegeljahre*, and the irony is compounded by the fact that the executor objects to Jean Paul using Vult's words instead of writing his own report.

Flegeljahre is therefore itself a double-novel in that *Hoppelpoppel* provides the counterpoint. It is from reading *Hoppelpoppel* that Vult decides that Walt is in love with Wina, the daughter of General Zablocki. And when Walt goes off on his romantic journey with the ostensible purpose of meeting up with Wina, everything becomes transformed in his mind into material for his novel. He meets what as a novelist he needs to meet: travelers of various kinds on the road of life, a beggar, a blue-eyed actress, a masked man, and finally Zablocki and Wina themselves. A picture seller sells him a composition in which all he has seen is transformed into an "anagram and epigram of life"[52] with a Janus-head, and an angel hovering above. Life may be double-faced, but Walt cannot cease to believe in supernatural benevolence, and never does. The episode with the picture seller is pure poetry, for what better description of poetry could there be than the "anagram and epigram of life"? And this is not the only scene in the novel where it draws near to poetry. The "prose" is always there, but it is transformed—transforms itself—into something of deeper, more basic significance.

The general plot-line is linear and chronological, and what digressions there are are either brief or projected into *Hoppelpoppel*. The treatment of digressions represents therefore a further development of the technique we have seen Jean Paul working toward in *Titan*, where in the last two volumes they had been embodied in speeches of the characters. In *Flegeljahre* they either occur in speeches of Vult or are implanted into *Hoppelpoppel* or in Jean Paul's "reports" to the executor (though there is one important arabesque early in the novel in which Walt's essay on the peaceful life of a Swedish parson prefigures the novel's envisioned "end"). The ecstatic passages, less frequent than in the earlier novels, appear either in *Hoppelpoppel* or as material intended for it, but there is one important such sequence in the real life of Walt. In all his novels Jean Paul carefully and effectively places climactic scenes at the end of each book of the novel. In *Flegeljahre* there is one such scene at the end of Book Three (Chapter 49), in which as they pass out of a dark cleft in the mountains into the morning sunlight breaking through a waterfall, Walt expresses first his usual delight at the glory of God but then extends his arms to Wina—"no longer toward Heaven alone but to what was most beautiful *on earth.*"[53] At the end of the preceding second book there is a marvelous scene which marks the end of Walt's attempts at male friendship. The awakening of love at the end of Book Three contrasts, therefore, with the disillusionment at the end of the second book, in which Walt realizes that his own clumsiness has prevented any rapprochement with the dashing Count Klothar (whom Vult has downplayed all along, partly in the attempt to open his brother's eyes but also because he was jealous, afraid that Klothar might usurp his place in his brother's affections). Walt has dressed up for his meeting with Klothar, trying to look his social equal by wearing an aristocratic theatrical costume and having his hair done appropriately. In this scene Vult restores Walt's hair to its normal pigtail—the coiffure of the bourgeois—while Walt vents his distress and Vult urges him to have more "egoism," to be more self-reliant. And urges him to hold the hair ribbon firmly in his teeth instead of lamenting lost fantasy, so that Vult can restore him to his normal self. It is a scene flooded by moonlight, and by love—nowhere in Jean Paul are the two worlds of his art, the poetry and the prose, more richly intertwined. Equally poetic is the great "mask-dance" [*Larven-Tanz*] toward the end of Book Four in which life transforms itself into pattern and music: "A *bal masqué* is perhaps the summit of what playful poetry can play after life. As for the poet all classes and times are the same, the external is merely dress but the internal is sound and delight, so here men make poetry of themselves and life. . . . All those that never came into contact . . . are encircled in *one* light happy round, driven on gloriously by rhythm, by music, that land of souls, as masks are the land of bodies."[54] It is Walt who speaks these words, which Wina says are themselves poetry. At the ball Vult tries at one point to become Walt by assuming his mask. But this does not work. He "goes as he came" and leaves Walt as he was. No reader, including Jean Paul himself, could really wish them otherwise.

Pigtails and moonlight—this conjunction seems to me to symbolize the essential nature of Jean Paul's art, which is thus elliptical in structure, as Friedrich Schlegel had suggested a novel should be. But does this mean that he had a poetic conception of the form? On moonlight he had the following to say: "To the eye, beauty without bounds appears mostly as moonlight, that wondrous light of spirits which is yet related to neither the beautiful nor the sublime, and which permeates us with painful longing, the dawn, as it were, of an eternity which can never rise on this earth."[55] And he once characterized poetry as painting "on the curtain of eternity the future spectacle of what transcends our reality, even the reality of the heart . . . no flat mirror of the present, but a magic mirror of time outside of time," drawing down from above what our thinking only glimpses fragmentarily, "the bright sweet eye from out of the cloud" [*das helle süsse Auge aus der Wolke*].[56] He continues with the assertion that the task of poetry is not to dissolve reality nor to reproduce it in its finitude but to decipher [*entziffern*] the eternal meaning that it must have, and the divine is perceptible by us only when transposed with (or into) reality; for "a world can arise from a god, but not a god from a world." By "world" Jean Paul obviously means here an integrated, meaningful world. The passages I have just been quoting are taken from an appendix to the *Vorschule der Ästhetik* and from Part Three of that treatise. Early on in the *Vorschule* he defines poetry as enveloping restricted nature with the unrestrictedness of an idea and allowing the latter to submerge itself in the former.[57] But this process must result in a fusion, not a subordination. Poetry must "totalize" reality and reify the Absolute. The poet's creative force combines self-consciousness (reflection, *Besonnenheit*) and the uncon-sciousness (instinct, *Instinkt*). Instinct intuits beyond space and time, it is a sort of divine force in the creative genius, it presages, opens up a bigger world, "senses a greater future than there is room for here below."[58] The comic he interprets as the obverse of the sublime, but the comic can be poetic only if the Absolute is somehow invoked. This occurs if the perceptions of the understanding are contrasted with the ideas of the reason, so that the finite becomes contrasted with the infinite. This is humor.

Humor, therefore, is a sort of reversed sublime in which the real is not elevated by reference to an idea but diminished thereby. It too should "totalize," dealing not with individual follies or fools but with folly itself ("Uncle Toby's campaigns do not ridicule just Uncle Toby or Louis XIV, but are the allegory of all human hobby-horses and the childishness in all of us").[59] Humor, in its recognition of the finite and the infinite factor in all of us, lays the path for the sublime, and irony is its objective representation.

René Wellek is probably right when he says that the most interest-ing section of the *Vorschule* is that dealing with wit which (in Wellek's words) is conceived of as "the metaphoric power in general, the poetic power itself, which is in the service of the symbolic view of the world."[60] Wit establishes similarities between incommensurable quan-tities (for example, between bodies and spirits). It is therefore essen-tially connected with the imagination and combines intuitively, where-as judgment [*Scharfsinn*] separates rationally and is the product of the understanding. The connections made by the latter (the under-

standing) are nonpictorial [*unbildlich*] and depend on partial similarities, on one common element in the predication, whereas those
made by the imagination are *bildlich* (graphic), so that *bildlich* wit can
either inspirit bodies or embody spirits.[61] Among such connections established by the imagination Jean Paul includes (and defends) wordplay. And he argues strongly for a cultivation of wit as the force
that gives freedom by its fluidifying powers, the faculty of dissociation that begets new associations and deeper perceptions, creating
new worlds—a sort of resurrection after a Last Judgment.[62]

In his discussion of plot, motivation, and characters Jean Paul
makes two interesting points. He downplays the importance of motivation as tending to produce a rather mechanical effect, and, secondly, he places therefore more emphasis on open characters, those
who can act this way or that. Fixed characters he thinks are not good
in a novel because their actions are far too easily predictable. What
interest there should be in a plot would seem for Jean Paul to derive
not from unpredictability of events or predictability of characters
but from unpredictability of characters. This throws light on the
preference we have seen in his novels for characters uncertain of
themselves—the unformed, fluid seekers. It also accounts for the
almost parodic nature of his external plots, his attitude of bemused
skepticism toward these, and the contrast we often feel in his novels
between inner development and external action, a contrast which is
close to ironic. The nearer a work is to prose (and consequently the
furthest from poetry) the more it is governed by the Law of Sufficient Reason. "It is a good idea to conceal true development behind
what is the apparent development"[63]—this is how he describes his
attitude to psychological action as contrasted with external plot, and
the novels themselves certainly bear this out.

Jean Paul seems to have read everything he could lay his hands
on, and this included novels of all types. In the *Vorschule* he attempts
a typology of the novel, distinguishing three types that he calls Italian, German, and Dutch. This categorization has been widely quoted,
especially in works on Jean Paul himself, but is actually not very
precise or very useful. The distinction between the "Italian" type,
which is characterized by intense feeling, lofty diction, noble characters, and a general elevated tone, and the "Dutch" type, which delin-
eates with loving care the ordinary and does so with great attention
to detail, is clear enough. On the other hand, the "German" type—
midway between the sublime and the everyday, with a hero who is
neither lofty nor comic, and "coloring bourgeois everydayness with

the evening glow of the romantic heaven," seems to be too much of a catchall. But Jean Paul obviously (and perhaps rightly) set his face against a too rigid concept of the novel. Its basic characteristic should be breadth "in which almost all forms can lie and clatter,"[64] and he recognizes its lyric, epic, and dramatic propensities, though without ever going so far as to advocate mixture of genres as Friedrich Schlegel had. But the tripartite typology does attempt to account for the mixture of styles in his own work, although it does not touch on the particular evasive poetry that emerges from the contrast and meeting of heaven and earth in the moonlight of the poetic imagination.

The great poet Hölderlin, according to two of his friends, was already working on his novel *Hyperion* in 1792, and in July 1793 he declared that he was writing it for the female sex in the hope that his hero would appeal to them more than "those wordy and adventure-ridden knights."[65] He seems to be referring to the protagonists of the *Ritterromane*, those popular novels involving "knights," and distinguishing his own work from such avidly read potboilers. Further testimony of his sense of departing from existing traditions of novelmaking is his statement, later in the same letter, that his novel is more a medley of occasional moods [*Gemengsel zufälliger Launen*] than the considered development of a fixed character, more a picture of ideas and feelings than a "regular psychological development," without explicit explanation of motivations but coming down eventually to the interaction of character and circumstances. He was planning it as a novel in two "books," and as such, though much changed, it eventually appeared, the first volume in 1797 and the second in 1799. The possibilities that the novel form offered were, Hölderlin said, still *terra incognita*,[66] with infinite opportunity for innovation and discovery. Nothing has been preserved of this 1793 version of *Hyperion*, which underwent radical revision as regards both the overall plan and the main character. But by October 1794 a first part was "almost finished," the "progress from youth to manhood, from feeling to reason, from fancy to truth and freedom" justifying lengthy treatment.[67] Schiller published the beginning of this version in his periodical *Thalia*. Hölderlin then began a metrical version, of which two fragments are preserved. The motivation behind this change would seem to have been his search for some kind of heightened language more appropriate to his lofty subject than ordinary novel-prose. But his prose had never been ordinary, and he soon aban-

Friedrich Hölderlin. Pastel by Franz K. Hiemer, 1792. Original in Schiller-Nationalmuseum, Marbach.

doned the metrical version and returned to prose. This new version is no longer in the epistolary form of the *Thalia* fragment; and presents Hyperion as an old man narrating his life in chronological sequence to a young visitor. But this in turn was abandoned as Hölderlin returned to the letter-form, though, as we shall see, a rather unconventional letter-form, in the final version.[68] Schiller, recognizing the novel as a work of genius, had persuaded Cotta, the most famous publisher of the day, to print it. When the first volume appeared, Hölderlin wrote to his sister that it was "a part of himself," and in the copy of the whole work that he sent to his beloved Susette Gontard (from whom he had meantime been finally separated) he underlined passages to indicate their relevance to them both, for this is a highly personal book.[69] But it is also a book about the times, with which Hölderlin felt increasingly out of tune. It is an elegiac book that constantly evokes ideals from which the modern world, the world of Hölderlin's own day as he saw it, had departed. Two images are persistently employed to emphasize this degeneration: modern society is contrasted with that of the great heroic age of Greece, and the divisiveness of modern man is contrasted with the unity of nature. The two images are, of course, connected, for Greek culture had frequently been interpreted as based on a sense of the unity of nature. The interesting thing about *Hyperion* is that the longing for *past* culture and the desire to become an integral part of the nature that is *present* all around him means overcoming both the opposition of culture and nature and that between past and present. The Greek setting, says Hölderlin in the short preface to the novel, was best suited to develop the hero's "elegiac" character—and, we must surely add, the particular thematic nexus of culture-and-nature, past-and-present. He warns against taking the book as a compendium of instruction or simply as a story, for it is neither: "The resolution of dissonances in a certain character is not just for reflecting on nor for mere pleasure" [*Lust*—entertainment, probably].[70] This is an important clue to what the novel is to be about: divisiveness *within* a character, which might seem different from division of present from past and alienation of man from nature, but is presented in *Hyperion* as an integral part of this central thematic concern. Greece is both metaphor and reality: the reality is modern Greece struggling to free itself from the Turks (the events in Volume Two refer to military engagements in 1770), the metaphor applies to the modern world in general, and, in the second volume, is narrowed into a devastating indictment of Germany. There is an extraordinary unity—perhaps even monotony—about the imagery of the book, and space and time become part of this imagery of unity.

Hyperion brilliantly combines two narrative modes, the epistolary and the retrospective. One of the main arguments in favor of the epistolary novel had been that it presented events and sentiments as they occurred or arose and thereby achieved an immediacy akin to that of drama. Opponents of the form asserted that such claims of greater illusion were themselves illusory, because it was impossible to combine immediacy of emotion with effective narration of events.[71] Hölderlin uses the letter-form but maintains a retrospective stance, elegiac and not immediate, except at one point where he wishes to convey the immediate nature of a situation, and does so by including in Hyperion's letters some old letters written at the time of the situation he is now recalling. The narrative stance is therefore consistently retrospective but becomes immediate at one moment without breaking the unity of the novel. Hölderlin's choice of technique makes this possible. After trying various narrative strategies, he decided to use neither a third-person narrator, nor a first-person narrator pretending to relate events as they occur—whereas in fact the sequence is completed before he begins his account which would affect the coloration of his account and destroy any illusion of immediacy. In an elegiac narration, such as Hölderlin most carefully and consciously constructs, such coloration is of the essence. And the letter-form means that Hyperion is not just talking to himself, nor to unknown readers, but to a specific person, Bellarmin, a German, for whom the fierce condemnation of Germany has special relevance, so that we have a fictive reader within the novel. Bellarmin never replies, or if he did, his answers are not given us. And he does not figure as a participant in the action that Hyperion describes—obviously not, or else Hyperion need not have told him about it. My point is that Bellarmin is in the novel, but is not a character in the novel. We know nothing about him, except that he is German—and that he is there, inquiring and receiving, the present learning about the past, but in his case the immediate past, not the past glory of antiquity. The fact that he has, so to speak, no face, and that he is a German means that Hölderlin, through Hyperion, is speaking not to a particular type of person (or reader) but to Germany. One could indeed argue that Hyperion is speaking to an alter ego and therefore to himself and that the whole book is an interior monologue with Hölderlin the Greek talking to Hölderlin the German.

As the novel begins, Hyperion has returned to his native Greece in search of a lost harmony, a desire which is reawakened in him by the Greek sunshine. But every moment of delight is succeeded by distress over mankind's severance from nature, and leads eventually to his recounting of his experiences. At the end of the book we return to the mood of the beginning. But all is not said. The last words to his silent partner are: "So dacht ich. Nächstens mehr"—"These were my thoughts. More soon."

So the book is circular in the sense that it returns to the spatial and temporal situation of the beginning, and yet not circular in that, through retrospective objectivation to Bellarmin, Hyperion has reached the resolution of dissonances which he only longed for at the beginning. The sense that everything was dead except nature, which had pervaded the beginning of the novel, is replaced by a realization that all is still there, in nature. "There is reconciliation in the midst of conflict and all that was separated finds itself again."[72] These are the "thoughts" he is referring to. And a new train of thoughts is thereby initiated. *Hyperion* is therefore not open-ended in the sense that *Florentin* is. *Florentin*, as we have seen, reaches no resolution and therefore permits various alternative resolutions in the thoughts of the reader. *Hyperion*, on the other hand, returns to its beginning but with the protagonist transfigured by objectivation through retrospective narration. Enriched by the recounting of memories, he moves on to a higher plane, like Wordsworth in *The Prelude*. The form of *Hyperion* is what M. H. Abrams has aptly called "the ascending circle, or spiral."[73] In the preface to the penultimate version of his novel Hölderlin used the image of the "eccentric path" leading away from the original unity "in order to restore it, through ourselves."[74]

In a sense a large part of the novel is "thoughts," which function like the reflections that eighteenth-century epistolary novelists liked to indulge in. But these are never real digressions where, as one eighteenth-century critic had put it, we see the author "peering through his characters" to the detriment of illusion, as in Julie's excursus on dueling in *La Nouvelle Héloïse*.[75] Even the analysis of how ancient Athens achieved such a high level of culture and the detailed condemnation of modern Germany are integral parts of the evolving action, for the first leads over into Hyperion's disillusionment with modern Athens and the second accounts for his decision to return to Greece. The elegiac mood makes the book largely lyrical, and the retrospective stance means that present and past are constantly reflecting on each other, and naturally, until all things come together at the end in the merging of divisions. The novel is therefore self-reflexive in that the synthesis proclaimed at the end is that achieved by the process of narration. The last thoughts are as much about the novel itself as about man's position in nature.

But *Hyperion* is not just thoughts. There is plenty of action. The conflict in Hyperion between a reflective self and one eager to engage in activity justifies the alternation between sentiments and events (to use Goethe's terms), to which one must add that the sentiments are conditioned by the retrospective stance and the events by Bellarmin's desire to know what happened. Immediacy and hindsight therefore mingle here too, and the mixture is by no means artificial. Hölderlin has combined traditional modes into a structure that is highly individual, a structure, one feels, that only a great poet could achieve. Every sentence of the prose resonates with poetic overtones. If ever one needed a proof that the novel can be a poetic form, then *Hyperion* provides it. And there is a good deal to be said in favor of Lawrence Ryan's assertion that Hyperion has, through his recollections, become a poet.[76]

Abrams describes the successive stages in Hyperion's narration "in which he periodically seems to approach a lost consonance with himself and with the outer world" but "at each stage . . . the equilibrium proves unstable and at once divides into opposites that press in turn toward a new integration."[77] The first stage is what Abrams calls the "Edenic self-unity of childhood." Characteristic of this are a sense of universal, unstrained [*mühelos*] order and a friendly creator whose heart beats within his creation. The word *mühelos* is used throughout the novel to characterize unity, in contrast to the strains of man's dichotomous existence. The second stage in Hyperion's development is his introduction to the world of ancient heroic Greece by his teacher Adamas, who gives direction to the child's roving thoughts and feelings not merely by evoking the glorious past but by indicating that what the old gods represented is still alive in the landscape of present-day Greece, drawing his attention particularly to Apollo, the sun-god (but also the god of poetry, though this is not emphasized at this point), and urging him to be like him. (In Homer the name Hyperion is given either to the son of Helios or to Helios himself.) There is a god in all of us who guides destiny, and all things are its "element," says Adomas.[78] Inspired by the desire to find this "element" on which to project his "god," Hyperion goes into the busy world, but is depressed by its busyness, its insensitivity, its unconcern for higher things, until he meets a godlike youth, Alabanda, actively engaged in trying to "save the fatherland," but practically minded and scornful of Hyperion's totally unpractical enthusiasm. Disconsolate, Hyperion returns to his father's farm, feeding on his own disillusionment and reduced to a sense of the fruitlessness of all higher endeavor, until spring returns and with it the stirrings of the god within him, not so self-confident as before, however, but entreating, seeking a way out of his nihilism. This comes to him through the encounter with Diotima, who represents harmony, love, and beauty. She is *mühelos*,[79] and for a time he returns to the Edenic stage, though with a heightened sense of its fragility. And indeed this mood begins to break up when Diotima tells him that he had felt isolated because he "wanted a world, not people."[80] She realizes that she too represents an ideal for him, and wonders whether she can live up to it. She charges him with inwardness, and when in sight of the ruins of Athens he expatiates on the glories of the past and the degeneration of the present, she tells him that the spirit of ancient Athens is still alive, alive in him, and he needs to apply it (to find what Adamas had called the element). "An artist can easily complete a torso for himself" [*Der Künstler ergänzt den Torso sich leicht*].[81] She directs him toward the people of *present* Athens, urging him to educate them, without, however, explicitly suggesting that he should do so as an artist. But the image I have just quoted seems to point in that direction, as does her reference in the same conversation to Apollo, and the fact that Hyperion's account of the past glory of Athens had culminated in the assertion that beauty, harmony, indeed *poetry* had been the basis from which Athenian religion, social organization, and philosophy had evolved. Beauty for Hölderlin means harmonious integration into unity. And this Diotima represents.

But Hyperion is still far from the achievement of such integration. In the second volume of the novel he tells Bellarmin how he joined the rebellious Greeks in their struggle against the Turks, and how he found none of his own idealistic motives among his companions in arms except in Alabanda. Diotima knew this was not the right thing for him to do, and asserted that spiritual freedom is not to be attained by the establishment of national freedom, unless the spiritual ideal behind the idea of a "free state" be maintained, which she doubts is possible. It is at this point that he sends Bellarmin the letters he and Diotima exchanged as the revolution ran its disastrous course, letters that make the past immediate. Realizing that in his actions he has fallen short of the ideal she has represented for him,

Hyperion decides to break with her. Then, at the urging of Alabanda that she still represents for him what she has always represented, he tries to revoke the separation, but she, equally disconsolate over her lover's disillusionment, which she had all too clearly foreseen, is already dead. In her last letter to him Diotima writes: "O sorrowing youth, soon you will be happier . . . for you will be a priest of divine nature and your days of poetry are growing within you already" [*die dichterischen Tage keimen dir schon*].[82] Hyperion had proposed to Diotima that they flee Greece together. Now he leaves alone. And comes amongst the Germans, a nation of fragmented, divided minds, specialists obsessed by immediate goals but without any sense of common humanity, or of harmony, or beauty, or the divine within and about them. But as spring returns so does Hyperion's consciousness of the stirrings of the god within him, and a sense of permanence and of organic unity pervades his spirit. Rotted fruit may fall to the ground but returns to nature's roots and the tree of life is green again. Sorrows and failures have taken their place in the scheme provided by his retrospective narrative, a meaningful place, contributive to the whole. The voice of Diotima still resounds; nature with its gods still lives; resolution comes from out of conflict, for the conflict of dissonances is like the quarrel between lovers, not like the strife of enemies. And unity is reestablished in his heightened vision, the vision of the poet who has found himself by retracing what he had thought were his unsuccessful attempts to find himself.

When *Hyperion* was first published, few critics had anything good to say about its form, which was considered a hodgepodge, chaotic, lacking rational connections. It was, as the *Tübinger Gelehrte Anzeigen* said, "more of a poem than a novel."[83] Such a statement shows how unprepared the critics and readers of the time were for the concept of the novel as poetry, for the idea that a work could simultaneously be both a novel and a poem. Hölderlin advanced further toward this ideal than did Jean Paul, because his novel is more consistently lyrical. The treatment of time is striking: by combining retrospective and on-going narration Hölderlin evolves an interpenetration of past and present in which neither exists without the other; each receives deeper illumination from the other, so that all divisions merge into the unity of the poetic vision. Jean Paul never attempted this because his vision was different: for him, wholeness consisted in the contrast of oppositions, necessary and enriching oppositions, and the only true unity was transcendental, not given to mortal man but nevertheless glimpsed by "higher" humans in their moments of greater illumination, their "poetic states." "Alles Getrennte findet sich wieder"—all that was separated finds itself again, in harmonious integration—this for Hölderlin is poetry, and this is the end point of his novel, the external manifestation of the god within. But for Jean Paul, the god is above, representing a transcendent undifferentiated unity, felt in the immanent world by select, poetic spirits, as a contrast to the differentiated, unharmonious, dualistic nature of earthly experience. Poetry for Jean Paul is rooted in the opposition of finite and infinite which begets the promise, the vision of transcendent unity, such as we have in Walt's dream. *Flegeljahre* ends with a dream, *Hyperion* with the actual achievement, of unity. Both these writers are working toward a realization of the novel as poetry and look toward a poeticization of the world—for Hölderlin in the poet, for Jean Paul in a broader class of humans, the *hohe Menschen*.

CHAPTER FIVE

The Novel as Poetry: Novalis

FRIEDRICH VON HARDENBERG, who adopted the pen name Novalis, was a very different person from Friedrich Schlegel, yet the
affinity that Schlegel felt with him was fully justified. They were
close friends and exchanged numerous letters. They also shared
many ideas on poetry and, what is more important, Novalis was the
poet that Schlegel wished to be, but, as his own poetic attempts show,
never could be. Novalis's lyrical output was not extensive, but nevertheless very remarkable. Most of his poems are mystical in character,
for his was a deeply religious nature, far more so than that of Friedrich Schlegel; and many of them are concerned with the transfiguration that comes through death, the return of the individuated self to
the primal unity, the confluence of the finite with the infinite. The
last few years of Novalis's short life (1772–1804) were as poetically
productive as the last months of John Keats. In these years he published his *Hymnen an die Nacht* [Hymns to Night], written first in free
verse and then converted into rhythmical prose of unusual power,
poems as intense as anything in German literature, which combine
personal grief at the death of a young girl, Sophie von Kühn, with
religious feeling, for she becomes through her death not only his
muse but the intermediary between this world and the beyond. He
also wrote two remarkable novels, *Die Lehrlinge zu Sais* [The Novices
at Saïs] and *Heinrich von Ofterdingen*, both of which remained unfinished and were published by Friedrich Schlegel and Ludwig Tieck
after Novalis's death.[1]

The statements of Novalis on the novel as a poetic form have been collated and interpreted by Gerhard Schulz in an admirable and comprehensive article which will serve as a basis for what I have to say on this subject, but on which I shall somewhat expand.[2] Schulz documents three successive stages in Novalis's elaboration of a poetics of the novel. The first began with his study of *Wilhelm Meister* during 1797. Schulz points out that these earliest theoretical statements on the novel as a genre were accompanied by his first sketches for a novel of his own, namely *Die Lehrlinge zu Sais*, an undertaking which received further impetus from his reading of *Lucinde* early in 1799. Novalis discussed *Lucinde* in a letter to Caroline Schlegel of 27 February. He realized that the novel was too much in advance of its time to be generally accepted, and considered its general tone to be cynical. In fact he suggested that the continuation should have more pieces like those on Little Wilhelmina and on Prometheus, and might well be called "Cynical Fantasies or Satanesques." He felt divided about it. What he mainly objected to was the treatment of dreams and fantasies, which robbed them of their essential fleetingness and gave them unsuitable lastingness. And he recognized that love meant something different for him, that his novel, the novel he was at that time already contemplating (*Ofterdingen*) would be quite different from Schlegel's, and from *Wilhelm Meisters Lehrjahre*, for whereas Goethe's novel dealt with the *Lehrjahre* of a person, his would deal with the "*Lehrjahre* of a nation." Implied here too is reference to the fact that the central section of *Lucinde* is entitled "Lehrjahre der Männlichkeit," though Novalis does not in his letter draw attention to this (which would, of course, have been known to Caroline). But the word *Lehrjahre* implies a definite direction toward a goal (a "whither," says Novalis), whereas what he has in mind is rather "Übergangs-Jahre," years of transition, transition "from the infinite to the finite" [*vom Unendlichen zum Endlichen*].[3] One might have expected him to say "from the finite to the infinite" but he does not, and the wording is significant. For *Ofterdingen* was to be concerned not with rising from the real to the ideal, such as we experience in the novels of Hölderlin and Jean Paul, but with bringing down an envisioned ideal into the texture of earthly reality, though as the novel finally developed, there was to be a movement upward again at the end (though this was never written).

The second stage was affected by Novalis's meeting with Ludwig Tieck, already a practicing novelist whose *Franz Sternbalds Wanderungen* (1798) was an artist novel approximating in some respects to the romantic conception of the genre, and by his visit to Goethe in July 1799. Novalis's misgivings about *Wilhelm Meister*, already apparent in the first period, now developed into a full-scale polemic against Goethe's novel, the idea for *Heinrich von Ofterdingen* was conceived, and the first part of the work written between December 1799 and April 1800. The third stage was that of his plans for the continuation of *Ofterdingen* and for other novels (never written), accompanied by further and deeper reflections on the potentialities of the genre, up to the moment of his death in March 1801, two months before his twenty-ninth birthday. The whole development of his thinking about the novel covered in all a period of only three to four years. Schulz's distinguishing of three distinct stages in his thinking may therefore be somewhat overschematic, but it nevertheless seems to me in general valid.

It is clear that this thinking began during the encounter with *Wilhelm Meister*, and that it was contemporaneous with Novalis's development of a transcendental philosophy, greatly assisted by the work of Fichte and yet essentially his own. In fragments written down in 1798 he developed the concept of the "transcendental" artist who re-creates the world in himself and himself in the world by individual combinatory activity, thereby "expanding his existence into infinity," joining up in meaningful combination what is individual and accidental with the necessary and absolute whole, and thereby creating "the most intimate community of finite and infinite."[4] He speaks also of this "transcendental" poetry as being concerned with the "*symbolic* construction of the transcendental world," and the novel as the form best suited to fulfill this ideal. "The epic continues, the novel grows—arithmetical progression in the former, geometrical in the latter."[5] Life itself becomes a novel made by the poet, and novel-writing a path toward knowledge of self and the world.[6] The novel represents life but its mimesis is a poetic mimesis, "masked events and personages which, stripped of these [poetic] masks, are events and persons well known [to us]." It does not present finite propositions or conclusions, it is the tangible realization of an idea, and an idea is an "infinite series of propositions—an irrational quantity, unpositable, incommensurable," but with an establishable law of progression.[7] Hence for Novalis the events and personages of a novel are allotropes of an idea, a series of variations on an idea. Its structure is a progression, but it should be a geometrical, not an arithmetical progression.

Among these fragments of 1798 there is a short essay on types

and structures of novels.⁸ In it Novalis seems to be taking issue with
Goethe's famous pronouncement in *Wilhelm Meister* that the novel
should deal with sentiments and events (in contrast to drama, which
deals with characters and deeds), that it should move slowly, re-
tarded by the sentiments of the main personage, who should be
more passive than active, that, again in contrast to drama, it can
legitimately deal with chance so long as this is somehow "guided and
directed by the sentiments of the personages."⁹ Novalis declares that
an individual is the "purely systematic" individuated by the chance
of an individual birth, and that all other chance aspects of his life are
determined by this original chance. From the outset, then, he relates
the individual to the Absolute. A novelist, he goes on to say, makes
an ordered series out of accidental events and situations. He then
considers various possible structures embodying different relationships between personage and events, but without expressing any
opinion on which relationship, and consequently which structure, is
best suited to his conception of what a novel should be. He does,
however, insist on the importance of unity as a structural principle.
A great poet will begin with a freely chosen initial contingency and
develop the imbalance in it, such as that between Wilhelm Meister's
higher strivings and his businessman's station, toward a resolution.
The ideas of beauty and usefulness, which had constituted the original imbalance in Wilhelm, finally fused when he met Natalie. It is
easier, says Novalis, for a novelist to make a connected series from
manifold contingencies than to develop from one simple idea outward to multiplicity. He speaks here of the centrifugal tendency of
things and the centripetal force of the *mind*, the former moving toward multiplicity and the latter toward unity. It is the fusion of both
that, like Friedrich Schlegel, he envisaged as the prime purpose of
the novel.

A digression on Novalis's use of the word "individual" and related
terms would seem to be in order at this point. By "das Individuelle"
he means something unitary and complete in itself: he equates it in
one Fragment with the Undivided, "das Ungeteilte."¹⁰ "In transcendental poetics" he observes in another place, "there is only one common (raw) Individual."¹¹ By "raw" he seems here to mean: not yet
fashioned into actual existences. The Absolute, spirit in the abstract,
is therefore, in his terms, individual, and that is why he can at times
talk about the "personality" or "personness" [*Personalität*, not *Persönlichkeit*] of the Universal, perhaps metaphorically and because Fichte
called the Absolute *das reine Ich*, pure Ego. But when Novalis speaks

of *Individualität* in "nature" (the world), he means individuation, separate individuals, each relatively complete in itself. Hence a statement such as the following: "Individuation [*Individualität*] in nature is infinite. This observation gives life to [*belebt*] our hopes of the personness [*Personalität*] of the universe [*Universum*].¹² In other words: individual existences, because they embody infinite variety, presuppose an undivided whole, an absolute "person," an infinite unity. Individuation produces accidentals and is therefore equivalent to chance: "A stone is different from a plant and an animal only in our world-system. The present determinacy [*Bestimmung*] and distribution [*Verteilung*] of each individual in this world-system are probably only apparent, or relative, accidental, historical, not moral? Each has acquired its place in the world-system according to the share it brought with it, its inferred relation of world (synthesis of quantity and quality)."¹³ Quantity and quality are Kantian categories, which apply only to the phenomenal world, the world of objects; but for romantic philosophers quantity applied to the world of objects, quality to the spirit—quantity to the object, quality to the subject. Hence the personness and unitary nature of the spirit or absolute intelligence.

Such, then, is Novalis's cosmology. But in the individuations of the finite world there are complete and incomplete individuals. An incomplete [*unvollständig*] individual is one that strives further, is unsatisfied, whereas a complete individual is without need or restlessness and fits into the system that rolls on its own course according to its own inherent laws.¹⁴ The Universal or Absolute is therefore a complete Individual. And all humans are "variations on one complete Individual,"¹⁵ some obviously more complete than others. Wilhelm Meister's initial imbalance was the sign of an incomplete individual—this is the conclusion we must surely draw from Novalis's cosmology. It is also clear that such a cosmology in one aspiring to write novels was bound to produce novels in which the nature and function of the individual personages would be quite different from what they had been in the practice of most novelists up to his time.

Novalis admired Goethe's artistry in its control of multiplicity, and perceived in *Wilhelm Meister* a foreshadowing of his concept of a (geometrical) series of variations. Thus he sees the Beautiful Soul of Book Six and Natalie as variations of the same "individual."¹⁶ In the *Allgemeines Brouillon* of the autumn of this same year, 1798, he extended this observation to include other characters of the novel. Lothario is now termed to be a male variation on Therese with a "transition to Meister," Wilhelm himself a combination of the Uncle and Lothario, Serlo is Jarno as an actor, and so on.[17] But Goethe is an "entirely practical poet" [*ein ganz practischer Dichter*]. These are the first words of a short essay on Goethe, written down in August 1798.[18] Like Josiah Wedgwood, says Novalis, Goethe "has [both] a natural business [*oeconomisch*] good taste, and a noble taste acquired through the understanding." The two are compatible, and have a close affinity "in the chemical sense," meaning, presumably, that they can be made to interact and combine. His greatest quality is the ability to give things final form, an "active empiricism"; he is an applied rather than a pure philosopher, endowed with an unusually sharp faculty for abstraction that simultaneously constructs the object to which the abstraction corresponds. Thus *Wilhelm Meister* is a construct of the understanding [*des Verstandes*], as rigorously fashioned as the works of the ancients and richer in content. But Goethe "must be surpassed in content and force, in variety and profundity," though his artistic rigor and security are unsurpassable. Novalis notes that the text (of *Wilhelm Meister*) is never "hurried" [*übereilt*], that dialogue alternates with description and reflection but with dialogue predominating, and that Goethe shows marvelous power in combining trivial "occurrences" [*Vorfälle*] with important "events" [*Begebenheiten*].[19]

It was in July or August 1799 that Novalis wrote down the summary statement: "A novel must be poetry through and through," and asserted that in a "poetic book" one should have the sense of discovering the world for the first time, of seeing what has always been there but one has never seen before. He speaks of our acquiring "der rechte Sinn für die Welt,"[20] a true sense of what "world" is, of the connections between things and their context *sub specie aeternitatis*. He begins to contemplate various subjects for such a "poetic" novel, some of them set at turning points of history, noting down basic situations and individualized partial manifestations of what he had earlier called "the complete Individual," representatives of the Absolute, variations in a series. He is working toward the composition of *Heinrich von Ofterdingen*, which was to embody all this. He seems to have settled on the subject of *Ofterdingen* late in 1799. As the composition of the novel progressed, his polemic against *Wilhelm Meister* intensified. It was in these months that his well-known characterizations of Goethe's novel as "thoroughly prosaic," "a Candide against poetry," destructive of "the romantic," "devoid of mysticism," "artistic atheism," occurred. At this time, perhaps under the influence of his reactions to *Wilhelm Meister*, he declared that the novel too has its unities, or should have, one of which shall be the "conflict of poetry and un-poetry" [*Kampf der Poësie und Unpoësie*].[21] Linking on to his earlier statements about geometrical progression and an infinite series of propositions expounding an idea as the desirable structure for a poetic, romantic novel, he now explicitly refers to the "inconveniences" of chronological, linear narration and advocates periodic structure rather than continuous structure: "The style [*Schreibart*] of a novel should not be a continuum—it must be a structure organized in separate periods. Every small piece must be something separate—contained—a whole in itself."[22] This is basically what Schiller and Goethe had said about the epic. There must, however, also be some overriding unity corresponding to the unity of our inner world ("*Poesie ist* Darstellung des Gemüts—der innern Welt in ihrer Gesamtheit")[23] but this need not, and probably should not, be the unity of a chronological sequence. It might be associative, it might seem totally disconnected—but it must all emerge from that original formative germ, the idea, of which the incidentals of plot and cast are variations and progressive manifestations, the Absolute of which every individuation is an embodiment, in which they are all sustained and to which they will all ultimately return in the transfiguring and defiguring synthetic statement to be achieved by the poetic novel. The seeming discreteness of the elements of a series in Novalis's ideal novel is really the means by which we are led to surmount everyday, finitely limited patterns of causal connection in time and space, to appreciate more fundamental, absolute connections in a landscape of infinity and thereby achieve a true sense of what "world" really is. But what does he mean by representation [*Darstellung*] "des Gemüts"? Several of the Fragments may help us to understand better what Novalis meant by *Gemüt*. Kant, he said, used the word to designate the faculty of the mind that combines perceptions into the unity of empirical apperception—a *faculty* of the mind, "not the substance of the soul (*anima*), but *animus*."[24] One can surely deduce from this that Novalis himself conceives *Gemüt* as *anima*. Elsewhere he states it thus: "*Gemüt*—harmony of all forces of the mind [*Geist*]—same disposition and harmonious play of the whole soul. Irony = manner [*Art und Weise*] of the *Gemüt*."[25] Or again: "In real poems the only unity is unity of the *Gemüt*. . . . Poetry = revealed *Gemüt*—active (productive) individuality."[26]

In the last year of his life Novalis decided that *Die Lehrlinge zu Sais* should become something different, namely "a truly symbolic nature-novel" [*ein ächt sinnbildlicher Naturroman*]—by which he presumably meant a novel about nature (certainly *not* a novel about *landscapes*!).

But, in the same context, he declared his intention of finishing *Ofter-dingen* first.[27] Neither intention was in fact fulfilled. But it would seem that the composition of *Ofterdingen*, combined with study of the writings of the seventeenth-century mystical writer Jakob Böhme[28] (who had much to say on nature), was leading him toward a reorganization of *Die Lehrlinge zu Sais*. The scheme for *Ofterdingen* was expanded to include lyrical and dramatic sections, moving toward that combination of genres advocated by Friedrich Schlegel. "Plastic arts, music and poetry relate to each other as do epic, lyric, and drama," Novalis had observed in 1798; "they are inseparable elements combined in relevant proportions in every free artistic structure [*Kunstwesen*]." "Nothing is more poetic than transitions and heterogeneous mixtures," he stated in one of his last fragmentary notes.[29] But the insistence on unity is still there, expressed now more than once by the term *Personalität*. At one point in these late notations he talks again of *Personalität des Universums*, at another of *Personalität* of the Spirit. Nature is "constricted [or "limited"—*gehemmt*] personification process," and therefore opposed to absolute, unlimited *Personalität*. Individual personalities are parts of this, but they can also partake of this absolute person-ness, can sense the absolute and infinite, especially in moral action where they act in productive freedom[30] (which is what the conversation with Sylvester in Part Two of *Ofterdingen* is about). In a way this is Novalis's own variation on Friedrich Schlegel's demand for absolute individuality combined with absolute universality. For Novalis, individuality is limited universality expressed as "imperfect" or "restricted" *Personalität*, and the universal, the "Spirit" is "perfect" *Personalität*. In these last fragments Novalis also speaks repeatedly of "mythology"—"mythology of history," "mythology of nature"—by which he means "free poetic invention which manifoldly symbolizes reality."[31] One of his very last notations runs as follows:

> The poet is really deprived of senses, but everything occurs within him. He most truly represents Subject-Object—mind [*Gemüth*] and world. Hence the infinitude of a good poetic work, its eternity. The poetic sense has close affinity with the prophetic and religious sense, with the vatic sense above all. The poet bestows order, he combines, selects, invents—and it is incomprehensible to him why [it should be] in this way and not otherwise.[32]

Mythology is recognition of refracted *Personalität*, of determinate Spirit in the phenomenal world; religion is concerned with absolute, undifferentiated, indeterminate *Personalität*. The former is therefore basically empirical, the latter necessarily spiritual and idealist. Poetry is the fusion of the two. Proceeding from an idealist basis it creates a new realism, a *Realidealismus*.

There is no evidence that *Die Lehrlinge zu Sais* was at its inception conceived as a novel. In a letter of February 1798 Novalis refers to "a beginning with the title 'Der Lehrling zu Sais'—also fragments—but all concerned with Nature," and in May he says he *might* later send Friedrich Schlegel a "novel in 16mo," which may refer to this work, or may not; but the only real designation of it as a novel is in a letter to Tieck of February 1800, where he speaks of refashioning it to become a "symbolic nature-novel."[33] It had always been concerned with nature; what is new is the description of its mode as "symbolic." A change in title—*Die Lehrlinge* (plural) replacing *Der Lehrling* (singular)—accompanies the envisaged change in structure, and is assumed to date from about the same time as the letter to Tieck. Probably it was an indication of one way the revision was to go. We have no other indication of how the revision was to work out, though we know that the manuscript (now lost) had marginal "annotations" by the author.[34] The text we have is based on a copy of this manuscript made by Karl von Hardenberg, the poet's brother, but without incorporation of the marginalia. It therefore represents the original, not the revised, form of the work, if indeed this latter were ever begun. It is definitely not a symbolic novel, for it is expository rather than imagistic, except for a short narrative that interrupts the sequence of speeches by the various unnamed characters. Some critics have found it hardly possible to speak of structure at all—let alone of symbolic structure—for the text consists of two fragments. The first is entitled *Der Lehrling* (the apprentice, pupil, or novice), which title refers to the first-person narrator (or rather reporter, for no action is narrated). The second, much longer section, entitled *Die Natur* (Nature), is in third-person "narration," in which various speakers advance various attitudes to nature. One of these speeches is in the form of a narrated story with symbolic overtones about two young lovers, which contrasts with the direct exposition of the others, the culminating statement being that of the Teacher himself who expounds the romantic view. Recently, however, two critics have asserted that there is indeed a structural principle that links together these two fragments (see note 44). If we take Novalis's statement of February 1798 literally, then this beginning was to be the beginning.

The Teacher's speech could be the conclusion in view of its climactic content, but we cannot be sure of that, for one of the Paralipomena suggests that Isis herself was to appear and various "transformations" occur, in which Greek, Egyptian, and finally Christian elements should play their part in the establishment of a "New Testament—and new Nature—as New Jerusalem."[35]

The legend of the veiled image of Isis in the temple at Saïs is a symbolic presentation of man's desire to penetrate the mystery of truth and the warning that no mortal should attempt this. Schiller, in a powerful poem that Novalis would surely have known, treated the subject as being an instance of hubris, the unjust stripping of the veil which destroys the sacrilegious seeker. He does not tell us what the miscreant saw, only that his impious act destroyed him. In *Die Lehrlinge zu Sais* the motif is treated in the story of Hyazinth and Rosenblütchen, where the young man strips the veil and finds his beloved, whom he had left behind in the search for "the mother of all things, the veiled virgin," Isis, here a nature-goddess, into whose sanctuary he is led in a dream—only to find Rosenblütchen behind the mysterious veil. His search for mother-nature leads him to love, his love, something in himself. And indeed in a distich, not part of this work, Novalis had suggested that behind the veil of Isis the ardent seeker will find himself.[36] The point would seem to be that Hyazinth seeking nature finds love and finds himself, for the love is part of him, was within him, but needed to be objectively realized. Is "Nature," then, love?

The real subject of this novel, if we may call it such, is how to attain true knowledge of nature. And this also implies a true knowledge of self. Hence the central position of the story of Hyazinth and Rosenblütchen. Confused by the various speeches he has heard on how to attain to an understanding of nature, the pupil (presumably the "I" of the first fragment) is addressed by a lively young man who chides him for his solitary brooding: "You are still young. Don't you feel the mandate of youth in your veins? Don't love and longing fill your breast? Why do you sit there in solitude? Is Nature solitary? Joy and desire flee those who maintain solitude, and without desire, what use is Nature to you? . . . You have not yet experienced love, poor fellow; at the first kiss a new world will be opened up to you and life will dart a thousand rays into your transported breast."[37] The experience of love is therefore the introit to the full understanding of nature. It happens when ratiocination ebbs. It is only in a dream-state that Hyazinth can penetrate the temple of Isis. "Thought," we are told shortly after the conclusion of this tale, "is but a dream of feeling, benumbed feeling, a pallid, gray, enfeebled life."[38] The implication is that the intellect, and its concomitants of analysis and rational exposition, will never achieve that communion with nature necessary for an understanding of nature. This is attainable only through feeling, desire, love—and, once attained, brings nature and self into that union symbolized by a kiss, a union in which subject and object are no longer discrete. The *Märchen* of Hyazinth and Rosenblütchen is therefore the structural center of *Die Lehrlinge zu Saïs* and its poetic summation. It contrasts with the rational argumentation of the rest, representing what eludes such argumentation.

The structure of the work, so far as we can perceive it, embodies Novalis's desideratum of a progression through variations, each representing different attitudes toward the general subject of nature. The variations are therefore themselves individuations of an absolute, but are presented not as a succession but as an interplay in dialogue, with two separate climaxes—the *Märchen*, and the final speech of the Teacher. To appreciate the relation of these two climaxes to each other within the total scheme of the novel and whether there is "geometrical" progression, we must examine how the argument proceeds.

The first fragment begins with reflections on the different paths traversed by men, the "figures" they observe in the cipher-language of nature, the intimations [*Ahndungen*] they derive from these, and their inability to combine them into a meaningful whole. The Teacher, however, has acquired over the years the sense of connections and now no longer sees anything in isolation. This is his superiority to the "pupils." The narrator of this fragment tells us that the treasures of nature elude his search because "everything leads him back into himself," everything is an image of a wondrous image of the divine which exists only in his thoughts. It is in these thoughts that he seeks "the sleeping maiden" his mind desires, to lift the veil, and if, as the inscription warns, no mortal may do this, to become immortal, lift the veil, and become a true novice of Saïs. The first fragment concludes with this statement and therefore points forward to the first climax, the *Märchen*.

The second fragment opens with a carefully expounded general statement on man's attempts throughout the ages to penetrate the mystery of nature and relate it to human experience, and the guidance received from naturalists and poets. The naturalists collected and classified—and nature died at their hands, leaving behind only "dead, twitching remains," whereas the poets gave increased life to nature and lifted it above the ordinary. He who wishes to know the soul [*Gemüt*] of nature should seek it in the company of the poets. Various attitudes to nature are then described,[39] and the point is made that when the striving to comprehend nature is transmuted into a humble longing, a pleasure, a warm sympathy, more understanding is achieved. But the result is different conceptions: nature as temple, as larder, as wilderness, as echo of a lost world. To understand nature man needs to have long acquaintance with it, the faculty of careful contemplation, simplicity of spirit and a god-fearing mind, active senses and imagination. Then the stars will revisit the earth, the past be renewed, and history become "the dream of an infinite, immeasurable present."[40]

Then various voices begin to make themselves heard and the dialogue begins. Some think it unnecessary to examine the varieties of nature, seeing in it a world of misery and death. Others consider it an adversary and try to make it subject to their will. Others turn away from it and explore their inner world, from which they then interpret the outer world. One "serious man" asserts that the outer world should be respected as a symbol [*Sinnbild*] of man's mind, developing in nobility, and nature will develop likewise for the man who exercises his moral sense. "Moral action is the one great endeavor [*Versuch*] in which all mysteries of the manifold world of phenomena are resolved,"[41] says this speaker, who obviously knows his Fichte. The exposition has moved toward a concept of nature that unites inner and outer worlds, making them interdependent, each transforming the other into something more "moral," more meaningful. One should recall here Novalis's aphorism: "We are on a mission: our calling—to educate the earth" [*Wir sind auf einer Mission: zur Bildung der Erde sind wir berufen*].[42]

Confused by all this, our *Lehrling* retires into brooding solitude and is thereupon told the tale of Hyazinth and Rosenblütchen. There then seems to be a break in the sequence, for what follows is an account of the pupils taking their leave, wishing they could understand the "inner music of nature" and replace their thinking by that feeling which brought harmony to man in the golden age of the state of nature. This passage, the final sentence of which (about thought and feeling) I have already quoted (see above, pp. 116–117) is followed by the arrival of several travelers who resume the argument in terms that suggest Novalis's own opinions, the various speeches progressing geometrically toward the final speech of the Teacher, not on what nature is, but on how to teach what nature is. The speeches of these travelers take up ideas expressed in the speeches of the pupils, presenting them in harmonically richer variations, for these men are more experienced than the pupils. The first returns to the theme of inner and outer worlds, asserting that exploration of the outer world demands not only careful contemplation but *undivided* attention and what results from such exploration is an interplay of the mobile waves of impressions with one's rigid attention. By this means man is made aware of his freedom (taking up a concept that had been advanced by another of the earlier speakers) and of his ability to *think and feel* (taking up another of the earlier points) simultaneously. By this means man attains deeper knowledge not only of the world but also of himself, and now operates, in complete freedom, between both worlds. Understanding of his own thinking and feeling will in turn lead him to the ability to decipher nature more completely. The second speaker objects to any theory that sees nature as a combination of external phenomena (the mechanistic view), asserting the binding power of suprasensual forces which link our finite world with others beyond it. The third speaker argues that simultaneous multiple interpretations are desirable but do not constitute knowledge unless they are compared and are accompanied by some sense of historical context and development. We need a history of nature, for nature has a past and a future. The fourth speaker returns to the subject of poets. They alone have sensed the true unity of nature, have seen in it "all the variations of an infinite soul" [*alle Abwechslungen eines unendlichen Gemüts*],[43] and are aware of its "soul," of the analogies between the movements of nature and those of the human heart, between natural and human phenomena.

In this first round of speeches by the travelers, the content is richer, the perception deeper, and the expression more articulately poetic than in the speeches of the pupils. There is a progression evident, a progression in power. In a second round, the first speaker claims that to understand nature one must re-create it in one's mind [*innerlich*], for in this creative contemplation of simultaneous production and perception the whole development of nature will appear, and inner and outer worlds fuse in the bonds of love. This is Novalis's concept of "productive imagination." The second speaker comments on the fact that all of nature seems to be present in each of its manifestations, and this presence embraces present, past, and future metamorphoses. The third speaker reiterates his belief in the value of multiple attitudes and interpretations and accepts the validity of those who experience nature through love, for they often come nearer to the truth than others. The fourth speaker, who, as the first round showed, was more of a poet than the others, enthusiastically takes up the point made by his predecessor, comparing in effect man's contact with nature and the sexual act itself, and elaborating on desire as a prevalent force in nature. But no one will ever understand nature without an organ that *creates* nature within himself and by which he can merge into nature, like a lover with his bride.

The Teacher and the pupils now approach the travelers. The travelers tell of their journeys to find traces of a lost primeval people reputedly of great culture, which have now brought them to Saïs. The Teacher himself has the last word, explaining what it means to be a "Verkündiger der Natur," one who proclaims nature, not just an investigator, not just an explicator, but one who reveres nature, becomes one with it by constant application in solitude and with patient mind, and then works to impart this understanding to others. It is what Novalis has been doing in this work. Like *Hyperion*, the book has become self-reflexive.[44]

The structure of *Heinrich von Ofterdingen* has some points of similarity with that of *Die Lehrlinge zu Sais*, but is basically different, though equally original.[45] We have already noted that Novalis intended to reorganize what was written of *Die Lehrlinge zu Sais* into a symbolic novel, and that this plan surfaced while he was composing *Ofterdingen*, which was conceived as a symbolic novel from the start. The very first chapter contains the famous symbol of the blue flower—a symbol, not an image, for it has no specific referent but hovers over the whole novel as something the true meaning of which is never established but always being sought—like Kafka's Castle.[46] The basic structure is therefore that of a quest, but a quest not so much for the blue flower as for what it means, a striving toward understanding as well as the desire for capture, embracing inner and outer worlds of experience, and essentially progressive. The progression reaches its climax and goal at the end of Part One of the novel, when Heinrich encounters Klingsohr, from whom he learns the nature and power of poetry, and his daughter Mathilde, with whom he becomes united in love. Both love and poetry are thereby revealed as aspects of the blue flower, aspects of the Universal individuated in these two personages, and Heinrich finds his fulfillment by incorporating both into himself. By the end of Part One of the novel, therefore, the individual characters (including others besides Klingsohr and his daughter) are merging into the main character, Heinrich himself.

But the novel has a second part, though this was never finished. And there was to have been a third part, for which we have only Novalis's jottings as to what it might have contained, with no clear indication of the overall structure. We also have a rather detailed account by Tieck of what he understood from Novalis to be his intentions, which does indicate the projected general structure of the third part but is of course second-hand and therefore perhaps not entirely reliable.[47] Part One is concerned with the quest and is entitled "Die Erwartung"—expectation, or anticipation. The second part bears the title "Die Erfüllung"—fulfillment—and presents what has been arrived at as a result of the quest, namely the translation of individual into absolute, finite into infinite, dissolving of time and space, fusing of inner and outer worlds—that poeticization of the world which was to overcome the dichotomousness of finitude and reveal true (that is to say, absolute) relations and connections. The first part of the novel moves in time and space and is therefore diachronic, the second part is synchronic, the third part would have been exochronic. Between Part One and Part Two there is a *Märchen* in which we move from the world of the first part to that of the second, and the end of the *Märchen* prefigures the third part. The *Märchen* is largely allegorical, and this too is a transition from the real world of the first part to the symbolic world of the second and the absolute world of the third, for allegory is not a poeticization of the world though it is a pointer toward it. The second part is intermediary: it represents a growing fusion of finite experience and infinite intimations. The third part was to play entirely in infinity. The structure of *Ofterdingen* is therefore progressive, and presents a truly geometrical progression.

Let us now consider the progression of Part One. It is essentially a progression through various spiritual landscapes. The first of these is home. The boy has heard tell of "ancient times, when beasts and trees and rocks spoke with man," the prelapsarian age before man's present dichotomous state emerged. He relives this in his imagination, and in dreams, one of which is broken off as he stands in wonder before the blue flower, broken off into the rude awakening by his mother's voice and his father's denigration of dreams. Heinrich defends dreams as access to the eternal, as a "bulwark against the regularity and triviality [*Gewöhnlichkeit*] of life," as a "friendly companion on the pilgrimage to the Holy Sepulcher."[48] It turns out that his father, a merchant, had also seen the flower in a dream—it might have been blue, but he cannot remember, and anyhow never followed up on it. Not so, however, Heinrich, for when he comes of age and is about to set out on a journey—a journey arranged by his father to make him less introverted—he has a vision of the blue flower, accompanied by the sense that his final destination is to return home. This quest, then, has the familiar romantic pattern of the circular quest, the journey from an actual home at the end of which man finds his spiritual home, a journey in which he indeed returns but not as the same person who set out.

Heinrich's first encounter on his journey is with a group of merchants. One might expect them to represent mercantile, antipoetic forces to set up a contrast between the world of business and the world of dreams, between material and poetic values. But this is not exactly the case, for their talk is of art *and* its social benefits as a refining force which counters both overseriousness and license by instilling in man a "gentle liveliness" [*milde Lebendigkeit*] and "calm modest joy" [*sanfte, bescheidene Freude*], so that love may become the guiding spirit in social life.[49] This orientation toward society is something new for the brooding youth, but he reacts for the moment by declaring that there are two forms of the full life, the contemplative and the social, and that knowledge of mankind can be acquired by either worldly experience or inner reflection, that is, by cultivation of outer or inner life. To which the merchants reply that he speaks like a poet. Whereupon Heinrich asks: What is poetry? And the merchants then tell him that it is more mysterious because less obviously mimetic than the arts of painting and music, that it creates from inside the mind and present a "new glorious world," a world of wonder where time is suspended, a world of magic disengagement from the familiarity of present reality. To explain what they mean, they have recourse to two *Märchen*, first the tale of the singer Arion and then, in the next chapter, a story of Novalis's own invention.

The tale of Arion is ushered in by a marvelous passage on the golden age, when nature was "more alive and meaningful" [*lebendiger und sinnvoller*] than today, and poets were interpreters, were prophets and priests, law-givers and physicians.[50] One of them was Arion, who aroused the envy of other men because of his special gifts, prophesied an ill fate for them if they kill him, remained unheard by them, but was received by nature, who returned to him his riches. The second tale concerns a princess and a young countryman, and is about art and nature. The king of a certain country had a passion for poetry and great love for his daughter, whose soul was itself a song of sadness and longing. She was the inspiration of all the poets at court. No one seemed worthy enough to be her husband, for the king was descended from mythical rulers of the world. But one day she stops for refreshment at a cottage inhabited by an old man instructing his son in the lore of nature, which makes her feel that she has entered a new, and somehow higher world. On subsequent visits she is inducted into the secrets of nature, how the world came into being by "wondrous sympathy" [*wundervolle Sympathie*] and the stars have united in "melodic rounds" [*melodischen Reigen*].[51] Deprived of her presence, for she does not return to court for a while, the king falls into a despair that none of the poets can dissipate. Without her their songs are empty for him. But one day she returns with her husband, the young countryman, and a child. The youth sings two songs, the first of which is not given us but we are told that it dealt with the golden age of love and poetry, their triumph over barbarism and hatred, and the final rejuvenation of nature and the return of the golden age. The second song deals with the loneliness of the poet and his need for love, and as the song progresses it describes what is happening, as the princess and the child appear, and what will happen. The king is joyfully reunited with his daughter, embraces the youth, and lifts up the child to heaven.

It is characteristic of Novalis to convey his deepest meaning in the form of a *Märchen*.[52] The relationship of poetry and nature is the theme of both these tales. In the first, nature proclaims its sanction of poetry; in the second, it unites with poetry and bears fruit. Inset narratives had always been a familiar feature of novels and had been used for a variety of structural purposes. But nowhere quite as here, where the insets do not just illustrate but epitomize, much as the lyrics in *Wilhelm Meister* do, and indeed the second tale culminates in a lyric, just as Goethe's own *Novelle* was (later) to do.

The next stage in Heinrich's quest involves the subjects of war and love, and the conflict and relationship between them. The theme of war presents itself in the form of the holy war of the Crusades to rescue the Holy Sepulcher. Love appears in the person of the grieving Saracen girl for whom the Crusades had been the invasion and destruction of paradise. Both themes culminate in songs, the crusading song of the warriors and the lament of the girl. A different aspect of love from that involved in the tale of the princess is here presented, and that is structurally comprehensible. But why war, at this stage in the argument? Of course the novel takes place vaguely at the time of the Crusades, but that would not seem to be the reason—rather that love and war were the recognized subjects of poetry as Ariosto had reminded us: "Le donne, i cavallier, l'arme, gli amori, / le cortesie, l'audaci impresse io canto." Heinrich is therefore experiencing that external enrichment which he needs, stuff for his as yet unsurfaced poetic urge. And a connection between the two themes—those of epic and romance—is expressly established in this chapter. For Heinrich, while listening to the crusaders' song, thinks of the Holy Sepulcher as a maiden in distress. The image is then ironically translated into reality when he encounters Zulima, the maiden in distress because of the ravages of war, in distress at the loss of her lover *and* of her homeland, which she describes as of "romantic beauty," like colonies of paradise, its inhabitants not the savage people of the crusaders' song, but generous souls, receptive to the "poetry of life and the wondrous, mysterious grace of nature."[53] A dialectical opposition is established here, whereas it was harmony that had been stressed in the previous chapters. War involves conflict and perhaps love does too; war demands passion, and this war is an undertaking of serious, religious fervor.

The fifth chapter is the great centerpiece of the first part of the novel. It contains two important encounters and involves a descent below the surface of life and backward in time, in which the dimensions of space and time become almost nonexistent. Heinrich meets a miner who tells him about his life and work and the satisfaction that he derives as he descends, with crucifix and lamp and after a celebration of the Mass, into the "hidden treasuries of nature," to those shafts and passages which become for him a metaphor of the twists and turns, perils and wonders of human life.[54] He sings two songs, the first celebrating the miner as lord of the earth, the second a mysterious haunting ballad about a palace of gold, and the disintegration of the power of gold in a materialistic world. Heinrich himself then makes the descent, which is also to a certain extent a descent into his own innermost self, bringing to consciousness the connections between the experiences of his "outer" journey so far, and leading him eventually to the inmost cave, where he encounters a man reading in a large book lying on a stone slab. There is a curious connection here with the dream recounted by Heinrich's father in the opening chapter of the novel, for he had had a similar experience, though in a dream. This man has fled the world not from dislike of humanity, for he greets Heinrich and his companions cordially, but in order to spend his time in contemplation. But time has no reality here, judging by the man's timeless appearance. He speaks of the difficulty of making a meaningful whole out of the disorder of individual experiences, of history and its importance in uniting past and future, of poets as the best historians, because they know how to connect [*zu verknüpfen*] and understand the "mysterious spirit of life" [*den geheimnisvollen Geist des Lebens*].[55] He speaks of the importance of memory and of hope, of his years of soldiery, and of his dead wife who lies buried here, Marie von Hohenzollern. For this hermit is the Count von Hohenzollern. He shows Heinrich his books of history and poetry containing images of life's vicissitudes, which capture Heinrich's attention. In one of them, written in a strange language, Heinrich sees his own life pictured, with all the persons who have so far played a part in it, but in costumes from another age, and some others he does not yet know. And the book lacks a conclusion. The count tells him it is the life of a poet, and indeed unfinished. His parting words are: "If your eyes are fixed on heaven, you will never lose the path to your home."[56]

Early on in the next chapter we are told that "Heinrich was by nature born to be a poet." But he has not yet become one. He has learnt what poetry is, from the merchants, from the Saracen girl, and from the Count von Hohenzollern but so far there has been no real dialogue with the outside, he has been mainly receptive. There is a turning outward at this point. Mathilde and Klingsohr, both of whom had figured as unknown quantities in the book in the cave, are to be the decisive encounters, and with them he has his crucial dialogue, in which he develops from a poetic nature to an active poet. This process fills the remaining three chapters of the first part of the novel.

At his first meeting with Mathilde, Heinrich tells her of his encounter with Zulima, and during the night he begins to connect Mathilde with the face in the blue flower, the image in the count's book, and the princess of the merchants' tale. Then, as he dreams, a connection is established with his dream at the beginning of the novel, with similar imagery but intensified content, for in the present dream Mathilde dies but returns to him as he searches through a strange, timeless landscape—all of which prefigures Part Two of the novel. Poetic re-creation and divination are already at work. In the big conversations with Klingsohr a whole series of themes is worked through in which intimations earlier in the book are more fully developed, with Heinrich raising the questions and Klingsohr replying and Heinrich then coming back with an articulate poetic statement of his own. To the question of the relationship between inner and outer worlds, Klingsohr replies that nature is to the soul [*Gemüt*] as bodies to light. Bodies arrest light and break it into colors, thereby either shining from within themselves and becoming transparent, or reflecting the light on to other bodies. To which Heinrich replies that people are crystals for our minds. The conversation moves on to the subject of various ways of reacting to nature, and the importance for a poet of an attentive mind, calm and sensitive like light, and equally elastic and penetrating—"a cool, enlivening warmth,"[57] says Klingsohr, which is his version of "emotion recollected in tranquillity." He then interprets poetically Heinrich's journey so far: "The realm of poetry, the romantic orient, has greeted you with its sweet sadness; war has spoken to you in all its wild glory, and nature and history came to you in the persons of a miner and a hermit." To which Heinrich replies that Klingsohr has left out love, which has come to him in Mathilde, whereupon Klingsohr blesses the union of Heinrich and Mathilde.[58]

In a second conversation Klingsohr and Heinrich talk about the poetic and antipoetic forces in "nature," the latter being characterized by sluggishness or dull desire, and of the poetic, romantic spirit embodied in war and the heroism of fighting for ideas, and the order imposed by poetry on experience—an order, however, in which chaos should always shimmer through,[59] for poetry should reveal in the world what is outside the world, and we are all in that sense sometimes poets. For instance, in love. There then follows a remarkable conversation between Heinrich and Mathilde—a conversation like nothing else in all literature, a communion of spirits, groping through their individual thoughts and feelings toward the Absolute, the unity of all experience that they represent. The images [Bilder] of life are all reflections of one basic image [Urbild] which is eternal and undifferentiated: *the* Person behind all personifications, *the* Individual behind all individuations. Dream and waking, past and present, life and death, being and becoming, mutability and eternity, all now become images of one primal image.

Klingsohr then narrates his *Märchen*, the most complicated in all romantic literature. Space does not permit me to go into all its fascinating ramifications, a task that has already been attempted by various critics.[60] Its theme is the rejuvenation of the world by the combined spirits of love and poetry, and not just our terrestrial world but the higher world, frozen into darkness since the departure of wisdom to the earth and waiting to be awakened from its spellbound torpor. The action involves numerous mythological and allegorical figures, and draws on legends of various origin, as well as

symbols from the natural sciences (which Novalis had studied extensively).[61] It falls into six main sections. The first takes place in the
frozen upper world eagerly waiting for deliverance; the second in
the "middle world," the earth, with allegorical representations of
mind, heart, fancy, love, and poetry—a divided household threatened by the Scribe, the incorporation of rationalism. The third section is a journey of Eros (love) and Ginnistan (fancy) to the kingdom
of the moon, Ginnistan's father, the realm of dreams and fancies.
The fourth depicts the decay of the middle world after the departure of Eros and Ginnistan. The fifth follows the journey of Fabel
(poetry), a journey to achieve salvation. And the last section returns
to the upper world where Eros and Fabel waken the sleeping princess of Peace, and become rulers of the kingdom, which enters on a
new golden age. The *Märchen* is much more interesting than this
summary sounds, for its myriad of details is presented with an infinite fecundity of imagination and marvelously subtle language of
evocative power.

The second part of the novel, "The Fulfillment," begins with a
poem spoken by the spirit of poetry, Astralis, who was to preside
over this second part and speak before each chapter, though unfortunately Novalis completed only the first chapter (and perhaps not
all of that). Astralis tells us she (or he) was born of the embrace of
Heinrich and Mathilde, and is the "center, the sacred spring," from
which all longing gushes forth impetuously and to which, after being
fragmented and refracted [*mannigfach gebrochen*], it ultimately calmly
retracts. The birth is described in flower imagery reminiscent of
Heinrich's two dreams—for the blue flower and Mathilde are both
present in Astralis. Time and space have now dissolved, a new world
has arisen, the world of love and poetry, of complete harmony,
where "world becomes dream and dream becomes world" and fancy
weaves its own rich carpet, wherein sorrow and joy, death and life
conjoin. But for this to occur the "old" world must die, as it did in
Klingsohr's *Märchen*. The poem leads into the first section of the
first chapter, which depicts Heinrich wandering in sorrow at the
death of Mathilde and then hearing her voice from a tree. She tells
him that if he sings a song in her honor—that is, if he exerts his
new-found poetic powers—a maiden will come and console him until
he too dies and joins "our friends." He then has a vision of Mathilde
with others in a wondrous palace, everything takes on new meaning,
and he becomes a poet again. The girl appears from out of her
timeless world, and as she speaks, various figures from Part One

reappear in her mysterious words. She speaks of a life possible only through death, transcending all divisions of time and space, in which all individuations merge into *Urbilder* (in the sense that word is used in the earlier conversation between Heinrich and Mathilde), earthly mothers—hers and Heinrich's—merge into "the Mother of God," earthly fathers—his, and hers who is Count Hohenzollern,—into the image of the father, and all progression is a movement "toward home." Her name is Zyane and she leads Heinrich to an old man, Sylvester, who reminds him of the miner and speaks of Heinrich's father and how the latter had been too much attached to the real world of objects to become anything more than a craftsman. Talk of education in terms taken from plant life leads Sylvester to speak of gardens, soil, fruition, and rejuvenation—and of clouds and storms, which bring a sense of supernatural powers and therefore of good and evil.

"There is certainly something very mysterious about clouds," says Sylvester. Heinrich has just said that they are for him somehow images or appearances [*Erscheinungen*] of a second *higher* childhood— uniting like terrestrial childhood the manifold of experience with a sense of the "golden future of all things," and affecting our earthly existence in a beneficial way. Their changing aspect—now pleasing, now frightening—invokes in us multiple sensations in which their pleasing form and brightness are counterbalanced by a sense of impending storm and destruction. What Novalis is here describing is the sublime, and he makes Sylvester continue with the assertion that this mixed feeling arouses in us our "moral superiority," the voice of "divine conscience" [*des himmlischen Gewissens*].[62] At this point the conversation becomes dense and difficult to follow, and yet it is obviously climactic and hence crucial for a right understanding of the novel. I shall therefore endeavor to elucidate its meaning as I understand it.

What makes this different from other eighteenth-century discussions of the sublime (for example, those by Burke, Kant, and Schiller) is that Novalis believes that nature is developing toward a "moral" state. By "moral," he means unified, undifferentiated, absolute, and therefore identical with spirit or, in his terms, God. The sublime is not the quality of an object, something within it, but the experience of or by an experiencing subject, as Kant had pointed out. But for Novalis the "mixed" nature of the experience derives from the fact that in it two stages in the *development* of nature are combined and are at odds, one more developed than the other. Stages in nature—or stages in our comprehension of nature? For Novalis the distinction is irrelevant because nonexistent. Just before this point in the conversation Heinrich had asserted that "fate and soul [*Schicksal und Gemüt*] were names for one and the same concept."[63] In other words, for him there is no distinction between inner and outer experience. Now Sylvester puts it thus: the anxieties evoked by dark clouds are "echoes of the old inhuman nature, but also wakening voices of higher nature, of heavenly conscience in us. The mortal [part of us] groans in its foundations, but the Immortal begins to shine brighter and acknowledges itself."[64] Such division will end only when nature is moral and "there is only *one* force—the force of conscience [*des Gewissens*]."

To Heinrich's request that Sylvester make the nature of *Gewissen* comprehensible, Sylvester replies that it emerges only while we comprehend it, it is both conscience and consciousness of conscience. Could *you*, he asks Heinrich, explain to me what poetry is? The connection between the two is therefore at this point established. Both are characterized by indivisibility [*Unteilbarkeit*]. In the external world of nature all worlds "lead to" one world; in the inner world of the *Gemüt* all senses are ultimately *one* sense. *Gewissen*, the moral and therefore unifying power in man, "creates" worlds and sense (by fusing the differentiated with the undifferentiated, the real with the ideal, the determinate with the absolute). It is "moral" because it involves freedom, it leads to mastery [*Meisterschaft*], *is* mastery. Through it, man acts as a person, as a whole, and mediates—mediates the Absolute, the Eternal, "God's Word"—in the sense of the primal, indivisible logos. Such action, says Sylvester, is true virtue [*Tugend*]. And so, says Heinrich, poetry is the embodiment or dress [*Verkleidung*] of the spirit of virtue, its task to rouse our highest activity as a person, as a unitary whole. And *Tugend* is, as a moral unifying force, the spirit of nature, of the whole external creation, including man—the indeterminate that sustains the determinate. *Gewissen* is "man's inmost being in full transfiguration, the divine *Urmensch*," it combines world with higher worlds—and it is the spirit of poetry in which "the higher voice of the cosmos" [*die höhere Stimme des Weltalls*] makes itself heard.[65]

It is this undifferentiated world of the Absolute that the third part of the novel was to portray. But most of the notations on the continuation of the novel would seem to refer to the rest of the second part, in which Heinrich was to spend some time in a monastery, experience war in Italy and art in Greece, visit Palestine, return to

Germany and go to the Emperor's court, and then write a poem on the conflict between good and evil. It is difficult to make much of all this material because it obviously embodies various stages in Novalis's thinking, which represent alternatives without a final choice.[66] The third part was to represent some kind of transfiguration, the blue flower was to become the final unifying symbol of this, and the work would seemingly have taken on more and more the form of a *Märchen*, and have culminated either in a poem (of which we have part) or another *Märchen* (of which we know only—and that from Tieck's report—what its general outline was to be, and that it was to represent, in Tieck's words, the "fulfillment" of the *Märchen* at the end of the first part). It is difficult to conceive of what this third part would have been like. In February 1800 Novalis had written to Tieck that "the whole [novel] is to be an apotheosis of poetry."[67] More need hardly be said. What better subject for a poetic novel than poetry itself?

CHAPTER SIX

A Visit with the Philosophers

THE ending of *Heinrich von Ofterdingen* would necessarily have been visionary in character, a transcendental epiphany in which all that had been separate should fuse into the indifferentiation of eternity. "Alles Getrennte findet sich wieder"—but whereas in *Hyperion* this harmony is declared to be realizable in earthly experience, for Novalis it is the "golden future" of moral unity. When Hölderlin spoke of the "eccentric path" of earthly experience, leading away from and out of unity in order to restore it, he was separating man off from God and validating the divisiveness of human existence from an eternal standpoint, suggesting that man must be alienated from the divine in order that he may know it, long for it, and return to it. But for Novalis man only knows the divine by communion with it, and this involves what Goethe had called "die and become," the falling away of earthly values such as Jean Paul's Viktor experiences in the presence of Emanuel as a prerequisite for entry into the higher state, though intuitions of eternity are vouchsafed to man within finite existence—as symbolized in the blue flower. In the first part of *Ofterdingen* Heinrich is constantly seeking some correlation of the discrete units of his experience, and in the second part of *Hyperion* the protagonist inveighs against the specialization of modern life. Both Hyperion and Ofterdingen only find fulfillment when they attain to a sense of the eternal unity inspiriting finite multiplicity. For Hyperion this amounts to an emanation or projection of the "God within him"; for Ofterdingen it is the acknowledgement of

Gewissen as the unifying force both within and without—the force itself, not product but process.

In my discussion of Friedrich Schlegel I stressed his search for a "center" to the multiplicity of experience, for a philosophy of the oneness behind the manifold of individuations—and his assertion that this is the prime task of poetry which by irony and "wit" presents such a view of the connectedness of all things in a universal fluidum and the interdependence, by connection or contrast, of the finite with the infinite, the determinate with the indeterminate. Jean Paul sees in the dualism of finite experience coexisting though alternating "moments" of the determinate and the indeterminate but accepts this as unity-in-polarity. Both Hölderlin and Novalis seek a synthesis, the former within finite experience, the latter beyond it but proceeding from it. Behind all this is a common sense of the fragmentation of modern life from which, as Hölderlin put it, the gods have retreated, and an equally strong concern about the warring tendencies of the human spirit—what Schiller had epitomized as inclination and duty, gratification of the senses and peace of soul. Schiller believed in the resolution of this discord in the "aesthetic state" induced by art. The Romantics aimed rather at the presentation of the discord in all its fullness, the contrast of higher and lower natures, higher and lower worlds—but linked this to a transcendent concept of undividedness, which is an Absolute but which nevertheless engenders the divided phenomenal world. Hence their striving for a "universal" poetry, their combinatory aspirations (including combination of genres), their "totalizing" endeavors, and their conception of the novel as an "encyclopedia of all poetic freedom" (Novalis).

This concern about divisions, coupled with the desire to establish an Indivisible, characterizes the philosophy and to a certain extent also the science of the period, as well as its literature. In philosophy it all proceeded from the impressions left by the philosophy of Kant which, in the opinion of several of his more thoughtful contemporaries, had established a number of distinctions and oppositions without maintaining a primal indivisible from which these divisions proceeded. In what follows I shall concentrate on those aspects of Kant's system which were of most importance for the romantic philosophers, and in particular for Fichte and Schelling. I shall also try to indicate briefly how these two philosophers attempted to overcome the divisiveness that they saw in Kant's philosophy, and the view of the world and of art that resulted therefrom, which was of significant importance to the romantic novelists and will help us better to understand their aims and achievements.[1]

In the *Critique of Pure Reason* Kant was concerned with how knowledge comes about, what the pure conditions in the human subject are for knowing objects ("pure" meaning not dependent on actual, empirical experience). This method of investigation, an investigation of the whole process of cognition, he called *transzendental*, and it is basically self-reflexive, the mind examining itself. He distinguishes between knowledge that is *immanent*—which is within the bounds of possible empirical experience—from that which is *transzendent* and overreaches such bounds, and both of these from the *transzendental* in which the mind seeks knowledge of itself. Out of this "transcendental" examination he hopes to arrive at an answer whether, and if so how, "transcendent" knowledge is possible. He accepts as a truth that the mind can and does make what he calls a priori judgments, that is: judgments independent of actual experience and based on "pure" reason (such as the axioms of mathematics)—and distinguishes these from a posteriori judgments, which are empirical judgments based on experience and valid only so far as experience goes (whereas a priori judgments have general validity). And he asserts that since metaphysics transcends empirical experience, its judgments—if it can make valid judgments at all, which is a question—must necessarily be a priori judgments.

Empirical judgments arise from unconscious intuitions [*Anschauungen*] in the subject of a manifold outside it, which then become representations [*Vorstellungen*] in the thinking process of the mind [*Verstand*] from which concepts [*Begriffe*] evolve, which represents an elementary unifying activity. These *Begriffe* are therefore limited and determinate. But Kant distinguishes the *Verstand* from a higher function of the mind, *Vernunft*, which can conceive of indeterminates, absolute principles or ideas, and is therefore transcendent in quality though its operations depend on the immanent origin of the representations of the understanding. But—and this was the crucial question for the romantic philosophers and poets—since we can talk of "mind" apart from the actual minds we experience (and in "transcendental" philosophy a mind can examine mind), do then the objects we experience have an absolute a priori existence, do they have existence apart from our representations of them, would they exist if they were never perceived? What is the relationship between objects and our representations of them? Kant believed that science had proved that there is a real world of objects outside us, but its reality is nevertheless encompassed by our experience of it. What we experience is therefore: things as they *appear* to us—*Erscheinungen*, or phenomena. But if they are things-as-they-*appear*, then there must be "things-in-themselves" [*Dinge an sich*] for them to be able to appear. Hence just as there must be "pure" conditions in the human mind, independent of empirical experience, for experience to be possible, so there must be "pure" *Dinge an sich* for "appearances" to be possible. For the Romantics this represented a basic division—between noumena and phenomena, and noumenal forms of both mind and "things"—but postulated no unity from which these divisions emerge.

In the transcendental inquiry of Kant's First Critique the mind is both subject and object, but his complex explanation of how the *Ding an sich* relates to phenomenal appearances need not concern us here because, as we shall see, the Romantics rejected the whole idea of a noumenal *Ding an sich*. Kant was, however, very much concerned with the question of what there is in "nature" (or the world of objects—all that is not "subject") that makes it perceivable by the mind. This was to become central, as we shall see, to Schelling's philosophy, and is embodied also in Novalis's conception of nature developing toward a "moral" state. Kant arrived at the conclusion that the same laws that unconsciously governed the flow of sense representations, became conscious in our thinking. The "laws" governing nature and those according to which the perceiving understanding operates, are certainly analogous, if not identical. At this point in Kant's argument, therefore, unconscious and conscious experience are considered in their relation to each other, and subject and object begin to approach each other, as do nature and spirit. Kant conceives of a universal, an absolute consciousness in which unconscious intuition and conscious thought merge, a noumenon that he calls transcendental apperception. This is the nearest he ever came to the positing of unity behind the divisions, but it is not a unitary principle or entity, we should notice, but a state, and a synthesis. It was, however, to points like this in Kant's system that the Romantics were to latch on, and especially to his relation of the unconscious to the conscious operations of the mind, of intuitions to thought.

Ultimately Kant's answer to the question of how experience (as empirical knowledge) is possible, is that it moves between the two poles of subjective apprehension of phenomena and the pure forms which are objective, in the sense that they are universally valid. The latter are noumenal and can never be known by "sensory intuition" [*sinnliche Anschauung*]; for this, an "intellectual intuition" [*intellektuelle Anschauung*] would be required and that, says Kant, we do not possess. (Fichte, as we shall see, disagreed.) Therefore metaphysics as knowledge of what transcends the physical, is, according to Kant, impossible, because we can never *know* universals. Nevertheless, he admits that we hanker after such knowledge because the knowledge that we can and do achieve never satisfies us, because our knowledge is confined to the determinate, and although the concept of determinacy necessarily implies a concept of indeterminacy, we never *reach* the Indeterminate in the progress of our knowledge. The Romantics disagreed. Fichte, as we shall see, actually *starts* from the Indeterminate, whereas for Kant the Indeterminate or Absolute is the goal—an ideal which we strive toward in our cognitive processes but which nevertheless remains an idea. Thus we talk about nature as a "whole," but we never experience it as that. All we do is to acquire more and more knowledge of its phenomenal reality, but behind this lies the idea of a whole which is noumenal, an "idea of pure reason." Such transcendental ideas—and for Kant there are three principal ones—world, soul, and God—are "regulative" of experience but are never objects of our experience. Romantic novelists showed that they are.

If we view nature teleologically, as many had done, then this idea of a whole would seem to precede the parts (so to speak) and the notion of a goal of nature be somehow anticipated. If this were the case, this goal could arise only in some infinite intelligence or spirit and the empirical objects of nature would be manifest thoughts of some such world spirit. But Kant emphasizes that only our own phenomenal knowledge leads us to such a concept, and this in itself neither proves nor disproves the existence of such an absolute intelligence. All we can say is that our own determinate experience leads us to *think* of some origin and goal, some sense of intention. But what sort of goal must this be? It must be unconditional, absolute, with its value lying within itself—and this for Kant means that it is "moral." Which will explain, perhaps better than anything else, what Novalis meant when he spoke of the "moral" goal of nature.

In the Second Critique, the *Critique of Practical Reason*, Kant investigates whether there are a priori principles in the will as there are in cognition. He distinguishes at the outset between acts of will directed toward a specific purpose and those which are not. These latter presuppose for him an a priori principle that he calls the moral law, which is not empirically conditioned but has general validity. All moral decisions involve choice for Kant, and freedom therefore is the essential *subjective* component in moral action. But there must also be an *objective* (universally valid) component as well. If we abstract all notions of purpose from the operations of the will, then we are left with the formal element, the form of the moral law, just as when we abstract from cognition the empirical content of specific experience we are left with the general a priori principles of the cognitive process. The moral law is therefore, for Kant, the a priori element of the will. The important point made here is that for Kant morality is autonomous, the moral quality of an action does not depend on something outside the action (its specific purpose, its result) but resides within it. The moral law is therefore noumenal, an absolute, and the fact that it often conflicts with the direction of our sensual natures means that here, in the moral sphere, we do somehow attain to the sense of an absolute. The will is its own legislator, does not depend on anything outside itself. In the *Critique of Pure Reason* Kant had argued that freedom is impossible in the phenomenal world and possible (thinkable) only in the noumenal. In the moral world there is freedom, in that we make choices, but the distinction between desire and obligation simply means that we are "citizens of two worlds," part sensual and part rational, and that what appears as necessity in the phenomenal world is freedom in the noumenal; man is both free and unfree. It is the concept of the moral law that gives us practical assurance of there being a noumenal reality and of our belonging to it as *rational* beings.

I have not followed Kant in all the complexities of his argument, but only highlighted those points that were to be of significance to romantic philosophers and the view of life and nature embodied in some of the romantic novels. It would seem clear that Novalis's concept of *Gewissen* is closely associated with Kant's "moral law," although it is wider and embraces, as we have seen, also the activity of the poet, so that for Novalis poetry becomes a form of moral activity. Kant himself, in the Third Critique, the *Critique of Judgment*, tries to establish a resolution of the conflict between necessity (in the laws of nature) and freedom (in the moral sphere) and finds this in the faculty of judgment, which mediates between the operations of the understanding (limited to the phenomenal world) and those of the reason (the noumenal world). Turning now to aesthetic judgments, he endeavors here too to distinguish between a posteriori and a priori elements, and between subjective reactions and objective principles. Kant asserts that the essential quality of aesthetic judgments is that they engage the faculties of the mind in pleasing interplay—either imagination and understanding (in the beautiful), or senses and reason (in the sublime). For the Romantics perhaps the most important part of his argument was the distinction he makes between the imagination and the understanding, the former being what produces intuitions, the latter being the power that forms representations, thoughts, and concepts. Intuitive experience, connected as it is with nonconsciousness and "prior" (so to speak) to the operations of conscious understanding, was obviously of prime importance to them. For they believed that such experience often brought knowledge that superseded conscious experience. Secondly: this whole emphasis on the free play of the mind in aesthetic activity and experience became, in part through the intermediary of romantic philosophers, an important aspect of their view of poetry and their conception of the novel. And thirdly, this same emphasis on freedom linked the aesthetic with the moral, as did Kant's assertion of the *autonomy* of the aesthetic as well as the moral (without reference to anything outside itself), and paralleled both the Romantics' rejection of the moralistic and utilitarian aesthetic of the Enlightenment and their assertion of the true moral nature of poetry. In a somewhat tortuous argument, Kant even went so far as to assert that beauty is a *symbol* of the good, by which he seems to mean that the beautiful, (and the aesthetic experience altogether) forms a link between the "sensual" world of nature and the "suprasensual" world of morality by its combination of sensual and suprasensual elements.

The main criticism of Kant's system in the years immediately following its appearance centered on two points: the lack of some primal unitary principle behind the oppositions (understanding and reason, phenomenal and noumenal, consciousness and unconsciousness), and the notion of the *Ding an sich.* If there is noumenal object as well as noumenal subject, we have *two* indeterminates or absolutes, which—it was asserted—is nonsense, if only because the concept "two" involves the category of quantity, a category of the *understanding* and therefore applicable only to the phenomenal world. Fichte therefore seeks a "first principle," a unitary noumenon which, since it is indeterminate, must be both subject and object, both receptive *and* spontaneous (faculties of the mind that Kant had distinguished between). This Absolute, intelligence-in-itself, he calls *das Ich*—it is not a state or an existence but an activity, transcendental ego or spirit, for it posits itself. It is not consciousness, but what makes consciousness possible. But if the Ego posits itself, it must do

this by oppositing to itself a non-Ego. Since there cannot by definition be anything *outside* this absolute Ego, the non-Ego must emerge
from the Ego. By spontaneous and autonomous activity the Ego
divides itself—not into two indeterminates, however, but into a determinate Ego and a determinate non-Ego, into subject and object,
and thereby consciousness evolves. Fichte speaks of this as the striving of the Ego to attain consciousness of itself. But the important
thing is that the non-Ego opposed to the Ego is opposed *by* the
Ego. There is no *Ding an sich*.

The relationship between Ego and non-Ego is one of reciprocal
limitation. By a curious notion that he called "transcendental affection," Kant had tried to explain how the *Ding an sich* affects the
noumenal intelligence to cause representations of phenomena in the
finite mind and make us believe in their absolute reality. Since he
has rejected the whole idea of the *Ding an sich*, Fichte cannot endue
the *Nicht-Ich* with autonomy and hence the power to limit the *Ich*,
for though it *appears* as though the *Nicht-Ich* limits the *Ich*, in fact this
is the *Ich* limiting itself. Hence for Fichte the "reality" of objects, of
the material or stuff of experience, does not have objective validity,
for it originates in the self-assertion of the intelligence. The sense of
being acted upon (Kant's "receptivity") is only the *finite* Ego's illusory
mode of operating. Why then do we think of objects as somehow
independent of the subject? To answer this Fichte evolves his concept of "productive imagination" [*produktive Einbildungskraft*].[2]

This concept, though somewhat obscurely formulated by Fichte, is
central to his whole system and of great significance for the relationship between subject and object, inner and outer worlds, consciousness and the unconscious as we find this embodied in the work of
romantic writers and particularly in the novel, which is essentially
concerned with the relationship of subject and object. The greatest
problem for all epistemologists had been to establish whether the
objects of our experience have autonomous existence apart from the
receiving mind. Fichte must believe that nothing can have autonomous existence outside the infinite and absolute *Ich*, and yet he does
recognize that our finite experience gives us the sense of receiving
impressions, of being affected by something outside ourselves. Kant
had distinguished between receptivity and spontaneity in the operations of the mind, passive and active functions of the intelligence.
But whereas he assumed the *Ding an sich* as the ground of the passive aspect of the mind, Fichte asserts that this passive aspect is not
provoked from outside of the *Ich* (there being nothing outside it) but

by self-limitation of the *Ich*. The *Ich* is indeterminate activity (*Tun*), striving—this is its "pure" activity, but for this to become actual, "objective" activity it must opposit something to itself, because striving implies some kind of check or hindrance, something striving against or being striven against, the *Nicht-Ich*, through which the *Ich* posits itself as passive, as receptive. Therefore receptivity is merely limited activity of the *Ich*. The *Nicht-Ich* brings the *Ich* to consciousness of itself by its opposition, so that the *Ich* is bent back on itself, returns into itself, and reflects on the sensation it has received, makes this an object, or *Nicht-ich*. The original intuitive *production* of the *Nicht-Ich* by spontaneous activity of the *Ich*, which is what Fichte means by "productive imagination," is therefore paralleled by the *reproduction* through reflection. In other words: consciousness reproduces what unconsciousness had produced, and being unaware of the latter, considers its representations to be those of a world of autonomous reality. Imagination is for Fichte the force that mediates between infinite and finite, determining the indeterminate.

We should note that for Fichte the Absolute is spirit, striving, unlimited activity, and therefore freedom. Since this activity is "pure" and has no external goal or purpose, it is therefore autonomous and moral. The objective activity of the *Ich* involves returning into itself. So the primal aspect of the Absolute, for Fichte, is activity, striving, will; cognition is secondary and the result of the "passive," self-limited aspect of the spirit. Hence will does not proceed from cognition, but vice versa. Consciousness is secondary to the free intuitive powers of the absolute intelligence or *Ich*. Reflection is freedom limiting itself by making itself an object. Productive imagination is the free positing of an object, the non-Ego, by the Ego, which then by its dependence on the Ego creates consciousness in and of itself in the Ego. Fichte's Absolute is therefore an indeterminate unity, in which the oppositions of subject/object, freedom/necessity, conscious/unconscious are not valid. Such oppositions occur only in the finite consciousness.

These formulations of Fichte are the basis of the romantic view of existence and experience as we find it in the novelists, even though some of them, notably Jean Paul, Schlegel, and Novalis, parted company with Fichte on several points. But they knew his work—or at least his earlier, more important work—well, and it is not difficult to see connections between their conceptions of unconscious and conscious knowledge, of the workings of the imagination, the self-reflective powers of the mind, the relation of determinates to the Indeterminate, and Fichte's philosophy. One major bone of contention however was his concept of nature (the world of objects, the *Nicht-Ich*) as something opposed, as a sort of obstacle to the free workings of the intelligence, albeit created by spontaneous unconscious activity of the intelligence—an opposition which is produced by the mind so that the mind may return to itself. This "degrading" (so to speak) of nature was not acceptable to most of the Romantics. Nor was the *unconscious* "productive imagination," the basic creative power of the spirit, from which, because it is below consciousness, all activity of the finite will must necessarily be excluded; Novalis, for instance, as we have seen, believed that the conscious creative will could modify nature and "educate" it toward a return to an undivided, moral state.

In many ways the early philosophy of Schelling (whose thinking developed through several distinguishable stages) is closer to the attitudes of the romantic novelists. For one thing his view of nature was more akin to theirs, as was his presentation of the relation between conscious and unconscious. And he built a philosophy of art into his system in such a way as to give it sovereign importance. Let us first consider briefly his philosophy of nature. Quite early on, in 1795, Schelling declared that the main task of philosophy was to account for the existence of the world.[3] Fichte had asserted that nature was the spontaneous unreflected product of the *Ich*. Schelling sees in nature the workings of an *unconscious* intelligence which develops into consciousness *through the mind of man*. By being perceived as representations in the human mind, nature attains to knowledge of itself and the mind to consciousness. Nature is therefore visible spirit, and spirit is invisible nature. There is no basic division between subject and object, and philosophy is the history of consciousness. Nature shows organization and this must presume an organizing force, but since this force is independent of the consciousness of the mind, it must be unconscious. Taking over terms from Spinoza, Schelling points out that nature is twofold: *natura naturans* as organizing or creating force, and *natura naturata*, the products—again, therefore, a fusion of subject and object. *Natura naturans* works by a polar opposition of counterbalancing forces: attraction and repulsion, receptivity and spontaneity, oxydation and deoxydation, and so forth. A dualistic principle, therefore, governs nature, a dualism resolved only in some unconscious intelligence that he calls world-soul [*Weltseele*]. It is a dynamic, developing universe, with the ultimate goal of indeterminacy, and indifferentiation of subject/object, nature/spirit, conscious/unconscious.

A Visit with the Philosophers

For Fichte there were two types of consciousness according to whether the subject (or *Ich*) is limited by the object (or *Nicht-Ich*) or object by subject, the former producing knowledge, the latter resulting in action, the former receptive and the latter spontaneous. Schelling can reconcile this distinction only by assuming that the activity basic to both is identical, though unconscious in cognition and conscious in action. He reformulates Fichte's concept of "productive imagination" by saying that what seems a division between subject and object is merely an indication of the limits of our consciousness, and his whole *System des transzendentalen Idealismus* (1800) is concerned with establishing the various stages in the development of self-consciousness, in which intuition and action, receptivity and spontaneity coalesce ultimately into an undifferentiated unity or "identity." From the transcendental standpoint the activity of the will is a continuation, or further development, of the activity that produces intuition of the world. In the process of history he postulates a similar combination of conscious action and unconscious forces. And in art—the section on which is the climax of the whole book—a similar fusion prevails, for every work of art, he says, contains in its completeness more than the artist consciously put into it, for in every artist there is a power greater than himself, something akin to fate or destiny, a force driving him. Like man in history, the artist is a compound of freedom and necessity. The same power that acts without consciousness in producing nature (which Schelling at one point calls the "unconscious poetry of the Spirit")[4] acts *with* consciousness or rather *through* the consciousness of the artist in producing the work of art. In artistic production the Ego can observe itself producing, and experiences the unity of free and driven activity, conscious and unconscious. In artistic creation the mind becomes an object to itself, and the distinction between subject and object no longer exists.

In lectures given at Jena during the winter of 1802–1803 (and subsequently repeated at Würzburg) Schelling developed his philosophy of art in more detail. He here postulates an *essence* [*Wesen*] of all things which is indivisible and undifferentiated, and determinate manifestations of this, which he calls *Potenzen*. Undifferentiation is identity-and-totality. All philosophy is concerned with this, the Absolute; but so is art, which he here calls "the most perfect objective reflex of philosophy."[5] In it basic essences appear in real things, ideas are objectified. It should represent the *Indifferenz* (nondifferentiation) of the real and the ideal, and represent it *as* "Indifferenz." Art therefore becomes the crown of Schelling's system because it represents the *Indifferenz* of the Absolute, and this is the final goal toward which all self-consciousness is progressing. Hence the importance of art as revealing the ultimate goal of everything—unity of nature and spirit, necessity and freedom, unconscious and conscious—the absence of all dichotomy and differentiation.

In the "Specific Part" of these same lectures Schelling has some remarks on how the novel should embody his conception of art.[6] As a form it represents a combination of the purposes of epic and drama. The epic has unrestricted action, in that it has no real beginning and could go on indefinitely. Drama, on the other hand, has a restricted action. The novel has a restricted action but unrestricted import—a specific plot being used to "show the Absolute."[7] Therefore the hero should be more symbolic than personal, and this can be intensified by irony toward the hero, because irony permits objectification of what is subjective in the hero, and retardation of the action by the hero imposes on the essentially dramatic nature of all plot that essentially epic quality of pondering and reflection on events. With reference to this latter point Schelling asserts that the novel is a vehicle for mature minds, conducive to calm reflection in the reader and representing for its author "that last refinement [*Läuterung*] of the mind which returns into itself and transforms life and experience into blossoms." As a mirror of the world it is therefore a "partial mythology," reflecting not just social conditions but wider concerns and higher values.[8] It can legitimately use the strange and uncommon [*das Abenteuerliche*] so long as it uses this, like all else, symbolically.[9] Common reality may well be used in a novel to set off uncommon reality. This is what happens in *Don Quixote*, the theme of which is "the real in conflict with the ideal,"[10] and this theme is the focus [*Mittelpunkt*] that every novel should have. In Part One of *Don Quixote*, the ideals of the hero come into conflict with the common world: in Part Two the world is "uncommon," "mystified," more idea than real. The Don and Sancho are "mythological characters." The adventure with the windmills, though specific, has mythological validity. In fact all the separate incidents are variations on the central theme, so that there is no sense of discontinuity or fragmentation—in other words, nothing episodic. In *Wilhelm Meister* Schelling perceives the same central conflict of real with ideal, although here it does not take the form of one theme appearing in manifold variations (as in *Don Quixote*); Goethe's novel is much more fragmented, yet general, eternal vistas open up at the end. Schelling interprets the secret Society of the Tower (which he recognizes as deriving from the *Trivialromane*) symbolically, for as soon as it becomes visible (instead of being a *felt* presence) it dissolves, leaving the hero with the realization that he has a mission and what it is—and so the "mystery" of the "apprenticeship" is revealed.[11] It is interesting, I think, that Schelling seems to have had a clearer sense of the really central irony of Goethe's novel than anyone else at the time—and many since.

The fact that our experience of determinates evokes in us the notion of the Indeterminate, and constantly does so, was reinterpreted by the German Romantics as an urge in us to *experience* the Indeterminate. For the philosopher Schleiermacher this was the basis of religious consciousness—"Religion is feeling and taste for the Infinite"[12]—and for many of the Romantics it was the essence of poetry. Contrary to Kant, the Romantics did not believe that we can never know the Indeterminate, but they did believe that such knowledge was of a different provenance from our knowledge of the Determinate. Some spoke of an inner sense in us supplementing our external or bodily senses; this combination is essentially what Novalis means by *Gemüt*, which combines consciousness derived from empirical experience with a higher form of consciousness that relates phenomena to noumena, the real to the ideal, the immanent to the transcendent, determinate to Absolute. For the Romantics believed that the inner life embraced certain intuitions and perceptions which are not empirically accountable, intimations of connection between seemingly quite disparate things, of a higher unity, of a transcendent, undifferentiated whole, of an Absolute. They observed that such higher experiences often come to us when our normal thinking apparatus, the *Verstand*, is dormant or suspended under the impress of some unusually strong emotion or experience. Hence the interest that all the Romantics manifested in states when normal consciousness is suspended: in dreams, trances, rapture, dislocations of the imagination, hallucinations, visions—even madness. It was they who made the first important excursions into the subconscious and the unconscious, believing that knowledge, together with truth, was to be found here too, knowledge that was not *less* than that of the consciousness, but perhaps a deeper, more basic revelation, uninhibited and unconstrained by the divisive and dichotomous operations of the waking reason. In such states of suspended consciousness man achieves some degree of approach to the whole, the Indeterminate from which all determinacy has evolved, the infinite that transcends the finite. The infinite is therefore accessible in subconscious or superconscious intuition. However, the Romantics never advocated a wholesale descent into the subconscious with a corresponding abandonment of rationality. What they were asserting was that rational consciousness was *incomplete* consciousness, limited by our determinate nature, that the subconscious extends such knowledge and feeds the consciousness, and complete knowledge is achievable only by the fusion of conscious and unconscious, interaction of outer and inner sense. If, as Schelling had asserted, philosophy is the history of consciousness, and primarily of self-consciousness,[13] then the ultimate goal of all striving is to attain complete consciousness in which the determinate distinction between rational and extrarational, conscious and unconscious no longer exists. And poetry is a means to this end. This is its educative function.

Some spoke of a *return* to a *primal* unity, using images such as that of a golden age or the chaos (of Genesis) that preceded the determinacy of the creation. Poetry was a conscious restoration of such unity, by virtue of its heightened sense of connections between determinate disparate things, its power to perceive, and represent, an undifferentiated unity behind the discrete and often conflicting individuations of existence. For the German Romantics firmly believed in a unitary Absolute "behind" a discordant and confused universe. Scientists too were seeking for some single force or principle operating in all the manifold phenomena of nature. There had been talk for some time of a possible universal fluid to account for the varieties of life in the universe. And recent discoveries, such as those of oxygen, magnetism, and electricity, had seemed to be pointing in the same direction. This was especially true of electricity, which brought with it the concept of the interdependence of positive and negative, thereby illustrating the complementary nature of apparent opposites and confirming what Schelling was to formulate as the dualistic principle operating in all nature, the resolution of which opposition was to be found only in the transcendent sphere of an absolute intelligence. The scientists were not concerned with an absolute intelligence, but rather with an absolute principle or universal force in nature. There were also psychologists among them who were concerned with mind rather than nature, though often relating the two analogically. The discovery of oxygen suggested that one vital element accounted for the apparent distinction, and diversity, of both organic and inorganic nature. Or was it not an element, but electricity? Or magnetism? Or was all life of volcanic or marine origin, following set lines of development? The Neo-Platonists of the Renaissance had believed that the universe was a living being with a soul, of which all individual existences were emanations. Much of this survived, through the mediation of mystical and occultist writers, to resurface in vitalist thinkers of the eighteenth century and the so-called "nature-philosophers" of the romantic period, the most notable of whom were Franz von Baader, Gotthilf Heinrich Schubert, Lorenz Oken, Johann Wilhelm Ritter, Henrik Steffens, and Carl Gustav Carus.

Common to these thinkers, according to Albert Béguin, was the conception of nature as an organism, not divisible into parts, and of life as a sort of cosmic circuit in which individual organisms interrupt the current and intensify it, so that an eternal movement is maintained toward the reestablishment of a "lost" unity for each individuation contains a "germ" of this lost unity and contributes toward its reestablishment.[14] Man as microcosm of the universe was originally endowed with an "inner" or "universal" sense which *knew* the universe by analogy (an old occultist doctrine). This sense still exists in us, though smothered, and all we have to do is to descend to it in order to regain attunement and integration, to return to our original harmony with nature. This involves a certain abandonment to the "rhythm of nature" (Schubert), to the subconscious level, such as we experience in hypnotic or somnambulistic states. "Everyone bears within himself his own somnambulist of which he is the magnetizer," Ritter once wrote to Baader.[15] Only in the unconscious do we now remain attuned to the whole. Ritter speaks elsewhere of the sense of something that infinitely transcends us and responds to our questions, and he calls it, in a phrase that recalls Hölderlin's Hyperion, "God in our heart." Steffens talks of the "dark dialogue of the whole with itself."[16] If we recall Schelling's assertion that artistic creation derives from an interplay of the conscious and the unconscious, then the relation of all this to poetry becomes apparent. Jean Paul speaks of the poet *listening* to a language inside him but strange to him, and Novalis of listening to an interior dialogue, Arnim of writing down what is dictated to him.[17] For Novalis the first stage of knowledge is inward: "inward leads the mysterious path" (*nach innen geht der geheimnisvolle Weg*)[18]—inward, listening to what the inner sense reveals, but then turning outward to the world, and finding emanations of the invisible in the visible, integrating these, and working toward a future unity. The path to unity is one of reintegration of spirit and nature by lifting the unconscious to the level of consciousness.

In her study of Mesmer, Maria Tatar shows that, according to

Mesmer, "the key to health . . . lay in recovering the wholly harmonious relationship that had once existed between man and nature."[19] Believing that the universal fluid in nature was magnetic, Mesmer asserted that disease resulted from obstruction of this fluid and could be cured by magnets or emanations of magnetic fluid. The important thing about this, for my present context, is that it represents an assertion that a force demonstrably present in nature (magnetism) also controlled the physical and psychic life of man. This was a question not of analogy or similarity, but of identity, for the concept of "animal magnetism" was not just a metaphor. It represented the force that inspirited both mind and nature, and linked the two. It was obviously below consciousness, and mediated between mind and nature, man and the cosmos. Mesmer posited an inner sense "in relation with the whole of the universe" to account for certain mental phenomena observed in his patients.[20] Hypnotic gestures could stimulate this sense, and the thereby induced "magnetic sleep" could be therapeutic, he believed. Whether the power of this inner sense resulted from contact with magnetism in nature (as some, but not all, believed), there was general belief that its revelations were of unusual clarity, transcending that of the impressions derived from external senses. For Novalis these were impulses from a spiritual world, for Fichte revelations of transcendence ("the suprasensual world is given to man by the inner sense").[21] For the Dutch philosopher Hemsterhuis (who had considerable influence on the Romantics) the inner sense was a "moral organ"—a phrase that suggests Novalis's *Gewissen*.

Which brings me finally to the subject of sleep and dreams. It was asserted that in man there were two nervous systems: a "cerebral" system which governed conscious behavior, and a "ganglionic" system which produced involuntary behavior. The cerebral system controls our waking life, the ganglionic is operative in sleep. According to Schubert, the ganglionic system was located in the solar plexus and resulted in intuitive knowledge; it was the physiological point of contact with the universal fluid (or organization) of the whole. Some of the nature-philosophers distinguished between a "telluric" state where imagination and feeling predominate, and a "solar" state governed by consciousness and reason—with the corollary that in sleep one is closer to the telluric state and, by loss of consciousness of self, to the universal (an old mystical idea). Sleep was therefore a sort of prefiguration of death, and dreams of the *unio mystica*, the return to primal unity. In *L'Ame romantique et le rêve*, one of the best books ever written on German romanticism, Albert Béguin has pointed to the enormous role played by dreams in this literature. I have already drawn attention to this in my accounts of Jean Paul and Novalis, and we shall see that dreams are an equally important element in the novels of the other Romantics. In a couple of essays written in the 1790s Jean Paul declared that dreams put us in contact with all that is more than individual within us.[22] Novalis said much the same in the beginning of *Ofterdingen* and Hoffmann was to speak later of the inner sense active in dreams and somnambulistic states in which we enter into communication with the "soul of the world," the "spiritual principle of all things." Arnim in the introduction to his novel *Die Kronenwächter* speaks of "what we seek, and what seeks us."[23] Dream and consciousness (telluric and solar) cease to oppose each other in the state of *full* consciousness that Ofterdingen attains to after the death of Mathilde and "world becomes dream and dream becomes world." The experience of another's death producing expansion of one's own consciousness, which Novalis himself had lived through at the death of Sophie von Kühn and vividly described in the *Hymnen an die Nacht*, involved the "transfiguration of life, living it fully, *hic et nunc*, according to the law of the beyond . . . the real transformation of the terrestrial world, finally reconciled with the general harmony and reintegrated into eternity" (Béguin's words).[24] But what distinguishes Novalis from most of his contemporaries, is that this reintegration is an act of will, not a state achieved involuntarily, in dream, ecstasy, or the unconscious. His "magic idealism" asserted that the world has only an *apparent* autonomy, that we can make what we will of the accidentals of life, that only our incomplete consciousness maintains a distinction between subject and object, that only when we understand ourselves can we understand the world, that *we* can reconstitute the original unity, and it is our moral task to do so.

Poetry, by its fusion of real and ideal, its combination of "absolute individuality and absolute universality" (to recall Schlegel's lapidary phrase), does just this. Dreams do too, and therefore prefigure poetry as sleep does death. By transcending both space and time they are divinatory and cosmic, as the dreams in the Old Testament and other religious writings as well as the experience of dreamlike states by various mystics show. Therefore dreams are akin to poetry. Jean Paul calls them "involuntary poetry." Hoffmann terms artistic activity a superior form of dream. Eichendorff speaks of poetry as expressing the sleeping melodies of the universe.[25] Schubert, in his treatise on the symbolism of dreams, *Die Symbolik des Traumes* (1814), links up the "symbolic" language of dreams with the metaphorical language of poetry, and the language of revelation. Beginning with the assertion that the language of dreams is more in accordance with the nature of our minds than normal "word-language" because it achieves combinations and associations that escape the waking reason, and also with whatever there is outside us—call it fate, *Schicksal*, or whatever—he speaks of its "higher sort of algebra" and of "the hidden poet within us" [*der versteckte Poet in unserm Innern*][26] who alone can "manipulate" this language which combines past, present, and future, and leaps across space. Dream, prophecy, and poetry speak the same language. Their images have universal relevance, their actions take on symbolic relevance as in religious cults, their language is essentially hieroglyphic. Nature itself is such a hieroglyphic language, but we have lost the power to interpret it, at least as regards the normal, "waking," operations of our mind, as the first revelation of God. Conscience, *das Gewissen*, is the "organ" in us of this "language" of God, this primal language, and the "hidden poet" within us is based on conscience in its *true* sense, for conscience, like all else, has become debased by human ratiocination and is no longer the instinctive voice of the divine in us.[27] We have become deaf to the symbolic language of nature, mistaking its actual sensual qualities for its meaning, and reducing ideas ("the objects of the spiritual region") to symbols of the objects of our sensual perception.[28] Only the language of dream returns to this true understanding of the divine language of nature. It *is* what the language of waking *should* be, but rarely is.[29] Schubert looks for a way by which man may return to a waking experience of what is now only vouchsafed him in dream or dreamlike states. In these states the ganglionic nervous system predominates over the cerebral, and the involuntary over the volitional. What we experience is the "opening up of an inner sense"[30] which brings us into contact with the rhythm of the universe—a barrier [*Scheidewand*, cf. Novalis's "mysterious curtain" in the opening chapter of *Ofterdingen*], that between ganglionic and cerebral systems, is removed, memory and foresight are given us, higher consciousness evolves, and we become once more part of the universal whole, able to comprehend nature and our part in nature as never before, thanks to the "hidden poet" within us, transformed in our innermost being. Without expressly saying so, Schubert is subscribing to the romantic notion of the sovereign power of poetry and its therapeutic moral force.

This little book was attentively read by Jean Paul, Schlegel, and

Hoffmann. Much in it is derived from other sources, but the shape of its argument (despite its somewhat tortuous style) and its alignment of dream, revelation, and poetry were timely and therefore influential. But for us it is time to return to the novelists, and specifically to Ludwig Tieck's investigations of the interplay of the conscious and the unconscious in the imagination, and his search for a poetic center.

CHAPTER SEVEN

Hazards of the Imagination: Tieck

LUDWIG TIECK (1773–1853) is certainly one of the most interesting writers of German romanticism, but he is one of the most difficult to write about.[1] His output was voluminous and in all genres, but is unequal in quality and so varied in its artistic intentions and in style, that it is difficult to arrive at an overall assessment even when one restricts oneself to a particular genre. It is his novels that concern us here, together with what he said about other novelists and about the novel as a form. He wrote two novels as a young man, namely *William Lovell* (1795–1796) and *Franz Sternbalds Wanderungen* [Franz Sternbald's Travels] (1798), and, in later life, three lengthy narratives, *Der Aufruhr in den Cevennen* [The Uprising in the Cevennes] (1826, unfinished), *Der junge Tischlermeister* [The Young Master Carpenter] (1836), and *Vittoria Accorombona* (1840), only the last of which is described on the title page as a novel, though it could be argued that the other two are also, in effect, novels. The two early novels are by far the most important for our context. The others, although they at times embody romantic preoccupations, are no longer romantic in form. They are scenic in structure, and, through their extensive use of conversations, are almost like extended dramas. Tieck also wrote a considerable number of novellas, the early ones dealing largely with experiences of an uncanny or supernatural nature, the later ones more grounded in the real than the fantastic, including some with historical subjects, one based on material from the life of Shakespeare (*Dichterleben* [Poet's Life], 1826–1831), and one on that of Camoëns (*Der Tod des Dichters* [The Death of the

Poet], 1833). He also wrote, in his earlier years, several *Märchen*, retellings of old folk-books (some in dramatic form), and some highly innovative dramas in which irony and alienation foreshadow the theater of Bertold Brecht. Brecht's epic theater also is prefigured by Tieck's long chronicle-dramas, panoramic and cinematographic in structure, with a use of lyrics similar to that of Brecht. These are really romances in dramatic form, and were undoubtedly inspired by Shakesperean romances, particularly *Pericles*. These plays show the fine line that divides drama of this kind from the novel. In addition, Tieck wrote a sizable amount of literary criticism, much of it of great interest. He was also a notable translator, his version of *Don Quixote* being the means by which Germans of his and succeeding generations became acquainted with Cervantes's masterpiece. He was an accomplished linguist, widely read in French, English, and Spanish literature. Quite early he showed evidence of acting talent, and acquired a great facility in writing. This latter was observed by one of his schoolteachers, who was turning out popular novels in his spare time and engaged Tieck to write the final chapter of a sensational potboiler. Tieck then did a good deal of hackwork, producing versions of French tales of a moralistic tenor for Friedrich Nicolai, a famous publicist of the time still eagerly promoting the Enlightenment ethos. But when his fancy took over too strongly, Tieck was, in effect, fired and left to indulge his own overpowering imagination, which he did very successfully. The connections between the young Tieck and the *Trivialliteratur* of the eighteenth century are therefore particularly strong. But although he took much, he always transformed it into something more interesting, and more romantic. The striking features about the early Tieck are his disturbed relationship to reality and the heightened sensitivity of his imagination, as Alfred Anger has pointed out.[2] These are the characteristics in himself that he objectifies in *William Lovell* and *Franz Sternbalds Wanderungen*. The latter, as we shall see, was considerably influenced by the personality and interests of his friend Wackenroder, with whom he cooperated on two major works of romantic aesthetics, the *Herzensergiessungen eines kunstliebenden Klosterbruders* [Outpourings of the Heart of an Art-Loving Monk] (1797), and *Phantasien über die Kunst* [Fantasias on Art] (1799), which advocated an attitude of religious reverence as the only true approach to the understanding of great art.

The *Geschichte des Herrn William Lovell* was published in three volumes in 1795 and 1796. Tieck revised it twice, first in 1813 and then for the Collected Works in 1828, but the general structure and movement remain the same. In my account I shall follow the first version.³ *William Lovell* is a transitional novel, traditional in form but romantic in much of what it describes, a novel about the dissolution of personality which moves into realms explored contemporaneously by Jean Paul but is much more sinister because no counterweight is given, no conclusion such as the closing mood of *Titan* was to offer. It deals with the systematic seduction and destruction of a human soul by forces both within and outside it, and can therefore legitimately be compared with both *Werther* and *Les Liaisons dangereuses*— not with one or the other but with both in combination. Like these it is a novel in letters, but without the monologue mood of *Werther*, for the letters are exchanged between a group of persons. Unlike the external action of *Les Liaisons dangereuses*, the forces from outside that contribute to Lovell's destruction are presented in a complicated plot of a sensational nature that derives from horror-novels, a subsection of the popular novels described above in Chapter 3. In fact *William Lovell* might well have been treated there, but it has seemed to me more apposite to consider it in the general context of Tieck's development as a novelist and a critic.⁴

Lovell is an Icarus nature, inflamed by enthusiasms that tend to lead him dangerously far from reality. He loves Amalie Wilmont of Bonstreet, Yorkshire, but his father wants him to marry a London society girl. For this reason and others he decides to go on a journey, accompanied by Old Willy, the trusty family servant, and Mortimer, a friend of Amalie's brother. So far everything is fairly conventional: the English setting, the journey, the contrast between town and country (London and Bonstreet), between father and son, sophisticated young men and simple but honest old servant. Lovell is a *Schwärmer*, the unworldly enthusiast dealt with both sympathetically and critically in so many German novels of the eighteenth century, and he and Amalie read Ossian together, for there is a melancholy embedded in his enthusiasms. Mortimer, on the other hand, is a rationalistic cynic, essentially man-of-the-world: also a type from novels of the eighteenth century. What is not traditional is Lovell's sense of some kind of dark fate, of something menacing that beckons from the future, of some misery attending his progress from childhood to manhood. At the same time he knows this feeling is irrational, but it is the "heart" in him, affording him both joy and torment:

> When this burning heart shall gradually cool off, this divine spark
> in me turn to ashes and the world perhaps consider me more

Ludwig Tieck. After a drawing by Karl Christian Vogel von Vogel-
stein, 1827. Whereabouts of original unknown.

sensible—what will replace the love within me seeking to embrace the world?—Reason will anatomize those beauties that now intoxicate me with their harmonies: I will know the world and human beings better, but I will love them less—as soon as a solution is found to a profound riddle, the riddle becomes insipid [*abgeschmackt*].[5]

The dichotomy of head and heart, also an eighteenth-century commonplace, is here given a romantic twist by being acclaimed: for Lovell, mysteries are better than solutions. Like Jean Paul, Tieck is very much concerned in this novel with dualism and alienation, and the passage I have quoted is illustrative of the psychological probing with which he presents his subject throughout the work. Lovell is given to that "chewing over" of misfortune which Werther had referred to, even here where no misfortune has as yet befallen him. He feeds on dark presentiments, speaks of "sweet melancholy," "the sad melody of changing feelings," and yet can realize that this self-centeredness will preclude any relations of friendship or love.[6] On the other hand the counterarguments of his father, who calls William's enthusiasms mere "childish ebullitions of the blood,"[7] must seem equally solipsistic to the reader, and are meant to, as also is the determination of Mortimer to cure him. There is a powerful dialectic at work in the novel. At one point Mortimer writes: "I am too happy for him [Lovell], too little what he calls serious. Which of us will first drive the other out of his defenses, that is the big question."[8] Mortimer uses the word *Verschanzungen*, which means an entrenched position, and his choice of words is apposite. Lovell, as we have seen, refers to his "changing feelings." It is this state of instability that constitutes the inner force which works to his destruction. His presentiment of an outer malevolent fate is to become reality in the course of the journey, and as he leaves England he expresses his determination to hold the reins of his own destiny, for if he once lets them drop a malevolent demon will drag him down into the abyss. The question is: what power does he have within him to keep a firm hold on the reins? He speaks of Amalie's love as such a power. If she were ever to forget him, then he would be lost. He does not contemplate his forgetting her, but that in fact is what is to happen.

The scene is now set, by the end of the first of the ten books of the novel (in its first version), for the journey into the abyss. The first stage is Paris, on which city we have simultaneous reports from Lovell, Mortimer, and Old Willy. One of the interesting technical features of *William Lovell* is the use of simultaneous reports on the same material by different persons to produce depth. (Something similar occurs in *Humphry Clinker*, where the aim is variety rather than depth.) Thus Lovell talks loftily about "slavery and oppression" and contrasts Paris with Greece and Rome, whereas Willy angrily describes how French aristocrats in their coaches purposely run over the poor people walking in the streets. The point is the same, but reinforced by the two different perspectives. The external plot now proceeds conventionally with Lovell's father embroiled in a lawsuit over estates, a mysterious and somewhat suspicious Italian named Rosa (a man) attaching himself to Lovell, Mortimer being called home to a dying uncle, and Lovell seduced by a Countess Blainville who affects a "sentimentality like that of Rousseau's Julie, a certain melancholy, a touch of Young's [*Night Thoughts*] and tedious talk of reason and morality like the heroines of English novels."[9] Lovell reports ironically to Rosa on what he considers his "conquest," aided by moonlight, red curtains and a piano, then remembers Amalie, and resolves never to trust his senses again. But Mortimer back home, is becoming increasingly attracted to Amalie, while Lovell continues his journey with Willy and a German named Balder, an enthusiast even more deeply steeped in melancholy than he.

More traditional elements now enter the external plot: highwaymen, Italian landscapes, the hallucinations of incipient madness (in Balder), the degenerate state of modern Rome, secret societies, *déjà vus*, and a mysterious messenger with a warning. All this is not particularly interesting, being all too familiar and of obvious provenance. More interesting is Lovell's own analysis of his states of mind: the flatness that invades his moments of highest exaltation, where enthusiasm so overreaches itself that it results in numbness and alienation: "Let us beware of that drunkenness of spirit which removes us too long from the earth, for we return as strangers dropped into an unknown world who have lost the power to lift themselves above it again."[10] He also notices his tendency to inject melancholy thoughts into pleasurable experiences in order to increase the pleasure by contrast. Balder becomes for Lovell an alarming mirror image, obsessed by death and decay, by a sense of life as a prison-house where all doors leading to ultimate truths are locked against us, and by the feeling that those who do persist in the search for absolutes find their reason strained to such a point that they face the specter of dissolution; they may catch a glimpse of the godhead, but their minds become closed to the things of the earth and the world deems them mad.[11] These are Balder's own words, in my paraphrase. Balder's melancholy, says Rosa, is a particular brand of enthusiasm that believes it has communion with spirits and "bathes in the pure gleam of the ether," a sensuality of heated fancy that creates ever new imaginary worlds and forgets the real world in which it lives "until the overstretched bow breaks and complete lethargy invades the spirit."[12] Lovell sees all this as self-indulgence in Balder, and fears that Balder is losing all sense of existence. He is, of course, vicariously reflecting on himself, but proudly asserts that his "inner sense" will enable him to control what his "outer senses" give him.[13] The idea has been planted in him by Rosa. And so while Balder is increasingly pursued by phantoms, Lovell plunges himself into the pleasures of the world, despite the warning from the mysterious messenger that Rosa is tricking him.

Persuaded by Rosa's arguments, he now declares that sensuality is the origin of all of man's higher aspirations, and yet, almost in the same breath, laments the loss of his illusions. Rosa next reports to a certain Andrea Cosimo on his "education" of Lovell. Cosimo replies that everything—"scorn and reverence, pride and vanity, humility and selfishness"—is a "blind mill driven by necessity, whose rumbling in the distance sounds like articulated tones. But man can hardly realize this because he himself is a cog turning and being turned somewhere in the machinery."[14] (This passage is characteristic of the powerful imagery that pervades the book and represents one of its greatest strengths.) Meanwhile Lovell is well set on his voluptuous path, becomes involved in seduction and murder, and ignores the pleas of his dying father to return home. He longs for new stormy excitements on the stage of life, for life has become a theater for him and he speaks of it in terms of theater imagery. All philosophies, he now decides, are but externalizations of feeling, and those feelings which project us into far unknown regions are our longing for eternity, our inability to conceive of nonexistence, a tendency toward the marvelous [*Hang zum Wunderbaren*] that speaks for the existence of "soul" and its continuance, of spirits, of a spirit of nature with which our own spirit is in communion.[15] This is Lovell's own version of Balder's loss of identity.

Lovell is now brought face to face with the mysterious Andrea Cosimo, and is assailed ever more strongly by the sense of some malevolent force surrounding him, which both terrifies and excites him. He feels that somehow this force is incorporated in Andrea, and the secret society he controls. And he is right, for Andrea, in a letter to Rosa, describes how he plays games with human souls, maliciously enslaving both reason and emotions and working on them to their destruction. The complications of the external plot begin to proliferate again at this point, and we do not need to follow its convolutions in detail. Suffice it to say that Lovell, feeling surrounded by spirits, returns to England, cynically seduces the sister of a friend, tries unsuccessfully to poison her brother, and abandons the girl, who subsequently dies. Her lover sets out to find Lovell, who has returned to the continent, and finally catches up with him in Rome, where Lovell, still obsessed by the phantom spirits that had surrounded him there, has returned to see Andrea again. There is a duel and Lovell is killed, while the other man, "satiated with life," decides to go to America to fight for the British.

As in this novel generally, the external action of these later sections is less interesting than the psychological action. Lovell's addiction, if one may call it such, to a world of spirits, malevolently encouraged by Andrea, makes the world of reality seem empty to him, and he becomes a cynical sensualist, which is exactly what Andrea wants. Dissatisfied with ordinary experiences, he longs for a more transcendent perturbation of his being: "Often I want to summon all those wondrous phantoms which passed by me there [in Italy]: I would like to plunge into that hideous night from which shudders arise that strongly grip the weak human heart and almost crush it. Or, if only the time were there once more when my impatient breast were sated with wonders so that I would forget the earth and its human inhabitants entirely—and also myself."[16] Andrea has engineered such supernatural "wonders" in order to confuse and destroy both Balder and Lovell. Toward the end of the novel one of Andrea's former disciples, who has defected from him in realization of his destructive power and has found satisfaction in married life, speaks of the strange moods of exaltation that Andrea had encouraged as "the forbidden tree in the garden of human life," the fruits of which do not enrich but in fact constrict, and induce dissatisfaction and nihilism.[17] And indeed the testament left by the dying Andrea reveals that he had been consumed by a lifelong hatred for Lovell's family (because he had not succeeded in seducing Lovell's mother) which he was determined to work out on William.

So the novel ends with a rationalization such as Jean Paul deplored and the readers of horror novels expected. But Lovell's downfall, though accelerated by Andrea, is produced by his own temperament. This is a powerful novel, and if it were not so long and were more concentrated on Lovell alone, it would be a terrifying novel. For its subject is a very serious one, namely the progressive disorientation and disintegration of the human mind under the influence of an overcharged imagination which is basically self-indulgent, probing beyond the restrictions imposed by finitude, seeking ecstasies that change with the course of time from ideals to phantoms. It reveals the dangers of "enthusiasm," in the eighteenth-century sense of the word, but not with the irony or critical distance that the eighteenth century maintained toward this subject. The seductive nature of enthusiasm, of the transcendental, of the marvelous, is presented in all its power, as is the longing to be shaken by some tremendous experience, especially by those from the dark pit. All this is presented sympathetically, but also the price that man must pay—alienation, despair, madness. The novel is full of the romantic dissatisfaction with the prose of life, the lure of the uncanny, and the fascination of the unknown, but it also presents the destructive nature of the dissatisfied imagination, the destruction of self in the attempt to transcend the limits of the self. The most disturbing thing about the book is its representation of imagination as a misleading rather than a guiding power. But Lovell's is a disorganized imagination from the start, stunted by belief in an evil fate which has no logical justification, an imagination therefore that is divorced from the reason.

In the preface to the first edition of *William Lovell* Tieck declared that the main interest of the book was intended to be in its portrayal of characters and it would not appeal to readers interested merely in "adventurous, disconnected events." When he published the second edition in 1813 he stated that the work had been concerned with the loss of a true sense of nature, art, and faith, due to the shallowness of the later Enlightenment, and in the preface to the final edition of 1828 he asserted that his purpose in writing *Lovell* had been to unmask hypocrisy, flabbiness, and falsehood, and mentioned that at that time he had been greatly affected by Restif de la Bretonne's novel *Le Paysan perverti* (1776).[18] Restif's novel is also concerned with the destruction of a human soul, in this case of a good-natured but naive young man from the country who is gradually destroyed by the seductive pleasures of Paris, his moral system being steadily undermined by advocates of sensualist philosophy, so that like Lovell he is finally converted to a life-creed that denies the validity of all higher moral values, virtue being in essence merely indulgent self-love. The novel is in letters, with various correspondents, and the sinister presentation of the sensualist argument has points of contact with *William Lovell*. There are also some resemblances of detail between the two novels,[19] but the general focus is quite different, Restif being concerned to show the dislocation of moral sense by false philosophy and addiction to pleasure whereas Tieck is far more concerned with the destructive effects of disordered imagination. The interest of Restif's novel lies predominantly in its depiction of the corruptive influence of civilized, urban society; Tieck is less socially oriented and far more concentrated on the depiction of aberrations of the mind caused by a deficient sense of reality and too much indulgence in fantasies. Rudolf Köpke in his memoir of Tieck reported that the latter had told him that irony was expressly articulated in *William Lovell*.[20] In a letter of March 1815 to his friend the Philosopher Solger, Tieck stated that he had written the book in a frame of mind that was mostly serene and yet he had become pleasurably immersed in confusion.[21] In 1838 he declared that in all his writings, from *William Lovell* on, he had dealt with true morality and good people (he meant presumably Lovell himself) and contrasted this fact with Jean Paul's *Titan*, which offended him by its "morality" of mawkishness, "exaggerated demands and ethereal aberrations."[22] This false transcendentalism is the butt of his attack in *Lovell*. In an important letter to Solger, written in September 1815, Tieck asserted that his hankering after all that was strange, mystic, and marvelous was always accompanied by doubt, "cool normality," and loathing at the thought of allowing himself to be intoxicated by such things, especially by hotness of the imagination and empty enthusiasms. In another letter to the same friend he admitted his easy impressionability, his loss of self in the fantasies of his imagination with all its changing moods.[23] From this we can see how much of himself had gone into Lovell and Sternbald.

The dualism and dissonance of *William Lovell* is romantic. Its form is more traditional and, despite the numerous poems that it contains, the book does not even approximate the criteria set by Friedrich Schlegel or Novalis for a truly romantic novel. And indeed Schlegel did not like it. He considered it boring, thin in characterization, nihilistic in both its prose and its poetry, and deemed the whole "a duel between poetry and prose" in which the prose is trampled and the poetry kills itself.[24] He was much more positive about Tieck's second novel, *Franz Sternbalds Wanderungen* (first version 1798; revised version 1843), praising it in the *Athenäum* Fragments for its

richness of fancy, its irony, and its "varied and yet unified coloration." It was, he wrote to his brother, the first romantic novel since
Cervantes.[25]

Franz Sternbalds Wanderungen is a very different novel from *William
Lovell*, but has points of contact with it.[26] It is an artist-novel, which
Lovell is not, but it also deals with the misleading capacity of imagination when this is not guided by some more rational power. That
enthusiasm or ecstasy alone does not produce paintings is something
Sternbald has to learn. He does learn it—to a certain degree, but he
never really replaces that knowledge by something else, by a more
productive personal engagement with the world of phenomena. So
this is a novel about an artist who never becomes a great artist—at
least not in what we have of the novel, for the work is unfinished.
Sternbald is inspired, and to some extent frustrated, by one persistent obsession of his mind, a memory of childhood and innocence,
connected with the figure of a young girl. At the end of the book
there are two climactic scenes: Sternbald stands in rapt wonder before Michelangelo's *Last Judgment* in the Sistine Chapel, and then, in
the next chapter encounters the girl of his vision. The real subject of
Sternbald would seem to me to be the relation between what the artist
sees and thinks and what he produces—between the inner vision and
its objectivation. In my analysis I shall follow the text of the first
version of the novel, which is in two parts.[27]

As the novel begins, Franz Sternbald is leaving Nuremberg and
the studio of Albrecht Dürer in order to achieve wider experience,
both of art and of life, and his ultimate destination is Rome. He
leaves behind his best friend Sebastian, also a student of Dürer's,
with whom he exchanges letters in the course of the novel, letters
that are merely one part of the novel's texture, as are also the numerous digressions and poems, for the narration is a traditional third-
person narrative and chronological, not retrospective. The letters
are part episode, part digression, and they are not the only episodic
elements in the structure which, as Friedrich Schlegel recognized, is
extremely rich. For the progress of Franz Sternbald's journey is
marked by numerous episodic encounters, each of which adds an
idea to the unfolding theme. Thus on the initial stage of his journey
Franz talks first with Sebastian, then with a journeyman-smith, then
with an aged peasant and his family and one of their neighbors, then
with a rich factory owner, then with a friend of Dürer's, and finally
with his mother and his dying father. Each of these encounters presents some aspect of the theme of art and the artist's life. The tech-

nique is familiar and basically picaresque, but it is here used differently: not to produce variety and breadth, but to promote unity and
depth. Sebastian urges Franz not to forget the example of Dürer and
what Nuremberg represents as a center of German art, the journey-
man discusses with Franz the uses of art and its validity independent
of usefulness, the peasant and his family represent the harmonious
peace of non-sophistication such as is denied Franz in his ambitions,
the neighbor directs his attention to religious legends as a subject for
art, to the simple piety also embodied in the peasant's family existence—a quality that Franz would like to paint but feels he does not
possess within himself. He has ideas for pictures, but ideas do not
make pictures, and the variety of impressions crowding in upon him
confuses rather than enriches him. The factory owner tries in vain to
deflect him toward a settled bourgeois existence, whereas the friend
of Dürer emphasizes the moral effect of great art on the spectator.
Franz's visit to his parents brings back memories of childhood, and
he has a second fleeting encounter with the young girl of his vision,
who this time drops her wallet in which are dried flowers, the same
flowers, we presume, that he had given her years ago. This persistence of the ideal reinforces his determination to follow his inner
desire to become an artist, and he sets out for the unknown with this
vision still in his mind, seeking his true self, for his putative father
on his deathbed has just told Franz that he is not his son. The motif
of unknown parentage is therefore linked with the quest for fulfillment, as in *Florentin*. The second encounter with the girl comes just
after he has painted a picture for the local church, a landscape with
figures in the setting sun but, on the other side of the canvas, a new
sun rising, the whole an image of grief at what has gone and joy at a
new dawning. Letters from Nuremberg suggest that instead of weakly
floating in a sea of impressions, he should use his reason more, take
a firmer hold on his tendency to enthusiasm and his urge to elevate
himself above the palpable realities of the world around him. And so
his real journey begins.

The second major section of the novel is set in the Low Countries.
Franz experiences Dutch paintings at first hand, and has an extensive conversation with Lukas van Leyden. The face of the young girl
constantly appears before his mind and in one of his dreams he
observes, much to his embarrassment, that Dürer is able to paint this
face whereas he was not. Franz tells Lukas that he lacks the courage
to paint what he sees, and Lukas suggests that this is because he is
too respectful of objects and too confused by too many objects, and

advises him to give up his journey and stay in Germany, for why experience even more impressions? But this, we can see, is only part of the problem: what inhibits Franz is not objects but ideals. Dürer visits Lukas while Franz is there, and there is a long conversation between them on the relation between ideas and objects in painting, between the configuration of reality and artistic design and composition. It is the inartistic combination of the parts, even when these are taken from nature, that creates unnaturalness, which all art must avoid. This statement (by Lukas) seems to Franz to be the answer to all his doubts about his own artistic powers, the dissatisfaction with his own work. Basically it is the realization that art depends not on subjects but on their transformation into a unified design. This conversation is a true digression, in the eighteenth-century sense, a break in the action but contributory to the overall design and general movement forward. The plot then resumes with Franz en route to Antwerp.

On this stage of his journey Franz meets a poet, Rudolf Florestan, and a merchant who collects works of art, named Vansen. Florestan is Italian, a lover of life in all its manifestations, and obviously intended as a contrast to the more introverted Sternbald. The German-Italian contrast takes up a theme touched on earlier in the conversations at Lukas's house. Florestan is returning home after traveling in various countries, including Germany; Sternbald was ultimately to return to Nuremberg, enriched by his experiences in Italy, though Tieck never got that far in the composition of his novel. Florestan recites various poems and provides an episode in the form of a story. Poems of Sternbald's own composition have already figured occasionally in the texture, but now, with the advent of Florestan, poems become a constantly recurrent feature. The episodic story is about a man who finds a picture of a girl and then sets out to find her, though he is urged by a friend not to let his fantasy obscure his reason in such a foolhardy venture. But he does find her. The episode is therefore a mirror image of Sternbald's own aspirations and fortifies him for his own quest. At Vansen's house in Antwerp there is an older man who argues that art is an ephemeral, useless, and devitalizing activity whereas all men should seek to serve the community and its needs. Sternbald gives a spirited defense of the disinteredness of art, though in the next chapter he unexpectedly reencounters the journeyman-smith of the beginning of the novel, rendered uncreative by the overpowering effect of Dürer upon him. A complex counterpoint would seem to be evolving, a combination of attitudes, but without any clear line of development as yet, though we have now reached the end of the first of the two completed parts of the novel.

Our confusion is hardly dispelled by Part Two. This deals with the adventures of Sternbald and Florestan on their progression to Italy, but Italy is not reached until almost the end. Franz and Rudolf pass through Alsace, and Franz paints a picture of the Holy Family for a rich man in Strasbourg, putting the face of the girl of his vision on the madonna. He now reinterprets the combination of clarity and uncertainty in his mind as a positive force, enabling him to avoid being both too particular and too general.[28] He realizes that his vision is an ideal, and that his striving toward it was the inspiration which had produced the painting. If he did find the girl of his vision, find the ideal in reality, would that spell the end of his artistic creativity, he wonders. He thinks not; or rather he hopes not. As the journey proceeds conversations multiply and poems proliferate. There are three important encounters. The first, with a sculptor named Bolz and a man dressed as a monk (but apparently not one), seems purely episodic, but these two characters are taken up in the plot-line later. Bolz tells Sternbald that his constant enthusiasms will prevent him from being a great painter. But Sternbald's enthusiastic description of the Strasbourg minster as an "allegorical poem"[29] embodying the necessary polarity of endlessness and order, of infinite and finite, unity and multiplicity, shows that he can now see the opposition of ideas and objects as a complementary rather than a conflicting relationship. The second encounter is with a countess, and the third with a hermit. These are not episodic but represent important stages in the unfolding theme of the novel.

Franz and Rudolf come upon a hunting party which includes the countess, who invites them to her castle. Franz is becoming more receptive to what he now calls the "immortal melody" of nature,[30] but the attempt to enter into it reduces him to exhaustion. All that art can achieve, he decides, is but intimation of nature, which is itself intimation of the godhead, its hieroglyph.[31] These thoughts are confirmed by his visit to the hermit, who is a painter and tells Franz that the highest thing man can achieve is to be at peace with himself and all things, for then "man transforms himself and everything around him into a divine [*himmlisches*: not earthly] work of art, and purifies himself with the fire of the godhead."[32] The relationship between man, nature, and God becomes, therefore, at this point in the novel, the central concern of art, which thereby acquires a strong religious grounding (which is essentially romantic). But this transformation through art can take place only in a mind that is at peace with itself and all things. Lack of such peace of mind was, as Bolz saw it, Franz's problem, and Dürer and Sebastian had said much the same. The hermit describes artistic inspiration as coming not from visions but from reality, from being stirred to the depths of one's being by reality, and then reducing this to the order of artistic presentation, telling others what nature tells the artist. In the hermit's cottage Franz finds a painting of the girl of his vision. He takes this to the countess, who tells him it is a picture of her dead sister. The hermit had merely said that it was a young girl who visited him a year previously.

Both the hermit and the countess are therefore inherently connected with Franz's inner vision. When he first meets the countess, Franz makes this connection himself; and when he hears that the girl is dead, the power of the ideal dies in him too. But it is not just this motif of the girl that integrates the countess and the hermit into the poetic unity of the whole, for both these characters are variations or arabesques on the theme of frustration through love of an idealizing kind. The countess represents an imagination disordered by an obsession—her abandonment by a knight—and uses others self-indulgently as adjuncts for her fantasy of being a Sigune or Isolde or some other abandoned heroine of medieval romance.[33] The hermit's despair at the loss of his wife had led him into madness, from which he had ultimately retrieved his senses in a life of religious contemplation. As the countess has retreated into fantasies and the hermit first into madness and then into isolation, so Franz now retreats from the "dead" ideal to the fleshly real in the person of a certain Emma. Neither he nor the countess has found that equilibrium of spirit to which the hermit had finally attained. Such is the counterpoint of this extremely rich novel. Franz is dubious about accepting the lure of the senses, but Rudolf tells him he will never be a painter if he maintains such doubts.[34] The real and the ideal in productive interplay continue to occupy their discussions as they proceed on their journey.

The reader may well feel by this time that this journey will never end—perhaps that it should never end. Franz can say that Lukas had put his finger on the problem and that the hermit's words are an articulate expression of his, Franz's, own thoughts, but despite all the advice he has been given, he does not seem to learn much to help him become a better painter. Is the journey then ultimately unproductive? Dürer tells us early on in the novel that Sternbald is his best pupil.[35] Maybe, then, he has nothing to learn? Perhaps the journey is not an education, but simply exposure to new subjects— new people, new landscapes? In that case there is no reason why it should ever end. The pattern is therefore quite different from that of *Hyperion*, for although Sternbald finds the girl of the vision alive in Rome, a resolution of the conflicting strains in his nature is never reached, except that he is to return to Nuremberg. But what happens to him there belongs to the unwritten part of the novel. This is, then, not really a *Bildungsroman*, for no *Bildung* is ever achieved. It is, however, the portrayal of the anguished search for wholeness, for that "peace with oneself and with all things" that the hermit had declared to be the necessary prerequisite for artistic creation.

What happens in the last quarter of the novel is the extension of Sternbald's worldly experience, culminating in Rome. First there is the meeting with a wounded knight, the "monk" of a previous encounter, Roderigo by name, who is the man who had abandoned the countess, and, later, his friend Ludoviko—both men of the world, both much influenced by amorous experiences (including the willing abduction by Ludoviko of a girl who is about to be made a nun). The complicated plot is moving away from the book's central concern with the experience of an artist, these secondary figures taking over the foreground and obviously intended as contrasts to Sternbald. Florestan himself represents the superficial "romantic" ideal of living life to the full without any encumbrance of obligations to others, moving from mood to mood, which he objectifies in extemporized poems. It has been said—rightly I think—that Sternbald's "study-journey" changes, under the influence of Florestan, into a romantic journey into the uncertain and mysterious, Italy becoming not the realm of great art but the land of romantic longing, the complete contrast to the settled world of Nuremberg, the land of carefree sensual enjoyment in contrast to the sober seriousness of Germany.[36] Sternbald seems to realize the tension between all that this romantic Italy represents and that with which he had set out on his journey, for when painting a Saint Genevieve he hesitates whether to give her the face of Emma or that of the girl in his inner vision. It is clear that he was never fully satisfied by Nuremberg, but it is also clear that the uninhibited openness of this "Italy" does not satisfy him either. One of the Italian painters talks of inspiration as being the mutation of the mind by the impact of some *higher* spirit.[37] But when Sternbald stands before Michelangelo's *Last Judgment*, what he says implies that there is something more than just transfiguration to great art: "Here you have transfigured yourself, Buonarotti, you great initiate: *here your terrible riddles are left in suspension, and you do not care who understands them*"[38] (my italics).

The novel might better have stopped here, with this confrontation between Franz and the greatest of all paintings. But unfortunately there is another chapter in which Franz finds the girl of his dreams, who is not dead at all and immediately recognizes him. If this were meant to be taken as imaginative and allegorical, it would be perhaps more satisfying. But it is not. The scene is cluttered with realistic detail, and in the fragment from the planned continuation, published in 1962 by Richard Alewyn, there is more of the same ilk, including the appearance of the girl's mother, a German, who wishes to be back in the land of the Marvelous.[39] In the afterword to the edition of 1843 Tieck indicated that Sternbald, after various adventures, was to find his father (= destiny) and the novel was to end in Nuremberg at Dürer's grave, with Sebastian there too.[40] But he never seriously worked at this conclusion, which would not really have made sense anyway. For the moment that the vision-girl becomes the real Marie, the romantic quest is over; this kind of yearning can never be satisfied, never reach finality without losing its meaning. So perhaps the prose kills the poetry here too, in this final chapter.

But the real interest of the book remains in its presentation of dualistic impulses. The discord on which it is built could never achieve resolution, and the last chapter solves nothing, unless we are to believe that this is the end of Sternbald as a painter, which the planned return to the world of Dürer would not suggest. It is obviously not a novel about a great artist (unlike Tieck's later novellas about Shakespeare and Camoëns) but about tensions in all of us which are heightened in someone aspiring to *express* these in art.

Tieck's extensive reading had brought him acquaintance with novels of all sorts. He did not articulate any precise conception of the genre, but seemed to consider it a literary form that could not be defined, and perhaps should not be. It remained for him *Erzählung*, narration—an extended narration and one of serious literary pretensions; but he did not delimit it clearly from the novella or from drama, and he never described it in the terms of Friedrich Schlegel or Novalis as a high form of poetry. The nearest he ever came to such a description was perhaps when, in 1800, he thought about embodying his *Letters on Shakespeare* in a novel, for he wrote to the

imaginary friend in that work that he could conceive of writing a
novel portraying the "poetic character" of Shakespeare, and that it
might contain poems, be a whole book illuminating a poet "in allegory, verses and stories." And this would be a viable novel so long
as everything in it had relation to everything else, was the "transformation of non-form into form."[41] He insisted elsewhere (in a long
essay of 1828, "Goethe and His Time") on the importance of a focal
point, *Mittelpunkt*, as organizing force, and said that this should preferably be internal to the narrative; otherwise, if such a center were
lacking, the only thing that could give a work form was some *exter-
nally* imposed "rule" to contain the recalcitrant parts. Rabelais, Jean
Paul, and Sterne, he said in this same essay, failed on both counts.[42]
He asserted that all Goethe's works, including the novels, were organized according to one governing idea, and he found such a center also in *Don Quixote*, the "poetic necessity" [*poetische Notwendigkeit*]
of which center could and did embrace the most disparate material.
What Tieck was demanding, was a *poetic* center, and this of course
applies also to drama. Thus he saw no basic difference between the
structure of Goethe's plays and that of his novels—in each case a
single "thought" governed the whole.[43] Tieck recognized the thin dividing line between novel and drama, instancing *La Celestina* and
Lope's *Dorothea*.[44]

In his early essay Shakespeare's treatment of the Supernatural
[*Shakespeares Behandlung des Wunderbaren*, 1793] Tieck compares the
all-pervasive marvelous in *The Tempest* with its treatment in *Don Quixote*, suggesting that the novel might better have ended with an incident which could not possibly have been transformed by the Don's
fancy, and would therefore have temporarily wrenched him out of his
illusions and allowed him to distinguish truth from error—a rather
rationalistic view for Tieck! Ten years later he talks about the mixture of poetry and "life" in the texture of Cervantes's novel which
demonstrates the opposition between them, so strongly that one remains in doubt whether the poetry is not parody.[45] In a later essay he
contrasts the "plan" inherent in the structure of *Don Quixote* with
what he considers the capriciousness of Rabelais—succession of incidents rather than coordinated development—and the alignment of
episodes in *Lazarillo de Tormes, Guzman de Alfarache* and *Gil Blas*.[46] He
does not seem, therefore, to accept the picaresque as a legitimate
form of novel-structure. In the same essay he lamented the way
Sterne in his "incomparable *Tristram Shandy*" proceeded purely will-
fully, neglecting "the basis [of the book] and those characters we

have gotten to like."[47] But Cervantes kept to a line of development and integrated the episodes into this overall unity. We have to respect the Don even while we laugh at him: the great originality of the book is its fusion of seriousness and parody.[48] Everything is controlled from the poetic center and held in place.[49] The genius of Cervantes was that he was able to imbue the ordinary and everyday elements of earthly experience with the "shimmer and color of the Marvelous."[50] Tieck admired *Simplicissimus* for its powerful depiction of the havoc created by the Thirty Years' War,[51] but he did not suggest that the book had anything akin to the poetry of *Don Quixote* (though it has). He planned at one time to bring it back to public awareness by producing a new edition of it—[52] as he was to do with other novels he thought unjustly neglected.

Tieck's historically important version of the eighteenth-century novel *Die Insel Felsenburg* [The Island of Felsenburg] by Johann Gottfried Schnabel (1731 to 1743) is prefaced by a long essay in dialogue form in which this interesting novel is placed in the general development of the European novel, as Tieck saw it. (The date of Tieck's version and of this essay is 1828). From our twentieth-century vantage point *Die Insel Felsenburg* is a curious mixture of baroque and Enlightenment features. It is a novel about a number of people shipwrecked on an island, pervaded not, as in *Robinson Crusoe*, by a sense of isolation from society but by that of willing removal from the corruption of society—asylum rather than exile, as has been well observed. It is not, as *Robinson Crusoe* is, concerned with the spiritual evolution of an individual confronted in his loneliness by eternity, but is the novel of a whole community established according to rational, humanitarian Enlightenment principles—a social, rather than a personal novel. The overriding ethos, then, is that of the earlier Enlightenment. But the form perpetuates seventeenth-century structure in its numerous sensational life stories told retrospectively by the characters—these being frequently broken off and resumed later, thereby creating an intricate interweaving of various narrative strands—as well as in its digressions and its vast length.

Starting from the opinion expressed by one of the fictive speakers in this dialogue that *Die Insel Felsenburg* was characteristic of the bad books that served as leisure reading in the earlier eighteenth century, Tieck suggests that all ages have had their entertainment reading, a study of which would provide an interesting history of the climate of taste of successive ages, for these works were read because they catered to needs of the time. A book exists both in itself and in its time, but a work of genius is one that, though of its time, is individual in that it works against its time. *Werther* and *La Nouvelle Héloïse* were revolutionary books because they expressed "the wound of-life, the sickness of love" more strongly than anyone had done hitherto, and in a new language; and "this opening up [*Auflösung*] of life, this unfolding of the mysteries of our breast, this anxiety and joy have continued to resound ever since—most penetratingly and destructively in that masterpiece of the same author [as that of *Werther*], *Die Wahlverwandtschaften*."[53] For Tieck the basic task of literature was to be new without becoming a slave to fashionable novelty, to combine "the wisdom of the permanent with the playful wit [*Witz*] of the changing [*des Wandelbaren*]."[54] He suggests that the revolution introduced by Rousseau and Goethe was the change from the naive (or direct) to the sentimental (in Schiller's sense; that is, reflective), that the *Insel Felsenburg* represents the naive, and therein lies its appeal for what Tieck calls his own "confused and disenchanted age" [*unserer verwirrten und verstimmten Zeit*].[55] This remark is but one example of Tieck's interest in simpler literature (or what he thought was simpler literature), in literature of more modest piety and beliefs, literature of a less blasé age than his own hypercultivated era, unencumbered by dualism, fragmentation, and dispiriting reflection and doubt.

In the course of this same essay Tieck contrasted the "barbaric style" of the *Insel Felsenburg* with contemporary English and French novelists. We also find remarks on Defoe, Swift, Richardson, Fielding, Smollett, Sterne, Goldsmith, and Scott in an essay of 1834. He paid tribute to Richardson's "narrative talent," but referred also, ambiguously, to his "analyses of the soul, patented prudery, loftiness of sentiments," which were then supplanted and "to a certain extent ridiculed" in the gaiety of *Tom Jones*.[56] He had great affection for Sterne and especially for his particular brand of humor, which combined laughter and pity.[57] He referred to Smollett's "often capricious but always colorful portraits," to the *Gemütlichkeit* of Goldsmith, and to Scott's demonstration of "how a narrative should be organized" (all this in the same essay).[58] He had, however, some reservations about Scott: he referred at one point (in 1827) to the value which Scott placed on what Tieck called "passive comfortableness" [*passive Behaglichkeit*],[59] and suggested that this indicated that Scott did not think of the novel as on the same artistic level as tragedy or epic. In other words: a novel for Scott did not seem to be aimed at the same higher emotions as epic or tragedy. On the other hand, he admired

Scott's ability to convert historical material into viable content for novels, his use of historical distancing, of retrospective narration often going back many years—this Tieck did term "poetic."[60] But, he compared him unfavorably with Shakespeare, especially with reference to the portrayal of deeper feelings.[61] As for French narrative fiction, Tieck had very little to say apart from his already quoted comments on Lesage and Rousseau. He was interested in Restif de la Bretonne for much the same reasons that he was interested in Grimmelshausen—for the portrayal of life of their times.[62]

On German eighteenth-century novels other than Goethe's, Tieck also had little to say.[63] His opinion of Jean Paul was mixed. He disliked his "mawkish morality."[64] He appreciated his humor but not his whimsy. He thought that the *Vorschule der Ästhetik* was simply the "report of a craftsman on his trade, a recipe on how to write Jean Paulish books," not books in general.[65] Karl Förster reports a conversation between Tieck and Jean Paul in 1822 at which he was present. When Jean Paul asked Tieck which of his works the latter liked least, Tieck replied "*Titan*: for in this I miss living characterization and that order and unity essential for a good novel." But he went on to give high praise to *Siebenkäs*: "full of strength, nature and fresh truth—for me your best work."[66] And on another occasion Tieck expressed his regret that *Flegeljahre* was never finished, calling it one of his favorite books.[67]

Köpke reports Tieck as having fairly strong views on the novels of the German Romantics.[68] Arnim was very talented but capricious, worked without a plan, shoveling in anecdotes and episodes without considering the whole, appealing at moments but distracting by his capricious *bizarrerie* at others, so that the general impression of such a novel as the *Gräfin Dolores* was bound to be unfavorable. Brentano was a real poet, even more talented than Arnim, but also sidetracked into diffuseness. Tieck told Köpke that artistically he had never felt close to either Arnim or Brentano, because neither had any real sense of nature or the natural, so that everything came out as artificial and contrived. Tieck wrote to Brentano late in 1801 expressing his admiration for the second part of *Godwi*, which he thought captured at times "the tone of the old romance," but urged him in future to concentrate his talents more and write less heatedly.[69] Hoffmann was too grotesque for Tieck: "poetry turned into caricature in Hoffmann."[70] All he had to say on Eichendorff was that almost everything in his fictions came out of *Sternbald*, and that his treatise on the German novel of the eighteenth century (see below, pages

247–249 was "very one-sided and full of misunderstandings."[71] As for *Lucinde*, he wrote to Solger on 16 December 1816 that if Schlegel had been really serious about it, he should have finished it.[72] An 1829 reference to it had the same tenor, for he charged Schlegel with being too eager to go to extremes, so that the novel had no real form, being neither lyrical nor a considered reflection, but made the impression of an undistanced confession, despite its flashes of wit, poetry, and real seriousness.[73] For *Florentin* he had nothing but contempt: "wretched stuff, Sternbald and all sorts of other things mixed in."[74] On the other hand he was full of respect for Novalis, declined to attempt to complete the unfinished *Ofterdingen* because he considered the fragment something sacred, but nevertheless persisted in his determination to see it published in the form in which Novalis had left it.[75]

In 1828 Tieck declared that Goethe and Shakespeare were the two authors who had always meant most to him.[76] On the whole he preferred the earlier Goethe to the "classical" Goethe, but he admired *Die Wahlverwandtschaften* for its psychological profundity even though he was made uncomfortable by it. He also saw it as a graphic portrayal of the spirit of the time at which it was written. He thought the book was "calculated, and carried to an extreme," according to Köpke,[77] but there seems no doubt that it had made a powerful impression on him, perhaps for the very reason that it *was* calculated and extreme. As for *Wilhelm Meister*, he preferred the beginning of the novel and disliked the practicality into which Wilhelm descends (according to Tieck) at the end.[78] In this opinion he was at one with Novalis, though he thought that Novalis was wrong in looking for, and hoping to find, absolute poetry in Goethe's novel. Tieck also objected to the symbolic overtones that the latter part of the book engenders. As for the *Wanderjahre*, that was for Tieck an even more disastrous descent into practicalities.[79] All this must be seen as part of his dislike of the way Goethe had, as Tieck thought, turned away from the national heritage of his homeland in mid-life.

Many of these comments date from Tieck's later years, but his attitude toward the novel as a form remained fairly consistent, in the sense that certain general lines are perceptible. He accepted the novel as a poetic form, or at least the possibility that it could be such. He demanded a poetic center even though the material be prose material, found this present in *Don Quixote*, Rousseau, and Goethe, but lacking in Rabelais, Jean Paul, Scott, and *Simplicissimus*. Ideally this focus should be *within* the novel—which is why *Don Quixote* would seem to be a model for him and—perhaps—why he preferred *Sie-benkäs* and *Flegeljahre* to *Titan*. It would also account for his venera-tion of Novalis and his disapproval of what he considered a lack of focus in Arnim, Brentano, *Lucinde*, and *Florentin*. Breadth and va-riety were not in themselves an ideal to be striven after; they ought to be somehow organized around a central idea. And this applied, in Tieck's view, to drama as well as the novel. We noted that, for him, only a thin dividing line separated the two genres. Most of his own longer works—his massive dramas and the two novels we have been considering—are, as regards form, romances. There is always a clear poetic center, out from which we move to the circumference, and the parts never fly off into outer space. The breadth achieved is that of multiple perspective, a formal principle inherent in all drama. William J. Lillyman presents a strong case for his assertion that the basic drive in Tieck was that of a man unsettled and dissatisfied in a narrow world and reaching out toward a more expansive domain of experience and imagination.[80] To that I would add that this move-ment outward is from a *poetic* center within himself, unwilling as he was to accept the surface circumference of life as the ultimate reality, seduced but bewildered by the multiplicity of experience, sometimes threatened by its instability, and by his own uncertainty, but always seeking some stable point of reference—and rarely finding it. The movement outward from what I have called a poetic center returns therefore upon itself as a search for a center.

CHAPTER EIGHT

Anxiety of the Spirit: Brentano and Arnim

TIECK's particular anguish and his longing for refuge from its torments led him toward a special affection for folktales, fairy tales, and the literature of earlier ages with its more stable system of beliefs and values, Arnim and Brentano were likewise deeply involved in the rediscovery and the propagation of folk literature, in part for the same reasons as Tieck but also for another reason that was historically determined. The great collection of German folksongs on which they cooperated with each other and published between 1805 and 1808 under the title *Des Knaben Wunderhorn* [The Boy's Magic Horn] must be seen against the background of the humiliation of the German states in these years, culminating in the disastrous defeat of Prussia and her allies at the Battle of Jena in 1806, and the subsequent occupation of Germany by Napoleon's forces. These events gave rise to an active realization among the intellectuals of the various German states of what they had in common, to the emergence of the concept "Germany" as a uniting and spiritual force, which, translated into action, eventually led to the defeat of Napoleon in 1813 at the Battle of Leipzig. *Des Knaben Wunderhorn* grew out of this mood, for what it presented was the reality of a great common heritage, a national heritage. The main impulse behind the advocation of folk literature by Brentano and Arnim was therefore, in contrast to Tieck's espousal of it, more historically than personally motivated.

There was, however, also a personal motivation—different in each case, for these were two very different personalities. Clemens Brentano (1778–1842) was basically a deeply religious nature tormented by strong sensual proclivities, constantly divided within himself, a brilliant but unstable genius who produced some of the finest lyrical poetry of the romantic movement, and a great deal of it. His natural medium of expression would seem to have been the lyric poem, but he also wrote comedies and tragedies, various shorter narrative prose works, including one masterly novella, *Kasperl und Annerl,* and several *Märchen,* which sophisticatedly expand folk legends into narrative structures of great complexity and irony and beauty. He also wrote, early in his writing career, a novel, *Godwi,* which is one of the most difficult but also one of the most remarkable of the German romantic novels. It would not be right to say that after a rather wild youth, to which *Godwi* is indeed ample testimony, he became intensely religious, for a religious temperament, though often thwarted, was there from the start, as the many childhood religious images in *Godwi* (which Béguin and others have connected up with early religious experiences) demonstrate. The religious poetry of Brentano's mature years belongs to the greatest—and most existentially anguished—in the German language. The central preoccupation of this poetry is man caught in the toils of sensual existence—be this passion, fear, or loneliness—longing for salvation, and seeking some kind of transcendent overcoming of the disharmony within his nature, with sometimes anguished appeals for help from God himself. In his later years Brentano was entirely taken up with religious activities and works of piety, and rejected his early writings, especially *Godwi,* as being too much of the flesh. His whole oeuvre is the expression, not of a tension between immanence and transcendence, as with Jean Paul, Hölderlin, and Novalis, but of a deeply personal conflict within a divided self.[1]

At first sight Ludwig Achim von Arnim (1781–1831) might seem a much more solid character, soldierly, aristocratic, more outgoing than introspective. But his work is full of terrors and horrors, the demonic, the unaccountable, and another form of anguish—namely that induced because the products (objects or actions) of the human will eventually control and subjugate the mind that created them. It is essentially the problem of the artist, that of losing control of the things he creates. Endowed by him with life, they themselves then become independent of him, and may even threaten or destroy him. Around the time of the Battle of Jena, Arnim was torn between the desire to pursue the reflective life of a writer and the urge to engage in practical political activity, for he was deeply concerned about the state of society and the future of his country. What he came to realize was that in either course man loses control over what he produces, and this recoils upon himself. He wrote three novels, two of which are major achievements in quite different veins, and a large number of novellas of consummate artistry and great human interest. He also wrote several plays, more epic than dramatic, which are not without interest, though not of the quality of his prose fiction. His achievements as a writer of fiction—particularly of novellas—have not been adequately appreciated until quite recently, though there were several important voices of the nineteenth century (Heine, Gautier, Kierkegaard, and Hebbel among them) who recognized his remarkable narrative talents. One of his most powerful stories, *Die Majoratsherren* (the title refers to the holders of an estate entailed to devolve on the eldest son), deals with a state of affairs in which the phantom images of a suppressed self well up into a man's consciousness and finally take over from reality. Voices from the subconscious force their way upward and eventually dominate all consciousness. In another novella, *Isabella von Ägypten,* a mandrake and a golem are created, with the initial purpose of serving the person who conjures them up, but they then take on an alarming life of their own which their "lord-and-master" is unable to control and finds difficult to terminate. The mandrake and the golem are folk incorporations of man's desire for greater power, but they also embody the lure of the uncanny, what is termed in *Isabella von Ägypten* "that unnameable world which does not yield to our experiments but uses us for its own experiments and amusement."[2]

Arnim's work is therefore as heterogeneous as his personality. Of the latter, Walter Migge asserts that behind the Apollonian exterior of his portraits there were dark emotions arising often from the subconscious. His work combines wild flights of fancy, leading him into dreams and nightmares of what Béguin calls "icy horror," with a tenacious clinging to the palpably visible and comprehensible.[3] He is therefore both a great realist and a great surrealist, but this is perhaps more apparent in the novellas than in the novels. In these latter we do, however, find dialogues between opposing selves—often between facts and doubts, immediate experience and presentiments as in the dream-monologues of Karl and of Dolores in the *Gräfin Dolores,* as if conscious and unconscious were in extended colloquy. Perhaps this is why Arnim was claimed by André Breton as a surrealist. Breton and the Surrealists spoke of the automatism of words in certain passages in Arnim to express the powers of the subconscious.[4] Several critics have seen in Count Karl, the central male character in the *Gräfin Dolores*, a self-portrait of Arnim: "a strange mixture of pride, rigidity, indecision, crippling deliberation, and inflamed sensitiveness in a noble and lovable character whose inner *gravitas* is always engaged in fighting to harmonize the inside with the outside."[5] Arnim once confessed to the brothers Grimm that there were unbridgeable conflicts in both *art* and life for him.[6] Unbridgeable in the here-and-now but he did believe in an ultimate higher resolution, a belief that proceeded from what was, in him as with Brentano, a deep religious sense—something that few have recognized in him (among these few, Eichendorff) but which was nevertheless there though rarely stated explicitly. There was therefore a common base to these two writers, so different but both so tormented—the one tormented by the demands of his sensual nature, the other by the visions of his creative imagination.

It was in 1801 that Brentano published his novel *Godwi*.[7] The full title was *Godwi oder das steinerne Bild der Mutter: Ein verwilderter Roman von Maria* [Godwi or the Stone Statue of the Mother: A Novel Run Wild, by Maria]. Run wild indeed it is, but very carefully and consciously so. No other novel of the romantic period demonstrates more convincingly that what might seem formless (and for many decades was considered so) was in reality formful—though only if we understand what romantic form is and approach the novel from this standpoint. It is the most bewildering and exasperating of all German romantic novels, but nevertheless a fascinating and significant book.

It begins apparently quite conventionally as an epistolary novel of a type all too familiar by 1801, with a letter from the restless and emotionally charged Godwi to his staid and mercantile-minded friend Römer, and the latter's reply. But any expectations that we are in for a correspondence between the two in which eventually imagination will win out over reason, or vice versa, or disaster befall the maladjusted hero in the form of madness, suicide, or natural death, are soon dispelled as more and more letter-writers and more and more recipients of letters turn up, some of them already mentioned in the correspondence between Godwi and Römer, but others not, and some of the latter as yet unknown quantities, so that we are left with several loose ends. The contrast between the adventurous Godwi and

Clemens Brentano. Bust by Christian Friedrich Tieck, 1803. On loan to Freies Deutsches Hochstift, Frankfurt. Photograph by Ursula Edelman, Frankfurt.

the solid Römer is clear enough, and recalls that between Wilhelm Meister and his brother-in-law Werner, for both Godwi and Wilhelm are would-be poets reacting against bourgeois domestic and utilitarian values. There are also several mysteries—a letter only to be opened at an as yet undecided future date, family skeletons in the cupboard, unexplained grief, sensed but unspecified relationships— which build on to the tradition of the sensational novels of the eighteenth century and the novelist's delight in mystification of his readers, this latter being also apparent in *Wilhelm Meister*. The reader looking for a clear plot-line becomes more and more confused, and that is Brentano's intention. We are projected into a maze of obscure events, both past and present, and a tangle of relationships between the oddest of persons with the oddest of names: Joduno von Eichenwehen, Werdo Senne, Lady Hodefield, Carl von Felsen, Franzesco Firmenti. And to add to the confusion there are two Godwis— father and son—although that is cleared up fairly early on. Scenes from the past are given us without their full context, and parts of various life stories without these being connected with each other. The action such as it is begins with Godwi's departure from Molly (Lady Hodefield, as we learn later), an older woman of intelligence, worldly experience, and highly developed sensuality, and his encounter with Joduno von Eichenwehen, who seems to him all innocence and truth compared with Molly. But the real turning point for him seems to be a second encounter, this time with Otilie, the daughter of Werdo Senne, who satisfies his need for love (something that in one letter he recognizes as narcissistic) and is more sympathetic to him, more open, more in tune with nature than the brooding, sentimental Joduno or the sophisticated and demanding Molly. In a crucial passage[8] Godwi speaks of the healing power of Otilie and likens this to the healing power of nature itself. He describes how his relationship with her has ceased to be a personal one because what was individual about it has become absorbed into something general, as Otilie herself into nature, and the moment into all of time. Throughout the novel there are poems (among them some of Brentano's finest lyrics) that point up the general significance of the specific mood or moment (as in Goethe's *Wilhelm Meister* or Shakespeare's plays), and at this particular point Godwi describes in a long poem a strange experience he had had as a child in which he saw a white marble statue of a sorrowing woman with a child on the edge of a lake, and the constant obsession that this memory had become for him.[9] This is the central image in a novel resplendent with power-

ful imagery in which the various characters are constantly transforming events into metaphors. The centrality of this image of the
marble statue demands that we analyze this poem rather carefully.

The poem, entitled *Szene aus meinen Kinderjahren* [Scene from My
Childhood Years], depicts the tension in Godwi between what is
fixed and what is mobile. As a child he had sought mobility, change,
the uncertainty of transitions, and this out of discontent at the rigid
monotony, the limitations of settled existence. He observed with delight the constant changing of nature and was obsessed by the desire
to make such transformations himself and to encompass them all in
a moment of experience. He played with a "glass" that reversed the
images of nature, bringing sky to earth and putting home and tutor
into the distance. But he soon learned that external things cannot be
transformed except by inner change in the observer. Watching the
transition from day to night, he longed both for alternation and
resolution, weaving ideals into reality as he watched the moon breaking through the night-clouds, dreaming of being in a boat on a dark
sea, and then suddenly encountering the marble image reflected in
the dark waters into which he plunged in a desire to bring life to its
marble, the life that it seemed to be asking for. Otilie, he tells us, is
like the image. She has made that childhood dream into reality.
When he awoke from that childhood vision, all seemed cold and
lifeless around him. He had asked his father who the marble woman
was, and why her tears were falling on the child she clasped so
sorrowfully. His father had left the room in silence, and left the boy
with the sense that all he desired was somehow embodied in that
marble statue.

What has here been described is the awakening of poetic sight in
Godwi, an awakening that has come about through his communion
with Otilie, much like that aroused in Heinrich von Ofterdingen by
Mathilde. The obsessive memory has been brought out into the open,
the reality of the present has reinforced vision of the past. This is
possible only because Otilie too is obsessed by the image he described. She too has lost her mother and grieves for her. So has
Joduno. But whereas Joduno's power to live as a free person has
been sapped by this persistent sense of loss, and Otilie's father is
near to distraction and longs only for the relief of death, Otilie is
conscious of her loss but as the loss of something that she seeks to
comprehend better. To bring out the full significance of this central
scene between Godwi and Otilie, Brentano has them both speak in
verse. The emergence of poetic sensibility is here being depicted.

Both are poets in relation to each other: but, one must add, neither is able to maintain this perspective in the world at large. Godwi is a poet only for Otilie or for himself. But even then he has problems, as he himself admits: he cannot absorb a landscape without reference to the infinite, he tends to see all objects as representations of something, not as values in themselves, and his experience of the present is vitiated by memories of the past. Hence the importance of this sequence in the novel, which shows both the powers and the limitations of his poetic sensibility.

The sequence ends peculiarly. They see lights that seem to come from a cottage and promise peace and repose. But there are no cottages hereabouts. Otilie says these are *stille Lichter* [calm lights], produced by nature and portending something important that is to happen. Godwi rejects such superstitiousness, but she then sings of the world of mystery that surrounds her always: "Sprich aus der Ferne / Heimliche Welt, / Die sich so gerne / Zu mir gesellt."[10] Then to her delight and his horror they both see the white marble woman with the child, Godwi sinks down exhausted, and she takes him home. I have traced this sequence in some detail, not only because it is central to Part One of the novel, but because it is returned to in Part Two. The figure of the dead mother appears in various manifestations—Godwi, Joduno, and Otilie all grieve for the loss of the mother, and a dead mother plays a decisive role in the letter of Antonio Firmenti to Godwi's father about the madness and disappearance of his brother Franzesco. This letter is a linear narrative of great violence and complexity, written in a sober clear style that contrasts with the highly figurative language of the rest. But its connection with the rest remains totally obscure. Indeed we are left with many mysteries at the end of Part One of the novel. Who is Römer and who was his father? Where is Godwi's father and who was his mother? Where did Lady Hodefield go every Saturday afternoon? What is the significance of the name Marie on the ring that Otilie suddenly finds on her finger when she wakes up one day? Who is the boy Eusebio, living with Werdo and Otilie Senne? Who is the Kornelia several times referred to? And why does this first part end with the pilgrimage on All Souls' Day to the grave of still another dead mother?

When Part Two begins, the author of Part One, Maria, is already dead. He becomes a *character* in the second part, a seeker for the truth about Godwi. For Römer's father had given Maria the materials out of which he had constructed Part One, and promised him the hand of his daughter if he did it well. Seeing the results, Römer's father sends Maria off to continue the story by his own efforts. This is not so hard as it might sound, for Godwi is still alive. So Maria travels to the estate of Godwi's father, where Godwi is living, his father being absent in Italy (maybe this has something to do with Antonio Firmenti's letter, we wonder). Unwilling to come straight out with the reason for his visit, Maria insinuates himself into the life of the estate and the persons living there which include a pseudo-poet Haber, a young girl Fiametta and various Mennonite tenant farmers. There are several carefully managed digressions in the form of conversations (on love and friendship, on the nature of "the romantic," on types of enthusiasm, on wit) and an elaborate masque. There is a certain amount of parody (particularly of Fichte) and several interspersed songs and poems, some of great beauty, Haber tells Maria that Godwi is a reticent man with no desire for close friendships, who seems to have some secret sorrow.[11] This leads to the digression on love and friendship. It is the masque that leads to the discussion on "the romantic," which centers on two topics: mediation and the nature of form.[12] Maria suggests that whatever mediates between our eye and a distant object, bringing us nearer to it and at the same time imparting to it something of itself (of the mediating agent), is romantic. A sort of telescope, says Godwi, or rather the color of the glass and the modification [*Bestimmung*] of the object by the shape of the glass. Haber protests that this would surely mean that the romantic has no form [*Gestalt*] of its own (but only takes its form from the mediating agent). But Maria replies that form is the proper delimitation [*Begrenzung*] of something thought, and Godwi adds that form has no form in itself but is the delimiting of a thought pressing outward in all directions from one point, whether this delimitation be in stone, sound, color, words—or thoughts themselves— all of which acquire form by this process. Maria then suggests a comparison with a soap bubble: its inner area is its thought, and its expansion is its form, and there is one particular moment when its relation to its own substance and its relation to outside light and colors are in complete harmony. In this moment it achieves perfect form. Then it breaks loose and floats through the air. Such is form: a delimitation preserving the idea but not proclaiming itself. [*eine Begrenzung, welche nur die Idee festhält, und von sich selbst nichts spricht*].[13] All else is non-form [*Ungestalt*], either too much or too little. Romanticism is therefore "translation," translation through an intermediary optic which both refracts and reflects, transforms, and imparts form.

The passage is self-reflexive, for its relevance to the structure of *Godwi* is apparent. The central idea, the inner space of the soap bubble, is that embodied in the marble statue, as the subtitle of the novel indicates. But what is the idea embodied in the statue? A sorrowing mother vainly trying to warm into life the child she holds in her cold marble arms—gazing down at her reflection in the water where things are moving, but unable to break the rigidity of the marble that shackles her. It would seem to be the monument to a dead mother, with a strong suggestion of death by drowning. But is the child dead too, or is he the observer, Godwi himself? In the poem he says that she seems to be expecting him to warm *her* into life by an embrace. But he does not; she vanishes into night; and he is left with a sense of deprivation, of longing to know what caused her sorrow, and of her representing something that he lacks. The memory of a dead mother is, as we have seen, a recurrent motif in the novel. Critics have associated it with Brentano's obsession with his own mother. When he first met Sophie Mereau, he wrote to his brother Franz that she was the very image of "our dead mother," and many of his female characters seem to be influenced by this mother-fixation.[14] But the significance of the statue in the novel is more than just autobiographical. It is an incursion into the finite of something beyond the finite, a message from the interior as it were, from the dark depths of the elemental, a warning, a concerned message, unspoken yet insistent, to someone who does not know how to live, to someone who needs to be warmed into life. The referential sphere of the statue is constantly expanding throughout the novel, extending to more and more persons, and becoming ever clearer. It is therefore not an image, but a symbol, constantly growing in ever widening circles.

When Maria arrives at the inn near Godwi's estate, he hears about another statue, on the estate, an elaborate monument to a girl named Violette, a person of ill repute who came to the estate, lived there for a while, went mad, and died. One moonlight night Maria finds his way to this statue, which is also of white marble, but quite different in character. It appears to him as "the apotheosis of a lost child who once wandered about here with pain in her heart and wild joy in her limbs."[15] At the base of the statue are four reliefs, depicting stages in her life, and always the struggle between spirit and flesh, with the flesh, allegorized as a tambourine, being finally crushed in death, but the spirit, imaged in a lyre, being held by an uplifted arm of the figure on the pedestal. It is after this experience that Maria tells

Godwi the reason for his visit, and hands him the first part of the novel. Discussing with him how the novel should proceed, Godwi gives Maria various papers relating to his, Godwi's, parents and to Werdo Senne and Lady Hodefield. Then, much later on, Godwi suggests that the novel should have begun with the poem about the marble mother and child and should end with verses that Maria had written about Violette's monument. The two are connected, for the mother was Godwi's mother and Violette a *fille de joie* who had played an important part in his life. Godwi puts it thus: "in that marble statue lay all my sorrow, I lay like the child in the cold arms of the image: what moved in the waters of the lake was the same, but seen in the mobility of life; but what here [in Violette's monument] is striving upward above the green bushes, that is my freedom; in Marie [his mother] pain and love were imprisoned, in Violette life became free."[16] His life, he goes on to say, moved between these two poles.

A good deal in the way of elucidation has emerged from the papers Godwi had given Maria. Godwi's mother, Marie, was one of two sisters, the calmer of the two, whereas her sister Annonciata was more passionate, complex, and mysterious. Joseph, the man Marie was to be married to, went on a journey to America, was no more heard of and thought dead. And so Marie married Godwi's father, bore him a son, and then one day, carrying the child in her arms, she saw Joseph returning on a ship in the harbor, stretched out her arms to him and was drowned. But the child was saved. Meanwhile Annonciata, some time before, had disappeared. Werdo Senne is Marie's first love, Joseph, and has recognized in Godwi her son.

Godwi now takes up the narrative himself while Maria records it. He describes how his father, after Marie's death, became an impassioned skeptic, always out to destroy everything and everybody, and that one day he met his match in Molly (Lady Hodefield) but seduced her, and she bore him a son, who is Römer. She moved from lover to lover, the last of whom, Carl von Felsen, tried to call Godwi's father to reckoning but was killed by him in a duel. Joseph was sent by Carl—they were good friends—to Molly to help her achieve some equilibrium in her life. Joseph himself married, but his wife died, and he retired from the world, as Werdo Senne, with his daughter Otilie. Eusebio is the child of the painter Franzesco, the brother of Antonio Firmenti, and a girl he abducted from a convent. Molly encountered this woman by chance in an inn, and after she died and Franzesco went off in despair, Molly cared for Eusebio and eventually took him to Werdo. And so on, and so on. At this point Maria declares that he is so bored with the whole story that it is agony just to listen to it.

In reply Godwi now criticizes Part One of the novel and what Maria had made out of the material. He asserts that Maria had made Eusebio far too fantastic, turned Joseph, as Werdo, into a gravestone, and got Otilie all wrong, for the way things were going he would have had either to kill himself because she refused him, or be unfaithful to her (which the public would not have liked), or marry her, which would have been impossible because she was so little flesh-and-blood. He then disassembles that central scene in the forest, revealing that the *stille Lichter* were simply a lantern held by Molly to light her way to the carriage, for Molly, with Eusebio, was the woman in white they had seen! Things are now tied up neatly: Joduno marries Römer, Otilie marries Franzesco Firmenti (now cured of his frenzy), and Molly and Godwi's father come back together again. Which leaves Godwi *fils*, who now brings Violette into the story by telling of his encounter with her and her lustful mother, of his disgust at the whole atmosphere, his falling to the mother, his anxiety about Violette (and her sister Fiametta) growing up in this atmosphere, and his inability or unwillingness to do anything about it, so that he abandoned Violette to her fate, which, when he returned to the house years later, he finds to have been what he had expected, and worse. He says he left her previously to "save himself":[17] now he saves her, taking her to the estate, but she goes mad and dies. The whole of this extraordinary sequence is built around the theme of someone craving for love, Godwi himself, but unwilling to meet the demands that love requires. All he can do is give Violette her monument, and point the connection to the statue of his mother.

While Godwi is telling this to Maria, and us, Maria is dying and talks of his barren life, its lack of any real achievement. He speaks of the difference between "dream of love," the essence of all true longing, the striving toward light and peace that he sees in all nature, and "love of dream," which plays with love vaguely, without specification, vapid and undefined, and ultimately a fruitless fantasy.[18] In the dream of love, spirit and body fuse in harmony. In the love of dream they remain at odds. And perhaps this dichotomy, this dissonance, is the theme of the novel, as it was the perpetual concern of all Brentano's poetry; perhaps all its many characters and twists and turns of the narrative are variations upon it. A postlude tells us that one Clemens Brentano was Maria's closest friend, and that the theme of all Maria's writings was, as Brentano well knew, fighting *for* love, whereas in his life he had had to struggle *against* it.[19]

I have dealt with *Godwi* at considerable length because in a way it is the romantic novel *par excellence*. Not that it is better than the others, but because it embodies so many romantic desiderata. It is built around the image of a dissonant world; its subject is the turmoil of the poetic mind, its basic tension that between spirit and senses. Its form is confessional with arabesques, theme and variations, using all genres, frequently self-reflexive, and combining individuality and universality in a structure both manifold and unified.

Examination of the various published collections of Brentano's letters (there is as yet no complete edition) yields very little in the way of comment on the novel as a form or on other novelists.[20] Indeed there is no particular evidence that Brentano was interested in the possibilities offered by the genre, and no sign that he had any ideal of what a novel should be. Nor does he seem to have been excited by what the novel had become at the hands of his contemporaries, his only comments of interest being on *Heinrich von Ofterdingen* and Arnim's *Gräfin Dolores*. He was never very satisfied with *Godwi*. On its completion he did indeed feel that it contained much that was "good" or "true," but he was dissatisfied with its form.[21] He called the first part "a strange brouillon" and as he proceeded with the second part he said that he felt it got worse and worse.[22] He told Tieck that he felt like a father who had given birth to a sickly, crippled child that was "partly not understood and mostly despised," and thanked him for his "kindly reading" of the novel.[23] To Arnim he wrote (in 1802) that the book was mere "flour and water."[24] And thirty-seven years later he was to look back on "that crazy Godwi" as "soaked in the poison of its time and nothing else."[25] But by far the most revealing comment of his on *Godwi* is in that same letter of 1802 to Arnim in response to Arnim's assertion that his portrayal of a young poet's development was far superior to that in *Ofterdingen*, though he did not approve of Brentano making his poet, Maria, die at the end.[26] To this Brentano replied:

> My young poet passes judgment on himself and on me, for I die in him. . . . In *Godwi* my destiny is writ large, and I find much in it that even the greatest [of authors] need hardly be ashamed of, but I also find that the whole book has no respect for itself, and that is a cunning ruse [*eine feine List*]. For he who keeps silent, or mocks himself, when others admire him, covers up bare patches and faults

with witty folds and stops up gaps with falsehoods—which is why only nakedness is really beautiful.[27]

It is difficult to decide whether this is ironical or straight: in other words, is Brentano here affirming his irony or deprecating it? The passage is typically self-assertive and self-abnegating at the same time, typical of Brentano's ambiguous attitude toward himself, his labile uncertainty.

Both Arnim and Brentano passed negative judgments on *Heinrich von Ofterdingen*. Arnim recognized individual things of beauty in it, but considered it mediocre as a whole.[28] To this Brentano replied that he was in agreement with Arnim's assessment, and went on to say that the characters were only half-human: "All the characters have fish-tails, all flesh is fish in the book. I feel a strange physical nausea in reading it. . . ."[29] That was in October 1802, and represents a revised opinion, perhaps prompted by Arnim's comments, for back in July of that same year he had written to his brother-in-law, the jurist Savigny, that "apart from its anachronisms and despite some platitudes" the book had "thoroughly gripped" him,[30] and, in writing to another friend sometime in the same year, he had described Novalis's novel as "full of innocence and deep wisdom, a book to be read a thousand times over."[31] This presumably all refers to Part One of the novel. For sometime early in 1803, in another letter to Arnim, Brentano expressed his dislike of Part Two, what there was of it, and of the "boring way" in which Tieck had described how the novel was to end.[32] On the other novels of the German Romantics Brentano had little to say, or at least said very little. He expressed his dislike of *Florentin,* made only passing references to Jean Paul and to *Lucinde,* and never mentioned the novels of Tieck, Eichendorff, or Hoffmann. He did, however, assert that *Hyperion* was "one of the finest books of the nation, indeed of the world."[33] One cannot help but conclude that the novel as a genre did not engage his interest, except as a vehicle for self-reflection in the multiple ironies of *Godwi*—and that even that was a one-shot attempt, which, in the religious absorption of his later years, he regretted. Nevertheless, from our point of view, *Godwi* amply demonstrates many of the new perspectives opened up by the romantic redefinition of the form.

Arnim's first novel, *Hollins Liebeleben* [Hollin's Love Life] (1802), also builds on to and out of the tradition of the epistolary novel.[34] It is an immature work, as Arnim himself was soon to recognize, and has

too much that is derivative for it to achieve a really personal statement, though it does seem to have sprung from something the author was seriously concerned about. Its hero fails in life, just as
Godwi and Maria had, but there are no tutelary statues, and there is
a sociological element, deriving from class differences, which is important in the structure. Arnim seems to have been far more conscious of sociological tensions than was Brentano, for these latter
play no notable part in *Godwi,* whereas Hollin's desired union with
his beloved is frustrated in life by their belonging to different social
classes and is only achieved as he is dying. But in other respects
Hollins Liebeleben echoes *Godwi.* The theme, stated at the outset as
"Our age is deficient in love and poor in love—youth hastens and is
soon followed by remembrances,"[35] recalls the statement at the end of
Godwi that "love is captive in our age and the limits of life more
respected than life itself."[36] Life (and love) is described by Hollin in
terms of a force striving toward realization of the "law" [*Gesetz*] of
one's being and compared with the mote in a sunbeam striving toward light and freedom,[37] which recalls Maria's image in *Godwi* of the
"dream of love." In both novels human aspirations are constantly
compared with forces in nature. Both Hollin and Godwi are equally
ill equipped to deal with life, but they are different persons. Hollin
dies in a sensational suicide, stabbing himself while acting the role of
Mortimer, the unhappy lover of Mary Stuart, in a performance of
Schiller's play. He does this because he believes himself ousted in his
love (called Marie in the novel) by a rival, just as Mortimer was by
Leicester in Schiller's play. But Hollin's parallelism is mistaken, for
although Marie plays Mary Stuart and his (as he believes, faithless)
friend Odoardo plays Leicester, Mary did love Leicester whereas
Marie loves not Odoardo but Hollin. By actually killing himself on
the stage Hollin is trying to make a point both to "Mary Stuart" and
to "Leicester," sacrificing himself as Mortimer did, but with the expectation of a different outcome. Or perhaps not? For Hollin certainly knew that at the end of Schiller's play Leicester deserts Mary.
In December 1802, when Brentano was reacting to Arnim's assertion
that the portrayal of the poet's development in *Godwi* was far superior to that in *Heinrich von Ofterdingen,* he returned the compliment
by saying that Arnim had beaten Schiller at his own game in *Hollins
Liebeleben,* for Hollin was, Brentano said, like Mortimer in Schiller's
Maria Stuart, but "in letting a lover get himself killed in Mortimer's
cold corpse you have won out over Schiller."[38]

  To write a novel, the climax of which was a performance of *Maria*

Achim von Arnim. Portrait by P. E. Stroehling, ca. 1804. Original in Freies Deutsches Hochstift, Frankfurt.

Stuart in which the characters of the novel act out what seems to Hollin, but only to him, an analogue of their own situation, was an original idea—especially when we consider that Schiller's play was brand new, published the year before Arnim composed *Hollins Liebeleben*. The parallel is false, as we have seen, like Wilhelm Meister's performance of *Hamlet*. Hollin, though expected to play Mortimer, arrives only when the play is in progress, like the Ghost in *Hamlet* in *Wilhelm Meister*, and when not on stage, he disappears and writes, in sections, a long last farewell to Marie. Structurally this recalls Werther's frequently interrupted long last letter to Lotte, as does the fact that the latter sequence of the main part of the novel is followed by an external narrator's report of the final train of events. But the character of Hollin is different from that of Werther, and the difference is essentially that of 1801 as against 1774. Arnim projects into Hollin the frustration of his contemporaries (and of himself). For Hollin starts out as a young man eager to serve his country in a time of national crisis, and trains himself physically (in a university national fraternity) to do so. But his fencing turns out as disastrously as Hamlet's, for he seriously wounds a friend. Odoardo writes to him that his mistake is in trying to lead others without being able to control himself. This is true, but the fencing incident leads to love in the person of his wounded friend's sister Marie. Love now takes over, a new sense of freedom invades him, a union with Marie replaces fighting for his country as the ultimate goal. He feels at peace with himself for the first time, no longer at odds with the world, attuned to nature at large. But Odoardo tells him this is delusion, the wish-fulfillment of his own restless dissatisfaction, and no indication that he has achieved a mature attitude to life. And so things turn out. For stupid jealousy, coupled with distrust in Marie and the inability to deal with a shabby intrigue, leads to the catastrophe, the ultimate *éclaircissement*, but also to the death of Hollin and Marie and the madness of Odoardo.

The narrative structure of *Hollins Liebeleben* contains much that is derivative—the epistolary form, the final report of the narrator, the performance of a play, negative vignettes of society, one interpolated story, and an intrigue involving a letter arriving too late. Like *Werther*, this novel is essentially the study of one character, but it is a romantic, not a sentimental, character, unfulfilled and therefore frustrated, unable to deal with life, caught between desire for action and desire for love, an echo of Schiller's Karl Moor and a foster-brother of Godwi and Julien Sorel. But he is presented critically. A child of the times, yes, but a child of no use to the times. In a curious appendix Arnim relates the life of a famous Swiss naturalist and geologist, Horace Benedikt von Saussure (1740–1799), who became not only a great and impassioned scientist but a public servant and benefactor, one who did not dwell solely in speculation but ventured boldly into practice, one whose life became a harmonious whole and was therefore a great life. The relevance to the theme of *Hollins Liebeleben* is apparent—and to Arnim's aspirations for himself.

Arnim, as we shall see, was later not enthusiastic about *Hollins Liebeleben*, but he vigorously defended his second novel, a much more ambitious work entitled *Armut, Reichtum, Schuld und Busse der Gräfin Dolores* [Poverty, Riches, Guilt, and Penance of the Countess Dolores], usually referred to as the *Gräfin Dolores* (1810).[39] Despite the immense length of this novel, its plot is fairly simple and is in fact summarized for us by the title. It traces the life of the daughter of an impoverished landed aristocrat—through marriage, worldly position, disaffection with her husband, seduction, adultery, self-recrimination, withdrawal and penance, and eventual death because she has been falsely persuaded that she has lost her devoted husband's affection. At the end of the novel a monument to Dolores is erected, showing her with one hand raised in warning and the other in blessing. It is placed at the top of a dangerous range of cliffs, a lighthouse to serve as a guide to sailors, who call it "The Holy Fire of the Countess"—or "The Holy Fire of the Mother," for she is surrounded by a group of children. So a statue hovers over this novel as in *Godwi*, though here retrospectively, whereas in Brentano's novel it was there almost from the beginning but had to be complemented by a second statue before its meaning could be fully understood. And we should recall that Godwi himself had said that the novel should have begun with the one statue and ended with the other. In a way the statue of Dolores combines aspects of both the women memorialized in *Godwi*, and all three statues radiate a message through the darkness of life, a guiding light for travelers over its turbulent ocean. The treatment of this motif is much more obvious in *Dolores*—perhaps too obvious in its didactic import, but Arnim's novel is a morality, whereas Brentano's is a poetic quest. Yet Dolores is no Violette, though each is the daughter of a countess. Dolores is much more class-conscious. She remains an aristocrat throughout, and her misfortunes stem from the fact that she embodies certain aspects of what Arnim considered the decline of the aristocracy—a tendency toward frivolity and a sheering away from what he considered the true, inherited responsibilities of the aristocracy: social and moral leadership. Like Eichendorff, he was a landed aristocrat himself, and, also like Eichendorff, he believed that the aristocracy still had a role of leadership to play, which for both of them was to be ethical leadership. Essentially what Arnim strove for was an aristocracy of the spirit, not the continuance of an antiquated social institution. He never worked for the revival of the political structure and values of the *ancien régime*. He deplored the destructive and anarchic tendencies of the French Revolution and recognized that it resulted in Napoleon Bonaparte, but he also recognized that the Revolution had promulgated important social and ethical values which the "old" aristocracy had to absorb if it was to maintain its spiritual importance. He was in fact what we would probably call a liberal aristocrat.[40]

Both in the *Gräfin Dolores* and in *Die Kronenwächter* he presents us with a contrast between what we might call fossilized aristocratism and true aristocracy, directly in the first novel and symbolically in the second. *Dolores* opens with a graphic contrast between the lifeless solidity of the prince's antiquatedly German *Schloss* and the italianate *Palast* of the neighboring count, at first sight more gracefully pleasing but disintegrating because of the count's spendthrift modernism. Both the prince and the count are absent at the beginning of the novel; both return toward the end and become strange allies. The action proper is concerned with the two daughters of the count, living in poverty in the one-time *Palast* until a certain Count Karl arrives and becomes engaged to the younger daughter, Dolores. Her sister Klelia, also attracted by Karl, goes off to stay with an aunt in Italy and eventually marries a Spanish duke and settles in Sicily. The whole is built on contrasts, not the least important of which is that between these two sisters. Dolores is less prepared in her mind to adapt to straitened circumstances than her sister is. She clings to what she conceives to be aristocratic-mindedness, dreams of riches, perhaps to be acquired by marriage; but Klelia is more practical, or tries to be, and would rather work than set her cap at a rich suitor. She believes in honesty rather than scheming and tells a tale of a man whom a single turn of fate brought into wealth and position. She soon emerges as the more cautious, sober, and pious of the two, whereas Dolores becomes increasingly lighthearted, spendthrift, and frivolous, feeling somehow that this is what is expected of a woman of her station. Karl tries to inject more seriousness into her and in one striking incident gives her a ring with Christ and the twelve apostles on it which used to belong to his mother, together with a rosary and other religious artifacts. But Dolores dislikes the ring because it cannot be worn in high society, and dismisses the rosary as useless. She seems to need constant social titillation, and when she finally marries Karl and they move to his country estate, she gradually surrounds herself with, or finds herself surrounded by, a strange collection of people, all of whom provide entertainment by the telling of stories. In some of these tales the grotesque side of Arnim's fancy emerges, but although he is here taking up a conventional element in novel structure, the stories relate to each other, reflect on the main plot, and serve to accentuate the difference between the characters of Dolores and her husband.

The first story purports to be about the long-lost son of the prince, whom Dolores and Klelia had known when they were all three children, but develops into a weird fantasy about old soldiers and prostitutes immured on an island and unable to get away. The second is about a Polish princess who jumps into the Vistula to save her country from becoming just a nation of "butchers" (that is, bourgeois merchants), floats downstream while many would-be rescuers drown, and is rescued by a priest, while the narrator, a true bourgeois and an art dealer, does good business because he is mistakenly thought to have helped save her. There is a frivolous tone to the first story, and an antireligious attitude in the second. Count Karl objects to both but Dolores defends them as consonant with the jocular tone of what she considers a "higher view of life."[41] She seems to disdain all seriousness, and when Karl persuades Pastor Frank, a neighbor of theirs, to tell the story of Hollin, which he does, more or less as it was in *Hollins Liebeleben* but without the epistolary framework, she is relatively unmoved, refuses to let a tragic story ruin her day, and calls for something lively. Pastor Frank then tells a story from what he asserts to be *his* love life. Karl is offended by what he calls the pastor's egocentric "vanity" and false dolling-up of a dull existence just to make an effect, but Dolores sees nothing wrong in the story— it was, after all, "entertaining" and that, for her, would seem to be what matters. Her values are social in a superficial way, whereas his are ethical in a somewhat doctrinaire form. This leads to the first serious altercation between Karl and Dolores, in which he calls Frank an "intellectual seducer" and she calls Karl a jealous spoilsport. Karl decides he is going to have to work at his marriage.

The stories so far told have been constantly interrupted by comments from Dolores and Karl, spiced by grotesque horrors (such as the countess who went to bed and disintegrated into a heap of ashes), and all turning somehow on the destruction of normal love-relationships. They often reflect back on each other and they act as a sort of mirror for the growing tension between Karl and Dolores. There now follow two protracted sections, both of the nature of episodes. The first is built around the marriage of a page and a maid on the estate, with songs composed by Karl for the occasion. He is given to venting his feelings in verse, and one of the most interesting features of this novel is the way in which the poems reveal what is going on inside the characters, especially Karl, alongside their articulated opinions—a series of interior monologues, a sort of dialogue between the external and the internal. Interplay, often between opposites, is a recurrent element in the structure of the *Gräfin Dolores*: thus in this episode Karl's poem on the joys of marriage is followed by a masque parodying the ceremony, serious songs by obscene jokes, and finally tales told by three nuns on the subject of marriage: one tells of missing it because she was always late for everything; the second relates that she never married because she liked to chatter and dance; and the third tells of the sister of a duke who dreamily embraced what she thought was a tree and then gave birth to a dusky-skinned baby. The second major "episode" is concerned with a poet and his family who arrive at the estate. But before this begins, a letter from Klelia, saying how unhappy she is because her uncle's house is full of gamblers and the only people she can talk to are nuns, arouses Karl's sympathy and Dolores's jealousy, for she thinks he might really find Klelia closer to his general outlook. This leads to an exchange in which Dolores wishes for a return to the good old days of aristocratic life whereas Karl argues for an "aristocratization of everybody" [*alle Welt zu adeln*], and for this to come about—as he puts it in a poem, since he has failed to talk his wife over to his opinions—"the aristocracy must become burghers."[42]

The episodic sequence concerned with the poet Waller and his family is one of the most curious parts of this very curious book. The fact that Waller makes poems out of everything suggests a sort of parallel to Karl, with the difference, however, that Karl's poems are private meditations whereas Waller's are for the public. At first sight Waller would seem to be intended as a portrait of the pseudopoet, like several similar figures in other romantic novels.[43] But things are not quite so simple as that: despite the facile, artificial nature of most of his work, and his view of everything, including his wife's death, as material for verses, some of his poems are not all that bad, and occasionally he makes remarks pregnant with truth. What he really lacks is a basis of seriousness, a firm ground, and in this respect he too is a reflection on Dolores, who defends him at moments, though finally rejecting him. Perhaps the most significant comments on Waller are made by Frank and Karl. When Frank counters Karl's objection that Waller is always shifting moods and perspectives and lacks all stability by asserting it is characteristic of an artistic temperament "to think simultaneously sadly and joyfully, seriously and jocularly," Karl's rejoinder is that in the process one thing destroys the other "like those two lions who bit each other so long that only their tails were left" (a characteristic Arnim horror-image).[44] This would suggest that for Karl, as for Arnim, aestheticism of this kind is not just the pleasing play of irony (such as Dolores would enjoy) but vicious destruction—nihilism, in fact. Art and the true artistic impulse are not thereby rejected, but art is not a balancing act of oppositions, or if it employs such equilibration it must do so from a firm unitary basis. And in Arnim's case this is a basis of belief, a belief in absolute values.

That this basis is ultimately religious is demonstrated not only by the further development of Dolores herself but, in the section of the novel that we are at present considering, by the character and fate of the boy Traugott, the son of Waller's wife by a previous marriage. After she dies, the boy, whose name, of course, means "trust in God," recalls experiences of his childhood when an old man rescued him from drowning and a comrade called Fear-God [Fürchtegott] showed him how to "build"—to order the elements of experience. The allegory is a little heavy, but the description of this childhood, of the boy's urge to rejoin his mother, and of his death on his mother's grave is of the utmost delicacy. It is significant that Karl says that Traugott's account of his childhood reminds him of his own early life. Traugott dies during harvest-time on the estate while Dolores awaits the birth of a child. The connection between fruition and death is made explicit—so explicit that Dolores says she fears that she may die in childbirth. It was but a passing remark to her husband and not very seriously offered. But, says the narrator, Dolores was like those persons who frighten others at midday with ghost stories which they would prefer to forget when they are alone at midnight.[45] It is with this striking characterization of Dolores that the second part of this four-part novel ends, the part entitled "Riches."

So far the novel's structure has combined a main plot told by a narrator, with constant authorial comments and a large number of interpolated episodes. These interpolations consist of stories, poems, short dramas, and even aphorisms, so that all genres are combined. Most striking perhaps is the fact that Arnim freely uses material from other authors—from older chronicles, from printed sermons, and even from his own works. On careful reflection the reader should appreciate that these seeming digressions are in fact arabesques: they act as a series of mirrors reflecting on the situation of Karl and Dolores. They proliferate in Part Two where, as a result of these numerous seeming interruptions, the main plot slows down almost to a standstill in comparison with the rather rapid process in the (shorter) first part, and chronological progression gives way to a swirling concentric pattern of parallels that certainly provides variety, but not breadth because everything radiates from one definite center, the Gräfin Dolores herself. But some sort of climax or crisis, or both, is obviously imminent, and therefore Part Three, entitled "Guilt," returns to progressive narration. Like the first part, it is relatively short, and the fourth part, like the second, again broadens out, also with extensive use of arabesques and digressions.

From Part Three on, the religious structure of the novel becomes apparent—sin, trials, and redemption. The progression is therefore geometrical, in Novalis's sense of that term. Karl and Dolores go back to town, though he hopes some day to persuade her of the superiority of life in the country. The child is born and named after his father. A letter from Klelia announces her marriage to the Spanish duke, which arouses Dolores's envy of her sister whom she imagines enjoying the high society she longs for. But a friend of the duke's, a marquis, tells them that both Klelia and her husband are in fact occupied with much the same concerns as Karl, namely the proper prosecution of their responsibilities as landed gentry. It is this marquis who is to become Dolores's seducer: he claims to be sent by a secret society to spread enlightenment, but in fact he is a political intriguer. He excites Dolores by persuading her that she too can have political influence, so that he soon has her completely in his power and frightens her with pseudo-Mesmerist tales of forces and spirits, of his being the incorporation of some god, and so on. During this period Karl has been out on his estate. He returns and tries to persuade Dolores to go back with him, but she declines and, surprisingly, the marquis goes with Karl instead. In a series of conversations between them, the worldliness of the marquis is contrasted with Karl's country solidity and probity. There is much talk of women and one night, after the marquis has left to take a letter from Karl to Dolores, Karl dreams that she has been unfaithful to him, hears a boy singing a song about the pain of parting, and then composes a poem which combines the dream with the song—one of the most striking examples of an inner dialogue in the book. This is followed by an equally remarkable sequence: full of misgivings Karl decides to take off into the blue, and the progression of his thoughts, which he writes down, is presented as stages on a journey, a sort of interior monologue that affords ample testimony to Arnim's obsession with the frightening specters that rise up from the subsoil of consciousness. Karl, like Dolores, is drawn for a time into the world of the occult—and like her, into a false occult, the imaginative refuge in fantasies that stop him from thinking and acting. But he pulls himself out of all this hocus-pocus and returns to Dolores who, in the meantime, has been deserted by the marquis. She is pregnant again—by the Marquis, she thinks—wonders whether to confess everything to her husband, decides not to, then blurts it all out, talking in her sleep. Again, just as in Karl's dream and musings on the journey, the subconscious comes to the fore—and takes over, suppressing all else. Part Three ends with a strange symbolic scene in which Dolores fires what she thought was an unloaded gun, hits Karl, and falls in a faint.

This third part obviously derives much in its external action from the *Trivialromane* of the time, some of which Arnim, like the other Romantics, must have read. But it is the inner action, what goes on in these two tormented souls, their colloquies with themselves, that interests us today. The characterization throughout the novel is of exceptional subtlety and depth, particularly as regards the two main characters, Karl and Dolores. There is, then, here perhaps a greater interest in character than in the other romantic novelists, and this in turn implies a greater realism, which also extends to depictive detail of setting. But what is most notable about this novel is its portrayal of what subsists below the surface, the interplay between conscious and unconscious.

The long last section of the novel, the fourth book, seems to me inferior to the rest, because there is too much digression from the central theme and too much concentration on figures other than the two protagonists. The "penance" extends to both Dolores and Karl, for it turns out that he had engineered the episode with the gun so that she should destroy him in a reification of what was happening internally. The progress of the penance is clear enough: it is ushered in by a pilgrimage in which both participate, and then takes them to

Klelia's estate in Sicily, where Dolores devotes herself to the rearing
of children—Klelia being, to her sorrow, childless—and Karl to estate duties, for Klelia's husband dies, but not before Klelia has told
Dolores that he was the marquis (though Klelia does not know of his
relations with her sister until Dolores tells her). One reason for the
journey to Sicily is to bring the child of Dolores and the "Marquis" to
his real father, but the father has died before they get there. Were it
not for the religious underpinning (strengthened by the fact that
this child becomes a monk), the novel would be drifting into sensa-
tionalism of a rather trivial kind. And this is the main trouble with
Part Four of the *Gräfin Dolores*: the sensational elements (which include a double poisoning of two subsidiary characters at the end)
detract from the concentration on the central moral theme of redemption; nor is even this brought to a satisfactory climax, because
Dolores dies after being falsely persuaded by a rival of Karl's infidel-
ity. So when the moment of rest is finally reached, it is not really a
resolution, certainly not a moral resolution. The apotheosis is brought
about too artificially, too violently to be really persuasive. Equally
distracting are the large number of interpolated tales, poems, and
other digressions. Some of these—for instance, the tale of Pope
Joan—are excellent novellas, and one can relate most of them to the
concerns expressed in the main plot, but too many others are more
diversions than arabesques. It could be that Arnim was trying to
lighten the texture, or simply that he could not control his "joy in
fabulating" (to use Goethe's phrase), but the result is a regrettable
loss of tension. The reintroduction of Dolores's father, and of the
prince and princess, seems hardly justified by the pseudosymbolism
of their abandoning their old residences for a new life and a new
understanding of each other's values, nor by the fact that the princess also goes to Sicily and, because of her designs on Karl, becomes the agent of Dolores's death. All this is stuff from a different kind of novel without the serious moral concerns of the *Gräfin
Dolores*. For all its good qualities Arnim's novel shows the dangers
of the arabesque form.

Brentano greeted the appearance of the *Gräfin Dolores* with enthusiasm, but later expressed disapproval of its loose structure. Knowing
that it was originally planned as a story or novella, he thought it
would have been artistically more compelling if it had remained a
novella.[46] But on the other hand he noted the added richness achieved
by its expansion into the dimensions of a novel. Arnim's novel had
appeared in May 1810, and in June Brentano recommended it to

the painter Philipp Otto Runge as being "as rich as very few other German novels" and signaling out for especial praise certain of the episodes, including that of the dusky child born of the embrace of a "tree," and the tale of Pope Joan.[47] The book had aroused mixed feelings among Arnim's closest friends, and we know that Jakob Grimm, one of the famous pair of brothers, had criticized it harshly. In November 1810 we find Brentano writing to the brothers Grimm, saying that he agreed with much of Jakob's criticism, for, despite the obvious seriousness of his intentions, Arnim had not paid enough attention to the structure, which was often little more than patch-work.[48] Brentano was referring specifically to the episodic narratives and characters of the book, and he contrasts its disorder with the shape of *Wilhelm Meister, Die Wahlverwandtschaften* (which neverthe-less bored him), *Titan, Siebenkäs,* and the "divine *Don Quixote.*" The beginning of *Dolores,* he said, was splendid—up to the point where the two girls part from each other; but he found the character of the marquis wooden and neither of the girls convincing, because "die Klelia schiesst ganz ins Kraut und die Dolores ins Fleisch, beide zusammen wären sie gut" ("Klelia runs too much to leaf and Dolores to flesh—their combination would be good").[49] He disapproves of the "ghastly childbed stuff" [*das entsetzliche Kindbetterwesen*] as "repulsive," as well as of the fact that Johannes (the child of Dolores and the marquis) "is already a subdeacon when he comes into the world" [*gleich als Subdiakonus auf die Welt kommt*].[50] In general, he charges the book with improbabilities and with irrelevancies in the form of inter-ruptions, but he pays tribute to its style, intelligence, and character. Brentano's criticism seems to me pretty close to the mark. Interest-ing as Arnim's use of arabesques is theoretically, it is less satisfying aesthetically and illustrates the danger of this structural technique if used excessively, as it undoubtedly is here. Brentano says nothing about its dialogues between conscious and unconscious, and this fact, combined with the remark (albeit jocularly phrased) about Klelia and Dolores, might well mean that he recognized the anguish of the spirit embedded in the book, which was not very different in charac-ter from his own.

Arnim's third novel, *Die Kronenwächter,* only the first volume of which was completed and published during his lifetime (in 1817), is every bit as ambitious as the *Gräfin Dolores,* but is quite different in character and is perhaps a greater, though more perplexing, achieve-ment.[51] Superficially it is a historical novel à la Walter Scott, set in an age of turmoil: Germany in the early sixteenth century, when established institutions were being assailed and the general social configuration was changing. Three persons, the Emperor Maximilian, Luther, and Dr. Faust, all of whom appear in Arnim's novel, epitomize the climate of this age of transition. Maximilian, "last of the knights," with his passion for hunting and tournaments, friend of scholars and universities, commissioner of manuscripts and collections of medieval poems, clung to old values in a world to which they no longer applied, the world of Luther and that restless adventurer Dr. Faust. As with Scott, the historical figures are kept in the background, though their presence is atmospheric and symbolic, whereas the foreground is occupied by fictional personages. As in the *Gräfin Dolores,* the novel is dominated by the tension between ancient values and rising values, and here too the old are disintegrating and the new not really stabilized. Though never explicitly stated, the parallel between the age of Maximilian and Arnim's own time is something we are meant to feel, especially as regards the role of the aristocracy, the validity of inherited traditions, and the acceptance or nonacceptance of middle-class (in this novel, burgher) values. As in *Dolores,* the heritage of the past is symbolized in castles: Burg Hohenstock, the residence of Graf Rappolt, a survivor of the great Hohenstauffen dynasty; the Kronenburg, where the ancient crown of the dynasty is kept; and the ruins of the palace of Barbarossa. But Hohenstock is overrun by farm animals and the illegitimate offspring of the half-crazed count and his domineering housekeeper-mistress, the Kronenburg is occupied by a secret society subversive to the rule of Maximilian, and the ruins of the palace of Barbarossa are converted by the hero of the novel, Berthold, into a weaving establishment. The action of the novel is set in the Swabian town of Waiblingen, which incorporates the burgher values and is striving to become a Free City. The focal theme is further intensified by the fact that Berthold himself is a descendant of the Hohenstauffens, and although eventually made burgomaster of Waiblingen, is vitiated in his burgher activities by obsessions deriving from his knightly lineage and what he conceives to be the call to a higher destiny.

The society of the Kronenburg, which gives the novel its title, impinges at intervals on life in Waiblingen, usually ominously and violently, much like the secret societies in some of the *Trivialromane.* But like these, its activities seem at times to be connected with some mission, though whether this is worthy or base remains at first obscure. Is it concerned to restore true leadership to the Emperorship to replace Maximilian's neglect of his proper duties, or does it simply want to subvert his position and replace him by someone they can control—in this case, Berthold? This ambiguity constitutes part of the excitement and mystery of the novel—which remains mysterious because it was never finished. For the "second volume" of the novel published by Arnim's widow Bettina in 1854 represents an earlier stage in composition, a text that Arnim had already heavily worked over in the first volume, which he published. In this first volume Maximilian is presented as a kindly person, albeit ineffectual as a ruler, and the inhabitants of the Kronenburg, the *Kronenwächter*, as sinister power-lords. The preservation of the Hohenstauffen crown is connected with the legend that the Emperor Frederick Barbarossa, whose burial place is unknown (he was drowned while on a Crusade in 1190), still sits surrounded by his knights in a cave in the Thuringian mountains, waiting until the need of his country should call him. But in most versions of this myth the knights are sleeping, whereas here they are active schemers.

The mystery and poetry of "this beautiful fiery book" as Bettina called it,[52] is mainly concentrated in these castles and the looming presence of the past and its self-appointed "guardians," as well as in the sense conveyed of subterranean or subconscious forces fashioning human destinies, and the bewilderment of those caught between dreams and reality, the higher aspirations of the mind and the hard facts of everyday existence. Basically this is another version of the tension in Jean Paul's heroes, though the tone is quite different and the treatment more grandiose. The tension exists not only in Berthold himself, but also in his wife Anna and, in a different form, in Maximilian. As in Jean Paul, both sides of the coin are presented with equal power. Arnim's "realism" is amply displayed in numerous scenes of burgher life, as well as by the great description of Maximilian's betrothal festivities in which the poetry of splendor combines with delicate prose details such as the tearing of Anna's dress in the pressure of the crowd. There is plenty of humor interwoven with the solemn seriousness of the theme of higher destiny, the counterpoint being almost Shakesperean. The farcical scenes, of which there are many, are structural arabesques, and one of the interesting things about this novel is that the arabesques are often grotesques, so that Arnim's subconscious preoccupations here come once again to the fore. The arabesques in *Die Kronenwächter* are, in my view, more successfully handled than those in the *Gräfin Dolores*, for here they do not halt the action or disperse the focus. The inset narratives and the poems are better integrated with the central theme, and even the series of pictures described at the end of ᴸook Two presents through episodes from the legendary past the notion of kingly responsibility, and is therefore organically related to the overall theme. The texture of the whole is extremely rich with plenty of fairy-tale and folk motifs, and the use of dialogue is comparable to that in the *Gräfin Dolores*.

The most striking grotesque scene in the novel concerns Dr. Faust, who performs a blood transfusion between Berthold, debilitated by the effects of a stroke, and Anton, the strapping painter's apprentice. This might seem at first sight to be a comic arabesque, but it results in a change of personality in both Berthold and Anton that becomes central to the development of the action. The symbolism of this scene—injection of blood into the comparatively bloodless Berthold, and infusion of some higher dimension into the rather crude Anton— is grotesque to the point of absurdity, but the deeper implication is that Berthold needs more guts and Anton more brains, for Anton too is of Hohenstauffen lineage. The motif is carried through to the end of the published part of the novel, for as Berthold dies in the vault where the Hohenstauffens are buried, blood spurts from the place where Faust had injected Anton's blood, and Anton is wounded in the place on his body where he received Berthold's blood—after a scuffle between burghers and knightly horse-soldiers, a rowdy climax to the celebrations of the baptism of the child of Anna and Berthold. The symbolism is a little heavy, but the implication is that these two characters—the artisan and the burgomaster—only realize their true selves when released from the artificial injection of otherness. The incursions of Faust and the Kronenwächter into the lives of both Anton and Berthold are therefore rejected by the symbolism of the novel, even though at the end of the 1817 text Anna's child is snatched away by Faust and given to Anton's brother Konrad, who is closely allied with the Kronenwächter. The subtitle of the novel is "Berthold's First and Second Life," his "second life" being his elevation to high burgher status and his marriage to Anna, *after* the blood transfusion, and as he dies bent over the tombs of the Hohenstauffens he murmurs, half-crazed, about a third life, presumably in eternity, out of the burgher world that he is rejecting. As the first volume ends Anna is praying for the recovery of Anton, for it was really the Anton in Berthold that she had married and she now realizes that she loves Anton. What will happen to Anton is left uncertain. But since, unlike Berthold, he has no inclination toward the world of the Kronenwächter (although equally connected by his past with it), one would assume that he is to recover, especially since he has been relieved of the blood of Berthold that had been forcibly put into him, and has entered on an active life unencumbered by obscurantist, mystical longings. The power of these latter is, however, never denied in *Die Kronenwächter,* and that is why Faust figures in it—as an evil force but one somehow belonging to a world of practical subversiveness masquerading as supernatural power, a world to which the Kronenwächter also belong.

It is difficult to know what to make of the continuation, which in several points is inconsistent with the first volume. Arnim was obviously engaged in recasting the whole novel, but completed only the first half. Also one cannot tell how much of the 1854 text is Arnim and how much Bettina. The first volume is a carefully constructed series of what Arnim calls "stories" [*Geschichten*] which are scenic in character, whereas the second is a continuous narrative plus various fragments. The action is of great complexity and hardly lends itself to a coherent summary, but its general lines are as follows. Anton recovers and marries Anna, but squanders their assets in gambling and drink under the influence of a sinister friend who turns out to be one of the illegitimate children of Graf Rappolt, and is therefore of Hohenstauffen lineage. Rappolt reenters the story and recounts his life and the history of the Hohenstauffens, Faust appears (here, inconsistently, for the first time) and gets Anton into his power by means of a demon phantom of sensuality. A Junker named Bluebeard, an illegitimate daughter of the Emperor Charles V, a dragon, the Peasants' War, the Anabaptists, iconoclasts, lansquenets, *filles de joie,* a lustful abbot, plus side references to Luther, Melanchthon and the mastersingers of Nuremberg—what have you—all this is brought in. But the real movement was eventually to lead back to the Kronenburg where, according to the fragmentary parts of the "text," Anton was first to take over leadership, but then, "longing for open contact with the spirit of the people."[53] go back to the real world, join the peasants in their war against the princes, and take part with them in their destruction of the Kronenburg. Arnim seems to have envisaged some mystical ending (or was this Bettina's idea?) in which the crown is divided and somehow becomes a spiritual symbol—" only to be regained by spiritual education [*geistige Bildung*] . . . a part of the human race works on in its mind until its time comes" [*Ein Teil des Menschengeschlechts arbeitet immer im Geist, bis seine Zeit gekommen*].[54] If this second volume is really all Arnim, then it shows an Arnim not yet in control of his material. It seems to me impossible to consider this text as a novelistic structure. For it has no structure, though judging from the first volume I feel fairly sure that it would have had a structure if Arnim had been able to work over it. One thing, however, seems quite clear and that is that it does not represent a hankering after old values. The society of the Kronenburg is expressly deprecated—in fact, destroyed. Could it be that Arnim, if he had been able to complete his novel, would have proclaimed the necessity of an aristocracy of the spirit, as in *Dolores*? Does the fragment about the divided crown point in this direction? Impossible to say. Certainly impossible to deduce anything conclusive from the hodgepodge of this "second volume." There are sections which are carefully worked out—such as Rappolt's narration, and a striking digression on presentiments and memories[55]—but on the whole it gives the impression of a *Trivialroman* structure insufficiently worked over and inadequately combined with a lofty, spiritual theme. It is full of horrors—arson, murder, decapitation of a monk by his fellows, and a hideous sequence in which Anna's child by Anton kills her child by Berthold and drinks its blood—demons from the subconscious not meaningfully integrated into an artistic structure, which is true also of the grotesquely farcical sequences all too obviously inspired by Arnim's reading of sixteenth- and seventeenth-century narrative fiction. *Die Kronenwächter* is a great imaginative venture of a troubled mind—perhaps of one that could find no answers to the conflicts within him.

In contrast to Brentano, Arnim had a good deal to say about novels and novelists. He obviously was much more interested in the possibilities of the genre than was his friend, and his knowledge of novels of the past was wider than that of most of his contemporaries. In 1809 he was systematically reading various older German narrative works in order to find material for inclusion in a collection of novellas entitled *Der Wintergarten* [The Winter Garden, a kind of conservatory], a curious work, ultimately unsuccessful because, despite a formal framework, there is no unifying principle behind its disparate material, except that of salvaging for the sake of conservation. Arnim worked over his materials, abbreviating, concentrating and, in some instances, purifying, throwing himself, as he wrote to Brentano, "into all sorts of historical masks"[56]—masks of various types of narrator and narrative stance. The most interesting thing about *Der Wintergarten* is the way it juxtaposes narratives, or parts of narratives, from different authors and periods, even in some cases combining them where he saw connections. It is a testimony to the permanence of the narrative voice, and to Arnim's interest in narratives of all kinds, but also to the aesthetic value of combining what to normal eyes might not seem to belong together—for instance, to use material from the eighteenth-century *Insel Felsenburg* to "explain" the late seventeenth-century picaresque novel *Schelmuffsky*, or to insert episodes from *Schelmuffsky* (1696) into a framework evolved from a fool-narrative of the same period, Christian Weise's *Die drei ärgsten Erznarren* [Three Worst Arch-Fools] (1672), or to combine parts of two major narrative treatments of war (by Moscherosch and Grimmelshausen). In *Der Wintergarten* there is a certain artificiality about all this and the result is, frankly, rather boring. But this combinatory activity, always going on in Arnim's mind, whether of contrasts or similarities, shows how he works outward from shorter contained units to broader structures and gives a foretaste of what was to be his prime structural principle in organizing his two major novels.

Arnim was interested not merely in German novels of the seventeenth century but also in those of other countries in that period. He expressed admiration for both Cervantes and Scarron. He objected to those who "misunderstood" *Don Quixote* as a satire on romances, and elsewhere expressed his affection for *Persiles.*[37] Scarron's *Roman comique* evoked his enthusiasm for its "heavenly characters" ("heavenly" simply in the sense of marvelously portrayed), and he suggested that Goethe should have let the actors in *Wilhelm Meister* read aloud from it—leaving out the inset novellas—which would have made Goethe's novel even more strikingly individual.[38] This is an interesting comment: it implies a situation in which actors in one novel read to one another a novel about actors which in turn reflects back on the novel in which they, the readers, figure. It also embodies the same principle of combination (and adaptation by condensation) that was operating in *Der Wintergarten.*

In general Arnim was more interested in these older novels than in those of the more immediate past or of his own contemporaries, though his interest was aroused by some of the romantic novels. In 1802 he met Mme. de Krüdener while she was writing her novel *Valérie* (published in 1803)—a personal, partly autobiographical novel with a hero who has been described as a "northern" version of Chateaubriand's celebrated René[59]—and told Brentano that it "will be good." He would have liked to give her *Godwi* to read, were it not for the "damn bed-scene" (meaning the sequence involving Godwi and Violette's mother).[60] Obviously he thought this unsuitable for the pious

Mme. de Krüdener. What he thought would be "good" about *Valérie*, is left unsaid; perhaps he saw it too as a demonstration of the root-lessness of the postrevolutionary psyche, the frustrations of transition between old and new. In this connection it is interesting to note that Arnim commented favorably on both novels of Mme. de Staël, praising the depiction of society and the delineation of the characters in *Delphine*,[61] and the way in which Mme. de Staël "divided herself" into the hero and heroine of *Corinne*.[62] He read Chateaubriand's *Atala* with enthusiasm, placing it along with *Delphine* as "the two most notable works that have appeared here recently." This comment was made in January 1803.[63] In these three novelists—Mme. de Krüdener, Chateaubriand, and Mme. de Staël—he sensed his own concern with the state of society caught between two worlds and man's (and woman's) efforts to adapt to this. The combinatory activity of his mind was always at work.

Arnim probably read a good deal of Scott. The whole conception of *Die Kronenwächter* is inconceivable without some knowledge of Scott. In December 1823 he wrote to his wife that he was reading *The Abbot*, "a novel of Walter Scott which I had not yet read" (which suggests that he already knew other novels by Scott), "which refashions stories [*Geschichten bearbeitet*] that I had once wanted to use myself [*die ich selbst einmal benutzen wollte*]. The tale is very attractive in its nature, repeating much from his [Scott's] earlier books, but nowhere is his method more visible of giving the appearance of credibility to the most improbable inventions by the truth of the details."[64] The comment seems to me interesting in various ways. It reflects, through what it says about Scott, Arnim's own compositional principle of combining fanciful inventions with truth of detail. The central sequence of *The Abbot* is concerned with the wild scheme that liberated Mary, Queen of Scots, from her imprisonment in Lochleven and her ill-advised decision to claim protection, in England, from Elizabeth. It also has a vacillating hero, caught between the old and the new, like Berthold. The image of a monarch reduced to anguished flight obviously epitomized for Arnim the plight of the aristocracy. He was particularly interested in Bonnie Prince Charlie; the last section of *Der Wintergarten* is a reworking of a famous account of his misfortunes. And in 1825 Arnim wrote to Bettina about some paintings he had found in a room in a place near his country estate, the work of a Prussian deserter who was in fact a Macdonald and had fled from England because of a duel and joined the Prussian army. Arnim's imagination immediately got to work: "If I were to combine this story with that of Prince Edward [Charles Edward Stuart, "Bonnie Prince Charlie"] and his expedition [the Jacobite invasion of 1745], as a result of which many Macdonalds had to flee, then I would have done a Walter Scott."[65] Although by this time Arnim was nearing the end of his productive life (his last big collection of novellas was published in 1826), we can see that the same old process of composition by combination is still at work.

There are passing references to German novelists of the eighteenth century, but none of significance except those concerning Goethe. He particularly admired Goethe's portrayal in the first part of *Die Wahlverwandtschaften* of what he called the "boredom of unoccupied, inactive good fortune," and went on in the same letter to describe how closely this portrayal corresponded to his own experience (he was, after all, like Eduard in that novel, a landed aristocrat). Arnim points to the fact that people of this station suffer from a particular kind of hypochondria, are too educated to have real rapport with the countryfolk, however much they may desire it, and so "cook their domestic soup so long that there is nothing more left in the pot." Nowhere are divorces more prevalent; everything new "disturbs them in their state of mutual ennui." The date of the letter (to Bettina) in which these remarks occur, is November 1809, one month after Goethe's novel had appeared and when Arnim was already working out the *Gräfin Dolores*.[66] Their relevance to his own novel is apparent. At this first encounter with *Die Wahlverwandtschaften* it was the social aspect of the novel that set his mind working. He was somewhat ironic about the ending: why close the chapel to stop miracles emanating from the dead Ottilie? If someone wants to perform miracles, who has the right to stop him? He returned to Goethe's novel in August 1817, now with more detachment and *Dolores* off his back, and wrote to Bettina that he now felt that the novel came, as it were, out of the stream of a hot spring. It had "a strange fateful effect, abandoning oneself so entirely to natural forces, but if one sees that some people do that quite comfortably, then one cannot but consider them as some kind of chemical substances waiting for some such encrustation of their damage [damaged parts]."[67] Obviously Arnim had now become aware of the moral implications of Goethe's novel. Both its social and its moral aspects had left their residue in the *Gräfin Dolores*.

On the novels of the other German Romantics, Arnim had various things to say. He claimed that Jean Paul suffered from a lack of "poetic seriousness" which no amount of caprice or wit could compensate for.[68] He found no such failing in Hölderlin's *Hyperion*, "that most glorious of all elegies,"[69] full of anger at the decline of Germany's glory and yet full of love for his unfortunate fatherland.[70] He praised *William Lovell* for what it had produced from out of "that arid old Richardsonian soil,"[71] but criticized the novelist Fouqué (who wrote several pseudohistorical novels) for unsuccessfully combining the machinery of older literature (meaning the use of the marvelous) with the climate of modern literature.[72] *Ofterdingen* he considered inferior to *Godwi* as the presentation of a poet's development, as we have seen. The former, he once said, was *pâté de foie gras* whereas *Godwi* was a proper meal.[73] The main thrust of his criticism (in which, as we have seen, Brentano concurred) was that the book was not gutsy enough, too rarefied with its "stupidly learned peasant chatter" and its boring and incomprehensible *Märchen*(!)[74] And the plans for the continuation amply demonstrated that such a work could not be written,[75] whereas *Godwi* was "one of the most perfect works I know" though the poet should not have been allowed to die at the end, and the (self-reflexive) devices of the final section diminished the seriousness of the novel.[76] The first part should have dealt with the apprenticeship of a poet, and the second with his fulfillment—in fact exactly what Novalis had done in *Ofterdingen* and Brentano had no intention of doing in *Godwi*, though of course Arnim did not recognize this.

Arnim also had interesting things to say about his own novels. In November 1802 he told Brentano that he thought he had made a mistake in publishing *Hollins Liebeleben* when he did, for what he liked about it was really only for himself, not for the public. He had been too much influenced by *Werther* in his use of the epistolary form and had first intended it to be "a kind of tragedy . . . laced through with narrative and letters"[77]—presumably coming close to Friedrich Schlegel's ideal of combination of genres, though Arnim does not say so. It was, he said, a transitional attempt in which his mind had not yet achieved full freedom. He did not feel apologetic about the *Gräfin Dolores*, and was prepared to defend it vigorously. He did so at length in a letter of October 1810 to Jakob Grimm, who felt the book was "untrue" [*unwahr*], lacked a sense of real life.[78] Arnim indignantly replied that the book was intensely true, that it was the result of "serious experience of the times," that everything in it had solid foundation in reality and its basic assertion of "God's hand in contingencies and rescue from sin" was valid.[79] He did, however, admit that the process of regeneration in Dolores could have been traced in more detail. Grimm replied that by "truth" he had meant not truth to life but poetic truth.[80] In a word, he found the novel *aesthetically* unconvincing. In reply to Wilhelm Grimm's review of the novel, Arnim defended the truthfulness of the characters, stating that in portraying the princess he had something of Catherine the Great in mind and that Potemkin was the model for another of the characters.[81] And he insisted once more on the validity of the novel's implied message, namely that no one is irretrievably lost because "every sinner carries a lost paradise within himself and as in the physical world there is no vacuum, so too in the realm of morality."[82] Arnim's comments on *Die Kronenwächter* are less interesting and are mostly confined to defending certain sections considered to be too compressed or too complex, and certain personages considered to be nongermane to the action, by explaining that these were to be further developed in the rest of the novel—in a word, Arnim defends what is published by reference to the total scheme in his mind, which, alas, was never to be fully realized.

CHAPTER NINE

A Visit to the Madhouse

WE now come to the mystery book of German romanticism. In 1804 there appeared at an obscure publishing house in Saxony a slim work entitled *Nachtwachen—Von Bonaventura* [Night Watches— by, or of, Bonaventura]. Nobody knows who "Bonaventura" was, but the writing is of such intensity and power that no one has been really satisfied by the report that its author was a minor writer of the period, one Friedrich Gottlob Wetzel. It was thought for a time to be a youthful indiscretion of the philosopher Schelling. Since then various other candidates for its authorship have been suggested, among them Brentano, Hoffmann, Jean Paul, even Caroline Schlegel, and most recently another minor author of the period, August Klingemann, but no one with persuasive proof.[1] The *Nachtwachen* remains one of the anonymous masterpieces of romantic literature. For a masterpiece it certainly is, a work of uncanny, disturbing, and profound poetry and significance, a collection of apocalyptic visions combined with gruesomely nihilistic reflections, serious and comic, moving and grotesquely absurdist at the same time.[2]

In using the word "collection" I do not mean to suggest that the work has no unity other than being an assemblage of parts. For it is a coherent whole, and it is a narrative of sorts, even though some critics have been unwilling to call it a novel. But looked at from the standpoint of the *romantic* conception of the novel, it is surely a novel, for it shows certain basic structural features that we have found in other romantic novels. It is circular in form, for at the end

[209]

of section 15 the narrator has arrived at that point in his life from which he started his narration at the beginning of section 1. The book is divided into fifteen sections, called "Night Watches" because the narrator is a night watchman or town crier, the vocal measurer of time. Appended is a "Hogarthian tailpiece" (section 16) which goes back further into the past, back to the narrator's birth. The time structure moves therefore from the present back into the recent past in various reflections and flashbacks, returns to the point from which it started, and then moves back to the distant past to "explain" the narrator's character and peculiarities. The fifteen sections of the "narrative" proper are arabesques but there is no central panel such as is provided by the "Lehrjahre der Männlichkeit" section of *Lucinde*. Rather what we have is variations on a theme that we are to hear in our minds, like the *Sphinxes* in Robert Schumann's *Carnaval* or the theme to be "read between the lines," but not played, in the second section of his Opus 20 *Humoresque*. The tailpiece is an absurdist afterword, set in a churchyard, the "suburban theater where death is the director and crazy poetic farces are performed as epilogues to the prose dramas performed in the Court and World Theater." The reference is to the distinction that prevailed, in Vienna actually, between the Burgtheater, which played a classical repertory, and the popular, suburban theaters, which performed less highfallutin, but sometimes more amusing and poetic spectacles. The tailpiece is itself such an epilogue, a commentary on what the fifteen night watches had presented, a reflection in a distorting mirror of what they are all about, of the unspoken theme. And this turns out to be "Nothing." The word echoes throughout the cemetery: worldly experience is ultimately the experience of nothingness. Nothing persists here below: but there is also nothing above in the beyond—except nothingness.

In the first section the narrator introduces himself as a poet turned night watchman in order to have something to live on. Being a night watchman is not without its own poetry. Thereby he has acquired distance and perspective toward those who sleep as though spellbound, like some solitary survivor of a general plague. As night wanderer he observes and reflects on human aspirations and disappointments; as a night-watchman he emphasizes the passing of time (night watchmen announced the hours on a horn) and the questionable nature of eternity. This is now the burden of his song. He interrupts a poet's dream of eternity by his stentorian reminder of transience and mutability, and eavesdrops on a freethinker's dying refusal to accept the idea of eternity proclaimed by a priest in the aspect of a devil. The second section moves firmly into the grotesque mode, as the watchman joins three devilish spirits around the bier of the freethinker, who dismember the corpse, carry off the rump, and leave a devil's mask beside the severed head. Our narrator has described himself in this section as a "humorist," as having become this in a world of excessive rationalism and diminished poetic frenzy. There is no longer any place in poetry for his madness, he says. So he "goes around" poetry, as a humorist.[3] His humor, as we see, is a crazed humor, with a taste for devilishness and an uncertainty as to what the devil really is. For the devilish spirits of this second section are in fact priests in disguise, who cross themselves and cry, "God be with us!" when he asserts that he is one of them, and threaten him in a clerical, excommunicating tone if he persists in interfering with their work. He desists, and as a result has only scattered information on the legal battles that ensued as to whether the severed head was the devil's or not. For, as he says in the next section, he had so far only believed in a "poetic devil," whereas nowadays the devil has become humanized and has lost his absolute quality.[4]

Reflecting thus, the narrator becomes witness to a strange rendezvous between a wife and her lover, with the husband asleep in bed, which the watchman interrupts by blowing on his horn and then indulges in a satirical legal discussion with the husband on what punishment should be meted out. He emphasizes that his profession of watchman allows him to do good in this and similar ways (preventing break-ins and so forth). But the episode is terminated by his return to his rounds, so that neither we nor the narrator know how it ended. The husband is a lawyer, and probably a magistrate, for when the watchman arrives (ahead of the wife) at his house he is sitting over piles of documents, mechanically signing death warrants. When his wife comes in he tells her he has done this because it is her birthday and she is so fond of tragedies. The watchman, mistaken for a statue by the lovers when they arranged the rendezvous, now assumes the same posture by mounting a pedestal intended for a statue of justice commissioned by the husband but not yet delivered. The scene develops into a parody of the final scene of *Don Giovanni* with the watchman as admonitory "stone guest." So the devil presides over this section too.

The fourth section is retrospective. The narrator looks at the book of his life, which has woodcuts. One of these depicts preparations for the raising of buried treasure by a shoemaker turning to alchemy

and a gypsy woman; a second woodcut shows the lifting of the treasure chest, inside which the narrator sees himself; and a third shows
the narrator sitting on a book by Hans Sachs and reading one by
Jakob Böhme (both were shoemakers and poets), with a commentary
by his own adopted father on the child's strange talk about conversation between stars, and the language of flowers and stones. Jeffrey
L. Sammons has suggested, rightly I think, that Sachs and Böhme
here "represent the world of clearly defined values and deep religious receptivity which has been left behind by the watchman . . .
aspects of the childhood paradise which is irretrievably lost," and
that the child's conversation implies that hopes placed in direct contact with nature also belong to this lost paradise.[5] The watchman is
interrupted in this reading of the book of his life, which takes place
in a church, by the sight of a strange sinister-looking figure apparently about to stab himself, his arm transfixed as midnight strikes,
and the dagger clattering to the floor as he laments that he can
never make the fatal final thrust. Attracted by the tragicomic nature
of the situation, Kreuzgang (our narrator) asks him about his life, so
as to have a good laugh. The man casts his life story in the form of a
marionette play about two brothers without hearts, both in love with
Columbine. One acquires a heart and returns from a journey to find
Columbine and the other brother already married. The *Hanswurst*,
the traditional fool-commentator of popular German drama of the
sixteenth century, tries to persuade the brother with the acquired
heart that we are all manipulated marionettes, and the brother in
turn tries to persuade Columbine that the Director has mixed up the
puppets and that *he* should have married her. But she refuses to
believe him, out of moral feeling and respect for the "Director."
Then the other brother, for no apparent reason but after delivery of
a "short, stiff tirade," stabs Columbine, her page, and himself, and
the brother with the heart tries to kill himself but the wire breaks,
because the Director pulls it too firmly; he fails in his attempt, and
an alien voice declares through his mouth that he will live forever.
Finally the *Hanswurst* denies free will and declares that it was all a
farce in which he was the only sensible character because he alone
took it for a farce and nothing more. The man now tells Kreuzgang
that he has always been trying to "jump out of the play and escape
the Director."[6] But the Director won't let him. He is an actor in the
Italian Comedy, has tried to die several times, tried to destroy time,
only to be always haunted by the threat of eternity.

In the fifth section the story is retold in clear normal prose, without the theological allegory and the satirical thrusts at Fichte's views on free will and the *Ding an sich*. It is a typical Spanish tale of two noblemen, Don Juan (the one who acquires a heart) and Don Ponce, brothers and rivals in their love for Donna [*sic*] Ines. The events of the story are the same as those of the puppet play, but the motivation is more explicit: it is because Juan tells Ponce that Ines, his wife, is unfaithful (whereas she has in fact repelled Juan's advances) that the triple murder takes place. At the end Juan stands "dumb and mad among the dead." The actor of the previous section is also mad.

Various critics, notably Sammons and Gerald Gillespie, have drawn attention to the irony of this double narration, pointing out that the seemingly logical motivation of the second narration is less convincing than the "savage mechanical farce" (Gillespie) of the first, its psychology affording merely a "superficial explanation for an action that is in actual fact wooden, cold, and not subject to free will, that emotions are not real but simply painted on and built in, and that the director of life (i.e., God) is an incompetent fumbler" (Sammons).[7] Technically the sequence is interesting as a pair of narrative variations or arabesques, puppets and men, a grotesque followed by normality. The two conflict and, in a way, undercut each other, as do the fantastic and the realistic sequences of the whole book. As a result the end of both these "tales" is a state of perplexity and a dislocation of rationality. Take it this way—or that—the book seems to be saying, and what Sammons calls the "cyclical structure" of the book and what Gillespie calls the "jaggedness" combined with the pretense of continuity, suggest that the whole structure is a conscious fusion of the logical and the illogical. The question is: which is the ultimate predominant view of life contained in the *Nachtwachen*? Or is the tension purposely left unresolved?

The sixth section begins with a confession by the narrator:

> In the years of my youth—and, as it were, in the bud—I was spoiled, for whereas other educated boys and promising youths make it their business to become ever more intelligent and sensible, I for my part always had a special preference for madness and sought to achieve a complete confusion within myself, so that, like the Lord God himself, I could build a complete and thorough chaos from which some time later, if I so desired, a tolerable world might be put together.

The argument for confusion is therefore that it can produce order, and a willed order ("if I so desired"). Confusion does not negate the idea of there being a God, for this narrator. Indeed the implication is surely that there is a God, a "Director." What went wrong, according to our watchman, was that mankind started, off its own bat, putting things in order too soon, so that nothing is in its right place and our world is botched and ripe for the scrap heap. This had become an *idée fixe* with him. He had often speculated on the Last Judgment and one day, instead of proclaiming time, he had announced the imminence of eternity, which caused general consternation—and frantic attempts by many to better their prospects by repairing past faults. In a parodic sermon to his fellowmen he asserts that the whole course of human history since Adam had achieved nothing, that they, his listeners, are not good enough for Heaven and too boring for Hell. Admitting his apocalyptic joke, he then suggested that it might be good to have periodic such reckonings and to start out right away improving the state. But his suggestion was rejected as impractical. So from now on he became a silent watchman, forbidden to *announce* time, and was considered a fool, or mad.

Having now "arrived at his madnesses,"[8] he recapitulates in the seventh night watch various incidents from his past life, beginning with a portrait of himself as "one of the graces, a monkey, and the devil" according to the angle that it is viewed from. Maybe he was the offspring of the devil and a "just canonized" nun. Full of contradictions, he sees everywhere materials to build madhouses. He then gives us samples of his writings: a funeral oration on life as gradual disintegration until we reach a second burial, and a satirical speech by a donkey on why there have to be donkeys. When his foster-father the shoemaker died, he had become a ballad singer with a specialty in murders. Legal actions were brought against him when he began to sing about the "lesser" murders of honor, love, truth, justice, and reason. He acted as his own defense (or, as he says, as his "own *advocatus diaboli*"), but when he questioned the competence of his judges he was committed to the madhouse.

In the eighth section we return to the poet of the first section, for poets too are basically idealists in conflict with reality. This poet had been writing a tragedy in which Love, Hate, Time, and Eternity were to appear as "lofty, mysterious figures." The Greeks had used the chorus to draw attention away from the horrors of the action into a realm of considered reflection. This poet uses the *Hanswurst* for the same purpose. The tragedy is rejected by the publisher, and the poet hangs himself with the string that was tied around the returned package. In a speech to the dead poet the watchman contrasts the poet's present distorted expression with the happy face on his portrait as a child, which is hanging in the room. He then reads the poet's farewell to life, which ends with these words: "I leave behind me nothing and defiantly stride toward you, o God, or Nothing."[90] O god, or Nothing—this is the basic question posed by the *Nachtwachen*. The watchman also gives us part of the prologue to the tragedy, to be spoken by the *Hanswurst*. Its subject is man's affinity with the apes. Man is a comic beast [*spasshafte Bestie*], and however seriously he struts on the stage of life, offstage he sheds his trappings and waits for the next role that the "Director" assigns to him. The prologue culminates in this impressive passage:

> The death's head is always there behind the smiling mask, and life is only the fool's cloak of bells [*Schellenkleid*] donned by Nothingness to tinkle until the time when its wearer tears it to pieces and hurls it away. Everything is Nothing, choking itself up and choking it down again, artful shadow-boxing to pretend that there really is Something, for if the choking should ever pause, then the Nothingness would appear in frightening clarity. Fools call such a pause "eternity," but it is really true Nothingness, absolute Death in contrast to the progressive dying by which Life arises.[10]

If one took this seriously, says the *Hanswurst*, one would be in the madhouse. He intends it merely as a counterblast to the idealism of the poet's tragedy. But we as readers do take it seriously, this combination of baroque *vanitas vanitatum* and existentialist perplexity. For this Fool is no fool, and for all his talk about consciously confusing the characters so that they do not know what they are and tend to think that they are more than they are, his is a philosophic madness, a madness North-North-West. So is the narrator's. And the image with which the next section begins, that of the various layers of an onion as the protective layers with which human beings envelop themselves, if thought through to its logical conclusion (as it was by Ibsen in *Peer Gynt*), means that when the layers are stripped off, nothing remains. "True Nothingness, absolute Death in contrast to the progressive dying by which Life arises" [*das eigentliche Nichts und der absolute Tod, da das Leben im Gegenteile nur durch ein fortlaufendes Sterben entsteht*]—life as progressive dying, as death-in-life preparatory to absolute Death, or extinction, or nothingness—with this Absolute or Eternity as what we die to and into and therefore a goal, an ultimate, unitary "Death" in which we overcome, absolve ourselves from, death-in-life—are we not here in the presence of a reformulation of the basic tenet of romantic philosophy, Schelling's "nondifferentiation," Novalis's "Immer nach Hause"? Is this then really an expression of nihilism? Surely not—no more than Jean Paul's speech of the dead Christ. And so behind this strange and seemingly negative book there is a belief in an Absolute—called Nothingness. But this Nothingness is the chaos from which all creation proceeded and to which all returns. Richard Brinkmann is certainly right when he says that the *Nachtwachen* is no less a romantic book than *Heinrich von Ofterdingen* for both show the way to the Absolute, though here by annihilation (in Novalis by transcendence) of the temporal.[11]

The ninth section takes place in the madhouse to which the watchman has been committed. Various types of madmen, each laboring under an *idée fixe*, are presented, but the narrator concentrates on Number Nine, who believes he is the creator of the world and gives a speech lamenting the way man has misused what was godlike in him to the extent of thinking himself a god, so that God doesn't know what to do with him, for man respects God only as someone as bright as himself. The narrator's own form of madness is that he finds all sense absurd and vice versa, thinks he is more rational than reason as deduced in philosophical systems, and wiser than all wisdom that is being taught. What then, he asks the doctor, is the cure? Who is to decide whether these people in the "madhouse" are wrong or the professors in lecture rooms? The doctor's prescription is: little or no thinking. We are close to the world of *Wozzeck* and *Marat-Sade*.

The tenth night watch describes a winter night with everything frozen and overshadowed by death-in-life. Three arabesques follow. First the sight of a beggar fighting against sleep and being frozen to death; then the tale of a youth who abandons one girl for another, a white rose for a red rose. The white rose dies and the red rose withers away at the thought of the white rose's bridal bed being her deathbed. Third we have the tale of a nun buried alive for having given birth to a child which the narrator hands over to a cloaked figure standing outside, the father. In the middle of this third arabesque there is a remarkable passage in which all the emotions of life flit past the narrator as distorted masks that he tries in vain to grasp and look beneath. But does he want to? What would he find? For when the mask drops, there is only the naked ego alone with itself, and how will it pass the time? The imagery of masks, of life as masquerade covering emptiness, constantly beneath the surface of all the previous sections, here comes right into the forefront of attention.

The eleventh section communicates a fragment from the life of the cloaked figure, the father of the previous chapter. Born blind, he had regained his sight, but then lost his beloved, an orphan ward of his mother, whom she had promised to the Church should he ever be cured of his blindness. So he longs for night again. The twelfth night watch is set appropriately on Twelfth Night, and deals with two more variations on the theme of masking: first the humorous speech of a poet seeking immortality by assuming personal paraphernalia of great authors (Kant's shoes, Lessing's wig, Goethe's hat), and second an encounter with a man apparently trying to shoot himself but actually rehearsing a part he is to play in the theater. The narrator, disillusioned and discomfited, for he has been expansively declaring to the seeming suicide the superiority of the certainties of this world over the uncertainties of the next, lapses back into his usual mood: "O false world, in which nothing any more is genuine, not even [this man's] hair, you empty absurd playground of fools and masks, is it then impossible to lift oneself up to some enthusiasm or other in you!"[12]

He tries again in the next section, with a "dithyramb on spring" and all the usual clichés come rolling out, until he gets to mankind, which stands there with nothing but the echoes of its own questionings. Tired of the "museum of nature," he turns to the temple of art where he observes a dilettante kissing the arse (as being artistically the best part) of the Medici Venus. The gods are all torsos in this "enlightened" age and should be buried again, the narrator exclaims. The torsos seem to come alive at his philippic, but then lapse again into silence while a chorus of furies stands watching ominously in the background.

In the fourteenth section we return to the madhouse, as the narrator comments on the twisted thread of his narration and promises now to "hatch out the nightingale's egg of his love."[13] Once he was playing Hamlet (to have the opportunity to vent his gall at the silent spectators) when the actress playing Ophelia went really mad and was carried off to the madhouse. Now he has encountered her in this madhouse, where she occupies the cell next to his. Deeply moved, he begins to write poetry, trying to work off the amorous emotion arising within him. Then he turns to writing letters to this Ophelia, confessing that he loves her and hoping for a like response from her. She confesses that she is unable to distinguish between truth and play. "Help me to read back through my role till I get to myself. . . . Bring me once more to my Ego and I will ask it if it loves you."[14]

He replies that everything is role-playing, and when this ceases there is nothing but a naked skeleton that grins at the other actors still performing. The Ego she seeks would be just such a naked skeleton. When he had pronounced Hamlet's words "To be or not to be," he had not really considered what "to be" meant. He had feared death because of the possibility of eternity which would be "a second boring *comédie larmoyante*,"[15] the first being life itself. So he suggests that they stop brooding, indulge in love as the farce that it is, and propagate so that others may play *their* roles after he and she are gone, extend the boredom until one last actor tears up his part so as no longer to have to play to an invisible public. But she insists on playing her role through to the end, to find out whether anything further exists. The night is stormy and Kreuzgang dreams he is encompassed by "the great terrible Ego" continually destroying itself and then being reborn, an endless cycle of monotony, Fichtean monotony. The Ego that he fears is the absolute Ego; that which she seeks is the personal, finite Ego. There is no confusion, but there is a distinction. She believes she was an Ego before she started playing roles, and to this she hopes to find her way back, whereas he believes there is nothing but roles until these are abandoned through absorption into the absolute Ego, which is the only true Ego and the negation of finiteness in infinite nothingness.

Kreuzgang wakes from his dream to hear Ophelia singing her songs, crouched over a stillborn child. So there *is* death without eternity, he thinks; but she tells him that what has died is her role, there is still the Ego "behind the play." Telling him now that she does love him, she dies. He is about to burst into wild laughter at the absurdity of it all, but tears well up, and looking around he sees the madmen standing silently around the corpse, and fear invades him.

Because he had attempted to propagate madmen, he is expelled from the madhouse and returns unwillingly to the world of "the sane ones." In the final (fifteenth) section he defends the satiric mask as the devil's revenge on the Creator. He is then engaged by the Director of a puppet theater to replace the *Hanswurst,* who had died of laughing. When the theater is dissolved by the town authorities because of "revolutionary tendencies," he takes a sad farewell from his role as *Hanswurst,* the "only person he had really loved besides Ophelia,"[16] and becomes a night watchman.

With that, the narrative proper is really at an end, but the "Hogarthian tailpiece" tells of his birth with the devil presiding. This "explains" his hatred of the world and his obsession with corruption (illustrated graphically as he walks through the churchyard). Once again he is Hamlet, but this time Hamlet addressing Yorick. This modern-day Hamlet, this nihilist with a positive view of the *nihil*, determines not to love, and to laugh "when the giant hand crushes him," as the giant hand of Shakespeare had seized "Ophelia." Everything falls into dust, nothing remains—not even the corpse of his alchemist father, which still has the same expression on its face as when he conjured up the devil long years ago, and has been preserved from decay by having its hands folded in prayer by well-meaning persons of some kind. But what is he praying for? What to? Whom or what should or could he pray to? Urging the corpse to join with him in defying "Heaven," Kreuzgang unclasps the hands, whereupon the corpse dissolves into dust. This nightmare phantasmagoria is more than a tailpiece; it is an allegorical commentary on the whole, an epilogue in the form of a baroque emblem. To put it last, rather than first, was one of the several strokes of genius in the structuring of this remarkable book. The title of this final section is taken from that of Hogarth's last engraving: *Tail-Piece. Finis or the End of the World,* the emblematic apotheosis and apocalypse of that transformation of the sublime into the ridiculous which is satire.[17] Kreuzgang tells us that the account of his birth is "the key to himself"—but "a dangerous psychological key." It is an explanation *propter hoc* and no more an explanation that the Spanish tale was of the puppet play. It is ironic in the best traditions of romanticism: if you want to know why I think as I do, well, here is the best explanation I could possibly give you. A true tailpiece.

The charge of formlessness has been brought against the *Nacht-wachen* as with so many of the novels of the German Romantics. Critics have debated whether it is structured at all, or if so, what this structure is. Is it merely a collection in which the parts are interchangeable? Pointing to the fact that there is no real development in the action (despite the biographical fiction) and no causal necessity between the parts, Dorothee Sölle-Nipperdey adduces only an additive structure without any central focus. Brinkmann speaks of a conscious dissolution of the fixed and ordered. Sammons perceives a cyclical structure of satire—catastrophe, nihilism and despair, bitter comedy—which is repeated five times. He does therefore see order of a sort where Sölle-Nipperdey does not, but claims that this cyclical pattern is "an artificial superstructure imposed upon the material . . . the result of an abstraction, in the aesthetic sense, from a given reality."[18] Some critics have questioned whether it is a novel at all, most interestingly Rita Terras, who thinks it is a book of satires modeled on the sixteen satires of Juvenal. Behind all these interpretations there is a model of coherent form from which the *Nachtwachen* is shown to depart. If, however, one does not proceed from a preconceived model of what a novel is usually supposed to be, but instead from what the Romantics wanted it to be, then the form becomes comprehensible, is organic (in August Wilhelm Schlegel's sense of that term), and is eminently romantic. Wolfgang Paulsen is on the right track, I believe, when he refers to the notion of the arabesque, and in this connection, specifically to *Lucinde*. And I believe one can go further in this direction.

Lucinde, as we saw, has a chronologically narrated centerpiece flanked by two sets of arabesques, six before and six after. The *Nachtwachen* has, in the sequence about "Hamlet" and "Ophelia," a central section, more or less chronologically narrated and, like the central section of *Lucinde*, "confessional" in Friedrich Schlegel's sense of that word. Add to this that the *Nachtwachen* as a whole consists of a tension between what purports to be a chronological biographical account and dislocation of this by discrete separate sections that are not chronologically arranged. So in the total structure as well, the confessional is balanced against the arabesques. The difference from *Lucinde* is that whereas in Schlegel's novel the confessional-chronological narration comes in the middle (seventh) section, in the *Nachtwachen* this is the penultimate, fourteenth section, if we count the sixteenth as an epilogue. But the fourteenth section (in the madhouse) is clearly prefigured by the ninth (the madmen in the madhouse). The structure of the *Nachtwachen* is therefore more of a "geometrical" progression (in Novalis's sense) than *Lucinde*—and certainly not merely arithmetical or additive. In fact it combines Novalis's prescription with Schlegel's—combining confessional and arabesque in a geometrical progression.

CHAPTER TEN

The Divided Self: Hoffmann

ERNST THEODOR WILHELM HOFFMANN (1776–1822), the greatest
teller of tales among the German Romantics, wrote mostly novellas,
and a great number of these. He was also a trained musician, and
apparently an excellent one, who wrote not only music, including
several operas, but also musical criticism of great interest, including
several essays on Beethoven. In respect for Mozart he replaced the
"Wilhelm" of his name by "Amadeus," and is therefore known as
E. T. A. Hoffmann. Almost all of his literary work was published in
the eight years between 1814 and his death, and it was to have immense influence on the literature of the world. He became the un-
disputed master of the uncanny, and it was to a story by Hoffmann
that Freud turned to illustrate his conception of the sources of the
uncanny. But Hoffmann is not just spookery: he was a master of
characterization, had a strong sardonic sense of humor, a taste for
the grotesque, a love of irony, and the power to evoke the shapes
and colors of real places and every hour of day or night, both in the
present or the past. It is the grounding of his fantasies in reality that
makes his presentation of the all-encompassing mysteries of life, like
that of Franz Kafka, so compelling. He was an absolute master of the
form of the novella, and it is through his novellas that he is best
known. But he did also write two remarkable novels, *Die Elixiere des
Teufels* [The Devil's Elixirs] (1815–1816), and *Lebens-Ansichten des
Katers Murr* [Life and Opinions of the Tom Cat Murr] (1820–1822).[1]
Despite the structural interest of his own two novels Hoffmann

never articulated a concept of the genre that might distinguish it from the novella of which he was such a masterly practitioner. And indeed it is sometimes not easy to draw the dividing line between those two genres with Hoffmann. Neither the *Elixiere* nor *Murr* is described on the title page as a novel, but elsewhere Hoffmann referred to them as novels. *Prinzessin Brambilla* and *Meister Floh* [Master Flea] might be considered by some critics to be novels of a sort, though Hoffmann himself called the former a capriccio and the latter a *Märchen*. Both of these designations refer partly to structure, though also to tone, and, to a certain extent, to content. *Klein Zaches* is a *Märchen* and Hoffmann categorized it as "the loose execution of a jocular idea,"[2] that is to say of *one* idea—which would put it in the domain of the novella. *Meister Floh* is more expansive, extensive, and complex in structure, and is subtitled "A *Märchen* in Seven Adventures." The concept of a narrative structure consisting of several adventures can also be applied to *Prinzessin Brambilla,* where the reader is explicitly charged to visualize the caricaturish engravings of Callot which are its basis, and to think of what a musician might demand of a capriccio.[3] The first of these remarks brings this work into relationship with Hoffmann's first major publication, the *Fantasiestücke in Callots Manier* [Fantasy Pieces in Callot's Manner] which could, if we think in musical terms, be conceived as a romantic fantasia. But there is a difference, for whereas the *Fantasiestücke* are a loosely connected series of stories and dialogues embodying various moods and preoccupations, *Prinzessin Brambilla* is a continuous narrative unified in mood and concerned with the same characters, who appear either in masks or not in masks according to the situation, which makes for interesting convolutions of the plot and gives the work both its tantalizing unity and deeply serious playfulness—a carnival of life. Like life, it is consciously unfinished, ending with the statement that only Master Callot himself could tell us what happened after the point that the author has chosen to lay down his pen. *Meister Floh* ends similarly with the statement that here is where we stop because there are no more documents. This is of course a fictive device to simulate reality. But it is also an admission of incompleteness which is at the same time a justification of incompleteness. *Murr* is similarly unfinished, but one could justifiably say that it is unfinishable or doesn't need to be finished. Much the same could be said for *Flegeljahre* and for *Hyperion;* and we recall what Dorothea Schlegel said about *Florentin.* Nevertheless it seems to me clear that *Murr* and *Flegeljahre* and *Hyperion* and *Florentin*—and we

E. T. A. Hoffmann. Drawing by Wilhelm Hensel, 1821. Original in Nationalgalerie, Berlin.

can add *Lucinde*—are novels in a sense that *Prinzessin Brambilla* and *Meister Floh* are not, because these latter are extrapolations of one single idea.

Of his published works, then, only the *Elixiere* and *Murr* were referred to by Hoffmann, though not on the title pages, as novels. He did, however, write, or begin to write, or just project, various other novels, about which we have only very sparse information. The earliest of these was entitled *Cornaro, Memoiren des Grafen Julius von S.* [Cornaro: Memoirs of Count Julius von S.], which he was writing in 1795, when he was in his nineteenth year. He sent the first part of it to his close friend Theodor Gottlieb von Hippel in April 1795, asking for criticism, which he apparently received, though Hippel's reply is not preserved. In the summer of 1796 he despatched the manuscript to a publisher, who rejected it. The manuscript has not survived, but in the letter to Hippel, Hoffmann spoke of the novel having two parts, and stated rather cryptically: "You will see that I preserve more or less the course of a certain story."[4] What story? And what was its shape? It could be that this refers to that famous horror-novel of the time, Grosse's *Der Genius*, because two months earlier Hoffmann had told Hippel how strongly that novel had affected him and that the passions aroused by its ending had mentally exhausted him.[5] We know from Tieck's letters to Wackenroder that the book had had a similar effect on the highly impressionable Tieck.[6] Hoffmann had also specifically mentioned the ecstatic portrayal of male friendship in Grosse's novel and how deeply moved he was by this in the light of Hippel's impending departure for another city. Be that as it may, the only other information about *Cornaro* that he gave in that letter, was to state that "the hubbub [*das Lärm*] in the first section is not without cause, but it will not be explained until the second part," which suggests the confusion with which *Murr* opens. A subsequent letter to Hippel asserted that the title *Cornaro* would also be explained in the second part, for which the first was all preparatory, which was perhaps, he suggested, why the whole seemed to him, Hoffmann, "somewhat motley" [*ein bischen buntschäckigt*][7] We have some evidence that, before the manuscript of *Cornaro* was rejected, Hoffmann had begun another novel. In October 1796 he told Hippel that he was sending him a book he was writing which would be "more jolly and witty" [*jovialischer und witziger*] than he himself was.[8] Earlier that year, in fact in March, he had quoted in a letter, also to Hippel, a long passage on friendship "from the novel I am now working on in my leisure hours and mostly on Sundays," entitled *Der Geheimnisvolle* [The Mystery Man].[9] Unfortunately the passage, which is a conventional eighteenth-century praise of male friendship, tells us nothing about what sort of novel this was to be, except to suggest that Grosse's praise of such friendship was still very much in his mind. There is no record that *Der Geheimnisvolle* was ever finished, and neither the manuscript of it, nor that of *Cornaro*, has survived.

Grosse's *Der Genius* had appeared in four volumes between 1791 and 1795. It was translated into English under the title *Horrid Mysteries* by the Reverend Peter Will, Lutheran minister of the German Chapel in the Savoy, in 1796, and was apparently widely read as part of the stock of "German Romances" in England, being explicitly mentioned by Jane Austen and Thomas Love Peacock.[10] Central to the book are the operations of a secret society identified by the translator with the Illuminati of Bavaria, a sect of Rosicrucian origins. The action of the novel recounts how various characters are brought into contact with this secret society which, under the guise of providing higher powers and communicating higher truths, is really concerned with extending its own power over public life and indulging the vengeful, sadistic passions of its members by elaborate rituals and machinations of delusive supernaturalism. The plot-line is full of startling twists and turns: disappearances, reappearances of the believed dead, "spirit presences," the sudden wilting away of a wife in her husband's arms, a girl hurled down a flight of stone steps to her apparent doom. The narrative structure consists of a series of intercalated life stories that break off or resume to keep the reader in continuous, attractive suspense. One such account begins with the sentence: "I awoke, at length, from that long swoon, and found myself stretched out in a coffin." There are also several scenes of what one critic has called "enraptured fleshliness."[11] In short: it has everything to keep one up nights. Tieck was frightened by it because he saw in it a mirror of his own youthful febrile imagination in which everything around him turned into horrors—the imaginative world of his own *William Lovell*. Basic to the novel is the theme of the friendship between two men, both of whom contribute by their life stories to the establishment of the prevailing mood of being constantly endangered—life-stories which intimate that the two of them are somehow more closely connected with each other than they had known—partial revelations which lead first to a straining of the friendship but then, as more and more comes to light, to an unmasking of the "powers" that have duped them and to the establishment of a lasting harmonious relationship between them. It would seem to be this that appealed particularly to Hoffmann, as did the gradual dispelling of "mysteries," the rejection of any sense of man being directed against his will by "secret" forces outside his control, and the return ultimately to a firm trust in responsibility for one's own fate and in one's power to direct it.

What else do we know about Hoffmann's taste in novels at this time? Not much. We know from later statements that he admired Schiller's unfinished but masterly story *Der Geisterseher* [The Spirit Seer], which, although on an infinitely higher plane than Grosse's novel, was not so different from it in mood. We know also that Hoffmann was acquainted with the work of Jean Paul, Sterne, Smollett, and Swift.[12] Quite early on, somewhere between 1796 and 1798, Hoffmann wrote a humorous sketch parodying both Jean Paul and Sterne. There are frequent references in his stories to these two novelists, but neither was a lasting influence on his structural patterns, although he retained his affection for Jean Paul up to and including the latter's last novel *Der Komet*.[13] German romanticism began to affect Hoffmann about the time of the Battle of Jena, when he was living in Warsaw. By 1815, the year that the complete *Fantasiestücke* and first part of the *Elixiere* were published, his reputation as an author was firmly established, and works flowed in rapid succession from his pen until his death in 1822. It is difficult therefore to speak of successive phases in his attitude to novels and novelists.

In February 1818 he planned a novel to be entitled *Die Meister des Gesanges* [The Masters of Song], with the subtitle "A Novel for Friends of Music," but wrote nothing of it.[14] A novel about musicians was a promising venture for Hoffmann, who of course had firsthand knowledge of German musical life. At one point in his writings he refers disparagingly to the treatment of music in Wilhelm Heinse's novel *Hildegard von Hohenthal* (1795) as being excessively dry.[15] Hoffmann himself could write so vividly about music and its effects, as we see in the sections of his writings dealing with the musician that he called Kreisler and in his own essays on Beethoven and other composers, that one regrets he did not execute this plan for a novel, which would surely have been far from dry, nor the projected third part of *Murr*, announced as "Bright Hours of a Mad Musician," to contain reflections on art, structured like a similar section in the *Fantasiestücke*. At the time of his death Hoffmann was supposed to have been working on still another novel, this one with the somewhat Jean-Paulesque title "Jacob Quickpepper's Honeymoon before

Marriage" [*Jakobus Schnellpfeffers Flitterwochen vor der Hochzeit*], to which there are several references.[16] But of this equally attractive-sounding plan nothing is preserved—if indeed any of it was ever written.

What then did Hoffmann have to say about other novels, and to what extent can we deduce from his comments an opinion on what a novel should be? Leaving aside occasional references to incidents in Rabelais, Cervantes, Lesage, *Jacques le fataliste*, Rousseau's *Confessions* and Mme. de Staël's *Corinne*, we find, as we would expect, that he was drawn toward those novelists who exploit fantasy and the super-natural, as for example his friend the minor romantic novelist Fouqué, in his novel *Der Zauberring* [The Magic Ring], which has a char-acter who encounters his seeming double and fears he is going mad (though everything is cleared up in the end, as in *Die Elixiere des Teufels,* which was to be published soon after).[17] Hoffmann seems to have been most impressed by those novelists who combined this supernatural streak with careful realism of background. Hence he repeatedly refers with approval to *Wilhelm Meisters Lehrjahre* and to Schiller's *Der Geisterseher.*[18] When *Prinzessin Brambilla* appeared in 1821, Hoffmann's friend Hitzig considered it a work of "haziness and mistiness, full of empty shadows in a space without ground or back-ground," and recommended that he should read Scott's *Guy Manner-ing.*[19] The point was to show the ailing Hoffmann what, in Hitzig's opinion, the public really wanted, and to indicate to him by contrast what was "wrong" with *Brambilla*. Hoffmann did read Scott's novel and declared it excellent, praising specifically its "vigorous vitality and powerful truth within great simplicity." But he continued: "And yet this spirit is far removed from me and I would do ill to manufac-ture such calm [*Ruhe*], for at the moment no such calm is given me."[20] He then went on to say that what he was and could be, would be shown by *Murr* and, God willing, by *Jakobus Schnellpfeffer*. So Hoff-mann, like Goethe, gave credit to Scott—but went his own way. One may well wonder why Hitzig recommended *Guy Mannering* rather than others of Scott's novels. This was the first of Scott's novels to be translated into German, under the title *Der Astrolog* (taking up the English subtitle). But by 1821, when Hitzig made his recommenda-tion, other novels by Scott were available in German,[21] and we have evidence that during these last months of his life Hoffmann asked to see some others (in particular *The Heart of Midlothian, The Antiquary,* and *Ivanhoe*), though he never said anything about them.[22] This in-creased curiosity about Scott's work may well have been stimulated by his own turning more frequently to historical subjects in his last years. When speaking of Scott's "calm," Hoffmann was probably referring to his artistic sovereignty vis-à-vis his subject matter. But Hitzig was making a definite point in urging *Guy Mannering* on Hoffmann. For although the astrological motif announced in its opening chapters is more of a framework than an essential element in the narrative structure, the supernatural plays a considerable part in the novel, though always as mystery arising out of realistically depicted settings and situations.

In the last volume of Hoffmann's great collection of stories entitled *Die Serapionsbrüder* [The Serapion Brothers] there is an interesting conversation about Scott between four of the framework characters.[23] This volume was published at Easter 1821, a few months after Hoffmann had been reading *Guy Mannering*. Two of the characters are discussing a story that has just been told by one of the company and praising its firm grounding in history. This is then contrasted with those works where the author's mind floats in a vacuum, with no solid foundation. Use of historical customs, manners, and traditions will give such a foundation, impart "a special color of life" [*eine besondere Lebensfarbe*] but only if there be a "skillful" use of such material, for the "rendering of historical truth, of reality, in a work whose events are entirely of the imagination [*Fantasie*]" demands a particular type of skill, without which all that will be produced is "a lusterless, cockeyed pseudo-life" [*ein mattes schielendes Scheinleben*]. Scott possessed this special skill. A third speaker declares that the exposition of *Guy Mannering* is based on Scottish manners and traditions, but one does not have to be well versed in these to follow the unfolding of the story, because the portrayal is so vivid that the characters emerge, in a few sharp strokes, from the frame of the picture. A fourth speaker adds that the methodical progression of the action is like the steady unraveling of a tangled skein, the firmly held thread of which never breaks in the author's hands. But the female characters are flat and pallid, except for the "sublimely gruesome gypsy who is more of a ghostly appearance than a woman." The reference is of course to Meg Merrilies, certainly one of Scott's greatest creations, a vagrant with the gift of prophecy, half woman and half spirit, intensely real but at the same time surrounded with mystery. There is indeed nothing like her in the *Prinzessin Brambilla*, the characters of which are based on those of the *commedia dell'arte*. But the settings are precisely located in the topography of Rome and the characters are in part real inhabitants

of that city and in part exotic fantasies, the whole point of the masterly construction being the interplay between these two worlds in
the carnival situation, so that one never quite knows what is real and
what is imagined. Hoffmann's artistic purpose here is to promote
this uncertainty in the reader by showing it in the characters. It is
indeed a capriccio, but a serious one, grounded in a reality as firm as
Scott's, and a reality that somehow promotes fantasy.

It was the combination of realism and fantasy that attracted Hoffmann to the engravings of Callot, and perhaps his most striking
quality as a narrative writer is this ability to demonstrate how the
supernatural emerges naturally from the real and everyday. Scott,
though in many ways so very different, had the same ability, which
may well account for Hoffmann's interest in *Guy Mannering.* And
probably for much the same reasons he was interested in Kleist's
novella *Das Bettelweib von Locarno* [The Beggar Woman of Locarno].
Hoffmann praises in this story the "marvelous coloration" and the
way that Kleist shows how one's fantasies can be aroused by very
simple means; "the horrifying exists often more in one's thoughts,"
he notes, "than in actual visible phenomena."[24] Similarly one of the
characters in the first version of *Die Serapionsbrüder* praises in Schiller's
Geisterseher and certain romantic narratives the way in which a higher
spiritual realm, part horrifying and part pleasing, is made to arise *inside* our own cramped, meager life and "surrounds us with the strange
sweet sorrow of distant premonitions."[25] The relation between reality
and fantasy can be seen as another form of that between "confessional" and "arabesque" which Friedrich Schlegel had talked about.
The work of Hoffmann has a clearly perceptible "confessional" element, but one that is always transformed by fantasy arabesques. This
is particularly evident in the Kreisler sections of *Murr,* for the figure
of Kreisler is an imaginative arabesque on Hoffmann himself. But so
is the cat. Hoffmann himself possessed such a cat, and August Klingemann, the author and theater director, reported that in November
1821 he was taken by the actor Ludwig Devrient to see Hoffmann,
who said he was very troubled about someone who was seriously ill.
On learning that the person in question was the cat, Klingemann
thought he had fallen a prey to Hoffmann's notorious sardonic humor. But Devrient assured him that this was a serious matter for
Hoffmann, because he had a sort of "magnetic rapport" with this cat
who had been elevated to a poetic character as Murr.[26] The origins of
the character of Murr were therefore not fantastic, but real. So too,
it would seem, was the highly unusual narrative structure of the

novel. For Hitzig reported that Hoffmann's cat was "strikingly beautiful" and "seemed to him [Hoffmann] to have more than usual animal intelligence," for it would "open the drawers of his desk with its paws *and settle itself on his papers.*"[27] The significance of this remark will only be apparent when we consider the structure of the novel later in this chapter.

In a letter of 24 March 1814, Hoffmann announced the completion of the first volume of *Die Elixiere des Teufels,* the theme of which was "nothing less than to trace in the tortuous and strange life of a man, over whose birth divine and demonic forces already presided, those mysterious connections of the human mind with all the higher principles latent in nature which flash forth on occasions, in flashes which we call 'Chance.' Expressed in musical terms the novel begins with a *grave sostenuto*—the hero is born in the cloister of the Holy Lime Tree in East Prussia, his birth being an expiation of his father's guilt—Joseph and the Christ Child appear to the aforesaid—then begins an *andante sostenuto e piano*—life in the cloister, his initiation—leaving the cloister he enters a world of manifold confusion—here begins an *allegro forte.*"[28] In a letter of September of the same year he said that the real "message" [*Tendenz*] of the work would not appear until the second volume.[29] The novel would seem therefore to have been planned with a structure similar to that of *Cornaro,* though we should remember that the idea of a confused and confusing first part to which the clue is given only in the second is a structural type that we have already encountered in various romantic novels, and may indeed be traced back to the *Trivialroman*—for instance to Grosse's *Der Genius.*

The *Elixiere des Teufels* can be read in various ways, each of which is legitimate and none of which completely excludes the others.[30] The suggestion, implicit in the passage quoted above, that the novel was to have a musical structure is not carried through, and the musical terms here used refer only to mood, not to structure. But there are in this passage valid clues to how the novel can be read. The reference to "divine and demonic forces" presiding over the hero's soul—a phrase that recalls Hoffmann's interpretation of Mozart's *Don Giovanni*—implies a morality-type structure akin to, say, the *Gräfin Dolores* (though "demonic" is too strong a word for what disturbs Dolores) or to a gothic novel like Matthew Lewis's *The Monk,* which was well known in Germany, and which the heroine of *Die Elixiere* is discovered reading at one point. This in turn, coupled with the reference to mysterious connections of the mind with "principles" of nature and the fact that this conflict was present at birth, prepares us for a plot-line on which transcendent forces will impinge, appearing as "Chance" and therefore curtailing human control. *Die Elixiere des Teufels* can therefore be read as a thriller full of violent and horrifying happenings, spiced with murder, rape, madness, and incest, and with a strong admixture of the mediated supernatural in characteristic romantic forms such as doubles, *déjà vus*, prophecies, and nightmares. There are no secret societies in it, but the constant sense of characters being manipulated by powers outside their control suggests the more sensational *Trivialromane*, such as *Der Genius*. Superimposed on this type of action is the elemental battle between divine and demonic forces as mediated in a particular life story. Hence the religious setting of the monastery, hence the fact that our hero is a monk, hence the climax of expiation. The thriller, therefore, combines with the morality play. But this novel has a third dimension namely the psychological. For Medardus, the hero, is not just the plaything of external forces. These forces are only able to "play" with him because of diverging tendencies within his own nature. Hence the reference to their presence at his birth. It is the psychological dimension that gives the novel its strength, and marks it off from ordinary shockers. To a considerable extent this dimension is also present in *The Monk*, though that work escapes into fantasy at the end. Hoffmann may have felt this, for his ending resolutely avoids fantasy. The whole novel is deeply rooted in the real world and the workings of the human spirit.

Let us now consider *Die Elixiere des Teufels* from these three different standpoints, beginning with what we have called the "morality" aspect. This is emphasized by the framework of the story, and by the narrative method. Medardus tells his own story, which is therefore a first-person narration. But the framework tells us that this "manuscript" was found after Medardus's death, and stresses the symbolic value of his story which is a testimony to the "secret thread that runs through our lives," any attempt to break which will necessarily result in disaster.[31] It is as an act of penance that Medardus writes it down. By reliving his life in narration he achieves redemption. The act of recapitulation is therefore therapeutic, and although the story is supposed to be written down in the same monastery from which he had set out on his life of turmoil and confusion, the structure is circular only in the sense of being, like *Hyperion*, an ascending spiral, for at the end Medardus has risen above what he was at the beginning. The pattern of the two novels is, however, somewhat different. For whereas *Hyperion* begins with divisiveness and ends with reconciliation (if only as an envisioned resolution to dichotomy), *Die Elixiere des Teufels* works outward from a primal unity, represented by childhood, diffracts into divisiveness, and then returns to unity—but to a higher unity. Medardus's narration is concerned with the various stages in this diffraction, and since his narration constitutes the bulk of the novel, this is essentially a novel about the divided self. As we have noted at various points, the Romantics often asserted that divisiveness was a necessary prerequisite for the attainment of higher unity. For Fichte it was even generated by the self. In Hoffmann's novel there is an added dimension, that of expiation for a father's guilt, the nature of which is not revealed until late in the book, by means of a manuscript about his family history which Medardus is given to read. This is part of his penitential exercises. The dark stirrings of his spirit now appear as being conditioned by heredity, and various ancestors appear as doubles of his self, except that he wins through to redemption whereas they did not. In this sense, but only in this sense, has he "expiated" the guilt of his ancestors. The old motif of a family curse has therefore been given an ethical and religious grounding. Only in that sense is there a conflict between divine and demonic forces. The forces are however not external, though the course of the narration makes them seem so at places. We should speak rather of proclivities, and the whole "fate motif" is best viewed symbolically, as a background mirroring of conflicting motions of the human spirit which Medardus experiences in all their intensity, and yet, unlike his "ancestors" and unlike Lewis's Monk, finally achieves peace.

Such is the moral purport of the book. I say "purport" rather than import, for the depiction of the divine forces is much less powerful than that of the "demonic"—and much less interesting, for Hoffmann knew as well as anybody that for most readers—and for most novelists—evil engages the attention more than good, especially when we can experience horrors vicariously. He therefore exploits to the full all the paraphernalia of the horror-novel, with the result that *Die Elixiere des Teufels* is undoubtedly the best thriller in German literature. All the horrors that haunted the imaginations of Tieck and Arnim are there—murders, rapes, ghosts, sinister appearances, doubles, *déjà vus*, revenants, prophetic dreams, chilling nightmares, visions of torture, auguries of disaster. But these are never fortuitous. They are always endowed with some deeper significance, and even when they are seemingly "explained away" by the time we reach the end of the novel, they remain meaningful as objectivations of what is going on in Medardus's mind. That he thinks he has murdered certain people, but actually hasn't, does not alter the fact that the desire to remove them was there—which leads me on to consider the third way of reading the novel, as a psychological study.

The most striking aspect of the novel read in this way is the use of doubles. Doubles in Jean Paul are usually hallucinations or manipulative tricks by others (including impersonations), though sometimes, especially when they appear in dreams or visions, they are the external appearances of inner anxieties. In Tieck's story *Der blonde Eckbert* doubles represent the repeated manifestation of some hostile force. In *Die Elixiere des Teufels* their function is somewhat different: they represent diffraction, not only of what seems to be some external force, but also of the self. The outstanding example of the former of these two uses of the double is the man in the purple cloak who is also a painter, and who as one or the other repeatedly appears to Medardus, always at important moments in his life. The most frightening of these appearances occurs when Medardus is jailed after having worked to conceal his true identity by fabricating a fictitious one. He dreams that he is trying to confess to a Dominican monk but cannot control his words, then learns he is to be tortured, tries to kill himself but fails, is then put on the rack, and awakes as he thinks his limbs are crumbling—and sees a real Dominican standing before him, who is the double of the painter. The monk now tells him that his various appearances were always to warn him, so this seeming demonic interloper was in fact a saving force, or at least was trying to be so. Diffraction of the self occurs when Medardus wittingly or unwittingly assumes another personality. This first occurs immediately after his departure from the monastery, when he comes upon a nobleman asleep on a ledge overhanging a deep gorge and about to fall over. In an attempt to prevent this from happening, Medardus wakes him, but this causes him to fall over the edge and, apparently, be killed. But when the noble's huntsman greets him as if he were the count himself (who was planning to go to a masquerade dressed as a monk) Medardus decides to "become" the count. This adventure must be viewed as a stroke of chance, if we read the novel solely as a tale of adventures; but it can also be interpreted psychologically. Count Viktorin is a worldly figure, and the exact physical resemblance between him and Medardus means that he is a worldly transmutation of the monk. When Medardus talks to the huntsman his voice seems not his own: "it was not I who spoke these words." For "Death had overtaken him [Viktorin] and some wondrous fate had put me in his place."[32] The assumption of the new personality seems to involve the destruction of Viktorin but in fact involves the displacement of Medardus, for Viktorin, as we learn later, is not dead. But for a time the monkish personality of Medardus is. He has now fully assumed his worldly aspect, which was always there as a tendency and had precipitated his leaving the monastery. New life proceeds from death. The divided personality rejects one part of itself in favor of the other. That the spiritual side is now abandoned for the sensual and that this involves what seems like murder and takes place on the edge of an abyss, marks the critical nature of this incident, which is no mere incident, and no chance occurrence but a profound psychological change.

Viktorin continues to haunt Medardus as a double. And there are others. At the castle to which as "Count Viktorin" he proceeds to go, he meets Hermogen, equally torn between the spiritual and the worldly, and obsessed by a sense of family crime that he must needs expiate. He recognizes Medardus in "Viktorin" and knows his reasons for wanting to leave the monastery. To rid himself of this disturbing double Medardus removes him in his thoughts and believes he kills him. Then later in the book another double appears in the person of a mad monk, so that the specter of madness is always before Medardus's mind. Madness is the extreme form of dislocation of the self, and the mad monk's life story disturbs Medardus by its many similarities to his own. His face presents a grotesque distortion of Medardus's own features. Medardus, Viktorin, Hermogen, and the mad monk are doubles, just as the painter, the man in the purple cloak and the Dominican monk are. A fictional device has been transformed into a representation of diffraction. When Medardus loses himself by the gorge, he loses control and the doubles crowd in on him, one after the other. And never leave him until he returns to the monastery.

That the external plot of *Die Elixiere des Teufels* is psychologically grounded and has nothing to do with chance is indicated by the nature of the elixirs referred to in the title and by the rationalization at the end. It is finally revealed that the murders Medardus believed he had perpetrated were in fact committed by others, and the physical similarities between the various doubles are "explained" by consanguinity through revelation of the family history, for almost everyone turns out to be related to everyone else. Such demystification is

Trivialroman technique, but it is used here to demonstrate that what seems like the incursion of irrational outside forces beyond man's control is in fact rationally accountable to "blood," to internal movements within the human psyche. The "divine and demonic forces" presiding over the "birth" of Medardus are therefore nothing more than potentialities of the human spirit, and "Chance" is indeed but the revelation of connections between the human mind and the "higher principles latent in nature." There is, for Hoffmann, no real division between self and world, except that the self, like Fichte's Ego, is divisible. Similarly the "elixirs" represent the temptations of the unknown, the urge to break out of the unity, the lure of the uncanny and the vicarious. Medardus is told to guard them, but never taste of them. When he does, he feels a strange burning power within him, a new strength, and he takes them with him on his journey. But the young count and his tutor who taste them in the monastery declare they are nothing more than good old Marsala. The "elixirs" are therefore no more responsible for Medardus's actions than the love potion in Gottfried's *Tristan and Isolde*. Both are merely external correlatives to inner drives.

The structure of *Die Elixiere* is clearly a geometrical progression. Arabesques and digressions are not found, though there is a sort of subplot involving comic and grotesque incidents, and there are interpolated narrations (some effectively left unfinished because they are broken off by some new turn of events) and a few episodic tales. All these episodes, however, are closely bound up with the main plot, and it is the unity and intensity of the book that make it such a compelling work. It is a study of the surfacing of the subconscious— perhaps the most powerful such study in the whole of German romanticism. In structure it is more traditional than other romantic novels, building on a novelistic heritage but transforming this into a more meaningful statement by its exploration of the inner depths of the human spirit.

Kater Murr on the other hand is a highly original structure, the most complex of all the romantic fictions.[33] It too purports to be a communicated manuscript—or rather a conflation of two, namely the life stories of Murr the cat and of Kreisler the musician (as its subtitle indicates). Murr, so the "editor" explains, in writing his memoirs had torn up a printed book which he found in his master's house, using the sheets "partly for backing and partly for blotting" (*teils zur Unterlage, teils zum Löschen*).[34] But these sheets remained in his manuscript and "by mistake" were considered part of it. "Hence" the apparent jumble of the form.The printed book "seems" never to have appeared: it was the life of the conductor and composer Johannes Kreisler. Murr in his prefatory note describes his own manuscript as "some leaves from life—of suffering, of hope, of longing," written for kindred "feeling souls" (the parallel with the preface to *Werther* is apparent!) and "pure childlike minds" (in which no such parallel can be asserted!).[35] No preface to Kreisler's story is included: perhaps, in reading Hoffmann's novel, we may decide that none is needed, for what Murr has said applies equally well to Kreisler. For he too is a "feeling soul," though perhaps not a "pure childlike mind."

But is that really so? The device of the double narration and the fact that the one narrator (the primary one) is an animal and the other (secondary?) a human, together with the fact that Murr's is a first-person narration whereas the story of Kreisler is related in the third person (presumably by someone other than he, though we are not told by whom), might naturally lead us to expect that the two stories will conflict, or at least subsist in an interplay of polar opposition. But this is not the case. What we have is a confluence with constant linkages, with none of the contrasts that we might expect. No question of animal self against spiritual self, for Kreisler is as driven by instincts as Murr and both are creative artists. No question of artist versus philistine, for it is in Murr's story that the attack on philistinism is contained. No question of higher feelings versus baser instincts, for Murr's idealized view of love and friendship is superior to Kreisler's. No question of rational versus irrational, for Murr's account is more connected than the torn-out leaves of Kreisler's. No question of tortuousness versus straightforward simplicity, for foul intrigues play just as large a part in Murr's life as in Kreisler's and both are involved in single combats with rivals. No question of development in the man and placidity in the animal, for Murr develops and even attains "culture" of a sort, whereas Kreisler remains essentially the same and never comes to terms either with the world or himself. None of the obvious expectations is therefore fulfilled. Instead we move in a circle of constant unexpectancy and unexpectedness, of connectedness within unconnectedness, promoted by the lateral narration of Murr, each section of which continues where the last left off, interlaced with the dislocated sections of Kreisler's story, which is no story but a series of fragments, and yet has just as much cohesion as Murr's account. In fact more, because whereas Murr "explains" everything as he writes, the account of Kreisler's doings moves from one mystery to another, unexplained by him because he is not writing it himself, and yet somehow "truer" because life as presented here is not thus explicable. That in the Kreisler sections we are dealing largely with the inexplicable and what cannot be rationally accounted for is emphasized by the narrative device of sections ending with such words as "for the stranger was none other than . . ." or "and she, strange to say, at that time . . ." or "they were interrupted by a noise . . ." or "and so. . . ." Murr's sections often end like that too, but he always completes the sentence in the next section. The narrator of the Kreisler sections never does. He doesn't need to, for the emotional connections are apparent, and any syntactical linkage would suggest a more rational succession than is in fact there. So both the method of the two narrations and their content present contrasting views of life, but the subtle connections, suggested but never explicitly stated, between them fuse them into a total unity that is essentially a unity of ironic reflection—not a simple matter of serious and comic parallelism but a rich texture of mutual interpenetration and interdependence.

The total structure of the novel is quite simple. It has four parts, entitled respectively: 1. "Feeling of Existence. The Months of Youth"; 2. "Life Experience of the Young Man. Et ego in Arcadia."; 3. "Months of Learning. Caprices of Fate"; and 4. "Productive Results of Higher Culture. Riper Months." There is also a short postscript by the "editor" communicating the sad news that Murr is dead and his autobiography is therefore unfinished. But he has left various fragments, and there is more from the book about Kreisler which the "editor" hopes to incorporate into a third volume (the novel is in two volumes, each with two parts). But Hoffmann, as we know, never did. And perhaps things are better left so.

Let me now illustrate the operation of this complex narrative technique by an analysis of the first of the four sections. It begins with apostrophes to life and to nature by Murr, followed by reflections on whether humans are really so superior to animals. Their "reason," of which they are so proud, is nothing more than consciousness, and that is simply something one acquires at birth, and one doesn't know how, just as he, Murr, does not know how he got to be born, though it must have been in a loft because of his lofty aspirations (my pun, not Hoffmann's), from which he is momentarily deflected by the memory of the good things he caught to eat up there—and breaks off after the first half of a sentence. The next section, from the

Kreisler book, starts with the second half of a sentence, but there is no syntactic or semantic connection between the two half-sentences. There is, however, a connection in the person of Meister Abraham who is telling an anecdote to the prince, for it is Abraham (a magician of sorts) who has brought up Murr. The anecdote concerns a lawyer robbed of his hat, coat, and stick by soldiers during a storm, the point being that it wasn't the wind but human agency that did the damage. The prince asks what this has to do with "that fateful night" when at a festivity a rocket fell into his toupet, his son fell into the fountain, and his daughter fled through the park. Abraham replies that it was all due to a windstorm, and that he, like the lawyer in the anecdote, had lost his hat and coat. Kreisler now interrupts to ask what really did happen at the festivity which Abraham arranged but Kreisler had not attended. Abraham replies that it was *because* Kreisler had run off like a madman that he had conjured up the storm to bring into the open the dangerous, destructive fires he had perceived in Kreisler's breast. But while Abraham was setting off a firework display, a real storm had broken out, which interfered with his carefully organized operations, deprived him of his hat and coat, but also led to his finding Murr, whom he now wants to entrust to Kreisler because he is going on a journey. Kreisler reflects on the mental capacity of animals—just as Murr had reflected on human reason. Do animals have minds or just instincts? Can they dream, for instance? Abraham asserts that Murr has reveries, a "somnambulic delirium" between sleep and waking, so he must either be in love or be writing a tragedy (because he has recently groaned and moaned a lot), and so . . .

Murr now describes his early education, his progress in reading and writing, and the first products of his pen—a "philosophic-sentimental-didactic novel, a political tract and a tragedy." The other narrator then describes the configuration of the prince's court. Prince Irenäus rules over a nonexistent territory but maintains the illusion of being a mighty ruler. He has two children, the Princess Hedwiga and the feebleminded Prince Ignaz. The most powerful people at court are Abraham and Mme. Benzon, whose daughter Julia has grown up with the princess. The section breaks off as we are about to be told how Irenäus lost his real kingdom and acquired an imaginary one, and switches to Murr's parents, and then back to the narrator of the Kreisler story, who apologizes for not proceeding chronologically. The information he has consists only of broken fragments *but* when the reader gets to the end he will perhaps pardon the "rhapsodic nature of the whole" and perceive a firm thread holding together the parts (self-reflexiveness with a vengeance!)[36] We now move to a description of the first encounter of Hedwiga and Julia with a wild musician frantically seeking for the "pure scale," who combines tragic intensity with irony. Hedwiga, full of a sense of evil forces threatening her, thinks he is mad; Julia, more composed, sees in him only an ironic rogue. Mme. Benzon says that from their description he must be. . . . But at this point Murr breaks in with the account of *his* important encounter with Ponto the poodle, who ironizes Murr's poetic productions, and then. . . . And Mme. Benzon tells Kreisler that his irony is destructive and has sown discord between the two girls. Equating discord with dissonance, Kreisler says that only music can subdue his inner tumult and that Julia's singing has had a strong effect on him. . . . Then Murr presents a sonnet on longing and an essay on mousetraps and their influence on cathood. After which he is prepared to pass on to the account of his adolescence. . . . Meanwhile Kreisler starts a mock narration of his childhood, of the musical propensities of some of his relatives, of his being forced into the legal profession, feeling imprisoned by it, but then, when liberated, unable to take advantage of his freedom. At which Abraham declares that only Kreisler himself was responsible for his misfortune, and. . . .

Such is the narrative texture of *Kater Murr*. The double narration results in our constantly moving between two centers. One recalls Friedrich Schlegel's image of the ellipse, which would seem apposite here, for the centers are foci of one ellipse, not of two separate circles. This basic pattern of oscillation between two points is maintained through the rest of the novel. There are digressions (such as did not figure in the *Elixiere*), there are intercalated narratives, there is parody, and satire, and there is a "mystery plot"—though this only in the Kreisler sections, as would be expected from what I have said above about the general nature of their narrative mood. There are in fact various mysteries: for instance, the striking resemblance of Kreisler to a painter named Ettlinger whom Hedwiga had loved as a child, who had fallen in love with her mother, gone mad, was put in chains and custody, once broke out and tried to kill Hedwiga, but was dragged away again. Hence her fear of Kreisler and her sense of being encompassed by threatening forces. Ettlinger is an ominous double to Kreisler. At one point he had thought he heard Ettlinger's voice speaking to him from the water (in which he had apparently drowned) and later in the novel the abbot of the monastery in which he has found temporary refuge urges him to take Ettlinger as a warning example. Hedwiga also feels threatened by the advances of Prince Hektor, whom her father intends her to marry, and she tells Benzon that while they were dancing together he changed into a monstrous dragon whose sharp gleaming tongue had stabbed her heart. Soon after this Hedwiga encounters a mysterious cloaked woman who calls her her child and hypnotizes her into sleep. All she knows is that she has seen this woman once before when she was a child and very sick. Julia feels equally threatened by Hektor and rightly so, for he intends to enjoy her before he marries Hedwiga. There is mystery surrounding Prince Hektor too, for Kreisler thwarts his attempted seduction of Julia by showing him a painting that sends him scurrying away with a curse. Hektor orders his adjutant to shoot Kreisler as the latter is on his way home alone. A shot is heard in the forest. Next morning Kreisler's blood-stained hat is found, but he has disappeared. And we have reached midpoint in the novel.

The second volume does much to dispel the mystery surrounding Prince Hektor by revealing the nature of the picture that had so disturbed him. In fact there are two pictures, the other in the possession of the abbot of the monastery in which Kreisler finds refuge after the incident at the end of Volume One, for it was the adjutant, not Kreisler, who had been shot. The first picture shows Hektor running away after stabbing his brother, the second shows the brother recovering by intervention of the Virgin. This brother became a monk and turns up at the monastery. Both brothers had been passionately in love with a girl named Angela, who died of poison which, according to the abbot, was administered by Hektor's brother in a fit of jealousy. This subplot, set in Naples and following a pattern familiar from sensational novels of the time and paralleled in the Firmenti story in *Godwi*, is tied up with other strands in *Murr*, for Angela is the daughter of Irenäus and Benzon. These two have secrets they do not reveal to us. So does Meister Abraham. Who is the mysterious Chiara, disappeared but still spiritistically contactable by him, the "invisible girl" of a piece of magical apparatus whom he married, and subsequently lost—but, so we later learn, was removed at the orders of Irenäus and Benzon? Why was she removed? The mystery surrounding all this, like that relating to Hedwiga, is never dispelled. Meanwhile Murr's progress is anything but mysterious. It embodies normal human emotions such as jealousy in love, and aspirations of social and cultural advancement. As the novel ends Murr is entrusted to Kreisler by Abraham, as we learned at the beginning of the novel, and the great festivity that was wrecked by the storm is about to begin. Kreisler in his monastery receives an urgent summons from Abraham to attend: all hell is loose—Benzon is ennobled, Julia is to marry the half-witted brother of Hedwiga, and Hedwiga herself is to marry Hektor. Something must be done. Kreisler must be there. We have arrived back at the beginning of the novel and now understand more about "that fateful night." But what happened *after* that we are never told, for the whole action of the novel is retrospective. Even then the past is not totally revealed. What we are given is a series of partial elucidations that superimpose themselves on each other but never add up to anything like full knowledge, a mirror of the workings of the human consciousness, a torn-up book of fate, never published because the life it describes has none of the "satisfying" shapeliness of Murr's straightforward externalization of a single consciousness—but nevertheless has its own deeper truth because it works from multiple perspectives, the product of a divided, but none the less unitary consciousness.

CHAPTER ELEVEN

Images on a Golden Ground: Eichendorff

JOSEPH VON EICHENDORFF (1788–1857) was and still is for many the quintessence of German romanticism. His exquisitely melodious songs of longing, of the lure of the unknown, of the urge to venture into appealing but perhaps dangerous realms, of *Wanderlust* that draws one away from home in search of a richer home, of the divine but also demonic power of nature—together with a handful of masterly novellas that deal with similar themes—these do indeed embody in a consummate way all the romantic excitements, expectations and, one must add, disappointments. No one has better described the call of the post horn, of the hunting horn, of the wandering minstrel; but these incursions into the normality of our lives are also presented as seductive forces. They may lead us out, but we may never return. Eichendorff has not forgotten the children who followed the Pied Piper of Hamelin. The greatness of Eichendorff consists in the fact that he portrays these enticements as exciting, beautiful, and poetic, but also as risks, leading we know not where. The poet follows the call, but only when he senses that it is genuine. Many such enticements are not, and indeed we are surrounded by such fascinating but deluding, even destructive, forces calling to our ennui, our vague longings, our hopes, intimating the path to richer, more beauteous experience. This is the particular form that romantic dualism assumes in Eichendorff. He questions the message of the half-heard melody and half-glimpsed vision, though simultaneously agreeing that it is a message. And he does this from out of a deep religious faith. He was a convinced Catholic, not a convert like others of the German Romantics but in continuance of the beliefs of his family lineage. His later works are, as we shall see, highly critical of romanticism, and always from his own intense religious sincerity. It is sometimes said that he outlived romanticism and yet stuck to it. This is not true, for his criticism of certain aspects of romanticism in these essays of his later years was trenchant. But he also did not turn against it just in those later years, when his own contributions to romanticism were substantially long past and the heyday of romanticism was over. In his own romantic works the dualism is everywhere apparent—the appeal and the suspicion of the appeal—for he evoked not merely the post horn, the hunting horn, and the minstrel but also the true mystic message of the silent forest and the moonlit night—God wandering through the world and the soul winging out to meet Him. For Eichendorff the infinite was attainable in the finite, and not necessarily outside it—attainable but not contained in the finite for he was no pantheist. The dualism of all romantic striving and the message of transcendence attainable to those who are rightly attuned, transcendence that does not involve being seduced, no matter how beautifully or persuasively, out of reality into a world of fantasy, illusion, and ultimately despair— these are the predominant ideas in Eichendorff's two novels *Ahnung und Gegenwart* [Presentiment and Present] (1815) and *Dichter und ihre Gesellen* [Poets and Their Companions] (1834).[1]

In contrast to Hoffmann, Eichendorff had a great deal to say about novels and novelists, though here again it is difficult to deduce any conception of the novel as a literary form that marks it off from other genres.[2] His major pronouncements on this subject are the treatise entitled *Der deutsche Roman des achtzehnten Jahrhunderts in seinem Verhältnis zum Christentum* [The German Novel of the Eighteenth Century in Its Relationship to Christianity] (1851) and the relevant parts of his *Geschichte der poetischen Literatur Deutschlands* [History of German poetic literature] (1857). There are also significant comments on romantic novels in the articles that he contributed to a militantly Catholic journal published in Munich, the *Historisch-politische Blätter für das katholische Deutschland,* in the years 1846 to 1848. All of these writings, we notice, belong to the last decade or so of his life, a good ten years or more after he had ceased publishing

Joseph von Eichendorff. Lithograph, from a portrait by Franz Kugler, 1832.

fiction of his own, and after the romantic movement in general had worked itself out.

For the earlier period, that of Eichendorff's own creative production, we have very sparse information on his taste in novels and his conception of the genre. The diaries, which run from 1798 to 1815, show that he was reading *Franz Sternbalds Wanderungen* in 1805, and Jean Paul in 1806 and 1807, with specific mentions of *Flegeljahre*, *Hesperus*, and "Gianozzo," and an oblique reference to *Titan*. There is also a record that, already in 1800, he had borrowed *Die unsichtbare Loge* from a lending library.[3] No critical remarks on Jean Paul are to be found in the diaries, but he was to comment extensively and perceptively on this novelist in the articles and treatises he wrote forty or fifty years later. We also know that Brentano sent him "two parts of the glorious *Simplicissimus*" in 1809, and that he bought his own copy in 1810.[4] He was also reading the popular novelists of the eighteenth century, as most other people were.

Let us now consider the late essays. In 1846 he contributed to the *Historisch-politische Blätter* a series of articles under the general title "On the History of Modern Romantic Poetry in Germany," which contain various comments on novels of the German Romantics.[5] Novalis is portrayed as a writer who believed in the reestablishment of true religion through poetry, by endowing poetry with a transcendental content without departing from real worldly substance, one who therefore particularly favored dreams and *Märchen*, both of which express the vast, mysterious expanses surrounding daylight reality. His novel *Ofterdingen* sought "to render real life with all its worldly relationships—marriage, the state, occupations, etc.—in its original higher meaning and veiled beauty."[6] Eichendorff regretfully noted in Novalis a certain indirection in religious content, expressing itself in pantheism and mystical nature-philosophy, which gave his work a vacillating ambiguity. This same crypto-pantheism he found combined with subjectivism in *Lucinde* to result in the assertion of a God-in-us which is genius, is individuality, and was formalized by Schlegel in his novel—formalized in the sense that it became the formative principle in that novel. But this was only the early stage, the Fichtean stage, of Schlegel's career, which eventually led him to fight his way through and beyond romanticism, recognizing that "romanticism is only true, can only fulfill its mission if it receives sanction and justification from the church."[7] Such a remark explains Eichendorff's guarded appreciation of *Ofterdingen* and mistrust of *Lucinde* at this time. Jean Paul's novels, says Eichendorff, also embodied "a poetry of the future, of expectation, of ennoblement of man through a reawakened faith in a higher, invisible world." This, presented as an educational process, conditioned the form of *Die unsichtbare Loge*; but what Jean Paul looked forward to was a secular "abstract religion of humanitarianism [*Humanität*]."[8] "Hence, since there is no firm gold ground [*Goldgrund*] to set off his earthly images, the fragmentation, inadequacy, and blurredness of reality and of his ideals—world-embracing, heaven-storming youths, and pallid, ethereally transparent, moonsick maidens, and that lachrymose sentimentality from which, because he is a true poet, he escapes from time to time by humorous capers."[9] In these same essays Eichendorff paid especial respect to the total lack of falsification in both of Arnim's novels, praising the "*inner* truth" of his portrayal of social morality in the *Gräfin Dolores,* and the *poetic* truth of the fictional characters in the *Kronenwächter* which makes this artifact "more historical" than many a work of history.[10] In a highly poetic passage Eichendorff praised the panoramic quality of Arnim's work, his portrayal of all the kingdoms of this world in which the finger of God is always visible. In other words Arnim, according to Eichendorff, had the gold background that Jean Paul lacked. Tieck did not. He lacked "confessional definiteness," existed in a dichotomy of mysticism and doubt, which sometimes emerged delightfully as irony but was sometimes merely neutral—and neutrality is the enemy of all romanticism which, according to Eichendorff, had to be based on firm religious faith.[11]

In a later article on Brentano's *Märchen* there is passage on *Godwi* that is of some interest.[12] Having characterized Brentano's chameleon nature with its constant alternations between light and shade, its vacillations between worshipful devotion and playful wit, Eichendorff asserted that Brentano's was a demonic personality that considered his own genius a burden of fate and hated it at times, was afraid of it and struggled with it as a sort of *Doppelgänger*—and that all this was expressed, albeit rather crudely and gloomily [*roh und düster*], in *Godwi*. He found in Brentano's novel the same *Weltschmerz,* the same emancipation of the flesh and revolutionary reversals that were to become prevalent in the 1840s, but combined with a deep religious faith. And "then the most deadly boredom invades the poet in the midst of this confusion, combined with loathing and disgust, so that he mercilessly destroys through bitter irony in the second volume all that he had created in the first, saying: 'I will take vengeance on the art in this book, or perish.'"[13] Eichendorff saw *Godwi,* then, as an expression of Brentano's struggle with himself, or rather of the struggle between his two selves, between his art and his anxiety over his art. Its irony was, for Eichendorff, the attempt to integrate two mutually annihilating tendencies, a moral force arising from inner outrage, bent on destroying what is bad and vulgar [*das Schlechte und Gemeine*] in life.[14] In another essay of this same year he compared *Godwi* with *William Lovell*; in both we have the work of gifted young men in their intellectual fledgling period [*Flegeljahren*], when fancy and reason are directly at odds with each other.[15] Since Eichendorff had elsewhere asserted that the protagonists of both these novels were reflections of their authors, one can safely assume that he detected this same tension in their heroes.

The long essay *Der deutsche Roman des achtzehnten Jahrhunderts in seinem Verhältnis zum Christentum* discusses various individual novels and offers some comments on the genre as a whole.[16] It was published as a book by Brockhaus in Leipzig in 1851. Important is the fact that it postdates the 1848 revolution. The historical setting is therefore quite different from that of the essays of 1846 and 1847. Old values were being opposed by new values, the future was uncertain, and literature was in the forefront of the battle. Eichendorff considered the passage from epic to novel to be indicative of a movement from interest in the external world of objects and actions to concentration on the inner world of states of feeling and characters. And he also thought that the German temperament, which tends more to reflection than action, is well served by what he called the "broad form or non-form [of the novel], in which the author, as if on a walk, can comfortably reflect on all sorts of things—nature and human beings, clouds and cabbages, palace and barnyard."[17] Eichendorff judged all novels according to whether or not they had a firm religious base. He used as an image the word *Goldgrund*, which means the gold background on which figures of various colors appear in illuminations and paintings of the Middle Ages. He distinguished in the romances of the Middle Ages between what he called an ideal type and a real type, as represented by Wolfram von Eschenbach and Gottfried von Strassburg respectively, the former being essentially religious, the latter devoid of religious grounding. The novel was, for Eichendorff, a prosaicization of both these types of medieval romance, but predominantly of the second. He recognized the emergence of humor from a situation in which chivalry had become robbed of its essentially religious basis, resulting in the portrayal of the "sharp contrast between higher needs and prosaic reality."[18] He instanced Moscherosch and the picaresque "rogue novels" of the later seventeenth century. And he appreciated the paradigmatic significance of Cervantes and Grimmelshausen. Cervantes's novel had a tragic subject—the death of chivalry—and Grimmelshausen's *Simplicissimus* was equally the product of reaction to the absurdities of the world of the time. But whereas Cervantes could build on to a national literary tradition, Grimmelshausen could not, was often clumsy, and yet always genuine, healthy [*kerngesund*], and natural [*naturwüchsig*]. His novel stands at the watershed of old and new times. It lives by the "subjective attitude" of its author, which is basically protesting and negative. And yet the book has a firm religious basis, its "basic harmony" being represented by a song of the hermit, "Komm, Trost der Nacht, o Nachtigall," which resounds throughout the novel until Simplex ends up as a hermit himself.[19]

Eichendorff treats the novel of the eighteenth century against the background of the various secularized religions of that age. Werther rejects religion in order to be his own god and succumbs to pantheism, which has always been the easiest way out for moral impotence. There is not even anything heroic or self-sacrificing about his suicide. He is "a modern Narcissus, always looking at his reflection bedded by the sky and framed with trees and flowers, and then, when he turns around, furious because the real sky and the real trees have other things to do than to deck him out."[20] Most of the novels of sensibility were superficial, he thought, because morality cannot be the basis for a religion but only its result, for the ground of all religion must be faith. The pietistic novel recognized this but tended toward self-indulgent subjectivism. In *Die Wahlverwandtschaften* he finds the same glorification of feeling, but with a different attitude on the part of the novelist: in *Werther* Goethe had alternated between enthusiasm and dry reporting, whereas in the later novel he was "a brilliant doctor conducting experiments and feeling the pulse of a sick soul."[21] Jean Paul was for Eichendorff *the* poet of the secular religion of humanism [*Humanitätsreligion*]. He believed in the perfectibility of man by his own efforts. He was the poet of dissonance and the "wit of melancholy" [*Witz der Melancholie*], obsessed by the conflict between ideal and reality, clearly portraying the shame and ruination of his times, but raising the banner of hope above the shambles.[22] He was an immensely serious writer, his only failing being his mistaken belief in humanism. Goethe accepted the religion of humanism too, but "whereas Jean Paul caught the whole world in a concave mirror of ideas, Goethe made the world as it is into a mirror of heaven. The finite in its manifold forms and manifestations was for him infinity, world-soul, god—and nature its revelation."[23] Immortality was for Goethe thirst for life, acceptance of natural order, the urge to praiseworthy thoughts and deeds, Man is an entelechy and this, the immortal part of himself, must follow its own direction. The transformation of demonic forces into productive powers in art means that Goethe's "religion" was fundamentally based on a poetical rather than an ethical conscience.[24] *Wilhelm Meister* displays the "veiled poetry of everyday life" [*die verhüllte Poesie des gewöhnlichen Lebens*],[25] but Eichendorff, like Novalis, found it pervaded by a pragmatic utilitarianism. Goethe was a great writer, one sustained by faith in beauty and harmony but one who stopped short of real understanding of the highest mysteries, which he attempted to grasp by metamorphosing them into symbols from nature.

In the later *Geschichte der poetischen Literatur Deutschlands* (1857) Eichendorff firmly states that all poetic literature depends for its value on its degree of closeness to a religious center, and he expands on ideas expressed in the earlier essays. He is even more skeptical about Goethe's humanism, asserting now that the educative system of the *Wanderjahre*, with its encouragement of natural inclinations and self-help, is basically what drove Werther to suicide, Wilhelm Meister to materialist philistinism, and the protagonists of *Die Wahlverwandtschaften* to spiritual adultery.[26] There is another tribute to the deep moral seriousness and the sagacious humor of Jean Paul. He has little good to say about Hoffmann, who for him represented that development of romanticism in which the imagination broke loose from its religious grounding and evaporated into empty play or caricature. In contrast to Brentano, says Eichendorff, Hoffmann did not fight the demonic strain in his nature: instead he cherished and coddled it, or turned it into the diabolic.[27] Religion was used simply as poetic adornment in his two novels. His failings were not aesthetic, but ethical. Eichendorff concludes by pointing to two destructive strains in romanticism: the tendency toward nature-philosophy and the tendency toward irony. Both consorted ill with the religious basis of the movement. An essentially ethical purpose had become aesthetic in the hands of the romantic poets (shades of Kierkegaard!) and irony in particular led to an elevation of form over content, and eventually to what could be called "romantic mannerism" [*eine romantische Manier*].[28]

There is a firm ethical basis to both of Eichendorff's own novels. They are religiously grounded, but in their use of multiple protagonists they present alternative answers to the question of what may constitute human fulfillment. The narration is chronological, but always geometrically progressive, rising in both novels to a striking climax in the final scene, in which the characters discover themselves more than ever before. In *Ahnung und Gegenwart* we follow the development of three male characters and several women; in *Dichter und ihre Gesellen* we are concerned primarily with four male characters.[29] Poems are used in both these novels to crystallize situations and moments (though, as we shall see in a moment, somewhat differently from in other romantic novels). Interpolated stories are used, sometimes as illustrations, sometimes as flashbacks, to illuminate the protagonists. Digressions do not occur in the form that they have in Jean Paul or Arnim, and arabesques are present only in the sense that the multiple heroes represent alternative or competing answers—variations, but central to the theme, not bordering arabesques around a central panel. Irony is used sparingly, though effectively, the contrast between ideal and reality being projected out of the narrative frame into the thoughts and actions of the characters but never representing a distanced attitude of the narrator, for there is really no narrative voice apart from the voices of the characters themselves. Hence there is really no self-reflexive irony in Eichendorff's novels, only ironization of would-be poets from the vantage point of a real poet.

It could, however, be argued that the double perspective which I mentioned at the beginning of this chapter as being characteristic of Eichendorff is a form of irony, in which something is both positive and negative according to the context or lack of context, whether it is viewed absolutely or relatively, on its own or with relation to other things. For instance: in the first chapter of *Ahnung und Gegenwart* the hero, Count Friedrich, is traveling with a group of students on a ship on the Danube and they pass a dark whirlpool enclosed by rocky slopes, a place of silence where no birds sing, its center looking up at one like the eye of death, a place that evokes feelings of isolation vis-à-vis the unknown, so that a cross has been placed on a rock in the midst of the stream. Friedrich's silent contemplation is broken by the sight of a beautiful girl on another boat, also gazing into the dark chasm of water: "He started inwardly. For it was as if her glance uncovered suddenly a whole new world of blooming splendor, age-old remembrances, and never known desires in his heart."[30] It is a sudden revelation of connections, a world of splendor woven of recollection and desire, of known and unknown—a revelation whose clarity (which startles him) contrasts with the dark indefinite-

ness of the whirlpool. On shore that night he encounters the girl
again briefly on the balcony of the inn where he is staying, and he
feels her breath, touches her arm, and then kisses her. She tells him
her name is Rosa. Next day he is awakened early by a nightingale
and thinks the encounter may have been a dream, until the inn-
keeper confirms that Rosa had indeed been staying there. He takes
leave of his travel companions, feeling suddenly alone and at a crossroads in his life. It is a sunny spring morning, the earth steaming in
green exuberance, and larks singing in the great expanse of clear
sky. Friedrich is happy, and a poem takes shape in his heart.

The present experience of the spring morning mingles with the
recollection of the encounter on the balcony at night, the image of
the beloved expresses itself in terms of the landscape, her absence in
terms of night, but in each case the images of the poem present real
sense-impressions that have come to him since the previous day, and
the whole poem is dominated by a paradoxical relationship between
day and night, light and dark. The poem, therefore, summarizes;
that he himself composes it, represents the conversion of his individual impressions into an organized whole and is, in that sense, a
crystallization. But when he attempts to write it down, Friedrich is
immediately invaded by a sense of dissatisfaction: "when he stopped
singing and began solemnly to write down the fleeting words [*die
flüchtigen Worte bedächtig aufzuzeichnen*] he had to laugh at himself
and rubbed them all out."[31] It was all right as a song, but not as
something written. The contrast between "die *flüchtigen* Worte" and
"*bedächtig* aufzeichnen" is meaningful. It implies that the poem was
too much of the moment to support the permanence of being recorded, that in Friedrich's view it did not have absolute validity, a
validity divorced from the circumstances. We readers may well take
a different view and accept such poems as valid configurations of
particular moments of general experience.

This peculiar double perspective is an important element in the
complexity of these novels. We are, however, not always made directly aware of this through some comment by the character who
sings the song. Consider for a moment the following well-known
lines:

> Laue Luft kommt blau geflossen,
> Frühling, Frühling soll es sein!
> Waldwärts Hörnerklang geschossen,
> Mut'ger Augen lichter Schein;
> Und das Wirren bunt und bunter

Wird ein magisch wilder Fluss,
In die schöne Welt hinunter
Lockt dich dieses Stromes Gruss

Und ich mag mich nicht bewahren!
Weit von euch treibt mich der Wind,
Auf dem Strome will ich fahren,
Von dem Glanze selig blind!
Tausend Stimmen lockend schlagen,
Hoch Aurora flammend weht,
Fahre zu! ich mag nicht fragen,
Wo die Fahrt zu Ende geht!

This is a poem about enticement out of the narrowness of circumstances and of self into a "schöne Welt," an enticement connoted by the image of hunting horns in the forest in springtime ringing out through the soft air, producing exciting confusion—a magic enticement that the speaker cannot withstand, and follows without asking where the call may lead. In his collected poems of 1837 Eichendorff placed this poem first, under the title *Frische Fahrt*. But it had already appeared in *Ahnung und Gegenwart* in a highly significant context.[32] The Countess Romana has taken charge of Rosa and carried her off to the *Residenz* and, hopefully, a more interesting existence than Rosa's uneventful and unromantic life in the country. But Romana too is disillusioned by life. She tells Rosa of the crucial episode in her early years, how she was enticed out of the garden of her family mansion by the sound of hunting horns, out into the forest, where she met a horseman who lifted her on to his saddle and to whom she gave her ring as a remembrance, but he brought her back to her home and vanished into the forest. Next spring, as she stood beside her mother in this same garden, she saw the horseman far off, her ring glittering on his finger. He tried to get to her, but as he jumped a ravine he fell into the chasm and was lost. She never saw him again, but the ring glitters every spring from the greenery and, as she says: "I cannot break the spell." Her mother too never forgot the incident and on the day before her death she had said to Romana:

Never jump out of the garden. It is bordered by the piety and godliness of roses, lilies, and rosemary. The sun shines brightly upon it and radiant children watch you from afar, wishing to walk with you there between the flower beds. For you shall experience more Grace and more heavenly splendor than others. And just because you will often be happy and bold and have wings I beg you never to jump out of the peace of the garden![33]

To Rosa's question whether she understands what her mother had meant by those words, Romana replies: "Sometimes . . . on misty autumn days," and taking up her guitar, walks to the window, and sings: "Laue Luft kommt blau geflossen. . . ." Seen in this setting, the poem remains the expression of the enticing beauty of the unknown, and as such it is positive and joyful; but the setting itself, with the warning of the mother, makes it a song of the *dangers* of such enticement. The fact that Eichendorff allowed this poem to speak for itself by placing it in such a prominent position in his collected *Gedichte* acknowledges its positive import; but what happens to Romana in the novel shows its other aspect. She remains frustrated and unfulfilled, and the promise of Grace contained in the mother's words never is bestowed on her, though it is on Rosa, whom we last meet kneeling penitently in prayer after a life characterized by basic piety thwarted through a similar desire for adventure.

Romana never recoils from the desire for excitement and for power. Her innermost self is revealed in the romance she sings at an "aesthetic tea party," about a princess who has enslaved the old heroes and lives in a forest, with a strange old man, whose mantle is full of playthings, to run the household. The princess wants to seduce the world anew, but the world has decayed, so that the worthies who now arrive in the wood and embrace the old heroes as friends are so weak that they are almost crushed by the embrace of these ancient warriors, and so unable to appreciate the strange activity of the old man that they try to bring order into it and are accordingly themselves turned into playthings, for they are not really heroes but just poets. "The world stays sober . . .

> And the enchantress with the old man
> Plays her former games anew
> Lonely for many a long, long year.[34]

In the novel there is some discussion at the tea party about the meaning of this romance. To us readers it is clearly Romana's wish-dream, a protestation of the impoverishment of the modern world as compared with the past, and therefore a romantic vision. But again we have a double perspective: taken for itself the poem is a positive statement, but seen in relationship to Romana it is wishful delusion. Her own castle is both an enchanted castle and a decaying feudal mansion. In it the seduction of Friedrich is unsuccessfully attempted; in it she dies by her own hand, stretched out over the decaying fragments of ancestral portraits. Her problem is that she is totally unable to harness her inherited strength of passion to the new circumstances of life. Unable to conquer Friedrich and refusing to accept his spiritual superiority over her, she sinks into a feeling of emptiness. Her life is a constant striking of romantic attitudes without serious romantic belief.

Enchantresses, *Waldhörner*, huntsmen—to which we may add gardens, post horns, lost brothers, wandering minstrels, people one seems to have met before, songs echoing from out of the past, standing at windows, nightingales, sunrises, splashing fountains, the sound of the guitar, and moonlight—these are some of the motifs that make up an Eichendorff work, and they occur in frequent and varying combination in both of the novels. It is, however, quite wrong in my opinion to construe them as elements of a consciously unreal world, a world of escapist fantasy. Eichendorff's novels are not fantasies: they deal with real people and real problems. And the motifs just listed are images of certain recurrent experiential situations. Thus when Romana hears the *Waldhorn*, meets her knight, and gives him her ring, this is not fairy-tale stuff but the description of a psychological experience—one that, in fact, turns into a trauma. Gretchen's spinning wheel is an image of monotony, of the *perpetuum mobile* of obsession with a particular thought; but the fact that spinning wheels are obsolete in no way diminishes the eternal validity of "Meine Ruh' ist hin." In reading a romantic novel it is important that we should realize that the elements of the plot itself function as images in this way. In Eichendorff the general situation of wandering and seeking is itself an image of a generation adrift, of a sense of aimlessness because established values have been cut away from under one's feet, because inherited guidelines are gone or have become questionable, a psychic situation which is certainly not confined to the early nineteenth century.

And so: these disguises, confusions, misplacings, discoveries, absurdities, and ironies, this imprecision, inconsistency, and discord, the apparent lack of motivation that we sometimes encounter, the frequent shiftings of perspective, and the immanence of chance and coincidence in this constantly mobile poetic world are the sincere expression of a view of life. They represent artistic form trying to embrace a vision whose order contains within itself disorder, and whose very lack of logic and absence of harmony represents a formal correspondence to real experience. That so many of these plot-elements derive from fairy tales is not whimsy or childishness, but a recognition of the mythic, archetypal nature of situations, and a recognition that apparent chance really represents a deeper organization not perceptible to those with rationalistic blinkers. That others of these motifs derive from the romances of adventure merely underscores the idea of life as adventure. That there are elements from chivalry testifies to a respect for basic moral values which have become lost, at least for the present. We can always read a romantic novel as pure plot, but to understand its full meaning we must always remain attuned to the image-quality of its events and situations. This is what makes Eichendorff's novels into examples of the novel as a *poetic* form.

In *Dichter und ihre Gesellen* there is a young man Otto rebelling against the idea of entering a settled profession.[35] He says he has heard the song of the minstrel, the *Spielmann*, coming from the hill of Venus with new enticing songs, and that he cannot but follow this stream of magic sound. He tries to be a poet, but is unsuccessful, and toward the end of the novel he is admonished to desist from these vain strivings by the real poet, Victor, who tells him: "There are but few poets in this world, and of those few hardly any drift unscathed up into the wondrous splendor of that magic night where wild fiery flowers grow and streams of song tumble into the ravines and the magic minstrel lures us from the rustling woods with heart-rending sounds into the mount of Venus where all joy is aflame and the soul is free as a dream, free with all its dark desires."[36] This passage is full of images associated frequently by Eichendorff with the poetic process (*Zaubernacht; wilde, feurige Blumen; Abgründe; Waldesrauschen; Traum*), but the most striking is that of the minstrel, the *Spielmann*. A real *Spielmann* had appeared in the very first chapter of *Dichter und ihre Gesellen*, and as this mysterious character goes out of sight, the observer has the feeling that his music is indeed drifting over the silence of the mountains. The connection between actual plot-elements and expressive images is so close in Eichendorff's work that the one becomes the other and there is hardly any difference between inner and outer worlds in this essentially poetic texture.

Music in one form or another is a constantly recurring image. There is a marvelous passage in *Ahnung und Gegenwart* where Friedrich and his friend Leontin observe through a closed window villagers dancing to musicians that the two men can see but not hear.[37] Leontin immediately turns the experience into an image: life as a room full of zealous musicians scraping away at the most difficult passages and people dancing to their beat, but not a sound being heard. Friedrich takes up the image: don't we all torment ourselves in trying to express our basic, individual melody, but never succeeding? True, says Leontin—so long as we have music within us, but most people saw away on wood without strings, determined to play to the end of the page. Here a specific moment in the plot has been converted into an image. This, to my mind, is how we should view the *Taugenichts* of Eichendorff's most famous novella, also a fiddler trying to reify the basic individual melody of his nature. It is also how we should interpret the various serenades, songs heard in the night, songs that one has not heard since childhood, or melodies to which one cannot hear or remember the words. These are all incidents in a plot structure, but they are also incursions of another world, shimmering beyond the confines of present space or welling up from the sleeping depths of memory.

Or take the image of the garden. Gardens play a large part in these two novels, but they are usually gardens of a particular type: formal, offering shade, containing statues, with a splashing fountain somewhere in the middle. They sometimes contain unusual or exotic flowers. More often than not they are overgrown, somewhat neglected, perhaps even deserted or abandoned, the statues are broken, the fountains dried up. We will recall Romana's mother's garden and how it functioned as a symbol of security and peace, but also of restriction. In the same novel, *Ahnung und Gegenwart*, Friedrich recalls his early years, which are also associated with a garden. One thinks automatically of the garden of innocence, the garden of childhood, the garden of Eden. But there is more to it than that. It has long dark avenues of closely cut trees running in all directions between beds of flowers, with fountains, at one of which a lovely young girl sits singing Italian songs while he stands for hours at the iron gates, looking out into the sunshine and light and the people journeying into the distance. Friedrich then converts this memory into an image: "All the quiet of that time lies far behind the bustle of days lived through since, like an old, sad, sweet song, and often when a single note of it reaches me again, I am seized by an indescribable longing, not just for gardens and mountains, but for a much farther and deeper home, of which this one seems but a pleasing reflection."[38]

The image of the garden is, as we see from this passage, connected with the image of the *Spielmann* and of song. But it is also a real garden to which Friedrich returns shortly before the climax of the novel, after long years of wandering. The crucial point in his development had been reached when, as he himself puts it, "that vague boyish longing, that wondrous *Spielmann* from the *Venusberg* turned into a sacred love and enthusiasm for a definite fixed goal."[39] This first takes the form of military activity for the state in the cause of freedom, but, disillusioned by the struggle, he finds his true calling as he kneels one day in a chapel and contrasts this sense of knowing what is right, with his previous life "when he was happy with his poetry." The "poetry" was never real poetry, and is no reliable companion on life's journey; and his love for Rosa must yield to a higher love. He reaches this decision at the very place where he had parted from the students and set out on his wanderings. Having now achieved a clear sense of what to do with his life, he admits to a feeling of moving backward through his past life to a real sense of home. And the final stage of this is when, from a high hill, he suddenly sees the garden of his childhood, his home in ruins, and a tomb-stone in the garden portraying a prostrate dead girl enveloped by a snake, with a broken sword and a broken coat of arms and a crucifix pressing down on the snake. The coat of arms is that of his family, the female figure on the tomb has the features of the girl who had sung Italian songs by the fountain. The hill on which he stands turns out to be a gathering place of madmen, persons warped by obsessions of one kind or another, presided over by Friedrich's wild, gloomy brother Rudolf whom he has not seen since childhood, though two landscapes—one wild and mountainous, associated with Rudolf, and the other pleasing and gentle, associated with the girl Angelina—have haunted his dreams ever since. The romantic quest, as we have seen, often leads one back to one's starting point, for when Friedrich now decides to embrace a religious life, we are told that this is the fulfillment of the basic urge of his soul, which was religious.

Gardens play an equally important part in *Dichter und ihre Gesellen*. When Baron Fortunat enters the garden of the celebrated poet Victor, who is away on a journey, he comments: "It was as if some wondrous magician had left all sorts of different signs on the greenery overnight, and was now dozing in the labyrinth, beside the plashing fountains, dreaming of the old time which he had conjured up and bound in his silent circles."[40] This time image turns into incident (instead of, as usually, vice versa) for what should he then encounter but a sleeping young man who, on awaking, leads him around the garden and explains that Victor wanted the garden kept as it was in his childhood. "Rightly so," says Fortunat, "for what else should a garden be but a poem with a quite distinct sound? In the monotonous splashing of these fountains, the ghostly symmetry of the allées and the silence of these statues there is a sadness enough to drive one mad."[41] In other words Fortunat sees in this garden, as in any other, the reminder of a former and ordered world. The sleeping young man is, as we find out much later, Victor himself, returned apparently to find peace in this place, for his life is restless. He has joined a company of actors in order to gain entrance to the castle of a prince, where he knows his beloved, the Spanish countess Juanna, has taken refuge. But she is drowned on a wild hunting expedition, trying to escape from the man she believes erroneously to be destined for her as a husband by the prince, while Victor is trying to save her. Her memory haunts him and at various points and in various places he thinks he sees her. These are not hallucinations, but other persons disguised as Juanna, each for her own purpose and each symbolically simulating her wild, free spirit. One of these false encounters takes place long after her death, in the garden of this same prince, now senile and living entirely in the picture books of his childhood. The masked figure whispers "Tomorrow!" to Victor, and he hears a strange poignant song, almost without melody. Then:

> Victor fled in horror through the garden, the moonlight shimmered dreamily on the bushes, the fountains swayed in the wind like fairies in long fluttering veils. Suddenly he heard the song again. On the stone basin of the fountain a man was dozing, without a hat, his head nodding, singing in his sleep. In the fleeting light of the moon he thought he recognized the pale sick prince.[42]

There is another section of *Dichter und ihre Gesellen* where a garden plays an important part. Otto, the would-be poet, after his crucial talk with Victor when he was urged to give up any such aspirations, seeks to make peace in his soul, and begins, without realizing it, to journey toward his home. Outside a town he falls asleep and dreams of the "cool forest beauty of his youth," but is wakened by the sound of a carriage with two young women in it who tell the coachman to drive to the "Bergvorstadt." That evening he sets out in search of them, hears the sound of a guitar and a strange song, follows this and finds himself in the dark garden of a *palais* where he finds again one of the ladies of the coach. When she learns his name, she brings him a volume of his poems and he reads to her his youthful poem on Melusina, the water sprite. The topic appeals to the lady for she says she herself is Melusina, never to be seen by day. But she falls asleep during his reading, for the poem is obviously not very good. Eventually he is led out of the garden; but the experience remains with him traumatically as something he cannot get out of his mind. And so he sinks into a febrile melancholy, and in his anguished dreams constantly hears the post horn, the rustling woods, and the bell of a distant hermit's cell. When he recovers, he is told that the *palais* in the "Bergvorstadt" has not been inhabited for years. He goes there but finds the garden overgrown, wild, empty. Grass grows in the cracks of the marble steps, doors and windows are firmly shut, and one half-broken shutter flaps in the wind. "My God," he asks himself, "where have I been all this time?" This garden—a garden of the imagination, a garden of feverish delusive self-fulfillment—has no real existence except in the dreams of the mind. And so he journeys home, but dies on a hill overlooking his home, surrounded by forests, where he had debated whether to follow the call of the *Spielmann*.

Other plot-elements could be considered in this same way. The motif of the hunt would then be an image of the desire for free activity, for action, for dangerous living, with its concomitant motif of the *Waldhorn*, associated with enticement, with wind, with echoes, with the depths of the forest or the heights of the mountains, with the magic horn and therefore with children, with the hunting horn and therefore with sex, with the post horn and therefore with adventure, the unknown, the flight from the domestic. Or the motif of actors, representing, as in Goethe's *Wilhelm Meister,* the pleasing assumption of personalities other than one's own, and of various personalities, the world of semblance, of play, and, to a certain extent, of escape. Or the motif of hermits: intended not just in a narrowly religious sense, though certainly in that sense too, but also in the wider sense of removing oneself from the everyday turmoil of the busy world in order to contemplate true values and develop inner strength. At the end of each of these novels one of the main characters enters the church. In *Ahnung und Gegenwart* Count Friedrich enters the monastery on the hill; in *Dichter und ihre Gesellen* Count Victor becomes a militant Catholic priest.

There is however, a difference in mood between the end of each of these novels. *Ahnung und Gegenwart* was begun in the fall of 1810, finished in 1812 and published in 1815 (when Eichendorff was twenty-seven). It was completed therefore, before the War of Liberation and published when the era of disruption was over and a whole new organization of European life had taken place, but uncertainty over the future prevailed—the year of the Congress of Vienna. It deals with various characters, all seeking some satisfying form of life against a background of shifting values, confusion, and turmoil. With three of these characters—Romana, Rosa, and Friedrich—we have already dealt in some measure. But there are two others who also occupy an important place in the novel—Leontin (Rosa's brother) and the poet or poetaster Faber. Leontin is an almost Shakespearean character, highly passionate but also endowed with a biting wit that often approaches self-irony. We are told at one point that Leontin's irony is the expression of despair. He vents his wit particularly on Faber and tells us that he needs Faber as a lightning-conductor. A "mountain and forest spirit," he is essentially a hunter, and it is in the hunt that he seems to find the nearest thing to fulfillment. He believes in living poetry rather than writing it and this provokes his skepticism toward Faber's literary efforts. Faber is the most complex and controversial character in the book. He believes in poetry, and is a poet, though at times his poetry conflicts with reality, is false, and he knows it. He too turns up on the hill of madmen at the end of the novel. The landscape of the final scene has three main components: the monastery, the distant view of the sea, and, below the hill, the flat land. In this final scene Leontin rejects the idea of sorrowing over the loss of past happiness and urges resolute looking into the future: he goes to the sea where a ship is waiting to take him and his bride to America. Faber goes down to the flat land to live in the world as a poet. Each makes his own testimony: Leontin to freedom, Faber to poetry, Friedrich to religion. As they depart from each other we feel a separation into what is ultimately the political life, the life of the poet, and the religious life. Since Friedrich stands on the hill and observes the others go, one must be left with the thought that the religious life is, for Eichendorff, the highest—which, in view of what I have said above, should not surprise us. But the others are not deprecated. In one last great speech Friedrich speaks to Leontin of the seriousness of the times they live in, the uncertain outcome of the battle between light and darkness, old and new values, a combat in which everyone must needs participate. This, we must remember, was written in 1812, the year of the retreat from Moscow. The emphasis is on *Kampf*, a necessity that Leontin also recognizes, on a battle between old and new from which a saddened but liberated world will rise to new glory—though maybe not in our times. Both

Friedrich and Leontin believe in the importance of maintaining old values, Leontin the true conception of freedom, Friedrich the true conception of right and righteousness. Leontin's immediate purpose is to "strengthen heart and eyes in the untouched forests of another continent," to remember the greatness of the past, retain his sorrow at the present, and thus make himself worthy of "the better future we all hope is coming—and to be ready and prepared for it." As for Faber, Friedrich proclaims that the poet is the heart of the world— *Der Dichter ist das Herz der Welt*—and through the poet's songs men's hearts become free, retain their innocence, and acknowledge honor and truth.

Dichter und Ihre Gesellen was published nineteen years later, in 1834, when Eichendorff was forty-six. It deals with four characters, all of whom are, in one way or another, poets: Count Victor, Baron Fortunat, Otto, and Dryander. At the end there is a parting of the ways similar to that in the earlier novel. Otto, as we have seen, ends in death. Victor forswears poetry for the church. Fortunat remains with poetry and goes to Italy. Dryander, the pseudo-poet, joins a company of traveling actors. Two other persons, who are not poets, are present in this final scene: Baron Manfred, who enters government service, and Walter, the friend of Fortunat's youth, who has heard the call of the *Spielmann* but resisted it and settled down in a life of satisfactory restrictedness. There are still battles to be fought. On that all are agreed. Victor justifies his choice, saying that poetry and yearning [*Sehnsucht*] are not enough. Who gives us the right to complain, when we are not prepared to help? What is needed is active participation—fresh bold spirits ready to do battle against the homemade idols that obscure the sight of God. Manfred recognizes that his purpose is similar, to be achieved by different means and with more concrete goals in view. And Fortunat says to Victor that what he wants for the world is, in the last analysis, the same: "But I have no other means of achieving it than my poetry, and with that I will live and die!" As Victor looks down on the earth he sees the conflict in his own terms of angels and devils, with the devil showing men the glories of the earth and saying: "Be free, then all shall be yours!" But in contrast to the worrisome anguish of Friedrich's speech on the times and its citing of Hamlet's

> The time is out of joint:—O cursed spite
> That ever I was born to set it right,

Victor, at the end of this novel, greets opportunity with exhilaration and joy: "O my friends, what a time this is! How happy is he who is born into it—to fight it out!" and the novel concludes with these lines:

> Wir ziehen treulich auf die Wacht,
> Wie bald kommt nicht die ew'ge Nacht
> Und löschet aus der Länder Pracht,
> Du schöne Welt, nimm dich in Acht![43]

It is the world that is at stake, the world of ultimate truth and lasting values, of transcendent premonitions and visions, the world of a poetry which embraces both conscious experience and the deeper revelations that emerge in the subconscious—the romantic world, the world of these romantic novels. These extraordinary books are not escapist fantasies that withdraw from reality into a realm of solipsistic play. They are rooted in dismay at the disorientation, fragmentation, and materialism of life as their authors saw it around them. They are inspired by the sense of an urgent calling to restore fullness and wholeness, and to open up wider vistas and deeper wells to a world sadly fraught with insensitivity and impoverishment, a shrinking world, a world that has somehow lost its groundings.

CHAPTER TWELVE

Conclusion

THE German romantic novelists were therefore not merely concerned with transforming the novel into poetry: they also hoped to redeem the world through poetry, to relate the manifold of experiences to a poetic center, to dissolve those divisions—nature and spirit, conscious and unconscious, finite and infinite—which, all too pervasive, militated against a clear understanding of the unity behind variety, the complementariness of oppositions, the interaction of past, present, and future, the relation of real to ideal, of conditioned to unconditional. Common to them all is the sense of a world that has gone adrift, explicitly articulated in Eichendorff, Arnim, and Hölderlin, and in the others implicit everywhere as the source from which all else proceeds. These are anguished, concerned, eloquently urgent voices—voices very different in timbre and range from each other, voices that resound in a variety of modes of expression. But everywhere we find the representation of divisiveness contrasted with envisioned unitariness, and confusion of spirit with clear-sightedness. In the novels of Jean Paul the two "worlds" are juxtaposed, each with its own specific reality. In *Hyperion* the higher world is recalled elegiacally and envisioned proleptically in the final emergence of poetic sight in the protagonist. Tieck shares the vision, but it remains a vision, never actually realized, in *Franz Sternbalds Wanderungen*. The powers of the imagination, lauded by Novalis, are mistrusted by the Tieck of *William Lovell* (and also to a certain extent in *Sternbald*) and displayed as dangerously seductive by Eichendorff and even as destructive by Hoffmann. So the imagination itself, the sovereign source of poetry, one would think, is also seen as the source both of visions of the higher world and of the divisions and frustrations of the present world. Even poetry itself is viewed variously: positively as the ultimate redeeming force by Novalis and Hölderlin, guardedly by Brentano and Tieck, skeptically by "Bonaventura" and Hoffmann, relatively by Eichendorff. Poetry for Eichendorff is the healing force only in a wide sense of the term: the practitioners, or would-be practitioners, of the art are relegated to a lesser status, but poetry in the sense of that higher state of mind which perceives connections between seemingly unconnected elements of experience, and relates finite to infinite, the presence of a "golden ground"—that is the redeeming force, but it is not confined to poets. Friedrich Schlegel is saying much the same with his concept of "universal poetry." The aesthetic statement of romanticism is therefore also an ethical statement, and nothing could be more wrong than to consider German romanticism as mere aestheticism. It speaks a clear "message" (to use an old-fashioned but not therefore ridiculous term), and a message whose relevance was not restricted to the era in which these writers lived.

But the aesthetic statement is there too, and it is important. Given this broader conception of "poetry," the novel is the vehicle best suited to express it in all its fullness. But not the novel in its traditional form. What was needed, sought after, and in part realized, was to present actual events and personages not as self-sufficiently "real," but always in relation to each other and to elements of experience that are not themselves events or personages, but that color and give perspective and deeper meaning to those actual events and personages. The particular is not merely shown as *related* to the general, the immanent to the transcendent, and the conditional to the unconditional, but as complementary aspects of one unitary whole which appears thus divided only in the phenomenal world. To convey this, a broad, elastic, comprehensive medium is required, combining genres, reacting to itself, relativizing the parts by irony, alternatives, multiple protagonists, and parallel actions which reflect upon each other, working toward an ultimate goal of totality but intentionally never reaching it. Images become events, and events turn into images. Characters develop counterparts or obverses, reality begets fantasies, and fantasies crystallize alarmingly into realities. Poetic boldness plays havoc with prose sobriety, confusion is heralded over the superficiality of superimposed order, and incompleteness over

Conclusion

completion as more expressive of the true nature of our experience.
For our few real moments of true understanding are fragmentary,
lightning flashes of illumination, unaccountable for in normal terms
of causality or chronology, sometimes visionary, sometimes coming
upon us when our rational powers are dormant, sometimes as seeming diversions from our normal paths of thought. Hence the re-
interpretation by these romantic novelists of certain traditional elements of novel-writing: the deeper meaning given to unexpected
incursions (whether thoughts or events or personages) into the steady
flow of life (and narration), the different function given to episodic
narratives and to digressions (which are now made into integral
parts, and important parts, of the total texture), and the changed
attitude toward whether chronological narration was a valid representation of the experience of time. And the desire, as Dorothea
Schlegel had said, not to aim at what was normally considered to
be a "satisfactory ending," but to leave the reader with something
to add, "in thoughts or in dreams"—to speculate on those further
thoughts of Hyperion, to continue wandering with Sternbald, reflect
on what will happen to Kreisler, and to Walt and Vult—and, of
course, on the circumstances that led to the untimely death of Kater
Murr. And to ponder the immense possibilities opened up by the
romantic view of the novel as poetry.

Notes

In these notes I concentrate on two things: giving explicit references to all the more important quotations in my text (in some cases with the original German), and suggesting further reading on the topics I discuss, without, however, attempting to refer to all the work that has been done on the individual novels. In what follows I use the normal (*PMLA*) abbreviations of certain titles, namely:

AF	*Anglistische Forschungen*
CL	*Comparative Literature*
DU	*Der Deutschunterricht*
DVLG	*Deutsche Vierteljahrsschrift für Literaturwissenschaft und Geistesgeschichte*
Fests.	*Festschrift*
GLL	*German Life and Letters*
GQ	*German Quarterly*
GR	*Germanic Review*
GRM	*Germanisch-Romanische Monatschrift*
JDSG	*Jahrbuch der Deutschen Schiller-Gesellschaft*
JEGP	*Journal of English and Germanic Philology*
JFDH	*Jahrbuch des Freien Deutschen Hochstifts*
JJPG	*Jahrbuch der Jean-Paul-Gesellschaft*
JWGV	*Jahrbuch des Wiener Goethe-Vereins*
LanM	*Les Langues Modernes*
MHG	*Mitteilungen der E.T.A. Hoffmann-Gesellschaft*

MLN	*Modern Language Notes*
MLQ	*Modern Language Quarterly*
Monatshefte	*Monatshefte für Deutschen Unterricht, Deutsche Sprache und Literatur.*
PLL	*Papers on Language and Literature*
PMLA	*Publications of the Modern Language Association of America*
Poetica	*Poetica: Zeitschrift für Sprach- und Literaturwissenschaft.*
WB	*Weimarer Beiträge*
WW	*Wirkendes Wort: Deutsche Sprache in Forschung und Lehre*
ZDP	*Zeitschrift für Deutsche Philologie*

Chapter One / Introduction

1. There is no book in English specifically on the novels of the German Romantics, but the collection of essays edited by Siegbert Prawer under the title *The Romantic Period in Germany* (New York: Schocken, 1970), contains an essay on "The Novel" by Hans Eichner. The individual novels are of course discussed in general treatments of German romanticism, and in monographs on the individual authors, the most important of which will be mentioned in succeeding chapters at the appropriate places. But, apart from Eichner's essay, there is, to my knowledge, nowhere any attempt to consider the novel-writing of the Romantics as a whole, or to delineate their concept of the genre.

In German the situation is not much better, though there are plenty of discussions (some of them very good) of individual romantic novels. There has been no comprehensive book on the romantic novel since Paula Scheidweiler's *Der Roman der deutschen Romantik* of 1916 (Leipzig and Berlin: Teubner), but there is an extensive treatment of the subject in H. A. Korff, *Geist der Goethezeit*, vol. III, (first published in 1940, the third revised edition of 1957 now available in a reprint, Leipzig: Koehler & Amelang) pp. 19–232. This deals only with the earlier Romantics but does treat *Hyperion* and Jean Paul (which Eichner does not). The later Romantics are treated in vol. IV of Korff, which includes a particularly extensive discussion of Hoffmann. Scheidweiler does recognize that the Romantics had a different conception of the novel from their predecessors, and she designates it as "musical," meaning thereby the expression of the universal in the particular, depicting a "feeling of world" rather than an empirical actuality, and therefore different from "epic" plasticity because it involves a denial of space and time in the search for what is beyond these. Korff speaks of a "changed attitude to life" [*Umwandlung des ganzen Lebensgefühls*] in the romantic period, by which man lives no longer in a "natural" world, but in a "supernatural" one (III, 7–8). The novels of the earlier Romantics are, for Korff, essentially self-portraiture [*Selbstdarstellung*] (III, 19), including what he calls "a new openness to infinity" [*Geöffnetheit der Phantasie gegen den neugefühlten Himmel der Ewigkeit*] (III, 33), but also its dualistic impulses, its fears and nihilistic tendencies—in other words, self-portrait of a generation. There is no real discussion in Korff of the romantic view of the novel as distinguished from other genres, except presumably the implication that it permits the fullest self-portraiture. Hans Heinrich Borcherdt, *Der Roman der Goethezeit* (Urach and Stuttgart: Port Verlag, 1949), draws heavily on Korff, and although, like Korff, he concentrates on analyses of the individual novels, mostly of their content, he does have a few pages (392–396) on the romantic concept of the novel as an artistic form; he does not, however, really go any further than Scheidweiler or Korff. Paul Böckmann, on the other hand, does attempt to do so in his interesting essay "Der Roman der Transzendentalpoesie in der Romantik" (in *Geschichte, Deutung, Kritik, Fests.* for Werner Kohlschmidt [Berne: Francke, 1969], pp. 165–185). He starts by saying that a new approach is needed to appreciate the romantic novels, asserting that their form is "transcendental," because they are basically concerned not with experience of the world but with the act of experiencing, the stages and processes of consciousness. Esther W. Hudgins, *Nicht-Epische Strukturen des romantischen Romans* (The Hague: Mouton, 1975), distinguishes Friedrich Schlegel's concept of the epic from his ideal for the novel, and demonstrates by the analysis of three romantic novels the nonepic structure of these. Unfortunately her concept of "nonepic" is not much more precise than Scheidweiler's "musical," with which it has various points of contact. Horst Meixner, *Romantischer Figuralismus: Kritische Studien zu Romanen von Arnim, Eichendorff und Hoffmann* (Frankfurt: Athenäum, 1971), asserts that in romantic novels, personages become "figures," i.e., representatives of religious and historical ideas, stylizations of "religiös-figurale Vorbilder aus dem christlichen Bereich" (p. 10).

2. Scott on Mrs. Radcliffe in *Lives of the Novelists* (prefatory essays to a series of novels published in Ballantyne's Novelists Library, this one in 1824). For an (abridged) reprint of this essay, see Ioan Williams, *Sir Walter Scott on Novelists and Fiction* (London: Routledge & Kegan Paul, 1968, pp. 102–119. Victor Hugo's review of *Quentin Durward* can be found in V. H., *Oeuvres complètes*, vol. 15, "Littérature et philosophie mêlées", ed. Michel Braspart (Givors: Martel 1952), pp. 171–188.

3. See my article "The Contemporary Background to a Passage in the *Lehrjahre*", in *Aspekte der Goethezeit* (Göttingen: Vandenhoeck & Ruprecht, 1977), pp. 138–139.

4. Schiller: Letter to Goethe, 20 October 1797. On the attitude of Schiller to the novel as a form, see my *Goethe and the Novel* (Ithaca: Cornell University Press, 1976), pp. 100–110.

5. Scott, *Miscellaneous Prose Works VI*, (Edinburgh: Cadell and London: Longman, Rees, Orme, Brown, and Greene, 1827), pp. 155–156.

6. Schiller, *Nationalausgabe*, vol. xx, ed. Benno von Wiese, (Weimar: Böhlau, 1962), pp. 459–460.

7. For Novalis's reactions to *Wilhelm Meister*, see Chapter 5 below.

8. Schlegel's essay: see *Kritische Friedrich-Schlegel-Ausgabe* (Munich-Paderborn-Vienna: Schöningh, vol. ii, 1967), ed. Hans Eichner, 126–146. The phrase "Sinn für das Universum" is on p. 134 of this edition of the text.

9. Schlegel, *Literary Notebooks 1797–1801*, ed. Hans Eichner (London: Athlone Press, 1957), No. 434.

Chapter Two / The Novel as Romantic Book

1. The best introduction to Friedrich Schlegel's life and works is undoubtedly Hans Eichner, *Friedrich Schlegel* (New York: Twayne, 1970).

2. I shall quote the works of Friedrich Schlegel from the *Kritische Friedrich-Schlegel-Ausgabe* [*KFSA*], edited by Ernst Behler with the cooperation of Jean-Jacques Anstett and Hans Eichner (Munich-Paderborn-Vienna: Schöningh, and

Zurich: Thomas-Verlag). This edition is still in progress, but well advanced. The text of the Athenäum Fragments is to be found in *KFSA*, vol. II, ed. Eichner (1967), pp. 165–255. For the 116th Fragment, see pp. 182–183. For Schlegel's theory of poetry, see Eichner's article "Friedrich Schlegel's Theory of Romantic Poetry," *PMLA* LXXI (1956), 1018–1041. Also Ernst Behler, "Friedrich Schlegels Theorie der Universalpoesie", *JDSG* I (1957), 211–252; Franz Norbert Mennemeier, *Friedrich Schlegels Poesiebegriff dargestellt anhand der literaturkritischen Schriften* (Munich: Fink, 1971), and Paul Böckmann's article "Zum Poesie-Begriff der Romantik" in *Wissen aus Erfahrungen, Fests.* for Herman Meyer (Tübingen: Niemeyer, 1976), pp. 371–383. Böckmann elaborates on Schelling's distinction between *Kunst* (conscious activity of the "genius") and *Poesie* (unconscious, "durch freie Gunst der Natur angeboren"), and, consequently between *Kunstpoesie* and *Naturpoesie.* Behler asserts that "poetry" for Schlegel is a very broad concept, the medium of communication of a whole "Bildungsprogramm," grounded in idealistic philosophy, the expression of spiritual reality and basically equivalent to "unbewusstes geniales Schöpfertum," the attempt at a synthesis between reflexion and speculation, finite consciousness and a sense of infinity. Mennemeier's extensive study is concerned primarily with the romantic concept of "objective poetry," which he, like Behler, interprets as a broad cultural concept aiming at a revolution of society. Basic to this concept is the idea of mediation between individual and whole, finite and infinite (see Mennemeier, pp. 98–99), such mediation being a creative act, progressive and continuous, and irony being one of its most potent forms.

3. But Eichner, in his volume on Schlegel in the Twayne series, translates these terms, I believe incorrectly, as "poetry of the educated" and "poetry of the people." On the distinction between *Kunst-* and *Naturpoesie*, see Böckmann's article cited in the previous note.

4. *KFSA* II, 284–285.

5. *KFSA* II, 257 and 258.

6. Eichner, "Schlegel's Theory of Romantic Poetry," pp. 1029–1032, and KFSA II, xcv.

7. Herder, *Sämtliche Werke*, ed. Bernhard Suphan, vol. XVIII (Berlin, 1883; reprint Hildesheim: Olms, 1967), pp. 59ff., and 109ff.

8. Eichner, "Schlegel's Theory of Romantic Poetry," p. 1021.

9. Friedrich Schlegel, *Literary Notebooks 1797–1801*, ed. Hans Eichner (London: Athlone Press, 1957; hereafter cited as *LN*), Nos. 76 and 86.

10. *LN*, No. 1096.

11. Boccaccio essay: *KFSA*, II, 373–396; *LN*, Nos. 427, 690, 860, 954, 1025.

12. *KFSA* II, 335. For Schlegel's "theory" of the novel, see Diana Behler, *The Theory of the Novel in Early German Romanticism* (Berne: Peter Lang, 1978). Earlier consideration of this topic is represented by Walter Bausch, *Theorien des epischen Erzählens in der deutschen Frühromantik* (Bonn: Bouvier, 1964), and Helmut Schanze's excellent article "Friedrich Schlegels Theorie des Romans" in *Deutsche Romantheorien*, ed. Reinhold Grimm (Frankfurt and Bonn: Athenäum, 1968), pp. 61–80 (2d ed., 1974, pp. 105–124.) See also Clemens Heselhaus, "Die Wilhelm-Meister-Kritik der Romantiker und die romantische Romantheorie," in *Nachahmung und Illusion*, ed. H. R. Jauss (Munich: Eidos, 1964), pp. 113–127.

13. *LN*, No. 69.

14. *LN*, No. 103.

15. *KFSA* II, 156.

16. *LN*, No. 288.

17. *LN*, No. 383. On *parekbasis*, see Bernhard Heimrich, *Fiktion und Fiktionsironie*

in Theorie und Dichtung der deutschen Romantik (Tübingen: Niemeyer, 1968), pp. 59–65.
18. *LN*, No. 340.
19. *LN*, Nos. 418, 511, 750, 794.
20. *KFSA* II, 333.
21. *LN*, No. 340.
22. *LN*, No. 358.
23. *LN*, No. 359.
24. *LN*, No. 379.
25. *LN*, No. 393. Cf. No. 419: "flung out without being integrated."
26. *LN*, No. 391.
27. *LN*, No. 612.
28. *KFSA* II, 149: Die Romane sind die sokratischen Dialoge unserer Zeit. In diese liberale Form hat sich die Lebensweisheit vor der Schulweisheit geflüchtet."
29. For this review, see *KFSA* II, 57–77.
30. *LN*, Nos. 754, 835, 774.
31. *LN*, No. 851.
32. *LN*, No. 1361; cf. No. 1339.
33. *LN*, No. 1352, with Eichner's transliteration of the mathematical symbols.
34. *LN*, Nos. 1339 and 1446.
35. *LN*, No. 1356.
36. On this point, see Schanze's article, p. 110.
37. *LN*, No. 1344.
38. For precise references, see Eichner's index at the back of *LN*.
39. Eichner, "Schlegel's Theory of Romantic Poetry," pp. 1024–1025.
40. *LN*, Nos. 289, 351, 584, 1096, 1583, 1703.
41. *LN*, No. 1728. On "elliptical", see Marshall Brown, *The Shape of German Romanticism* (Ithaca: Cornell University Press, 1979), pp. 127–179. Brown traces the romantic concept of elliptical form back to Jakob Böhme's doctrine of two centers.
42. The *Wilhelm Meister* essay is to be found in *KFSA* II (126–146).
43. *KFSA* II, 183 (No. 118).
44. *KFSA* II, 181 (No. 111).
45. *KFSA* II, 245 (No. 418).
46. *KFSA* II, 246–247 (No. 421).
47. *KFSA* II, 285.
48. *KFSA* II, 286.
49. *KFSA* II, 263.
50. *KFSA* II, 315.
51. *KFSA* II, 318–319.
52. *KFSA* II, 317.
53. *KFSA* II, 331. There is a detailed analysis of the *Brief über den Roman* in Karl Konrad Polheim, *Die Arabeske* (Munich-Paderborn-Vienna: Schöningh, 1966), pp. 134–197. See also Raymond Immerwahr's excellent essay "Die symbolische Form des 'Briefes über den Roman,'" *ZDP* 88 (1969) Sonderheft pp. 41–60.
54. *KFSA* II, 332; cf. *KFSA* XVIII, 303: "An Richter ist die tiefe Kränklichkeit und der Sinn fürs Kranke das Interessante und der superlative Grad der Individualität das Achtungswürdige."
55. *KFSA* II, 333.
56. *KFSA* II, 334.
57. *KFSA* III, 84. Schanze (p. 117) says that *Witz* in Friedrich Schlegel's use of the term means the creative principle itself ("das schöpferische Prinzip schlechthin").

58. *KFSA* II, 337–338.
59. *KFSA* II, 338.
60. *KFSA* II, 299.
61. *KFSA* XI, 159–160. See also Schlegel's review of Part One of Tieck's translation of *Don Quixote*, which accords high praise not only to *Don Quixote*, but also to *Galatea* and *Persiles* (*KFSA* II, 282–283).
62. *KFSA* VI, 274–276; "magic mirror," 276.
63. *KFSA* VI, 331; 395.
64. Friedrich Schlegel, *Neue philosophische Schriften*, ed. Josef Körner (Frankfurt: Schulte-Bumke, 1935), pp. 363–387.
65. Eichner, *Friedrich Schlegel*, pp. 35–36.
66. *KFSA* XVIII, xxvi ff.
67. *KFSA* V, 77. There is a considerable literature on the subject of romantic irony. Helmut Prang gives a useful overview of the more important treatments of this subject in *Die romantische Ironie* (Darmstadt: Wissenschaftliche Buchgesellschaft, 1972). The most extensive treatments are those by Ingrid Strohschneider-Kohrs, *Die romantische Ironie in Theorie und Gestaltung* (Tübingen: Niemeyer, 1960), and Heimrich, *Fiktion und Fiktionsironie*. See also Raymond Immerwahr, "The Subjectivity or Objectivity of Friedrich Schlegel's Poetic Irony," *GR* XXVI (1951), 173–190.
68. *KFSA* III, 12.
69. *KFSA* II, 318.
70. *KFSA* III, 84–85.
71. *KFSA* V, xvii–xviii.
72. The text of this essay is to be found in *KFSA* I, 70–115.
73. *KFSA* V, 7–9. On the form of *Lucinde*, see pp. 31–32 in Peter Virchow's introduction to his translation of the novel (Minneapolis: University of Minnesota Press, 1971): "the first six sections are a preparation for the central section and . . . the last six represent either some sort of further growth of the ideas contained in the central section or a denouement of the action of that section," and "the first six parts of the novel provide us with a picture of what Julius is, the central part shows us how he came to be what he is, and the last six parts adumbrate the further directions of his growth." Borcherdt, (*Der Roman der Goethezeit*, p. 428) speaks of "Arabesken." The standard treatment of the "arabesque" in romantic literature is Polheim, *Die Arabeske*, and it deals extensively with Friedrich Schlegel. Polheim distinguishes between "arabesques" as ornamental variations (or digressions) and "arabesque" as a total form. There is some evidence that the latter may have represented Schlegel's *ideal* form of the concept, but he undoubtedly also used the term in the former sense with reference to actual novels, as did Jean Paul and most of the other Romantics. Polheim defines the concept of the *Arabeske* as a *total* form as representing "infinite fulness in infinite unity" [*die unendliche Fülle in der unendlichen Einheit*] (p. 13). This, however, describes, to my mind, what the goal of representation might be, not the representation itself, and "arabesque," in either sense (as total form or as partial form) is surely a category of form, not of content, though Polheim disagrees, at least with reference to Schlegel, saying that the term can also be applied to content (p. 150).

Among the more perceptive interpretations of *Lucinde* are Wolfgang Paulsen, "Friedrich Schlegels *Lucinde* als Roman," *GR* XXI (1946), 173–190, who sees the work as a search for harmony, and therefore interprets the turning outward at the end of the novel as groping toward some kind of equilibrium between amorality and bourgeois values; [*Psychologisch und moralisch aber lag dieses Gleichgewicht zwischen Amoralität und Bürgerlichkeit, und die ganze* Lucinde *ist daher letzten Endes nichts als ein dynamisches Abtasten aller Existenzmöglichkeiten innerhalb dieser polaren Lebensformen"* (p. 189), which seems to me questionable. Esther Hudgins offers a long analysis of the "nonepic" elements in the novel (*Nicht-Epische Strukturen,* pp. 44–89). But by far the most elaborate interpretation of the interaction between form and content of *Lucinde* to be found in Polheim's article "Friedrich Schlegels *Lucinde*," *ZDP* 88 (1969), Sonderheft pp. 61–90.

74. *KFSA* v, 35.
75. *KFSA* v, 71.
76. *KFSA* v, 77.
77. *KFSA* v, xix, letter to Novalis, 20 October 1798.
78. On the reception of Lucinde, see *KFSA* v, xlvi–lv.

Chapter Three / Traditions and Innovations

1. *KFSA* v, lix and lx.
2. The material for Part Two of *Lucinde,* including the poems, is all to be found in KFSA v.
3. I quote *Florentin* from the only available modern reprint, that in the series Deutsche Literatur in Entwicklungsreihen, in vol. 7 of the section dealing with the Romantics (Leipzig: Reclam, 1933). This volume was edited by Paul Kluckhohn and is referred to hereafter as "Kluckhohn."
4. Kluckhohn, p. 10.
5. Kluckhohn, p. 99.
6. Kluckhohn, p. 138.
7. Kluckhohn, p. 167.
8. Kluckhohn, p. 239.
9. Kluckhohn, p. 240.
10. Kluckhohn, p. 241.
11. Ludwig Jonas and Wilhelm Dilthey, eds., *Aus Schleiermachers Leben,* vol. III (Berlin: Reimer, 1861), pp. 248, 253, 268; and *Krisenjahre der Frühromantik,* ed. Josef Körner (Brno: Rohrer, vol. 1, 1936), p. 215.
12. Hans Eichner, "*Camilla.* Eine unbekannte Fortsetzung von Dorothea Schlegels *Florentin.*" *JFDH,* 1965, pp. 314–368.
13. On this aspect of the novel, see J. Hibberd's excellent article "Dorothea Schlegel's *Florentin* and the Precarious Idyll," *GLL* N.S. XXX (1977), 198–207.
14. Kluckhohn, p. 228.
15. Not much has been written on *Florentin,* but, in addition to Kluckhohn's notes and introduction in his edition, the eager reader is referred to Scheidweiler, *Der Roman der deutschen Romantik,* pp. 24–29, and Borcherdt, *Der Roman der Goethezeit,* pp. 414–421.
16. Erich Kahler, *The Inward Turn of Narrative* (Princeton: Princeton University Press, 1973). Ian P. Watt, *The Rise of the Novel,* (Berkeley: University of California Press, 2d ed., 1959).
17. These are the opening sentences of, respectively, Crébillon's *Les Egarements du coeur et de l'esprit* (1736–1738), Prévost's *Manon Lescaut* (1731), *Gulliver's Travels* (1726), and Godwin's *Caleb Williams* (1794).
18. Peter Brooks, *The Novel of Worldliness* (Princeton: Princeton University Press, 1969), p. 4.
19. *Tristram Shandy,* Book 1, ch. 22.
20. Peter Michelsen, *Laurence Sterne und der deutsche Roman des achtzehnten Jahrhunderts* (Göttingen: Vandenhoeck & Ruprecht, 1962), p. 42.

21. "Eine freie Ansicht des Lebens," in a review of 1806. See my *Goethe and the Novel*, p. 152, and what Goethe had to say on Goldsmith and Sterne (summarized in chapter 9 of my Goethe book).

22. Book iv, ch. 22.

23. Cf. Alice Green Fredman, *Diderot and Sterne* (New York: Columbia University Press, 1955).

24. In Diderot, *Oeuvres romanesques* (Paris: Garnier, 1962), p. ii.

25. Fredman, p. 83.

26. Fredman, p. 204.

27. Sterne, *Letters*, ed. L. P. Curtis (Oxford: Clarendon Press, 1935), p. 77.

28. Book i, ch. 10.

29. Book iv, ch. 32 and ch. 22.

30. *Oeuvres romanesques*, p. 553.

31. Roland Mortier in his distinguished book *Diderot en Allemagne* (Paris: Presses Universitaires de France, 1954), says that it was Diderot's technique, rather than the content, that appealed to Schlegel: "Ce qui a séduit Schlegel en Diderot, ce n'est pas tant sa pensée ou sa vision du monde que sa technique, d'une liberté désinvolte, un peu folle, qui fait craquer de toutes parts les structures littéraires traditionelles" (p. 236). He also notes direct echoes of *Jacques le fataliste* in Hoffmann (who, as a musician, was also interested in *Le Neveu de Rameau*.) I have not come across anything really definitive on the relations of the Romantics to Sterne. Gertrude Joyce Hallamore's study *Das Bild Laurence Sternes in Deutschland von der Aufklärung bis zur Romantik* (Berlin: Ebering, 1936) has some useful references. Michelsen's book (see note 20 to this chapter) includes, of the authors I discuss, only Jean Paul. Johann Czerny, *Sterne, Hippel und Jean Paul* (Berlin: Duncker, 1904), contains some useful material. In the vast literature on Jean Paul there are of course constant references to that author's indebtedness to Sterne, and there are similar statements regarding Friedrich Schlegel, but nothing really searching or wide-ranging on Sterne's significance for the German romantic novelists as a whole has come to my notice.

32. KFSA ii, 152: "An geselligem Witz und geselliger Fröhlichkeit sind wenige Bücher mit dem Roman Faublas zu vergleichen. Er ist der Champagner seiner Gattung." Cf. *Literary Notebooks*, ed. Eichner, No. 1966.

33. The three parts of Louvet's novel were: *Une année de la vie du Chevalier de Faublas* (1787), *Six Semaines de la vie du Chevalier de Faublas* (1788) and *La Fin des amours du Chevalier de Faublas* (1790). The complete text is readily available in *Romanciers du XVIIIe. siècle*, vol. ii (Paris: Pléiade edition, 1965), ed. Marguerite du Cheyron.

34. Pléiade ii, 535.

35. Pléiade ii, 746ff.

36. Pléiade ii, 608. Here is an attempt at a translation of this passage: "I wanted to implant a kiss on the vicomte. "Mademoiselle," he said, "it's for me to make the attack." He took me by the hand, made me leave the table, and tried to kiss me. I repelled him vigorously: "Leave me alone, monsieur, you are impertinent." The vicomte, more stubborn than enterprising, seemed only to want to steal a kiss, and kept laughing at the resistance he encountered. Apparently more accustomed to resist than to pursue, he showed much skill and little vigor in his attack. Mlle. de Portail on the other hand, reversing all the usual behavior, displayed much strength and little grace in her defense. The vicomte, soon exhausted, collapsed on to a sofa. "That girl is a real dragon," he cried. "One would have to be Hercules to subdue her! How wise is Mother Nature. She has made us women sweet and weak. I see now that all is for the best in the better

of all possible worlds. Let's put things right again. Mischievous young lady, calm yourself! I am now just the Marquise de B***; the Vicomte de Florville yields up all his rights to you."

37. Marion Beaujean, *Der Trivialroman in der zweiten Hälfte des 18. Jahrhunderts* (Bonn: Bouvier, 1964). An earlier study, still very valuable, of this subject is Marianne Thalmann, *Der Trivialroman des 18. Jahrhunderts und der romantische Roman* (Berlin: Ebering, 1923). There is a good section in Borcherdt on the subject (pp. 239–252). Otto Rommel has an article in *DVLG* 17 (1939), 183–220, entitled "Rationalistische Dämonie. Die Geisterromane des ausgehenden 18. Jahrhunderts."

38. Beaujean, pp. 107–118.
39. Beaujean, pp. 115ff.
40. Beaujean, p. 123.

Chapter Four / Toward a Poetic Novel

1. See my *Goethe and the Novel*, pp. 159–160.

2. For a general introduction in English to Jean Paul, see Dorothea Berger, *Jean Paul Friedrich Richter* (New York: Twayne, 1972), and, in German, Uwe Schweikert, *Jean Paul* (Stuttgart: Metzler, 1970). The secondary literature on this author is vast: for a bibliography (up to 1963) see Eduard Berend, *Jean-Paul-Bibliographie*, newly edited and expanded by Johannes Krogoll (Stuttgart: Klett, 1963). A supplement to this is provided by Eike Fuhrmann, "Jean-Paul-Bibliographie, 1963–1965," *JJPG* 1 (1966) 163–179. Dorothea Berger includes in her book a selected list of translations into English of Jean Paul's novels, and a useful select bibliography of secondary literature, with some comments. Schweikert's account of Jean Paul's life and artistic development is excellent. He also lists the more important studies on the individual novels, and deals with their historical, political, and literary background. The standard biography of Jean Paul is that by Walther Harich (Leipzig: Haessel, 1925). A recent book by Rüdiger Scholz, *Welt und Form des Romans bei Jean Paul* (Berne: Francke, 1973), gives a good critical overview of the subject, which builds on to earlier criticism, taking issue particularly with the treatments by Max Kommerell (*Jean Paul* [Frankfurt: Klostermann, 1933]) and Peter Michelsen (in *Laurence Sterne und der deutsche Roman des achtzehnten Jahrhunderts*). It also contains an excellent bibliography. On Jean Paul's conception of the novel, there is a good article by Bernhard Böschenstein ("Jean Pauls Romankonzeption," in B. B., *Studien zur Dichtung des Absoluten* [Zurich: Atlantis, 1968], pp. 25–44). Ulrich Profitlich, *Der seelige Leser. Untersuchungen zur Dichtungstheorie Jean Pauls.* (Bonn: Bouvier, 1968), deals specifically with how Jean Paul wanted his works to be read, and his structural methods of assuring the required effect. Wolfdietrich Rasch's essay entitled *Die Erzählweise Jean Pauls* (Munich: Hanser, 1961), demonstrates how what Rasch calls Jean Paul's "interruptive" style is the expression of his central theme of the disharmony of the world. Albert Béguin's treatment of Jean Paul in *L'Ame romantique et le rêve* (Paris: Corti, 2d ed., 1939), is one of the best sections in a very remarkable book.

I quote Jean Paul's novels from the edition edited by Norbert Miller and Walter Höllerer and published by the Hanser Verlag of Munich between 1960 and 1963 (hereafter Hanser). I also refer to the Prussian Academy edition of the *Sämtliche Werke* (hereafter *SW*) at various points.

3. Baudelaire, *Oeuvres complètes* (Paris: Gallimard, Pléiade ed., 1975–1976), II, 88.

4. E.g., letter to Thomas Beddoes, 21 March 1806 (*SW*, Abt. III, vol. 5, p.

Notes to Chapter 4

84): "Ihr Sterne und Swift—dieses Zwillingsgestirn des Humors—waren meine wegweisenden Sterne". Cf. Hanser II, 537.

5. *Der Komet* was long in composition. Originally it was to have combined three things: the story of an apothecary and Jean Paul's own biography, these two alternating "narratives" linked in a structure inspired by the English eighteenth-century moral weeklies which was to take the form of a jocular journey through the planets. From the outset it was conceived as a humorous novel, a "pantheon of humor." Rabelais and Cervantes are mentioned as models. But the autobiographical element was eventually taken out (and published separately after Jean Paul's death), the "moral weekly" arabesques were relegated to an appendix, the planets were replaced by earthly towns with ordinary inhabitants—and, in general, the original far-ranging plan of a fantasy became a much more limited, satirical-realistic journey-novel. The work was never finished, and although it contains marvelous things, one misses that tension between the immanent and the transcendent which had given the earlier novels their special power. And if humor is the attempt to resolve this tension, then one must surely agree that the humor is not rich enough to do so. *Der Komet* has its admirers, but it is not the great German humorous novel that it was intended to be. There are two full-scale studies of this novel: Uwe Schweikert, *Jean Pauls "Komet": Selbstparodie der Kunst* (Stuttgart: Metzler, 1971), and Susanne Gierlich, *Jean Paul: "Der Komet oder Nikolaus Marggraf. Eine komische Geschichte"* (Göppingen: Kümmerle, 1972).

6. For the genesis of *Die unsichtbare Loge*, see Berend's introduction to his edition of it in *SW*, Abt. I, vol. 2. For critical analyses of this novel, the reader is referred to Borcherdt, *Der Roman der Goethezeit*, pp. 167–183, and Berger, pp. 38–48 (Korff does not discuss it). See also P. D. Rowson's short but perceptive article "The Opening Scene of Jean Paul's *Die unsichtbare Loge*," *GLL*, N.S. XXXI (1978), 221–227, which demonstrates "the wealth of relationships and perspectives from which Jean Paul constructs the world of his novels" (p. 226), and Wulf Köpke, "Jean Pauls *Unsichtbare Loge*. Die Aufklärung des Lesers durch 'Anti-Roman,'" *JJPG* 10, (1975), 49–67, who asserts that here the form of the novel is used to replace a false ideal of the genre by true poetry [*umfunktioniert zur Demontage des falschen Romans im Bewusstsein des Lesers und zugleich zur Erscheinung der wahren Poesie des Lebens*] (p. 67).

7. Hanser I, 28.
8. Hanser I, 30.
9. Hanser I, 221.
10. Hanser I, 223.
11. Hanser I, 135.
12. Hanser I, 435.
13. Hanser I, 1317.
14. Hanser I, 1026.
15. Hanser I, 555.
16. *SW*, Abt. I, vol. 2, v. Diary entry for 7 May 1791. See also *SW* Abt. I, vol. 3, pp. xxxiv–xxxvi.
17. Hans Bach gives a full account of the genesis of *Hesperus* in his introduction to the relevant volume of *SW*, namely Abt. I, vol. 3.
18. Hanser I, 583.
19. Hanser I, 590.
20. *SW*, Abt. I, vol. 3, xxxvi.
21. Hanser I, 681.
22. Hanser I, 891.

23. Hanser I, 683.
24. Hanser I, 936–941.
25. Hanser I, 827.
26. For treatments of *Hesperus*, see Borcherdt, pp. 183–203, which includes an elaborate analysis of the character of Viktor, though I find it hard to agree with his statement that Viktor is a rounded character from the outset: "schon zu Anfang eine durchaus abgerundete und originelle Persönlichkeit, die nicht erst durch Irrtümer in ihren Lehrjahren erzogen werden muss." Korff (*Geist der Goethezeit* III, 25–35), asserts (p. 31) that rescue from romantic ennui [*innere Rettung vor dem Lebensweh des Romantikers*] is the main theme of the novel—which also seems dubious to me. For Béguin, who calls Jean Paul the great master of dreams: "le maître incontesté du rêve, le poète des grands songes cosmiques, le peintre des paysages fabuleux où le moi se perd voluptueusement dans les espaces infinis" (p. 167), *Hesperus* is Jean Paul's central work, and Béguin devotes to it some of his most vibrant pages. See also Hans Bach, *Jean Pauls Hesperus* (Leipzig: Mayer & Müller, 1929), and Dorothee Hedinger-Fröhner, *Jean Paul: der utopische Gehalt des Hesperus* (Bonn: Bouvier, 1977).
27. Hanser II, 344.
28. Hanser II, 348.
29. Hanser II, 538.
30. Hanser II, 553.
31. Hanser II, 558.
32. Hanser II, 565.
33. Hanser II, 408.
34. Hanser II, 259–265.
35. Hanser II, 267.
36. On *Siebenkäs*, see Borcherdt, pp. 214–223, and Korff III, 42–48, neither of whom seems to me to do justice to the very serious, almost tragic nature of this novel. For Korff it is the development of the humoristic idyll (which is how he describes *Wutz*—wrongly, I think) into a "tragicomic novel," which is ultimately humorous, with Siebenkäs's humor being the expression of "high culture of the intellect" (!) and Leibgeber as the type of the "absolute humorist" (p. 45) (whatever that may be). Dorothea Berger, on the other hand, does appreciate the tragic dimension (pp. 83–95) as does Gerhard Schulz in his essay "Jean Pauls *Siebenkäs*," in *Aspekte der Goethezeit* (Göttingen: Vandenhoeck & Ruprecht, 1977), pp. 215–239—an excellent analysis, though it perhaps rather overdoes the "religious" aspect of the novel. There is also an older and fuller study of the novel by Hans Dahler, *Jean Pauls Siebenkäs. Struktur und Grundbild* (Berne: Francke, 1962).
37. For a detailed account of the various stages in the composition and development of *Titan*, see Berend's introduction to vol. 8 of the first *Abteilung* of *SW*. See also, for a full assessment of the novel, the extensive treatment of it in Korff (III, 122–169), who interprets it as romantic man's coming to terms with his own romanticism [*die Auseinandersetzung des romantischen Menschen mit seinem Romantikertum*] (p. 123) and sees in it the *classical* tendencies of Jean Paul's ideal of education (126), and these represent in a way a denial of the specifically Jean-Paulesque: "Wenn der Titan ein Erziehungsroman ist, dann bedeutet das, dass sein Held im Laufe der Entwicklung das spezifisch Jean Paulsche verliert und statt dessen einen zunehmend idealen und allgemeinen Charakter bekommt" (p. 170). Borcherdt's discussion of the novel (pp. 303–334) embodies a similar interpretation. Both are more convinced by the ending than I am, and neither takes the Giannozzo appendix into account, which would seem to me to be a falsification of the true tenor of the complete work, to which the Giannozzo section

inherently belongs (see my discussion of it later in the chapter). In his 1970 book on Jean Paul, Schweikert states (pp. 41–42): "Die Einkräftigkeit steht im Roman das Ideal einer harmonischen Bildung, die Allkräftigkeit des tätigen Menschentums gegenüber, zu welchem Albano sich durchringen muss." He considers the ending of the novel a "compromise": "Jean Paul lässt zwar die Titanide Linda untergehen, rettet aber inkonsequenterweise den Titanen Albano, indem er dessen genialischen Idealismus harmonisiert, ihn aufs normale Menschenmass herabmindert" (p. 42). Schweikert lists the more important studies of *Titan* on pp. 50–51, including some on the *Komischer Anhang*.

38. Letter to Fritz Jacobi, 8 September 1803.
39. Hanser iii, 801.
40. Hanser iii, 663.
41. Borcherdt (p. 321) sees her as a combination of Natalie and Therese in Goethe's novel.
42. On the various stages in the composition of *Flegeljahre*, see *SW*, Abt. i, Introduction to vol. 10. For critical assessments of this novel see Borcherdt, pp. 453–562, and Korff iii, 170–196. Whereas Korff to my mind does not do sufficient justice to the tragic dimension of *Siebenkäs*, he overplays what he considers the tragic nature of *Flegeljahre*, speaking for instance (p. 185) of the "Tragödie vom vergeblichen Brüderbund," and stating that in the two brothers we have both potentialities, ecstatic and sardonic, of romantic man: "die Seligkeit des schwärmenden Herzens und die in Humor verwandelte Unseligkeit des enttäuschten [Herzens]" (p. 186). Jean Paul embodies in the twins both sides of his poetic nature and, in more general terms, the tragedy of human separation: "die Tragödie der hoffnungslosen menschlichen Getrenntheit" (p. 187). Gerhart Mayer, "Die humorgeprägte Struktur von Jean Pauls "Flegeljahren" ZDP 83 (1964), 409–426, interprets the combination of devaluation and transfiguration, of "desillusionierender Abwertung des endlichen Daseins und schwärmerischgläubiger Verklärung der Welt" as demonstrative of a humorous structure. Herman Meyer's discussion of the novel in *Zarte Empirie* (Stuttgart: Metzler, 1963), is the best account of its structure that I have read. Peter Horst Neumann, *Jean Pauls "Flegeljahre"* (Göttingen: Vandenhoeck &Ruprecht, 1966), builds heavily on Meyer, and is really a series of individual essays on crucial episodes. On the ending, see the excellent essay by Heinrich Bosse, "Der offene Schluss der 'Flegeljahre,'" *JJPG* 2 (1967), 73–84.
43. *SW*, Abt. iii, vol. 3, 193 (Letter to Christian Otto, 24 or 25 May 1799).
44. Hanser ii, 1058.
45. *SW* Abt. i, vol. 10, p. lix.
46. *SW*, Abt. i, vol. 10, p. lxx.
47. Hanser ii, 793.
48. Hanser ii, 1032.
49. Hanser ii, 655.
50. Hanser ii, 680.
51. Hanser ii, 979.
52. Hanser ii, 860.
53. Hanser ii, 902.
54. Hanser ii, 1051.
55. Hanser v, 467.
56. Hanser v, 447.
57. Hanser v, 43.
58. Hanser v, 89.
59. Hanser v, 126.

60. René Wellek, *A History of Modern Criticism*, vol. 2 (New Haven: Yale University Press, 1955), pp. 105–108.

61. Hanser v, 184–185.

62. Hanser v, 201–202.

63. Hanser v, 264.

64. Hanser v, 248.

65. For a general introduction to Hölderlin in English see Ronald Peacock, *Hölderlin* (London: Methuen, 1938), Agnes Stansfield, *Hölderlin* (Manchester: Manchester University Press, 1944), and the two essays on him in Michael Hamburger, *Contraries: Studies in German Literature* (New York: Dutton, 1970). In German there is a good general introduction by Lawrence Ryan (*Friedrich Hölderlin* [Stuttgart: Metzler, 2d ed., 1967]), with a bibliography of the extensive literature on Hölderlin.

There is a translation into English of *Hyperion* by Willard R. Trask (New York: Ungar, 1965) and a critical reading of it by Walter Silz, *Hölderlin's Hyperion: A Critical Reading*, (Philadelphia: University of Pennsylvania Press, 1969), which does not do justice to the structural excellence of the novel. In German there are many discussions of it, including elaborate ones by Scheidweiler (*Der Roman der deutschen Romantik*, pp. 83–109), Borcherdt (pp. 334–362), and Korff (III, 96–122). There is also an important book on it by Lawrence Ryan, *Hölderlins Hyperion. Exzentrische Bahn und Dichterberuf* (Stuttgart: Metzler, 1965), and an extensive study by Friedbert Aspetsberger, *Welteinheit und Epische Gestaltung. Studien zur Ichform von Hölderlins Roman "Hyperion"* (Munich: Fink, 1971). Ryan comments on the fact that the novel expands the expressive potentialities of the epistolary form by allowing the narrator to develop as he narrates. This is a "progressiver Roman . . . indem sich das erzählende Ich als Selbstreflexion des handelnden Ich konstituiert" (p. 6). Aspetsberger has an excellent bibliography of relevant literature and discusses it at length in the course of his own exposition.

I quote *Hyperion* from the text in the so-called *Kleine Stuttgarter Ausgabe*, ed. Friedrich Beissner, vol. 3 (Stuttgart: Kohlhammer, 1958). An account of the genesis of *Hyperion* and the various versions of it is to be found on pp. 311–328 of Beissner's edition (hereafter Beissner III). Other material on Hölderlin is cited from the same edition. The letter of July 1793 is in Beissner VI (Stuttgart: Kohlhammer, 1959), pp. 94–97.

66. Beissner VI, 96.

67. Beissner VI, 149.

68. All these versions are to be found in Beissner III.

69. Beissner VI, 259; Beissner III, 322–323.

70. Beissner III, 5.

71. See my *Goethe and the Novel*, pp. 40–41.

72. Beissner III, 166: "Versöhnung ist mitten im Streit und alles Getrennte findet sich wieder."

73. M. H. Abrams, *Natural Supernaturalism* (New York: Norton, 1971), p. 184. Abrams gives an acute analysis of *Hyperion* on pp. 237–244 of the same book.

74. Beissner III, 249: "Wir durchlaufen alle eine exzentrische Bahn, und es ist kein anderer Weg möglich von der Kindheit zur Vollendung . . . Wir reissen uns los vom friedlichen En Kai Pan der Welt, um es herzustellen, durch uns Selbst." On the cyclical structure of *Hyperion*: Ryan, *Hölderlins Hyperion*, pp. 215–216.

75. Friedrich von Blanckenburg, *Versuch über den Roman* (Leipzig and Liegnitz: bey David Siegberts Wittwe, 1774), p. 412.

76. Ryan, *Hölderlins Hyperion*, p. 228.

77. Abrams, p. 239.

78. Beissner III, 18.
79. Beissner III, 61.
80. Beissner III, 70.
81. Beissner III, 89.
82. Beissner III, 155.
83. Beissner III, 333: "mehr ein Poëm, als ein Roman."

Chapter Five / The Novel as Poetry

1. The best introduction in English to the work of Novalis is John Neubauer, *Novalis* (New York: Twayne, 1980). An earlier general study is Friedrich Hiebel, *Novalis* (Chapel Hill: University of North Carolina Press, 1954). Bruce Haywood has written on Novalis's images in *Novalis: The Veil of Imagery* (The Hague: Mouton, 1959), which includes a full treatment of *Heinrich von Ofterdingen* (Neubauer's treatment of that novel is rather thin). Neubauer includes a list of English translations of Novalis's works (pp. 176–177).

In German the secondary literature on Novalis is vast. Of particular significance for a consideration of him as a novelist are Oskar Serge Ehrensperger, *Die epische Struktur in Novalis' "Heinrich von Ofterdingen"* (Winterthur: Schellenberg, 1965); Hans-Joachim Beck, *Friedrich von Hardenberg: "Oeconomie des Styls"* (Bonn: Grundmann, 1976), which deals with the "reception" of *Wilhelm Meister* "into" *Ofterdingen*, and Gerhard Schulz, "Die Poetik des Romans bei Novalis", *JFDH*, 1964, pp. 120–157.

2. Schulz's article has been reprinted in *Deutsche Romantheorien*, ed. Reinhold Grimm (Frankfurt and Bonn: Athenäum, 1968), pp. 81–110. I quote from the second edition (1974) where the article appears on pp. 125–154.

3. Novalis, *Schriften*, ed. Paul Kluckhohn and Richard Samuel, 2d revised and extended edition (Stuttgart: Kohlhammer, 4 vols. [so far], 1960–1975). I shall quote throughout from this edition. The letter to Caroline is to be found in IV, 277–281.

4. *Schriften* II, 528 and 533–535.
5. II, 536 and 534.
6. II, 563 and 544.
7. II, 570.
8. II, 579–582.
9. For a discussion of this passage, see my *Goethe and the Novel*, pp. 77 ff., and my article in *Aspekte der Goethezeit* (Göttingen: Vandenhoeck & Ruprecht, 1977), entitled "The Contemporary Background to a Passage in the *Lehrjahre*" (pp. 137–145).
10. *Schriften* III, 65.
11. III, 248.
12. III, 665.
13. III, 254; cf. II, 501.
14. III, 334.
15. II, 564.
16. II, 564; cf. II, 647.
17. III, 312.
18. II, 640–642.
19. III, 326; II, 425.
20. III, 558.
21. III, 639.

22. III, 562; cf. III, 645: "Unbequemlichkeiten einer chronologisch fortschreitenden Erzählung."
23. III, 650.
24. II, 380.
25. II, 613.
26. III, 683.
27. IV, 323. Letter to Tieck of 23 February 1800.
28. On Novalis and Böhme, see Carl Paschek, "Novalis und Böhme," *JFDH*, 1976, pp. 138–167, which lists earlier treatments of this subject on p. 140, fn. 8. On the general subject of Böhme and the Romantics, see Marshall Brown, *The Shape of German Romanticism*, pp. 133–141.
29. *Schriften* II, 564, and III, 587.
30. III, 665–669.
31. III, 668.
32. III, 686: "Der Dichter ist wahrhaft sinnberaubt—dafür kommt alles in ihm vor. Er stellt im eigentlichsten Sinn Sub[ject] Obj[ect] vor—Gemüth und Welt. Daher die Unendlichkeit eines guten Gedichts, die Ewigkeit. Der Sinn für P[oësie] hat nahe Verwandtschaft mit dem Sinn der Weissagung und dem religiösen, dem Sehersinn überhaupt. Der Dichter ordnet, vereinigt, wählt, erfindet—und es ist ihm selbst unbegreiflich, warum gerade so und nicht anders." I have not attempted to reproduce the play on various meanings of the word *Sinn* in this passage. The square brackets represent the editors' extensions of Novalis's abbreviations.
33. IV, 251, 254, 323.
34. I, 71.
35. I, 111, Paralipomenon 7.
36. II, 584:   Einem gelang es—er hob den Schleyer der Göttin zu Sais—
   Aber was sah er? er sah—Wunder des Wunders—Sich Selbst.
37. I, 91.
38. I, 96.
39. These different attitudes to nature may well represent those of Schelling, Goethe, Hemsterhuis, Tieck, alchemists and Fichte. See *Schriften* I, 73–74.
40. I, 87.
41. I, 90.
42. II, 427.
43. I, 99.
44. Neubauer finds the *Lehrlinge zu Sais* inconclusive, believing that Novalis himself had not yet found the solution. He does not consider the possibility that the work intentionally presents various attitudes side by side without wishing to suggest a *true* answer. Other discussions of this work are: Heinz Bollinger, *Novalis, Die Lehrlinge zu Sais; Versuch einer Erläuterung* (Winterthur: 1954) which I have not been able to see; Juri Striedter's article, "Die Komposition der 'Lehrlinge zu Sais,'" in *DU* 7/2 (1955), 5–23; and, most extensive, Ulrich Gaier's book, *Krumme Regel* (Tübingen: Niemeyer, 1970). Both Striedter and Gaier demonstrate that there is a real structural principle embodied in *Die Lehrlinge zu Sais*.
45. On *Ofterdingen*, see Scheidweiler, *Der Roman der deutschen Romantik*, pp. 55–83, Borcherdt, *Der Roman der Goethezeit*, pp. 363–382, the elaborate discussion in Korff (*Geist der Goethezeit* III, 559–596), and especially Richard Samuel's excellent essay in *Der deutsche Roman*, ed. Benno von Wiese (Düsseldorf: Bagel, 1963), pp. 252–300. Also: Johannes Mahr, *Übergang zum Endlichen. Der Weg des Dichters in Novalis' "Heinrich von Ofterdingen"* (Munich: Fink, 1970), with a good bibliography, but dealing only with Part One of the novel; and the older essay

by Oskar Walzel, "Die Formkunst von Hardenbergs 'Heinrich von Ofterdingen,'" *GRM* 7 (1915–1919), 403–444 and 465–479.

46. A comparison between Novalis and Kafka, though not with regard to the use of images, is also made by Neubauer (p. 135).

47. See *Schriften* I, 359–369. Most of the secondary literature on *Ofterdingen* speaks only of two parts to the novel.

48. I, 199.

49. I, 206.

50. I, 210–211.

51. I, 220.

52. Cf. III, 377: "Im Märchen glaube ich am besten meine Gemütsstimmung ausdrücken zu können."

53. I, 236.

54. I, 246.

55. I, 259.

56. I, 266.

57. I, 281.

58. I, 283–284.

59. I, 286.

60. See particularly the interpretation by Kluckhohn in *Schriften* I, 43–67.

61. For Novalis's interest in and knowledge of science, see Neubauer, *Novalis,* chapter 3. See also Neubauer, *Bifocal Vision: Novalis' Philosophy of Nature and Disease* (Chapel Hill: University of North Carolina Press, 1971).

62. *Schriften* I, 330.

63. I, 328.

64. I, 330.

65. I, 333. There is an excellent discussion of this conversation with Sylvester in Charles M. Barrack's article "Conscience in *Heinrich von Ofterdingen:* Novalis' Metaphysic of the Poet," *GR* 46 (1971), 257–284. Barrack is of the opinion that "Conscience, like love and poetry, is another term which expresses absolute conscious ego [in Fichte's sense of "ego"; see my next chapter]. . . . For the hero, conscience appears as duty because the hero lives partly under the domination of raw nature. This prevents conscience from appearing in its true essence, i.e., the autonomous will of absolute ego. But for the poet, who is a "free guest" [*Schriften* I, 267] in this world, conscience appears in its true form, our absolute freedom, ego's consciousness of itself. In other words, conscience, for the poet, appears in its most intimate form, poetry" (p. 284).

66. This is the opinion of Johannes Mahr (pp. 15–18). But see Samuel's valiant attempt to reconstruct the rest of the novel in his essay on the novel, the farthest that anyone has ever gone in this direction and, on the whole, very persuasive.

67. *Schriften* IV, 322. And, as Novalis wrote elsewhere (II, 545), poetry is the romanticization of the world": "Die Welt muss romantisiert werden. So findet man den urspr [ünglichen] Sinn wieder. Romantisieren ist nichts, als eine quallit[ative] Potenzirung. Das niedre Selbst wird mit einem bessern Selbst in dieser Operation identificirt. So wie wir selbst eine solche qualit[ative] Potenzenreihe sind. Diese Operation ist noch ganz unbekannt. Indem ich dem Gemeinen einen hohen Sinn, dem Gewöhnlichen ein geheimnissvolles Ansehn, dem Bekannten die Würde des Unbekannten, dem Endlichen einen unendlichen Schein gebe so romantisire ich es—Umgekehrt ist die Operation für das Höhere, Unbekannte, Mystische, Unendliche—dies wird durch diese Verknüpfung logarythmisirt—Es bekommt einen geläufigen Ausdruck, romantische Philosophie. *Lingua romana.* Wechselerhöhung und Erniedrigung."

Chapter Six / A Visit with the Philosophers.

1. A good account in English of the German romantic philosophers is that by Frederick Copleston in vol. 7, part 1 of his *History of Philosophy* (available in Image Books, New York: Doubleday, 1965). In German the clearest account is probably still that of Nicolai Hartmann, *Philosophie des deutschen Idealismus* (Berlin: De Gruyter, 2d ed., 1960). Neither Copleston nor Hartmann deals with romantic *literature*, but Korff has a good account in *Geist der Goethezeit* III, 235–346, which does connect romantic philosophy with romantic literature, and particularly with the novel.

2. Fichte, *Grundlage der gesammten Wissenschaftslehre* (1794). See Fichte, *Sämtliche Werke*, ed. J. H. Fichte (Berlin: Veit, 1845; reprint De Gruyter, 1965), I, 225–227.

3. *Schellings Werke*, ed. Manfred Schröter (Munich: Beck, 1927; reprint, 1965) I, 237. Subsequent references to Schelling in my notes to this chapter refer to this edition [*Werke*].

4. *Werke* II, 349.

5. *Werke* III, 189.

6. *Werke, Ergänzungsband* III, 325; 329.

7. *Werke, Ergänzungsband* III, 325.

8. *Werke, Ergänzungsband* III, 327.

9. *Werke, Ergänzungsband* III, 328.

10. *Werke, Ergänzungsband* III, 330–331.

11. *Werke, Ergänzungsband* III, 332.

12. Friedrich Schleiermacher, *Werke* (Berlin: Reimer, 1835–1864), IV, 242: cf. Copleston vol. 7, part 1 p. 188.

13. "Fortgehende Geschichte des Selbstbewusstseins," *Werke* II, 331.

14. Béguin, *L'Ame romantique et le rêve*, pp. 67–68.

15. Quoted in Béguin, p. 76.

16. Béguin, pp. 76–77.

17. Béguin, pp. 189 (Jean Paul), 206 (Novalis), 253 (Arnim).

18. Novalis, *Schriften* II, 419.

19. Maria Tatar, *Spellbound* (Princeton: Princeton University Press, 1978), p. xii.

20. Tatar, p. 45.

21. Fichte, *Sämtliche Werke*, v, 268.

22. "Über die natürliche Magie der Einbildungskraft" (1795) and "Über das Träumen" (1799). On this subject, see J. W. Smeed, *Jean Paul's Dreams* (London: Oxford University Press, 1966).

23. For Hoffmann, see Béguin, pp. 303–304; for Arnim, Hanser I, 519: "was wir suchen, was uns sucht."

24. Béguin, p. 200.

25. Jean Paul; "unwillkürliche Dichtkunst," in the essay "Über das Träumen" (*SW*, Abt. I, vol. 7, p. 405); for Hoffmann, see Béguin, 303; Eichendorff: "Schläft ein Lied in allen Dingen, /Die da träumen fort und fort / Und die Welt hebt an zu singen, / Triffst du nur das Zauberwort" (*Werke und Schriften*, ed. Gerhart Baumann and Siegfried Grosse, [Stuttgart: Cotta, I, 1957], p. 112).

26. Gotthilf Heinrich Schubert, *Die Symbolik des Traumes* (Bamberg: Kunz, 1814; facsimile reprint Heidelberg: Lambert Schneider, 1968), pp. 2–3.

27. Schubert, p. 57.

28. Schubert, p. 77.

29. Schubert, p. 89.

30. Schubert, p. 103.

Chapter Seven / Hazards of the Imagination.

1. There are several studies of Tieck in English. The most relevant to my subject is William J. Lillyman, *Reality's Dark Dream: The Narrative Fiction of Ludwig Tieck* (Berlin: De Gruyter, 1979). See also Alfred Edwin Lussky, *Tieck's Romantic Irony* (Chapel Hill: University of North Carolina Press, 1932); Edwin Hermann Zeydel, *Ludwig Tieck, the German Romanticist* (Princeton: Princeton University Press, 1935; reprint Hildesheim/New York: Olms, 1971, with a preface to this new edition by the author); and James Trainer, *Ludwig Tieck: From Gothic to Romantic* (The Hague: Mouton, 1964). In German, Wulf Segebrecht has edited a volume of essays on Tieck by various contributors (Darmstadt: Wissenschaftliche Buchgesellschaft, 1976). Other recent work includes Armin Giese, "Die Phantasie bei Ludwig Tieck" (Diss., Hamburg, 1973), and Ernst Ribbat, *Ludwig Tieck, Studien zur Konzeption und Praxis romantischer Poesie* (Bonn: Athenäum, 1977). Both Lillyman and Ribbat include extensive bibliographies of secondary literature on Tieck. Tieck's comments on his own works are conveniently collected in *Dichter über ihre Dichtungen, vol. 9, Ludwig Tieck*, in three parts, ed. Uwe Schweikert (Munich: Heimeran, 1971; hereafter Schweikert).

2. In his excellent edition of *Franz Sternbalds Wanderungen* (Stuttgart: Reclam, 1966), pp. 550–551.

3. There is no modern reprint of this edition. I have used the copy in the British Library. The 1828 text is available in volume I of the four-volume edition of selected works by Tieck, ed. Marianne Thalmann (Munich: Winkler, 1963–1966). My references are to the first edition, which is in three volumes, but, for convenience, I also give references to the corresponding text in the 1828 version, using Thalmann's edition. It should be noted that the text is often somewhat different in the 1828 version.

4. For discussions of *William Lovell*, see Lillyman, pp. 21–41; Korff, *Geist der Goethezeit* III, 48–54; Borcherdt, *Der Roman der Goethezeit*, pp. 138–148; Giese, pp. 90–125, and Ribbat, pp. 46–65. There are two recent full-length studies of *Lovell*: Karlheinz Weigand, *Tiecks "William Lovell." Studie zur frühromantischen Antithese* (Heidelberg: Winter, 1975), and Walter Münz, *Individuum und Symbol in Tiecks "William Lovell." Materialien zum frühromantischen Subjektivismus* (Berne: Herbert Lang, 1975) The subtitles of both indicate their general tenor.

5. I, 23–24; Thalmann, p. 244.
6. I, 37–38; Thalmann, p. 251.
7. I, 40; Thalmann, p. 251–"kindische Aufwallungen des Bluts."
8. I, 62; Thalmann, pp. 259–260.
9. I, 140; Thalmann, p. 287.
10. I, 237; Thalmann, pp. 321–322.
11. I, 267–274; Thalmann, pp. 332–337.
12. I, 300; Thalmann, pp. 345–346.
13. I, 321; Thalmann, p. 353.
14. II, 67; Thalmann, p. 398.
15. II, 256–261; Thalmann, pp. 467–468.
16. III, 102; Thalmann, p. 569.
17. III, 358; Thalmann, p. 654 (abridged).
18. Schweikert I, 64.
19. On this matter see Lillyman, p. 21, fn. 3.
20. Rudolf Köpke, *Ludwig Tieck. Erinnerungen aus dem Leben des Dichters*, 2 vols. (Leipzig: Brockhaus, 1855; hereafter Köpke), II, 173–174.
21. Percy Matenko, *Tieck and Solger, The Complete Correspondence* (New York and Berlin: Westermann, 1933), p. 167.

22. Schweikert I, 279.
23. Matenko, pp. 182, 209.
24. Friedrich Schlegel, *Literary Notebooks,* ed. Eichner, No. 529.
25. *KFSA* II, 245; Letter of March 1799.
26. Anger has an excellent discussion of *Sternbald* in his edition of the novel. Giese (pp. 291–332) asserts the crucial importance for the novel of the difference between Dürer and Lukas in their views of art, the former seeking new things and stressing inner vision, the latter proceeding in the continuity of a tradition and stressing craftmanship. See also Scheidweiler, *Der Roman der deutschen Romantik,* pp. 42–54; Korff III, 66–82; Borcherdt, pp. 402–414; Ribbat, pp. 99–112, and Lillyman, pp. 61–76. Jeffrey L. Sammons, "Tieck's *Franz Sternbald:* The Loss of Thematic Control," *Studies in Romanticism* 5 (1965), 30–43; Hans Geulen, "Zeit und Allegorie im Erzählvorgang von Ludwig Tiecks Roman 'Franz Sternbalds Wanderungen,'" *GRM* 18 (1968), 281–298; and Gonthier-Louis Fink, "L'Ambiguité du message romantique dans *Franz Sternbalds Wanderungen* de Ludwig Tieck," *Recherches Germaniques* 4 (1974), 16–70; each approach the novel from different standpoints (reflected in the titles). All three of these articles are notable interpretations of the novel and, taken together, illustrate the difficulties that any consistent interpretation of it presents.
27. The text of the first edition is available in the edition by Alfred Anger, with excellent notes and commentary (hereafter Anger). The text of the final version is readily available in volume I of Thalmann's edition.
28. Anger, pp. 201–202.
29. Anger, pp. 217–218.
30. Anger, p. 249.
31. Anger, p. 250.
32. Anger, p. 254.
33. Anger, p. 479; Thalmann, p. 886 (expanded).
34. Anger, pp. 277–278.
35. Anger, pp. 132–133.
36. Anger, pp. 568–572.
37. Anger, p. 385.
38. Anger, p. 397.
39. Richard Alewyn, "Ein Fragment der Fortsetzung von Tiecks 'Sternbald,'" *JFDH,* 1962, pp. 58–68.
40. Anger, p. 501; Thalmann, p. 986.
41. Ludwig Tieck, *Kritische Schriften,* 4 vols. (Leipzig: Brockhaus, 1848–1852; reprint Berlin: De Gruyter, 1974; hereafter KS), I, 147–148.
42. *KS* II, 181–182.
43. *KS* II, 214. As a result Tieck called *Götz von Berlichingen* more a "dramatic novel or scenic novella" than a play for the stage, and the form of *Werther* "not basically different" from that of Goethe's dramas (*KS* II, 207 and 210). In 1829 he referred to Goethe's *Die Wahlverwandtschaften* as a "*tragedy* of family life and modern times" (Schweikert III, 217).
44. *KS* II, 209.
45. *KS* I, 47f. and 207f.
46. *KS* II, 68ff.
47. *KS* II, 69.
48. *KS* II, 149–150.
49. *KS* II, 184.
50. *KS* II, 381.
51. *KS* II, 153ff.
52. Schweikert I, 136.

53. *KS* II, 161 and 163.
54. *KS* II, 165–166.
55. *KS* II, 168–169.
56. *KS* II, 382.
57. On Tieck's appreciation of Sterne, see Lussky, pp. 124–125.
58. *KS* II, 382.
59. *KS* II, 78.
60. *KS* II, 102.
61. Letter to Solger, 15 February 1819 (Matenko, p. 522).
62. *KS* II, 385–386.
63. He recognized the narrative talent of Schiller and regretted that he never finished *Der Geisterseher* (*KS* II, 387). He admitted the combination of inwardness with a popular tone of writing in the first books of Jung-Stilling's famous pietistic novel-like autobiography, and appreciated correctly how much its author had learnt from his friend Goethe (*KS* II, 245). He thought that Heinse's importance as a novelist (he speaks only of *Ardinghello*) was primarily historical in his having been the first to embody feelings and ideas about art in a novel, even though his novel was uneven, combining some things that were good with others that were ugly (*KS* IV, 276). Wieland, he thought, though formerly overestimated was now unjustly slighted (especially by the Schlegels) for he was the first to write really readable elegant prose, though a prose modeled on French.
64. Köpke II, 182–183.
65. On Jean Paul, see *KS* II, 163–164, 181–182; Schweikert I, 280, Matenko, pp. 264–265.
66. Eduard Berend, *Jean Pauls Persönlichkeit in Berichten der Zeitgenossen* (Berlin: Akademie-Verlag, 1956), pp. 292–293.
67. Berend, p. 265.
68. Köpke II, 203–204.
69. *Letters of Ludwig Tieck, Hitherto Unpublished,* ed. Edwin H. Zeydel, Percy Matenko, and Robert Herndon Fife (New York: MLA, 1937), p. 44.
70. Köpke II, 206.
71. Schweikert I, 179 (letter to Brockhaus, February 1852).
72. Matenko, p. 317.
73. Schweikert I, 234–235.
74. Schweikert I, 175.
75. Letter to Friedrich Schlegel, 23 April 1801.
76. *KS* II, 174.
77. *KS* II, 212; Köpke II, 191.
78. Köpke II, 191.
79. Köpke II, 191.
80. Lillyman, p. 28.

Chapter Eight / Anxiety of the Spirit

1. The best general introduction in English to Brentano is John F. Fetzer, *Romantic Orpheus: Profiles of Clemens Brentano* (Berkeley: University of California Press, 1974). In French there is René Guignard's overview of Brentano's work, entitled *Un Poète romantique allemand: C. Brentano* (Paris: Les Belles Lettres, 1933). Béguin's chapter in *L'Ame romantique et le rêve* is excellent, particularly as regards the religious basis of Brentano's imagery. In German there is a good bibliography of secondary literature on Brentano in the first volume, pp. 1249–1267, of the four-volume edition of Brentano's works published by the Hanser Verlag,

and a good *Nachwort* (by Friedhelm Kemp) in the same volume. The secondary literature is surveyed critically by Bernhard Gajek in *Homo Poeta: Zur Kontinuität der Problematik bei Clemens Brentano* (Frankfurt: Athenäum, 1971), which is excellent but deals predominantly with the poetry, and is thin on *Godwi*. Werner Hoffmann, *Clemens Brentano: Leben und Werk* (Berne and Munich: Francke, 1966), is the most recent study of all of Brentano's work, but with a biographical approach.

2. "Ein Grauen wohnt in der Tiefe des hochmütigsten Menschen vor der unnennbaren Welt, die sich nicht unseren Versuchen fügt, sondern uns zu ihren Versuchen und Belustigungen braucht"—quoted by Walter Migge in the *Nachwort* to vol. 3 of Achim von Arnim, *Sämtliche Romane und Erzählungen* (Munich: Hanser, 1962–1965). I shall quote Arnim's novels from this edition (hereafter Hanser).

There is as yet no general study of Arnim in English or in German, and René Guignard's *Achim von Arnim* (Paris: Presses Universitaires de France, 1936) is unfortunately nothing like as good as his study of Brentano. He considers Arnim more interesting as a man than as a writer. Béguin, on the other hand, has the highest regard for this author, and his chapter on Arnim in *L'Ame romantique et le rêve* is extremely interesting and stresses him as a poet of the unconscious. In German the best succinct overview is probably that of Walter Migge's *Nachwort* to the Hanser edition, which pays true respect to the novels as well as to the stories, whereas most of the secondary literature in German on Arnim concentrates on him as a writer of novellas (for instance Wolfdietrich Rasch in his article "Achim von Arnims Erzählkunst," *DU* 7/2 [1955], 38–55). A very full critical bibliography of recent work on Arnim is to be found in Volker Hoffmann, "Die Arnim-Forschung, 1945–1972," *DVLG* 47 (1973) Sonderheft pp. 270–342. See also Gerhard Rudolph, *Studien zur dichterischen Welt Achim von Arnims* (Berlin: De Gruyter, 1958), and Helene M. Kastinger Riley, *Idee und Gestaltung: Das konfigurative Strukturprinzip bei L. A. von Arnim* (Berne and Frankfurt: Herbert Lang, 1977). Critical assessments of Arnim are divided between those which consider him uncentered, improvisatory, lacking in some overriding structural principle, and those which assert that his work is controlled by a strong, if unusual, such principle. Rudolph represents the former view and Riley the latter. Of the two, I find Mrs. Riley's book the more convincing.

3. Migge, see Hanser III, 831; Béguin, p. 259 ("frisson glacial").
4. Hanser III, 846.
5. Hanser III, 831.
6. Hanser III, 831.
7. I quote *Godwi* from the text, edited by Friedhelm Kemp, in the second volume of the Hanser edition of Brentano's works.
Scheidweiler's treatment of *Godwi* (*Der Roman der deutschen Romantik*, pp. 29–42) is still worth reading, but neither Korff nor Borcherdt seems to me to appreciate the poetic structure of the work. On the other hand there are perceptive analyses in both Guignard and Fetzer, and Benno von Wiese's article "Brentanos *Godwi*: Analyse eines 'romantischen' Romans," in B.v.W., *Von Lessing bis Grabbe* (Düsseldorf: Bagel, 1968) pp. 191–247, is excellent. See also Eugene E. Reed, "The Union of the Arts in Brentano's *Godwi*," *GR* 29 (1954), 102–118; Franz Norbert Mennemeier, "Rückblick auf Brentanos *Godwi*: Ein Roman ohne Tendenz," *WW* 16 (1966), 24–33; Horst Meixner, "Denkstein und Bildersaal in Clemens Brentanos *Godwi*," *JDSG* 11 (1967), 435–468, and Gerhard Storz, "Beobachtungen zu Brentanos *Godwi*", in *Fests.* for Friedrich Beissner (Babenhausen: Rotsch, 1974), pp. 436–446.
8. Hanser II, 137ff.

9. Hanser II, 142–7.
10. Hanser II, 155.
11. Hanser II, 237–238.
12. Hanser II, 258–262.
13. Hanser II, 259.
14. Clemens Brentano, *Briefe*, ed. Friedrich Seebass, 2 vols. (Nuremberg: Hans Carl, 1951), I, 21; cf. Rolf Nägele, *Die Muttersymbolik bei Clemens Brentano* (Winterthur: Keller, 1959), which treats this subject extensively and well, with good sections on the marble statue and Violette's monument.
15. Hanser II, 292.
16. Hanser II, 373.
17. Hanser II, 439.
18. Hanser II, 415–416.
19. Hanser II, 450 and 453.
20. I quote from the following collections of Brentano's letters: Reinhold Steig, *Achim von Arnim und die ihm nahe standen* (Stuttgart: Cotta, vol. 1 [Arnim and Brentano], 1894; hereafter Steig I); *Clemens Brentanos Liebesleben*, ed. Lujo Brentano (Frankfurt: Frankfurter Verlags-Anstalt, 1921; (hereafter *Liebesleben*); *Das unsterbliche Leben: Unbekannte Briefe von C.B.*, ed. Wilhelm Schelling and Friedrich Fuchs (Jena: Diederichs, 1939; hereafter *UL*); *C.B. Briefe*, 2 vols. ed. Friedrich Seebass (Nuremberg: Hans Carl, 1951; hereafter Seebass); and *Clemens Brentanos Gesammelte Briefe*, 2 vols. (Frankfurt: Sauerländer, 1955; hereafter *Ges. Briefe*).
21. Steig I, 26; *UL*, p. 158.
22. *UL*, p. 217.
23. Seebass I, 97.
24. Seebass I, 162.
25. "Von . . . dem Gifte der Zeit besudelt," Seebass II, 387–388.
26. *JFDH*, 1934–1935, pp. 402f.
27. Seebass I, 163.
28. Steig I, 41.
29. Steig I, 51.
30. *UL*, p. 266.
31. *Liebesleben*, p. 38.
32. Steig I, 66.
33. Letter to Rahel Varnhagen, 1 October 1814. See *Varnhagen von Ense, Biographische Portraits* (Leipzig: Brockhaus, 1871), p. 116.
34. *Hollins Liebeleben* is contained in vol. II of the Hanser edition (ed. Walter Migge, 1963) and the other two novels in vol. I (ed. Migge, 1962). There has been very little discussion of *Hollins Liebeleben*, but there is an interesting section on it in Hans Steffen's article "Lichtsymbolik und Figuration in Arnims erzählender Dichtung," in *Die deutsche Romantik*, ed. Steffen (Göttingen: Vandenhoeck & Ruprecht, 1967), pp. 180–199, and a good article on it by Heinz Härtl in the *Wissenschaftliche Zeitschrift der Martin-Luther-Universität, Halle-Wittenberg, Gesellschafts- und Sprachwissenschaftliche Reihe* 18 (1969), 171–182.
35. Arnim, Hanser II, 10.
36. Brentano, Hanser II, 453–454.
37. Arnim, Hanser II, 12.
38. Brentano's letter: Seebass I, 163.
39. On the *Gräfin Dolores*, see Borcherdt, *Der Roman der Goethezeit*, pp. 540–550, Renate Moering, *Die offene Romanform von Arnims "Gräfin Dolores"* (Heidelberg: Winter, 1978), and Horst Meixner, *Romantischer Figuralismus*, pp. 13–101. Surprisingly little in the way of a detailed study of this novel is available in pub-

Notes to Chapter 8

lished form, though there are several (typescript) dissertations, which Moering discusses.

40. On this topic: Klaus Peter, "Adel und Revolution als Thema der Romantik," in *Literaturwissenschaft und Sozialwissenschaften II: Legitimationskrisen des deutschen Adels 1200–1900*, ed. Peter Uwe Hohendahl and Paul Michael Lützeler (Stuttgart: Metzler, 1979), pp. 197–217.

41. "höhere Ansicht des Lebens . . . wo alles Scherz wird" (Hanser I, 81).

42. Hanser I, 172–173.

43. E.g., Haber in *Godwi*, and Dryander in *Dichter und ihre Gesellen*.

44. Hanser I, 192.

45. Hanser I, 235.

46. Seebass II, 29.

47. *Ges. Briefe* I, 160.

48. Seebass II, 53f.

49. Seebass II, 54.

50. Seebass II, 54.

51. On *Die Kronenwächter*, see especially Werner Vordtriede's article on it in *Deutsche Romane von Grimmelshausen bis Musil*, ed. Jost Schillemeit (Frankfurt: Fischer 1966), pp. 155–163, and Karol Sauerland, "*Die Kronenwächter*. Auflösung eines Mythos," *WB* 14 (1968), 868–883. Most of the other secondary literature on this novel deals with the portrayal of history in it, or with Arnim's historical sources, neither of which concerns me here.

52. Hanser I, 801.

53. Hanser I, 1035.

54. Hanser I, 1040 and 1051.

55. Hanser I, 1025ff.

56. Hanser II, 880.

57. Steig I, 211 and 264.

58. Steig I, 264 and 211.

59. P. E. Charvet in vol. v of *A Literary History of France* (London: Benn, 1967), p. 78.

60. *JFDH*, 1934–1935, p. 406.

61. *JFDH*, 1934–1935, p. 418.

62. Steig II, 69.

63. *JFDH*, 1934–1935, p. 418.

64. *Achim und Bettina in ihren Briefen* ed. Werner Vordtriede (Frankfurt: Suhrkamp, 1961; hereafter *Achim und Bettina*), I, 437. On Arnim and Scott, see R. F. Holt's article in *GLL*, N. S. xxvi (1972–73), 142–160.

65. *Achim und Bettina*, II, 553.

66. Steig II, 349.

67. *Achim und Bettina*, I, 86.

68. Steig I, 230.

69. Steig III, 402.

70. From Arnim's essay "Ausflüge mit Hölderlin" (1828), quoted by Beissner in Hölderlin, *Kleine Stuttgarter Ausgabe* III, 329–330.

71. Steig I, 41.

72. Steig III, 83.

73. *JFDH*, 1934–1935, p. 403.

74. Steig I, 41.

75. Steig I, 136.

76. *JFDH*, 1934–1935, p. 402.

77. *JFDH*, 1934–1935, pp. 399–401.

Notes to Chapter 9

78. Steig III, 72.
79. Steig III, 75–76.
80. Steig III, 78.
81. Steig III, 86.
82. Steig III, 87.

Chapter Nine / A Visit to the Madhouse

1. For an account of the various suggestions for authorship of the *Nachtwachen*, see Jost Schillemeit, *Bonaventura. Der Verfasser der Nachtwachen* (Munich: Beck, 1973).

2 The most important critical studies in English of the *Nachtwachen* are: Jeffrey L. Sammons, *The Nachtwachen des Bonaventura: A Structural Interpretation* (The Hague: Mouton, 1965), and Gerald Gillespie's lengthy introduction to his translation of the work (Austin: University of Texas Press, 1971).

The more important studies in German are Dorothee Sölle-Nipperdey, *Untersuchungen zur Struktur der Nachtwachen von Bonaventura* (Göttingen: Vandenhoeck & Ruprecht, 1959); Werner Kohlschmidt, "Das Hamlet-Motiv in den "Nachtwachen" des Bonaventura," in *German Studies Presented to Walter Horace Bruford* (London: Harrap, 1962), pp. 163–175; Wolfgang Paulsen, "Bonaventuras Nachtwachen im literarischen Raum", *JDSG* IX (1965), 447–510; Klaus Joachim Heinisch, "Bonaventura: Nachtwachen," in K. J. H., *Deutsche Romantik, Interpretationen* (Paderborn: Schöningh, 1966), pp. 181–200; Richard Brinkmann, "Nachtwachen des Bonaventura: Kehrseite der Frühromantik," in *Die Deutsche Romantik*, ed. Hans Steffen (Göttingen: Vandenhoeck & Ruprecht, 1967), pp. 134–158; Peter Küpper, "Unfromme Vigilien. Bonaventuras Nachtwachen," in *Fests. für Richard Alewyn* (Cologne and Graz: Böhlau, 1967), pp. 309–327; Rita Terras, "Juvenal und die satirische Struktur der Nachtwachen von Bonaventura," *GQ* 52 (1979), 18–31; Korff (*Geist der Goethezeit* III 204–218) cannot make much of it. For him it breathes a "völlig nihilistischer Geist" and is "ganz ohne Plan, mit souveräner Willkür hingeworfen"—a view that few would share nowadays.

I shall quote the *Nachtwachen* from the excellent edition by Wolfgang Paulsen (Stuttgart: Reclam, 1972; hereafter Paulsen), which has a valuable *Nachwort*.

3. Paulsen, p. 11.
4. Paulsen, p. 17.
5. Sammons, p. 61.
6. Paulsen, p. 39.
7. Gillespie, p. 8; Sammons, p. 42.
8. Paulsen, p. 56.
9. Paulsen, p. 71.
10. Paulsen, p. 75.
11. Brinkmann, pp. 152–153.
12. Paulsen, p. 105.
13. Paulsen, p. 112.
14. Paulsen, pp. 118–119.
15. Paulsen, p. 120.
16. Paulsen, p. 131.
17. The engraving has a subtitle: *The Bathos. Manner of Sinking in Sublime Paintings.* This work of Hogarth's was well known to Jean Paul, who refers to it in various places. See, for instance, Jean Paul, Hanser edition II, 452, and the relevant note by the editor of the volume.
18. Sammons, p. 78.

Chapter Ten / The Divided Self

1. General introductions to Hoffmann in English include: H. W. Hewett-Thayer, *Hoffmann: Author of the Tales* (Princeton: Princeton University Press, 1948); Ronald Taylor, *Hoffmann* (London: Bowes and Bowes, 1963); Kenneth Negus, E. T. A. *Hoffmann's Other World* (Philadelphia: University of Pennsylvania Press, 1965); Horst S. Daemmrich, *The Shattered Self: E. T. A. Hoffmann's Tragic Vision* (Detroit: Wayne State University Press, 1973), and Steven Paul Scher, Hoffmann and Sterne: Unmediated Parallels in Narrative Method," *CL* xxviii (1976), 309–325.

In German see: Walter Harich, *E. T. A. Hoffmann: Das Leben eines Künstlers*, 2 vols. (Berlin: E. Reiss, 1921—the standard biography, which also contains critical assessments of the works); Karl Ochsner, *E. T. A. Hoffmann als Dichter des Unbewussten* (Frauenfeld and Leipzig: Huber, 1936—connects Hoffmann's work with romantic philosophers, especially with Schelling and Schubert, and has a good final chapter on *Die Elixiere des Teufels*); Lothar Köhn, *Vieldeutige Welt: Studien zur Struktur der Erzählungen E. T. A. Hoffmanns und zur Entwicklung seines Werkes* (Tübingen: Niemeyer, 1966—speaks of "rational-irrational structures," and has an extensive analysis of *Die Elixiere*). Margot Kutter, *Die Gestaltung des Individualitätsproblems bei E. T. A. Hoffmann* (Düsseldorf: Nolte, 1936), and Dietrich Raff, *Ich-Bewusstsein und Wirklichkeitsauffassung bei E. T. A. Hoffmann* (Rottweil: Emmanuel, 1971), both deal with the relation between individuality and reality in Hoffmann, and Raff deals only with the two novels. Thomas Cramer, *Das Groteske bei E. T. A. Hoffmann* (Munich: Fink, 1966), and Erwin Rotermund, "Musikalische und dichterische 'Arabeske' bei E. T. A. Hoffmann," *Poetica* 2 (1968), 48–69, approach Hoffmann's literary work from his music criticism. For a Marxist view of Hoffmann, see Hans-Georg Werner, *E. T. A. Hoffmann* (Berlin and Weimar: Aufbau-Verlag, 2d ed., 1971.

2. In the preface to *Prinzessin Brambilla*. See Hoffmann, *Späte Werke*, ed. Walter Müller-Seidel and Wulf Segebrecht (Munich: Winkler, 1969), p. 211.

3. *Späte Werke*, p. 211.

4. E. T. A. Hoffmann, *Briefwechsel*, ed. Hans von Müller and Friedrich Schnapp (Munich: Winkler, 1967–1969, 3 vols.; hereafter *Briefw.*), 1, 60.

5. *Briefw.* 1, 53–54.

6. W. H. Wackenroder, *Werke und Briefe*, ed. Lambert Schneider (1938, rpt. Heidelberg: Lambert Schneider, 1967), pp. 315–320.

7. *Briefw.* 1, 61.

8. *Briefw.* 1, 110.

9. *Briefw.* 1, 87–88.

10. *Horrid Mysteries*, reprint with introduction by Devendra P. Varma (London: Folio Press, 1968).

11. *Horrid Mysteries*, p. 195.

12. George Ellinger, *E. T. A. Hoffmanns Werke* (Berlin and Leipzig: Bong, n.d.; hereafter Ellinger), 1, xv–xvi.

13. See the references in *Briefw.* iii, 462 (Namenregister), and Robert Herndon Fife, "Jean Paul Friedrich Richter and E. T. A. Hoffmann," *PMLA* xxii (1907), 1–32.

14. *Briefw.* ii, 157.

15. Hoffmann, *Schriften zur Musik. Nachlese*, ed. Friedrich Schnapp, (Munich: Winkler, 1963), 345.

16. *Briefw.* ii, 288, 324 (with name changed to Timotheus instead of Jacobus), 328, 349, 372.

17. Ellinger, I, xv-xvi.
18. Ellinger xv, 159.
19. Briefw. II, 287–288.
20. Briefw. II, 288.
21. This is confirmed by Rainer Schürer in his study of Scott's novels in Germany ("Die Romane Walter Scotts in Deutschland," Diss. Freie Universität Berlin, 1969), which tells us that *Rob Roy* appeared in German translation in 1818, *The Black Dwarf* and *Old Mortality* in 1819, *The Bride of Lammermoor* and *Ivanhoe* in 1820, and *Waverley* in 1821 (though Tieck had tried unsuccessfully to reach an agreement with a publisher to translate it in 1818). The translation of *Guy Mannering* had appeared in 1817. According to Luise Sigmann, "Die englische Literatur von 1800 bis 1850 im Urteil der zeitgenössischen deutschen Kritik," *AF* LV (1918), 58, the real enthusiasm for Scott does not seem to have set in until 1820, after which date translations of the novels followed thick and fast.
22. See *Briefw.* II, 340 [*Midlothian*], 356 and 362 [*Antiquary*], 356 [*Ivanhoe*]—all in 1821–1822.
23. *Serapionsbrüder* (Munich: Winkler, 1966), pp. 924–926.
24. Ellinger xv, 159.
25. *Serapionsbrüder*, p. 928.
26. *E. T. A. Hoffmann in Aufzeichnungen seiner Freunde und Bekannten*, ed. Friedrich Schnapp (Munich: Winkler, 1974; (hereafter *Aufzeichnungen*), p. 606.
27. *Aufzeichnungen*, p. 512, my italics.
28. *Briefw.* I, 454.
29. *Briefw.* I, 483.
30. There is a translation of the *Elixiere des Teufels* by Ronald Taylor (London: John Calder, 1963). Recent treatments of this novel include Horst Daemmrich, "*The Devil's Elixirs:* Precursor of the Modern Psychological Novel," *PLL* 6 (1970), 374–386; Charles E. Passage, "E. T. A. Hoffmann's *The Devil's Elixirs:* A Flawed Masterpiece," *JEGP* 75 (1976), 531–545; Karin Cramer, "Bewusstseinsspaltung in E. T. A. Hoffmanns Roman *Die Elixiere des Teufels*," *MHG* 16 (1970), 8–18, and Renate Moering, "Musikalität und Zwielicht: Zwei Formprinzipien in E. T. A. Hoffmanns *Elixieren des Teufels, JWGV* 75 (1971), 56–73. See also Jean-F.-A. Ricci, "Le Problème de la vraisemblance dans les Elixirs du Diable de E. T. A. Hoffmann," *LanM* 46 (1952), 28–34, and Harich I, 267–290; Korff, *Geist der Goethezeit* IV, 572–582; Borcherdt, *Der Roman der Goethezeit*, pp. 503–510; Meixner, *Romantischer Figuralismus*, 155–230; Ochsner, pp. 112–137; Cramer, pp. 44–90; and Raff.
31. Hoffmann, *Die Elixiere des Teufels* [and] *Lebens-Ansichten des Katers Murr*, ed. Walter Müller-Seidel and Wolfgang Kron (Munich: Winkler, 1964; (hereafter, *Elixiere* etc.), p. 8.
32. Winkler, *Elixiere* etc., pp. 47–48.
33. There is a translation of *Murr* in vol. 2 of *Selected Writings of E. T. A. Hoffmann*, ed. and trans. Leonard J. Kent and Elizabeth C. Knight (Chicago: University of Chicago Press, 1960). There is an excellent edition of the novel, edited by Harmut Steinecke (Stuttgart: Reclam, 1972) with valuable notes and a selection of contemporary reviews. Discussions in English include: Lawrence O. Frye, "The Language of Romantic High Feeling: A Case of Dialogue Technique in Hoffmann's *Kater Murr* and Novalis' *Heinrich von Ofterdingen*," *DVLG* 49 (1975), 520–545; Peter J. Graves, "E. T. A. Hoffmann's Johannes Kreisler: 'Verrückter Musikus'?" *MLQ* 30 (1969), 222–233; Michael T. Jones, "Hoffmann and the Problem of Social Reality; a study of *Kater Murr*," *Monatshefte* 69 (1977), 45–57.
   In German, there is a long discussion in Harich II, 211–286, and in Korff,

Geist der Goethezeit IV, 543–639. See also Hudgins, *Nicht-epische Strukturen*, pp. 90–133, Rotermund, and Raff. There are briefer discussions in Borcherdt, *Der Roman der Goethezeit*, pp. 511–522, in Herman Meyer's interesting book *Das Zitat in der Erzählkunst* (Stuttgart: Metzler, 1961), pp. 114–134, and in Wolfgang Preisendanz's *Humor als dichterische Einbildungskraft* (Munich: Fink, 1976), pp. 74–83. Herbert Singer has an essay on the novel in *Der Deutsche Roman*, ed. Benno von Wiese (Düsseldorf: Bagel, 1963), and von Wiese himself has one in his *Von Lessing bis Grabbe* (Düsseldorf: Bagel, 1968). Two recent fuller studies are Robert S. Rosen, *E. T. A. Hoffmanns "Kater Murr". Aufbauformen und Erzählsituationen* (Bonn: Bouvier, 1970), which includes discussion of space and time in this novel, and Ute Späth, *Gebrochene Identität: Stilistische Untersuchungen zum Parallelismus in E. T. A. Hoffmanns "Lebens-Ansichten des Katers Murr"* (Göttingen: Kümmerle, 1970).
    34. Winkler, *Elixiere* etc., p. 298.
    35. Winkler, *Elixiere* etc., p. 300.
    36. Winkler, *Elixiere* etc., p. 336.

Chapter Eleven / Images on a Golden Ground

    1. The best introduction in English to the work of Eichendorff is that by Egon Schwarz (New York: Twayne, 1972), which has a chapter on "The Novelist" but discusses only *Ahnung und Gegenwart*. See also Lawrence Radner, *Eichendorff: The Spiritual Geometer* (Lafayette, Ind.: Purdue University Studies, 1970). Readers of German are referred to the various articles in *Eichendorff Heute*, ed. Paul Stöcklein (Darmstadt: Wissenschaftliche Buchgesellschaft, 1966), and to the perceptive essays by Oskar Seidlin, collected as *Versuche über Eichendorff* (Göttingen: Vandenhoeck & Ruprecht, 1965). Also Hans Jürg Lüthi, *Dichtung und Dichter bei Joseph von Eichendorff* (Berne: Francke, 1966); Wilhelm Emrich, "Dichtung und Gesellschaft bei Eichendorff," *Aurora* 18 (1958), 11–17 (also in *Eichendorff Heute*); Walter Rehm, "Prinz Rokoko im alten Garten: Eine Eichendorffstudie," in W. R., *Späte Studien* (Berne: Francke, 1964), pp. 124–214; Dietmar Köhler, "Wiederholung und Variation: Zu einem Grundphänomen der Eichendorffschen Erzählkunst," *Aurora* 27 (1967), 26–43; Peter P. Schwarz, *Aurora: Zur romantischen Zeitstruktur bei Eichendorff* (Bad Homburg: Gehlen, 1970). On Eichendorffs "Geschichte des Romans," see Eugen Thurnher's article in *Stoffe, Formen, Struktur,* (*Fests.* for Borcherdt) (Munich: Huber, 1962), pp. 361–379.
    2. Lüthi (p. 24) confirms this: "Obgleich er [Eichendorff] die grosse Bedeutung der Form erkennt und besonders hervorhebt, interessiert ihn bei der Darstellung und Beurteilung der Werke das Formale viel weniger als der Inhalt, die Gesinnung und die Weltanschauung, die darin zum Ausdruck kommt."
    3. Joseph Freiherr von Eichendorff, *Werke und Schriften*, ed. Gerhart Baumann and Siegfried Grosse, 4 vols. (Stuttgart: Cotta, 1957–1958; hereafter Cotta). The diaries are in vol. 3 of this edition. For these references, see Cotta III, 106 (*Sternbald*), 139 (*Flegeljahre*), 168 (*Hesperus*), 176 ("Gianozzo"), 179 (*Titan*). See also *Sämtliche Werke*, Historisch-kritische Ausgabe (hereafter *SW*), vol. XI, *Tagebücher* (Regensburg: Habbel, n.d. [1908]), 317 (*Unsichtbare Loge*).
    4. Cotta III, 243 and 248.
    5. These articles can be found in *SW* VIII/I, 5–52. They are not included in complete form in Cotta.
    6. *SW* VIII/I, 26.
    7. *SW* VIII/I, 31.
    8. *SW* VIII/I, 33–34.

9. *SW* VIII/I, 34.
10. *SW* VIII/I, 35–36.
11. On Tieck: *SW* VIII/I, 37–39.
12. "Brentano und seine Märchen" (Cotta IV, 883–893; *SW* VIII/I, 53–62).
13. Cotta IV, 889.
14. Cotta IV, 893.
15. Cotta IV, 911.
16. Cotta IV, 645–859.
17. Cotta IV, 648.
18. Cotta IV, 694.
19. Cotta IV, 694–697.
20. Cotta IV, 713.
21. Cotta IV, 715–716.
22. Cotta IV, 786–788.
23. Cotta IV, 789.
24. Cotta IV, 791.
25. Cotta IV, 795.
26. Cotta IV, 239.
27. Cotta IV, 385–386.
28. Cotta IV, 403.
29. For literature on *Ahnung und Gegenwart* see: Borcherdt, *Der Roman der Goethezeit*, pp. 526–540; Scheidweiler, *Der Roman der deutschen Romantik*, pp. 109–131; Korff, *Geist der Goethezeit* IV, 441–446; Erika Jansen, *Ahnung und Gegenwart im Werke Eichendorffs* (Giessen: Kindt, 1937); Paul Requadt in *DU* 7 (1955), 79–92 (also in P. R., *Bildlichkeit der Dichtung* [Munich: Fink, 1974], pp. 35–48); Walter Killy, "Der Roman als romantisches Buch: Über Eichendorffs *Ahnung und Gegenwart*," in *Deutsche Romane von Grimmelshausen bis Musil*, ed. Jost Schillemeit (Frankfurt: Fischer, 1976), pp. 136–154, and Meixner, *Romantischer Figuralismus*, pp. 102–154.
   On gardens: Rehm's article (listed above in note 1), and Lawrence R. Radner, "The Garden Symbol in *Ahnung und Gegenwart*," *MLQ* 21 (1960), 253–260. On the opening sequence: Brigitte Kayser in *Aurora* 35 (1975), 45–57 ("vorübergehende Verblendung"). On Faber: Dieter Kafitz's excellent article in *DVLG* 45 (1971), 350–374.
   See also Detlev W. Schumann, "Some Scenic Motifs in Eichendorff's *Ahnung und Gegenwart*," *JEGP* LVI (1957), 550–569.
   For literature on *Dichter und ihre Gesellen* see note 35 below. There is, to date, no translation into English of either of Eichendorff's novels.
30. Cotta II, 10.
31. Cotta II, 16.
32. Cotta II, 124.
33. Cotta II, 124.
34. Cotta II, 140: "Und die Zaub'rin bei dem Alten
                    Spielt die vor'gen Spiele wieder
                    Einsam wohl noch lange Jahre."
35. Egon Schwarz considers *Dichter und ihre Gesellen*—wrongly, I think—"merely a more orderly reprise of old narrative techniques, motifs, themes and plots" (p. 24). Radner, however, takes quite a different view: "In *Dichter und ihre Gesellen* he [Eichendorff] gives a picture of the twentieth century; the nations of the world united against the common enemy, God" (p. 12), which seems to me to go too far in the other direction. See also Scheidweiler, pp. 109–131; Hudgins, *Nicht-Epische Strukturen*, pp. 134–169, Hans Kaboth, "Eichendorffs *Dichter und ihre*

Gesellen," *Aurora* 4 (1934), 57–62; Christian Strauch, "Satirische Elemente im Aufbau von Eichendorffs *Dichter und ihre Gesellen," JWGV* 72 (1968), 87–112; Klaus Kindermann, "Lustspielhandlung und Romanstruktur: Untersuchungen zu Eichendorffs *Dichter und ihre Gesellen"* (Berlin, 1973); and Ernst L. Offermanns's article in *Literaturwissenschaft und Geschichtsphilosophie, (Fests.* for Emrich) (Berlin: De Gruyter, 1975), pp. 373–387.

36. Cotta II, 656–657: "Es gibt nur wenige Dichter in der Welt, und von den wenigen kaum einer steigt unversehrt in diese märchenhafte, prächt'ge Zaubernacht, wo die wilden, feurigen Blumen stehen und die Liederquellen verworren nach den Abgründen gehen, und der zauberische Spielmann zwischen dem Waldesrauschen mit herzzerreissenden Klängen nach dem Venusberg verlockt, in welchem alle Lust und Pracht der Erde entzündet, und wo die Seele wie im Traum frei wird mit ihren dunklen Gelüsten."

37. Cotta II, 63–65.

38. Cotta II, 48.

39. Cotta II, 165: "die unbestimmte Knabensehnsucht, jener wunderbare Spielmann vom Venusberge, verwandelte sich in eine heilige Liebe und Begeisterung für den bestimmten und festen Zweck."

40. Cotta II, 517.

41. Cotta II, 518.

42. Cotta II, 655.

43. "Trustily we take up the watch,
For soon the deepest night may fall,
Obscure the glory of the lands.
O beauteous world, be on your guard!"

Bibliography

PRIMARY TEXTS

ARNIM, ACHIM VON. *Sämtliche Romane und Erzählungen.* Ed. Walter Migge. Munich: Hanser, 1962–1965. [Hanser]

BONAVENTURA. *Nachtwachen.* Ed. Wolfgang Paulsen. Stuttgart: Reclam, 1972. [Paulsen]

BRENTANO, CLEMENS. *Briefe.* Ed. Friedrich Seebass. 2 vols. Nuremberg: Hans Carl, 1951. [Seebass]

——. *Clemens Brentanos Gesammelte Briefe.* 2 vols. Frankfurt: Sauerländer, 1955. [*Ges. Briefe*]

——. *Clemens Brentanos Liebesleben.* Ed. Lujo Brentano. Frankfurt: Frankfurter Verlags-Anstalt, 1921. [*Liebesleben*]

——. *Das unsterbliche Leben: Unbekannte Briefe von Clemens Brentano.* Ed. Wilhelm Schelling and Friedrich Fuchs. Jena: Diedrichs, 1939. [*UL*]

——. *Werke.* Ed. Friedhelm Kemp. 4 vols. Munich: Hanser, 1963–1968.

EICHENDORFF, JOSEPH FREIHERR VON. *Sämtliche Werke.* Historisch-kritische Ausgabe. Regensburg: Habbel, n.d. [1908]. [*SW*]

——. *Werke und Schriften.* Ed. Gerhard Baumann and Siegfried Grosse. 4 vols. Stuttgart: Cotta, 1957–1958. [Cotta]

HOFFMANN, E. T. A. *Briefwechsel.* Ed. Hans von Müller and Friedrich Schnapp. 3 vols. Munich: Winkler, 1967–1969. [*Briefw.*]

——. *Die Elixiere des Teufels* [and] *Lebens-Ansichten des Katers Murr.* Ed. Walter Müller-Seidel and Wolfgang Kron. Munich: Winkler, 1964. [Winkler, *Elixiere* etc.]

——. *Lebens-Ansichten des Katers Murr.* Ed. Hartmut Steinecke. Stuttgart: Reclam, 1972.

——. *Schriften zur Musik. Nachlese.* Ed. Friedrich Schnapp. Munich: Winkler, 1963.

[297]

Bibliography

——. *Die Serapionsbrüder.* Ed. Walter Müller-Seidel and Wulf Segebrecht. Munich: Winkler, 1966.

——. *Späte Werke.* Ed. Walter Müller-Seidel and Wulf Segebrecht. Munich: Winkler, 1969.

HÖLDERLIN, FRIEDRICH.

——. *Sämtliche Werke, Kleine Stuttgarter Ausgabe.* Ed. Friedrich Beissner. Vols. III and VI. Stuttgart: Kohlhammer, 1958, 1959 [Beissner III, VI]

MATENKO, PERCY. *Tieck and Solger, The Complete Correspondence.* New York and Berlin: Westermann, 1933.

NOVALIS. *Schriften.* Ed. Paul Kluckhohn and Richard Samuel. 2d revised and extended edition. Stuttgart: Kohlhammer, 1960–1975. 4 vols. completed.

RICHTER, JEAN PAUL FRIEDRICH. *Jean Pauls sämtliche Werke: historisch-kritische Ausgabe.* Weimar: H. Böhlaus Nachfolger, 1927–1964. [*SW*]

——. *Werke.* Ed. Norbert Miller and Walter Höllerer. Munich: Hanser, 1960–1963. [Hanser]

SCHLEGEL, DOROTHEA. *Florentin.* Ed. Paul Kluckhohn. In Deutsche Literatur in Entwicklungsreihen, Reihe Romantik, vol. 7. Leipzig: Reclam, 1933. [Kluckhohn]

SCHLEGEL, FRIEDRICH. *Kritische Friedrich-Schlegel-Ausgabe.* Ed. Ernst Behler with Jean-Jacques Anstett and Hans Eichner. Munich-Paderborn-Vienna: Schöningh, and Zurich: Thomas-Verlag, 1958– [*KFSA*]

——. *Literary Notebooks 1797–1801.* Ed. Hans Eichner. London: Athlone Press, 1957. [*LN*]

——. *Neue philosophische Schriften.* Ed. Josef Körner. Frankfurt: Schulte-Bumke, 1935.

STEIG, REINHOLD, ed. *Achim von Arnim und die ihm nahe standen.* Vol. I. Stuttgart: Cotta, 1894. [Steig I]

TIECK, LUDWIG. *Dichter über ihre Dichtungen, vol. 9, Ludwig Tieck.* Ed. Uwe Schweikert. Munich: Heimeran, 1971. [Schweikert]

——. *Franz Sternbalds Wanderungen.* Ed. Alfred Anger. Stuttgart: Reclam, 1966. [Anger]

——. *Geschichte des Herrn William Lovell.* 3 vols. Berlin and Leipzig: Nicolai, 1795–1796.

——. *Kritische Schriften.* Leipzig: Brockhaus, 1848–1852; repr. Berlin: De Gruyter, 1974. [*KS*]

——. *Letters of Ludwig Tieck, Hitherto Unpublished.* Ed. Edwin H. Zeydel, Percy Matenko, and Robert Herndon Fife. New York: MLA, 1937.

——. *Werke in 4 Bänden,* Ed. Marianne Thalmann. Munich: Winkler, 1963–1966. [Thalmann]

VORDTRIEDE, WERNER, ed. *Achim und Bettina in ihren Briefen.* Frankfurt: Suhrkamp, 1961. [*Achim und Bettina*]

Bibliography

SECONDARY LITERATURE

ABRAMS, M. H. *Natural Supernaturalism.* New York: Norton, 1971.

ALEWYN, RICHARD. "Ein Fragment der Fortsetzung von Tiecks 'Sternbald.'" *JFDH,* 1962, pp. 58–68.

ASPETSBERGER, FRIEDBERT. *Welteinheit und Epische Gestaltung. Studien zur Ichform von Hölderlins Roman "Hyperion."* Munich: Fink, 1971.

BACH, HANS. *Jean Pauls Hesperus.* Leipzig: Mayer & Müller, 1929.

BARRACK, CHARLES M. "Conscience in *Heinrich von Ofterdingen*: Novalis' Metaphysic of the Poet." *GR* 46 (1971), 257–284.

BAUSCH, WALTER. *Theorien des epischen Erzählens in der deutschen Frühromantik.* Bonn: Bouvier, 1964.

BEAUJEAN, MARION. *Der Trivialroman in der zweiten Hälfte des 18. Jahrhunderts: Die Ursprünge des modernen Unterhaltungsromans.* Bonn: Bouvier, 1964.

BECK, HANS-JOACHIM. *Friedrich von Hardenberg: "Oeconomie des Styls."* Bonn: Grundmann, 1976.

BÉGUIN, ALBERT. *L'Ame romantique et le rêve.* Paris: Corti, 2d ed., 1939.

BEHLER, DIANA. *The Theory of the Novel in Early German Romanticism.* Berne: Peter Lang, 1978.

BEHLER, ERNST. "Friedrich Schlegels Theorie der Universalpoesie" *JDSG* I (1957), 211–252.

BEREND, EDUARD. *Jean-Paul-Bibliographie.* Ed. and expanded by Johannes Krogoll. Stuttgart: Klett, 1963.

———. *Jean Pauls Persönlichkeit in Berichten der Zeitgenossen.* Berlin: Akademie-Verlag, 1956.

BERGER, DOROTHEA. *Jean Paul Friedrich Richter.* New York: Twayne, 1972.

BLACKALL, ERIC A. "The Contemporary Background to a Passage in the *Lehrjahre.*" In *Aspekte der Goethezeit.* Göttingen: Vandenhoeck & Ruprecht, 1977. Pp. 137–145.

———. *Goethe and the Novel.* Ithaca: Cornell University Press, 1976.

BLANCKENBURG, FRIEDRICH VON. *Versuch über den Roman.* Leipzig and Liegnitz: bey David Siegberts Wittwe, 1774.

BÖCKMANN, PAUL. "Der Roman der Transzendentalpoesie in der Romantik." In *Geschichte, Deutung, Kritik. Literaturwissenschaftliche Beiträge, dargebracht zum 65. Geburtstag Werner Kohlschmidts.* Ed. Maria Bindschedler and Paul Zinsli. Berne: Francke, 1969. Pp. 165–185.

———. "Zum Poesie-Begriff der Romantik." In *Wissen aus Erfahrungen. Werkbegriff und Interpretation heute. Festschrift für Herman Meyer zum 65. Geburtstag.* Ed. Alexander von Bormann in association with Karl Robert Mandelkow and Anthonius H. Touber. Tübingen: Niemeyer, 1976. pp. 371–383.

BOLLINGER, HEINZ. *Novalis, Die Lehrlinge zu Sais; Versuch einer Erläuterung.* Winterthur: 1954.

BORCHERDT, HANS HEINRICH. *Der Roman der Goethezeit.* Urach and Stuttgart: Port, 1949.

Bibliography

BÖSCHENSTEIN, BERNHARD. "Jean Pauls Romankonzeption." In B. B., *Studien zur Dichtung des Absoluten.* Zurich: Atlantis, 1968. Pp. 25–44.

BOSSE, HEINRICH. "Der offene Schluss der 'Flegeljahre.'" *JJPG* 2 (1967), 73–84.

BRINKMANN, RICHARD. "Nachtwachen des Bonaventura: Kehrseite der Frühromantik." In *Die deutsche Romantik.* Ed. Hans Steffen. Göttingen: Vandenhoeck & Ruprecht, 1967. Pp. 134–158.

BROOKS, PETER. *The Novel of Worldliness.* Princeton: Princeton University Press, 1969.

BROWN, MARSHALL. *The Shape of German Romanticism.* Ithaca: Cornell University Press, 1979.

CHARVET, P. E. *A Literary History of France.* Vol. v. London: Benn, 1967.

COPLESTON, FREDERICK. *A History of Philosophy.* Vol. 7, part 1. New York: Doubleday Image Books, 1965.

CRAMER, KARIN. "Bewusstseinsspaltung in E. T. A. Hoffmanns Roman *Die Elixiere des Teufels.*" *MHG* 16 (1970), 8–18.

CRAMER, THOMAS. *Das Groteske bei E. T. A. Hoffmann.* Munich: Fink, 1966.

CZERNY, JOHANN. *Sterne, Hippel und Jean Paul. Ein Beitrag zur Geschichte des humoristischen Romans in Deutschland.* Berlin: Duncker, 1904.

DAEMMRICH, HORST S. "*The Devil's Elixirs:* Precursor of the Modern Psychological Novel." *PLL* 6 (1970), 374–386.

——. *The Shattered Self: E. T. A. Hoffmann's Tragic Vision.* Detroit: Wayne State University Press, 1973.

DAHLER, HANS. *Jean Pauls Siebenkäs: Struktur und Grundbild.* Berne: Francke, 1962.

EHRENSPERGER, OSKAR SERGE. *Die epische Struktur in Novalis' "Heinrich von Ofterdingen."* Winterthur: Schellenberg, 1965.

EICHNER, HANS. "*Camilla:* Eine unbekannte Fortsetzung von Dorothea Schlegels *Florentin.*" *JFDH,* 1965, pp. 314–368.

——. *Friedrich Schlegel.* New York: Twayne, 1970.

——. "Friedrich Schlegel's Theory of Romantic Poetry." *PMLA* LXXI (1956), 1018–1041.

——. "The Novel." In *The Romantic Period in Germany.* Ed. Siegbert Prawer. New York: Schocken 1970. Pp. 64–96.

ELLINGER, George. *E. T. A. Hoffmanns Werke.* Berlin and Leipzig: Bong, n.d.

EMRICH, WILHELM. "Dichtung und Gesellschaft bei Eichendorff." *Aurora* 18 (1958), 11–17. Also in *Eichendorff Heute,* ed. Paul Stöcklein. Darmstadt: Wissenschaftliche Buchgesellschaft, 1966.

FETZER, JOHN F. *Romantic Orpheus: Profiles of Clemens Brentano.* Berkeley: University of California Press, 1974.

FIFE, ROBERT HERNDON. "Jean Paul Friedrich Richter and E. T. A. Hoffmann." *PMLA* XXII (1907), 1–32.

FINK, GONTHIER-LOUIS. "L'Ambiguïté du message romantique dans *Franz Sternbalds Wanderungen* de Ludwig Tieck."*Recherches Germaniques* 4 (1974), 16–70.

FREDMAN, ALICE GREEN. *Diderot and Sterne.* New York: Columbia University Press, 1955.

FRYE, LAWRENCE O. "The Language of Romantic High Feeling: A Case of Dialogue technique in Hoffmann's *Kater Murr* and Novalis' *Heinrich von Ofterdingen.*" *DVLG* 49 (1975), 520–545.

FUHRMANN, EIKE. "Jean-Paul-Bibliographie, 1963–1965" *JJPG* 1 (1966), 163–179.

GAIER, ULRICH. *Krumme Regel.* Tübingen: Niemeyer, 1970.

GAJEK, BERNHARD. *Homo Poeta: Zur Kontinuität der Problematik bei Clemens Brentano.* Frankfurt: Athenäum, 1971.

GEULEN, HANS. "Zeit und Allegorie im Erzählvorgang von Ludwig Tiecks Roman 'Franz Sternbalds Wanderungen.'" *GRM* 18 (1968), 281–298.

GIERLICH, SUSANNE. *Jean Paul: "Der Komet oder Nikolaus Marggraf. Eine komische Geschichte."* Göppingen: Kümmerle, 1972.

GIESE, ARMIN. "Die Phantasie bei Ludwig Tieck—ihre Bedeutung für den Menschen und sein Werk." Diss. Hamburg, 1973.

GILLESPIE, GERALD ERNEST PAUL, ed. and tr. *Die Nachtwachen des Bonaventura. The Night Watches of Bonaventura.* Austin: University of Texas Press, 1971.

GRAVES, PETER J. "E. T. A. Hoffmann's Johannes Kreisler: 'Verrückter Musikus'?" *MLQ* 30 (1969), 222–233.

GUIGNARD, RENÉ. *Achim von Arnim.* Paris: Presses Universitaires de France, 1936.

———. *Un Poète romantique allemand: C. Brentano.* Paris: Les Belles Lettres, 1933.

HAMBURGER, MICHAEL. *Contraries: Studies in German Literature.* New York: Dutton, 1970.

HARICH, WALTHER. *E. T. A. Hoffmann: Das Leben eines Künstlers.* 2 vols. Berlin: E. Reiss, 1921.

HÄRTL, HEINZ. "Ludwig Achim von Arnims kleiner Roman 'Hollins Liebeleben.'" *Wissenschaftliche Zeitschrift der Martin-Luther Universität, Halle-Wittenberg, Gesellschafts- und Sprachwissenschaftliche Reihe* 18 (1969), 171–182.

HARTMANN, NICOLAI. *Philosophie des deutschen Idealismus.* Berlin: De Gruyter, 2d ed. 1960.

HAYWOOD, BRUCE. *Novalis: The Veil of Imagery.* The Hague: Mouton, 1959.

Bibliography

HEDINGER-FRÖHNER, DOROTHEE. *Jean Paul: der utopische Gehalt des Hesperus.* Bonn: Bouvier, 1977.

HEIMRICH, BERNHARD. *Fiktion und Fiktionsironie in Theorie und Dichtung der deutschen Romantik.* Tübingen: Niemeyer, 1968.

HEINISCH, KLAUS JOACHIM. "Bonaventura. Nachtwachen." In K. J. H. *Deutsche Romantik, Interpretationen.* (Paderborn: Schöningh, 1966), Pp. 181–200.

HESELHAUS, CLEMENS. "Die Wilhelm-Meister-kritik der Romantiker und die romantische Romantheorie." In *Nachahmung und Illusion.* Ed. H. R. Jauss. Munich: Eidos, 1964. Pp. 113–127.

HEWETT-THAYER, H. W. *Hoffmann: Author of the Tales.* Princeton: Princeton University Press, 1948.

HIBBERD, J. "Dorothea Schlegel's *Florentin* and the Precarious Idyll." *GLL* N.S. XXX (1977), 198–207.

HIEBEL, FRIEDRICH. *Novalis.* Chapel Hill: University of North Carolina Press, 1954.

HOFFMANN, VOLKER. "Die Arnim-Forschung, 1945–1972." *DVLG* 47 (1973) Sonderheft pp. 270–342.

HOFFMANN, WERNER. *Clemens Brentano. Leben und Werk.* Berne and Munich: Francke, 1966.

HUDGINS, ESTHER W. *Nicht-Epische Strukturen des romantischen Romans.* The Hague: Mouton, 1975.

IMMERWAHR, RAYMOND. "The Subjectivity or Objectivity of Friedrich Schlegel's Poetic Irony." *GR* XXVI (1951), 173–190.

——. "Die symbolische Form des 'Briefes über den Roman.'" *ZDP* 88 (1969), Sonderheft 41–60.

JANSEN, ERIKA. *Ahnung und Gegenwart im Werke Eichendorffs.* Giessen: Kindt, 1937.

JONAS, LUDWIG, AND WILHELM DILTHEY, eds. *Aus Schleiermachers Leben.* Vol. III. Berlin: Reimer, 1861.

JONES, MICHAEL T. "Hoffmann and the Problem of Social Reality: A Study of *Kater Murr.*" *Monatshefte* 69 (1977), 45–57.

KABOTH, HANS. "Eichendorffs *Dichter und ihre Gesellen.*" *Aurora* 4 (1934), 57–62.

KAFITZ, DIETER. "Wirklichkeit und Dichtertum in Eichendorffs *Ahnung und Gegenwart*: Zur Gestalt Fabers." *DVLG* 45 (1971), 350–374.

KAHLER, ERICH. *The Inward Turn of Narrative.* Princeton: Princeton University Press, 1973.

KAYSER, BRIGITTE. "Joseph von Eichendorff: *Ahnung und Gegenwart.* Interpretation der Begegnung Friedrichs mit Rosa als Stadium vorübergehender Verblendung." *Aurora* 35 (1975), 45–57.

Bibliography

KILLY, WALTER. "Der Roman als romantisches Buch: Über Eichendorffs *Ahnung und Gegenwart*." In *Deutsche Romane von Grimmelshausen bis Musil*, ed. Jost Schillemeit. Frankfurt: Fischer, 1976. Pp. 136–154.

KINDERMANN, KLAUS. "Lustspielhandlung und Romanstruktur. Untersuchungen zu Eichendorffs *Dichter und ihre Gesellen*." Berlin, Freie Universität, 1973.

KÖHLER, DIETMAR. "Wiederholung und Variation: Zu einem Grundphänomen der Eichendorffschen Erzählkunst." *Aurora* 27 (1967), 26–43.

KOHLSCHMIDT, WERNER. "Das Hamlet-Motiv in den "Nachtwachen" des Bonaventura." In *German Studies Presented to Walter Horace Bruford*. London: Harrap, 1962. Pp. 163–175.

KÖHN, LOTHAR. *Vieldeutige Welt: Studien zur Struktur der Erzählungen E. T. A. Hoffmanns und zur Entwicklung seines Werkes*. Tübingen: Niemeyer, 1966.

KOMMERELL, MAX. *Jean Paul*. Frankfurt: Klostermann, 1933.

KÖPKE, RUDOLF. *Ludwig Tieck. Erinnerungen aus dem Leben des Dichters*. 2 vols. Leipzig: Brockhaus, 1855.

KÖPKE, WULF. "Jean Pauls *Unsichtbare Loge*. Die Aufklärung des Lesers durch 'Anti-Roman.'" *JJPG* 10 (1975), 49–67.

KORFF, H. A. *Geist der Goethezeit. Versuch einer ideellen Entwicklung der klassisch-romantischen Literaturgeschichte*. Vols. III and IV. Leipzig: Koehler & Amelang, 1957, 1958. First published 1940, 1953.

KÖRNER, JOSEF, ed. *Krisenjahre der Frühromantik*. Vol. I. Brno: Rohrer, 1936.

KÜPPER, PETER. "Unfromme Vigilien. Bonaventuras Nachtwachen." In *Festschrift für Richard Alewyn*. Ed. Herbert Singer and Benno von Wiese. Cologne and Graz: Böhlau, 1967. Pp. 309–327.

KUTTER, MARGOT. *Die Gestaltung des Individualitätsproblems bei E. T. A. Hoffmann*. Düsseldorf: Nolte, 1936.

LILLYMAN, WILLIAM J. *Reality's Dark Dream: The Narrative Fiction of Ludwig Tieck*. Berlin: De Gruyter, 1979.

LUSSKY, ALFRED EDWIN. *Tieck's Romantic Irony: With Special Emphasis upon the Influence of Cervantes, Sterne and Goethe*. Chapel Hill: University of North Carolina Press, 1932.

LÜTHI, HANS JÜRG. *Dichtung und Dichter bei Joseph von Eichendorff*. Berne: Francke, 1966.

MAHR, JOHANNES. *Übergang zum Endlichen. Der Weg des Dichters in Novalis' "Heinrich von Ofterdingen."* Munich: Fink, 1970.

MAYER, GERHART. "Die humorgeprägte Struktur von Jean Pauls *Flegeljahren*." *ZDP* 83 (1964), 409–426.

Bibliography

MEIXNER, HORST. "Denkstein und Bildersaal in Clemens Brentanos *Godwi.*" *JDSG* 11 (1967), 435–468.

——. *Romantischer Figuralismus: Kritische Studien zu Romanen von Arnim, Eichendorff und Hoffmann.* Frankfurt: Athenäum, 1971.

MENNEMEIER, FRANZ NORBERT. *Friedrich Schlegels Poesiebegriff dargestellt anhand der literaturkritischen Schriften: Die romantische Konzeption einer objektiven Poesie.* Munich: Fink, 1971.

——. "Rückblick auf Brentanos *Godwi*: Ein Roman ohne Tendenz." *WW* 16 (1966), 24–33.

MEYER, HERMAN. "Jean Pauls *Flegeljahre.*" In H. M., *Zarte Empirie.* Stuttgart: Metzler, 1963. Pp. 57–112.

——. "Zitierkunst in E. T. A. Hoffmanns Kater Murr." In H. M., *Das Zitat in der Erzählkunst.* Stuttgart: Metzler, 1961. Pp. 114–134.

MICHELSEN, PETER. *Laurence Sterne und der deutsche Roman des achtzehnten Jahrhunderts.* Göttingen: Vandenhoeck & Ruprecht, 1962.

MOERING, RENATE. "Musikalität und Zwielicht: Zwei Formprinzipien in E. T. A. Hoffmanns *Elixieren des Teufels.*" *JWGV* 75 (1971), 56–73.

——. *Die offene Romanform von Arnims "Gräfin Dolores."* Heidelberg: Winter, 1978.

MORTIER, ROLAND. *Diderot en Allemagne.* Paris: Presses Universitaires de France, 1954.

MÜNZ, WALTER. *Individuum und Symbol in Tiecks "William Lovell." Materialien zum frühromantischen Subjektivismus.* Berne and Frankfurt: Lang, 1975.

NÄGELE, ROLF. *Die Muttersymbolik bei Clemens Brentano.* Winterthur: Keller, 1959).

NEGUS, KENNETH. *E. T. A. Hoffmann's Other World.* Philadelphia: University of Pennsylvania Press, 1965.

NEUBAUER, JOHN. *Biofocal Vision: Novalis' Philosophy of Nature and Disease.* Chapel Hill: University of North Carolina Press, 1971.

——. *Novalis.* New York: Twayne, 1980.

NEUMANN, PETER HORST. *Jean Pauls "Flegeljahre."* Göttingen: Vandenhoeck & Ruprecht, 1966.

OCHSNER, KARL. *E. T. A. Hoffmann als Dichter des Unbewussten. Ein Beitrag zur Geistesgeschichte der Romantik.* Leipzig: Huber, 1936.

OFFERMANNS, ERNST L. "Eichendorffs Roman *Dichter und ihre Gesellen.*" In *Literaturwissenschaft und Geschichtsphilosophie. Festschrift für Wilhelm Emrich.* Ed. Helmut Arntzen, Bernd Balzer, Karl Pestalozzi and Rainer Wagner. Berlin: De Gruyter, 1975. Pp. 373–387.

PASCHEK, CARL. "Novalis und Böhme." *JFDH*, 1976, pp. 138–167.

PASSAGE, CHARLES E. "E. T. A. Hoffmann's *The Devil's Elixirs:* A Flawed Masterpiece." *JEGP* 75 (1976), 531–545.

Bibliography

PAULSEN, WOLFGANG. "Bonaventuras Nachtwachen im literarischen Raum." *JDSG* IX (1965), 447–510.

———. "Friedrich Schlegels *Lucinde* als Roman." *GR* XXI (1946), 173–190.

PEACOCK, RONALD. *Hölderlin.* London: Methuen, 1938.

PETER, KLAUS. "Adel und Revolution als Thema der Romantik." In *Literaturwissenschaft und Sozialwissenschaften II: Legitimationskrisen des deutschen Adels 1200–1900.* Ed. Peter Uwe Hohendahl and Paul Michael Lützeler. Stuttgart: Metzler, 1979. Pp. 197–217.

POLHEIM, KARL KONRAD. *Die Arabeske. Ansichten und Ideen aus Friedrich Schlegels Poetik.* Munich, Paderborn, Vienna: Schöningh, 1966.

———. "Friedrich Schlegels *Lucinde.*" *ZDP* 88 (1969), Sonderheft pp. 61–90.

PRANG, HELMUT. *Die romantische Ironie.* Darmstadt: Wissenschaftliche Buchgesellschaft, 1972.

PREISENDANZ, WOLFGANG. *Humor als dichterische Einbildungskraft.* Munich: Fink, 1976.

PROFITLICH, ULRICH. *Der seelige Leser. Untersuchungen zur Dichtungstheorie Jean Pauls.* Bonn: Bouvier, 1968.

RADNER, LAWRENCE R. *Eichendorff: The Spiritual Geometer.* Lafayette, Ind.: Purdue University Studies, 1970.

———. "The Garden Symbol in *Ahnung und Gegenwart.*" *MLQ* 21 (1960), 253–260.

RAFF, DIETRICH *Ich-Bewusstsein und Wirklichkeitsauffassung bei E. T. A. Hoffmann. Eine Untersuchung der "Elixiere des Teufels" und des "Kater Murr."* Rottweil: Emmanuel, 1971.

RASCH, WOLFDIETRICH. "Achim von Arnims Erzählkunst." *DU* 7/2 (1955), 38–55.

———. *Die Erzählweise Jean Pauls: Metaphernspiele und dissonante Strukturen.* Munich: Hanser, 1961.

REED, EUGENE E. "The Union of the Arts in Brentano's *Godwi.*" *GR* 29 (1954), 102–118.

REHM, WALTER. "Prinz Rokoko im alten Garten: Eine Eichendorffstudie." In W. R., *Späte Studien.* Berne: Francke, 1964. Pp. 124–214.

REQUADT, P. "Eichendorffs *Ahnung und Gegenwart.*" *DU* 7 (1955), 79–92. Also in P. R., *Bildlichkeit der Dichtung. Aufsätze zur deutschen Literatur vom 18. bis 20. Jahrhundert.* Ed. Hans-Henrik Kummacher and Herbert Ohl. Munich: Fink, 1974. Pp. 35–48.

RIBBAT, ERNST. *Ludwig Tieck, Studien zur Konzeption und Praxis romantischer Poesie.* Bonn: Athenäum, 1977.

RICCI, JEAN F.-A. "Le Problème de la vraisemblance dans les Elixirs du Diable de E. T. A. Hoffmann." *LanM* 46 (1952), 28–34.

RILEY, HELENE M. KASTINGER. *Idee und Gestaltung: Das konfigurative Struk-*

turprinzip bei L. A. von Arnim. Berne and Frankfurt: Herbert Lang, 1977.

ROMMEL, OTTO. "Rationalistische Dämonie. Die Geisterromane des ausgehenden 18. Jahrhunderts." *DVLG* 17 (1939), 183–220.

ROSEN, ROBERT S. *E. T. A. Hoffmanns "Kater Murr": Aufbauformen und Erzählsituationen.* Bonn: Bouvier, 1970.

ROTERMUND, ERWIN. "Musikalische und dichterische 'Arabeske' bei E. T. A. Hoffmann." *Poetica* 2 (1968), 48–69.

ROWSON, P. D. "The Opening Scene of Jean Paul's *Die unsichtbare Loge.*" *GLL* N.S. XXXI (1978), 221–227.

RUDOLPH, GERHARD. *Studien zur dichterischen Welt Achim von Arnims.* Berlin: De Gruyter, 1958.

RYAN, LAWRENCE JOHN. *Friedrich Hölderlin.* Stuttgart: Metzler, 2d ed., 1967.

——. *Hölderlins Hyperion: Exzentrische Bahn und Dichterberuf.* Stuttgart: Metzler, 1965.

SAMMONS, JEFFREY L. *The Nachtwachen des Bonaventura: A Structural Interpretation.* The Hague: Mouton, 1965.

——. "Tieck's *Franz Sternbald*: The Loss of Thematic Control." *Studies in Romanticism* 5 (1965), 30–43.

SAMUEL, RICHARD. "Novalis: Heinrich von Ofterdingen." In *Der deutsche Roman: Struktur und Geschichte.* Ed. Benno von Wiese. Düsseldorf: Bagel, 1963. Pp. 252–300.

SAUERLAND, KAROL. "*Die Kronenwächter.* Auflösung eines Mythos." *WB* 14 (1968), 868–883.

SCHANZE, HELMUT. "Friedrich Schlegels Theorie des Romans." In *Deutsche Romantheorien. Beiträge zu einer historischen Poetik in Deutschland.* Ed. Reinhold Grimm. Frankfurt and Bonn: Athenäum, 1968. Pp. 61–80. (2d ed. 1974, pp. 105–124.)

SCHEIDWEILER, PAULA. *Der Roman der deutschen Romantik.* Leipzig and Berlin: Teubner, 1916.

SCHER, STEVEN PAUL. "Hoffmann and Sterne: Unmediated Parallels in Narrative Method." *CL* 28 (1976), 309–325.

SCHILLEMEIT, JOST. *Bonaventura. Der Verfasser der Nachtwachen.* Munich: Beck, 1973.

SCHNAPP, FRIEDRICH, ed. *E. T. A. Hoffmann in Aufzeichnungen seiner Freunde und Bekannten.* Munich: Winkler, 1974.

SCHOLZ, RÜDIGER. *Welt und Form des Romans bei Jean Paul.* Berne: Francke, 1973.

SCHUBERT, GOTTHILF HEINRICH. *Die Symbolik des Traumes.* Bamberg: Kunz, 1814; facsimile repr. Heidelberg: Lambert Schneider, 1968.

Bibliography

SCHULZ, GERHARD. "Jean Pauls *Siebenkäs*." In *Aspekte der Goethezeit*. Ed.
Stanley A. Corngold, Michael Curschmann and Theodor J. Ziolkow-
ski. Göttingen: Vandenhoeck & Ruprecht, 1977. Pp. 215–239.

——. "Die Poetik des Romans bei Novalis." *JFDH*, (1964, pp. 120–157.
SCHUMANN, DETLEV W. "Some Scenic Motifs in Eichendorff's *Ahnung
und Gegenwart*." *JEGP* LVI (1957), 550–569.
SCHÜRER, RAINER. "Die Romane Walter Scotts in Deutschland." Diss.
Freie Universität Berlin, 1969.
SCHWARZ, EGON. *Joseph von Eichendorff*. New York: Twayne, 1972.
SCHWARZ, PETER P. *Aurora: Zur romantischen Zeitstruktur bei Eichendorff*.
Bad Homburg: Gehlen, 1970.
SCHWEIKERT, UWE. *Jean Paul*. Stuttgart: Metzler, 1970.
——. *Jean Pauls "Komet": Selbstparodie der Kunst*. Stultgart: Metzler,
1971.
SEGEBRECHT, WULF, ed. *Ludwig Tieck*. Darmstadt: Wissenschaftliche
Buchgesellschaft, 1976.
SEIDLIN, OSKAR. *Versuche über Eichendorff*. Göttingen: Vandenhoeck &
Ruprecht, 1965.
SIGMANN, LUISE. "Die englische Literatur von 1800 bis 1850 im Urteil
der zeitgenössischen deutschen Kritik." *AF* LV (1918).
SILZ, WALTER. *Hölderlin's Hyperion: A Critical Reading*. Philadelphia: Uni-
versity of Pennsylvania Press, 1969.
SINGER, HERBERT. "Hoffmann, *Kater Murr*." In *Der deutsche Roman. Vom
Barock bis zur Gegenwart. Struktur und Geschichte*. Ed Benno von Wiese.
Düsseldorf: Bagel, 1963 Vol. I, 301–328.
SMEED, J. W. *Jean Paul's Dreams*. London: Oxford University Press,
1966.
SÖLLE-NIPPERDEY, DOROTHEE. *Untersuchungen zur Struktur der Nachtwa-
chen von Bonaventura*. Göttingen: Vandenhoeck & Ruprecht, 1959.
SPÄTH, UTE. *Gebrochene Identität: Stilistische Untersuchungen zum Parallelis-
mus in E. T. A. Hoffmanns "Lebens-Ansichten des Katers Murr."* Göt-
tingen: Kümmerle, 1970.
STANSFIELD, AGNES. *Hölderlin*. Manchester: Manchester University Press,
1944.
STEFFEN, HANS. "Lichtsymbolik und Figuration in Arnims erzählender
Dichtung." In *Die deutsche Romantik. Poetik, Formen und Motive*. Ed.
Hans Steffen. Göttingen: Vandenhoeck & Ruprecht, 1967. Pp. 180–
199.
STÖCKLEIN, PAUL, ed. *Eichendorff Heute*. Darmstadt:Wissenschaftliche
Buchgesellschaft, 1966.
STORZ, GERHARD. "Beobachtungen zu Brentanos *Godwi*." In *Festschrift*

for Friedrich Beissner. Ed. Ulrich Gaier and Werner Volke. Babenhausen: Rotsch, 1974. Pp. 436–446.

STRAUCH, CHRISTIAN. "Satirische Elemente im Aufbau von Eichendorffs
Dichter und ihre Gesellen." *JWGV* 72 (1968), 87–112.

STRIEDTER, JURI. "Die Komposition der 'Lehrlinge zu Sais.'" *DU* 7/2
(1955), 5–23.

STROHSCHNEIDER-KOHRS, INGRID. *Die romantische Ironie in Theorie und
Gestaltung.* Tübingen: Niemeyer, 1960.

TATAR, MARIA. *Spellbound.* Princeton: Princeton University Press, 1978.

TAYLOR, RONALD. *Hoffmann.* London: Bowes and Bowes, 1963.

TERRAS, RITA. "Juvenal und die satirische Struktur der Nachtwachen
von Bonaventura." *GQ* 52 (1979), 18–31.

THALMANN, MARIANNE. *Der Trivialroman des 18. Jahrhunderts und der romantische Roman.* Berlin: Ebering, 1923.

THURNHER, EUGEN. "Eichendorffs *Geschichte des Romans.*" In *Stoffe, For-
men, Struktur. Studien zur deutschen Literatur.* Ed. Albert Fuchs and
Helmut Motekat. *Hans Heinrich Borcherdt zum 75. Geburtstag.* Munich:
Huber, 1962. Pp. 361–379.

TRAINER, JAMES. *Ludwig Tieck: From Gothic to Romantic.* The Hague:
Mouton, 1964.

VIRCHOW, PETER, tr. Friedrich Schlegel, *Lucinde.* Minneapolis: University of Minnesota Press, 1971. Introduction.

VORDTRIEDE, WERNER. "Achim von Arnims Kronenwächter." In *Deutsche
Romane von Grimmelshausen bis Musil.* Ed. Jost Schillemeit. Frankfurt:
Fischer, 1966. Pp. 155–163.

WALZEL, OSKAR. "Die Formkunst von Hardenbergs 'Heinrich von Ofterdingen.'" *GRM* 7 (1915–1919), 403–444 and 465–479.

WATT, IAN P. *The Rise of the Novel.* Berkeley: University of California
Press, 2d ed., 1959.

WEIGAND, KARLHEINZ. *Tiecks "William Lovell." Studie zur frühromantischen
Antithese.* Heidelberg: Winter, 1975.

WELLEK, RENÉ. *A History of Modern Criticism.* Vol. 2. New Haven: Yale
University Press, 1955.

WERNER, HANS-GEORG. *E. T. A. Hoffmann.* Berlin and Weimar: Aufbau-
Verlag, 2d ed., 1971.

WIESE, BENNO VON. "Brentanos *Godwi.* Analyse eines 'romantischen' Romans." In B. v. W., *Von Lessing bis Grabbe.* Düsseldorf: Bagel, 1968.
Pp. 191–247,

———. "E. T. A. Hoffmanns Doppelroman Kater Murr. Die Phantasie des
Humors." In B. v. W., *Von Lessing bis Grabbe.* Düsseldorf: Bagel, 1968.
Pp. 248–267.

WILLIAMS, IOAN. *Sir Walter Scott on Novelists and Fiction*. London: Routledge & Kegan Paul, 1968. Pp. 102–119.

ZEYDEL, EDWIN HERMANN. *Ludwig Tieck, the German Romanticist: A Critical Study*. Princeton: Princeton University Press, 1935; repr. Hildesheim and New York: Olms, 1971, with a preface to the 2d ed. by the author.

Index

Index

Index

Neo-Platonists, 145
Nicolai, Friedrich, 151
Novalis, 16, 18–19, 107–130, 134, 145, 147, 171, 216, 245; *Allgemeines Brouillon*, 111; *Heinrich von Ofterdingen*, 18–19, 37, 47, 109, 112, 114, 120–131, 148, 171, 185–186, 207, 216, 245; *Hymnen an die Nacht*, 42, 147, 179; *Die Lehrlinge zu Sais*, 113–120

Organic form, 19, 201, 220
Ossian, 152

Parekbasis, 24, 30
Paulsen, Wolfgang, 220
Peacock, Thomas Love, 225
Physics, physical sciences, 31–33, 37, 144
Plato, 27
Productive imagination, 119, 138–141
Prose sobriety and poetic boldness, 17, 94, 264

Rabelais, 167, 276
Radcliffe, Ann, 16
Restif del la Bretonne, 170; *Le Paysan perverti*, 158–159
Retrospective narration, 101–105, 168, 211, 241
Reuter, Christian, *Schelmuffsky*, 204
Richardson, Samuel, 36, 169; *Clarissa*, 16, 52; *Pamela*, 51
Richter, Jean Paul, 30, 33, 36, 54, 59, 66–98, 105–106, 132, 145, 147–148, 154, 157, 167, 170, 186, 200, 206, 209, 226, 245–249; *Auswahl aus des Teufels Papieren*, 80; *Clavis Fichtiana*, 87; *Flegeljahre*, 90–95, 106, 170, 245; *Hesperus*, 74–79, 131, 245; *Der Komet*, 70, 226, 276; *Des Luftschiffers Giannozzo Seebuch*, 86–87, 245; *Siebenkäs*, 79–84, 170, 198, 216; *Titan*, 69, 84–90, 92, 159, 170, 198, 245; *Die unsichtbare Loge*, 70–74, 245; *Vorschule der Ästhetik*, 96–98, 170
Ritter, Johann Wilhelm, 145
Romance, 17, 23, 170, 172

Rousseau, 36, 53; *Confessions*, 28, 35; *La Nouvelle Héloïse*, 16, 35, 49, 52, 102, 155, 169
Runge, Philipp Otto, 198
Ryan, Lawrence, 103

Sachs, Hans, 212
Sakuntala, 77
Sammons, Jeffrey L., 212–213
Saussure, Horace Benedikt von, 190
Scarron, *Le Roman comique*, 204
Schelling, Friedrich Wilhelm Joseph von, 134, 140–145, 209, 281; Jena lectures, 141; *System des transzendentalen Idealismus*, 141
Schiller, Friedrich, 17–19, 98, 116, 132; *Der Geisterseher*, 226, 227, 229, 286; *Maria Stuart*, 188–189; *sentimentalisch*, 26, 169; *Über naive und sentimentalische Dichtung*, 26
Schlegel, August Wilhelm, Berlin lectures, 23; *see also* Organic form
Schlegel, Caroline, 38, 108, 209
Schlegel, Dorothea, 38; *Florentin*, 44–50, 64, 102, 161, 171, 186
Schlegel, Friedrich, 16, 21–43, 107, 110; *Athenäumsfragmente*, 21, 30, 159–160; Boccaccio essay, 23; *Brief über den Roman*, 24, 33–35; *Über die Diotima*, 38–39; *Gespräch über die Poesie*, 21, 30–35, 44; *Über Goethes Meister*, 19; *Lucinde*, 38–43, 59, 61, 108, 171, 186, 210, 245; *Lyzeumsfragmente*, 60; Notebooks, 29; Paris lectures, 35; *Über das Studium der griechischen Poesie*, 21; Vienna lectures, 24, 36
Schleiermacher, Friedrich, 42, 143
Schnabel, Johann Gottfried, *Die Insel Felsenburg*, 168–169, 204
Schubert, Gotthilf Heinrich, *Die Symbolik des Traumes*, 145–149
Schulz, Gerhard, 108–109
Schumann, Robert, 91; *Carnaval*, 210; *Humoresque, Op. 20*, 210; *Papillons*, 91
Scott, Sir Walter, 16, 63, 169–170, 198, 205–206, 292; *The Abbot*, 206; *The Antiquary*, 227; *Essay on Romance*,

Index

17; *Guy Mannering*, 227–228; *The Heart of Midlothian*, 227; *Ivanhoe*, 227; *Quentin Durward*, 16
Second world, 72, 74, 78, 84
Self-reflexiveness, 19, 58, 84, 103, 120, 133, 139, 182, 185, 250
Sentimental, 26, 30, 33–34
Shakespeare, 22–23, 28–29, 33, 178, 219; *Hamlet*, 189, 217–219, 261; *Pericles*, 151; *Romeo and Juliet*, 28–29; *The Tempest*, 167
Smollett, Tobias, 17, 169, 226; *Humphry Clinker*, 155
Solger, Karl Friedrich, 159, 171
Spielmann, 255–257, 259, 261
Spinoza, 32–33, 37, 140
Staël, Mme. de, 16; *Corinne*, 205; *Delphine*, 61, 205
Steffens, Henrik, 145
Sterne, Laurence, 17, 28, 33, 69, 167, 169, 226; *Sentimental Journey*, 71; *Tristram Shandy*, 53, 55–56, 167
Subconscious, the, 143, 175, 196, 235, 262
Surrealists, 176
Swift, Jonathan, 33, 69, 226
Symbolic (form, poetry, language); Symbols, 109, 113–115, 118, 120, 137, 142, 148, 182, 201, 202

Tasso, 28
Tatar, Maria, 145
Telluric state, 146–147
Thalmann, Marianne, 63–64
Tieck, Ludwig, 107–109, 121, 130, 150–172, 186, 224, 232, 246, 281; *Der Aufruhr in den Cevennen*, 150; *Der blonde Eckbert*, 233; *Dichterleben*, 150; *Franz Sternbalds Wanderungen*, 30, 50, 160–166, 170, 245, 263; *Goethe und seine Zeit*, 167; *Letters on Shakespeare*, 166; *Der junge Tischlermeister*, 150; *Shakespeares Behandlung des Wunderbaren*, 167; *Der Tod des*

Dichters, 150; *Vittoria Accorombona*, 150; *William Lovell*, 151–158, 207, 225, 247, 263; (with Wackenroder) *Herzensergiessungen eines kunstliebenden Klosterbruders* and *Phantasien über die Kunst*, 151
Transcendental poetry and poetics, 109–111
Trivialliteratur, Trivialromane, 62–65, 69, 73, 75, 143, 151, 196, 199, 203, 230, 231, 235
Tübinger Gelehrte Anzeigen, 105
Typology (of the novel), 24–29, 97–98, 109–110

Unconscious, the, 134, 137, 139, 140, 143, 145
Universal poetry, 21, 132, 264

Verstand, 17, 39, 42, 112, 133, 143
Voltaire, 36, 54; *Candide*, 19

Wächter, Leopold (= Veit Weber), 63–64
Wackenroder, Wilhelm Heinrich, 151, 224
Wagner, Richard, 42
Walpole, Horace, *Castle of Otranto*, 17
Watt, Ian, 51
Weber, Veit, *see* Wächter, Leopold
Wedgwood, Josiah, 112
Weise, Christian, *Die drei ärgsten Erznarren*, 204
Wellek, René, 96
Wetzel, Friedrich Gottlob, 209
Wieland, Christoph Martin, 53, 59, 286
Witz, wit, 31, 34–38, 40, 73, 91, 97, 169, 248
Wolff, Christian, 34
Wolfram von Eschenbach, 247
Wordsworth, William, *The Prelude*, 102

Young, Edward, *Night Thoughts*, 155

[315]

The Novels of the
German Romantics

Designed by G. T. Whipple, Jr.
Composed by Eastern Graphics
in 10 point Baskerville, 2 points leaded,
with display lines in Baskerville.
Printed offset by Thomson-Shore, Inc.
on Warren's Number 66 text, 50 pound basis.

Library of Congress Cataloging in Publication Data

BLACKALL, ERIC A. (Eric Albert)
   The novels of the German romantics.

   Bibliography: p.
   Includes index.
      1. German fiction—18th century—History and criticism.
   2. German fiction—19th century—History and criticism.
   3. Romanticism—Germany. II. Title.
PT759.B55 1983   833'.6'09145   82-22104
ISBN 0-8014-1523-3